The Amazing QUIZ Challenge

More Than 12,000 Questions and Answers to Tempt, Tease, Tickle, and Test Your Brain

Reader's Digest

The Reader's Digest Association, Inc.
Pleasantville, New York | Montreal

Project Staff

Executive Editor
Elissa Altman

Writers
Sharon Bowers
Shea Zukowski
Susan Randol
Jeff Bredenberg

Cover Designer
Richard Kershner

Interior Page Designer
Erick Swindell

Illustrations
Chuck Rekow

Copy Editor
Marcia Mangum Cronin

Reader's Digest Home & Health Books

VP, Editor in Chief
Neil Wertheimer

Creative Director
Michele Laseau

Executive Managing Editor
Donna Ruvituso

Associate Director, North America Prepress
Douglas A. Croll

Manufacturing Manager
John L. Cassidy

Marketing Director
Dawn Nelson

The Reader's Digest Association, Inc.

President and Chief Executive Officer
Mary G. Berner

President, Home & Garden and Health & Wellness
Alyce C. Alston

SVP, Chief Marketing Officer
Amy J. Radin

President, Global Consumer Marketing and CEO, Direct Holdings
Dawn M. Zier

Library of Congress Data has been applied for.

ISBN: 978-1-60652-984-3

Address any comments about *The Amazing Quiz Challenge* to:

The Reader's Digest Association, Inc.
Editor in Chief, Home & Health Books
Reader's Digest Road
Pleasantville, NY 10570-7000

To order copies of *The Amazing Quiz Challenge*, call 1-800-846-2100.

Visit our online store at **rdstore.com**

Printed in the United States of America

1 3 5 7 9 10 8 6 4 2

US 5092/L

Note to Readers
The contributors, editors, and proofreaders who created **The Amazing Quiz Challenge** have taken all reasonable measures to confirm and verify the accuracy of the information contained in this volume. However, some statements of fact can be open to interpretation. Similarly, new learnings and research often reveal that information long held to be true isn't. We welcome your input on any answers for which you have sound evidence that they may be incorrect. We will research all such queries and make any necessary corrections in subsequent editions. Send queries to:

The Amazing Quiz Challenge
c/o Donna Ruvituso
Home & Health Books
The Reader's Digest Association, Inc.
Reader's Digest Road
Pleasantville, NY 10570-7000

Can it *really* be true?

Just what's so special about *The Amazing Quiz Challenge*? Take this quiz to find out!

True or **False**:

 1 There are more **fascinating facts** packed into these pages than in almost any other book.

 2 This book will **keep you entertained** for months to come.

 3 The facts in this book will often **surprise and amaze** you.

 4 You will be sprinkling **fun questions** from this pages into many of your conversations.

 5 You will **smile and chuckle** frequently while reading this book.

 6 After every reading, you will **feel smarter** and more clever.

 7 Reading this book will help keep your brain **young and agile**.

8 This book will bring back **countless wonderful memories**.

We're happy to report that the answer to all eight questions is "true"! *The Amazing Quiz Challenge* is among the most delightful and comprehensive trivia books ever put together. Just turn the page, and let the fun begin!

Contents

Introduction: **Riddle Me *This*! 7**

Chapter 1: **Americana 8**

From the Founding Fathers to college mascots, presidential goof-ups to war heroics, favorite rivers to greatest cities, we'll test your knowledge of America in more ways than you can shake 50 stars at.

Chapter 2: **Entertainment 44**

Get ready for your screen test! You'll be on the edge of your seat trying to answer these questions on everything from Hollywood luminaries to Broadway musicals to the television shows that we so love to talk about.

Chapter 3: **Sports 82**

Batter up! Tease and test your mettle by answering these competition-quality questions and quizzes about the Olympics, NASCAR, fishing, sailing, golf, and much more.

Chapter 4: **Food and Drink 122**

Does absinthe really make the heart grow fonder? Find out the truth about all things edible and drinkable in this delectable collection of quizzes. You'll never look at food the same way again!

Chapter 5:
Around the World 156

Whether you've traveled the world by plane, train, or arm-chair, these globe-trotting tests will enlighten, inspire, and delight. Do you really think that The Doolittle Raid had to do with a man who talked to animals? (Wrong!)

Chapter 6:
Religion and Mythology 200

Any idea who the Oracle at Delphi was or what Norse god gave his name to a day of the week? Whether you're quizzed about Martin Luther, the Apostles, or Zeus, you may find yourself stumped but you'll still be smiling at these divine questions!

Chapter 7: **Science 228**

Even if you failed science class in high school, fear not! You probably know more than you think on scientific subjects ranging from the animal kingdom and crazy chemical compounds (like the ascorbic acid you have with breakfast every morning) to which bone, exactly, the hipbone is connected to.

Chapter 8:
The Wonderful World of Business 262

This terrific tally of tests covers everything from the legends of Wall Street to brilliant inventors and their prize creations. You deal with money everyday; now it's time to find out how much you really know about the stuff!

Chapter 9: The Arts 304

"A rose is a rose is a rose is a rose," wrote one of the greatest poets of the twentieth century. But do you know which one? From museums to famous houses like the Alhambra, no artsy subject goes untouched in this entertaining and fascinating look at the beauty we humans have created.

Chapter 10: World Play 344

You say tomAto and I say tomAHHto, but that doesn't mean I'm right and you're wrong. Or does it? The fine art of word play is brain-teasing and tongue-tying at best, and a sure way to dazzle your mental skill and fill your day with fun!

Q Riddle Me *This*!

What do the following have in common?

Jeopardy, The $64,000 Question, Name That Tune, The Price Is Right, The Wheel of Fortune, Gambit, Jackpot, What's My Line?, The $25,000 Pyramid, The Hollywood Squares

Sorry, but that's probably the easiest question in this book: Each is a television game show based on the tried and true, favorite ol' American pastime of trivia!

Young and old, rich and poor, east and west, Americans have long loved sharing obscure knowledge, and (let's admit it!) getting answers right and proving our friends wrong. But it goes far beyond television, doesn't it? We stump ourselves with crossword puzzles, test our mettle at family parties by hauling out *Trivial Pursuit*, banter at work or over dinner about the little details we discover in the movies, sports, celebrities, and news stories of the day.

Why do we do this? In part because we love to learn, and to share what we've learned. We also do this because we love the challenge of knowing lots of stuff, the joys of testing our mental capacitiy, our savvy, our memories. If brains could do jumping jacks, we want to be the first ones signed up for gym class. The fact is that even while we're having fun answering these brainteasers, we're exercising our knowledge and our minds, and that's a wonderful thing.

Of course, this love of trivia leaves our brains crammed full of knowledge we'll probably never need, like:

- What was Dr. Frankenstein's first name?
- What famous novelist wrote all of her mysteries in the bathtub?
- What was the Allies' password on D-Day?

And you know what? You're right: None of these facts are important unto themselves. But knowing them is great joy nonetheless, and an important reassurance that our noggins are in great working order.

Welcome, then, to *The Amazing Quiz Challenge*! We at Reader's Digest have assembled a massive collection of mind-boggling questions that will make you smile, make you guffaw, and help you wake up that sleepy gray matter! Perfect for quiz-a-day fun to have with your morning coffee, and ideal for that long car trip that you and your honey are taking on your next vacation, *The Amazing Quiz Challenge* will fill countless hours with facts and fun. Now, *that's* enterBRAINment.

Elissa Altman
Executive Editor,
Reader's Digest Home Books

Americana

America offers freedom, opportunity...and a treasure trove of trivia! Here are colonists, presidents, astronauts, singers, comedians, and so many more who shaped this great country, as well as the events that led us to where we are today.

The Road to Independence

Kings, colonists, tea parties, and traitors: The road to independence is lined with colorful characters and critical moments in our nation's history. Test your knowledge of these important people, places, and events in the pages that follow.

Life in the Colonies

Who, What, Where: Do you know the answers to questions about life in the colonies?

1 What was the name of the first permanent English settlement in North America, named after England's Scottish king in 1607?

2 Which colony was established in part as a place to send English debtors from prison?

3 Who were put on trial at Salem, Massachusetts, in 1692?

4 Which colony did the Pilgrims found in 1620?

5 Which school, later one of America's great universities, was the first college founded in the colonies?

6 How is the killing by British troops of five colonists in Massachusetts in 1770 known?

7 Which was the last of the 13 English colonies to be founded in 1733?

8 What notable first did the *Boston News-Letter* achieve in 1704?

9 Where was the Mayflower originally headed?

10 What was the original cash crop for Virginia colonists?

Early Americans

American history is incomplete without Native American history. How much do you know about the country's original inhabitants?

1 What was the nationality of the Acadians who, during the late 1700s, moved to Louisiana?

2 How many Native Americans are thought to have died from infections within a century of the Europeans' arrival: 10 percent, 50 percent, or 90 percent?

3 Where did the Makah Indians live: on the East Coast or the West Coast?

4 Did Native Americans have horses before the Europeans arrived?

5 What year was the first Thanksgiving celebrated at Plymouth, Massachusetts?

6 What tribe did Chief Tecumseh belong to?

Lucky 13

Every schoolchild has to memorize the 13 colonies. Can you name them?

War and Peace

History textbooks are filled with details about battles, commanders, and peace treaties. How much do you remember?

1 When did the Battle of Lexington and Concord take place?
a. April 1, 1775
b. April 12, 1775
c. April 19, 1775
d. April 30, 1775

2 Who was the military commander for the Revolutionary forces at the Battle of Bunker Hill?
a. Israel Putnam
b. George Washington
c. Benedict Arnold
d. William Howe

3 What formally ended the American Revolutionary War?
a. The Adams-Onis Treaty
b. The Treaty of Madrid
c. The Treaty of York
d. The Treaty of Paris

4 When did the Boston Tea Party take place?
a. December 16, 1771
b. December 16, 1772
c. December 16, 1773
d. December 16, 1774

5 Who read the Declaration of Independence in the yard of Independence Hall on July 8, 1776?
a. John Nixon
b. George Washington
c. Thomas Jefferson
d. John Hancock

6 Who built Fort Ticonderoga?
a. The British
b. The French
c. The Spanish
d. The Americans

7 What animal was featured in the "Join, or Die" sketch Benjamin Franklin created?
a. Bear
b. Moose
c. Alligator
d. Snake

8 How many lanterns meant the British were coming by land?
a. One
b. Two
c. Three
d. Four

9 What nickname was give to the women who delivered water to their men in battle?
a. Anna Glass
b. Mary Carry
c. Molly Pitcher
d. Sarah Vase

10 What did "doodle" in "Yankee Doodle" originally mean, when sung by the Redcoats?
a. Soldier
b. Fool
c. Commander
d. Hero

Names to Know

You've heard of these people, but do you know what they did? Label each statement true or false.

1 George Washington signed the Declaration of Independence.   TRUE ○   FALSE ○

2 Anne Hutchinson told a court that God had spoken to her.   TRUE ○   FALSE ○

3 Roger Williams founded Connecticut.   TRUE ○   FALSE ○

4 Pro-British colonists were called Loyalists.   TRUE ○   FALSE ○

5 William Bradford was elected governor of Plymouth 30 times.   TRUE ○   FALSE ○

6 Henry Hudson claimed territory in the New World for England.   TRUE ○   FALSE ○

7 Pocahontas is buried in England.   TRUE ○   FALSE ○

8 Crispus Attucks, a black man, was killed in the Boston Massacre.   TRUE ○   FALSE ○

9 William Penn, an English Quaker, made a treaty with the Indians in 1682.   TRUE ○   FALSE ○

10 Benedict Arnold hatched a plan to surrender Fort Ticonderoga to the British.   TRUE ○   FALSE ○

Who Founded What?

Match the location of the colony with its founder.

Connecticut_____   **A** William Penn

Delaware_____   **B** London Company

Georgia_____   **C** Virginians

Maryland_____   **D** John Wheelwright

Massachusetts_____   **E** Lord Baltimore

New Hampshire_____   **F** Thomas Hooker

New Jersey_____   **G** Puritans

New York_____   **H** James Oglethorpe

North Carolina_____   **I** Eight English nobles

Pennsylvania_____   **J** Peter Minuit and New Sweden Company

Rhode Island_____   **K** Duke of York

South Carolina_____   **L** Lord Berkeley and Sir George Carteret

Virginia_____   **M** Roger Williams

First, Last, and In-Between

Colonial "firsts" seem obvious—but sometimes they're a surprise. And "seconds" and "lasts" can be fun, too. Can you identify these surprises?

1 Which colony became the first state?

2 Which state first flew the flag with 13 stars?

3 Which colony became the second state?

4 Which of the original 13 colonies was the last to become a state?

5 Four of the first five presidents came from which colony?

6 Which colony claimed the first child born in America?

7 What is the name of the first child born in America?

8 Which colony was the first to authorize its delegates to the Continental Congress to vote for independence?

Our Presidents

The good, the bad, and the ugly: they're all represented in this section about presidents! You'll find heroes, scoundrels, and honest men simply doing their best in trying situations. See how much you know about the most powerful men on earth.

Mr. President!

Even if you can list the presidents in succession, you may find it more difficult to answer presidential questions when they're thrown at you in random order. How well will you do on this quiz?

1 What is the name of America's second president?

2 Which president in 1804 authorized the Lewis-Clark expedition to find a route to the Pacific Ocean?

3 Who became president in 1923?

4 Who was president at the time of the Cuban missile crisis in 1962?

5 What was the name of the president of the Confederacy during the Civil War?

6 Whom did Franklin D. Roosevelt replace as president?

7 The White House has been the home for every American president except for whom?

8 Who was the longest-serving president?

9 Who is second in line (after the vice president) to the presidency?

10 Which president offered the American people a "New Deal"?

Second in Line

Vice presidents are often forgotten, but we'll remember them here. Try your hand at this round on vice presidents.

1 What links Jalan Diponegoro 2, Tai-an Street, and the Naval Observatory?

2 What connects Charles Dawes—Calvin Coolidge's VP—to Jose Ramos-Horta and David Trimble?

3 Who was vice president under Lyndon Johnson between 1963 and 1965?

4 Who was the only 19th-century vice president to become president through election?

5 What links Al Gore, Walter Mondale, Gerald Ford, and Hubert Humphrey?

6 Who was the first female vice presidential candidate representing a major political party?

7 Which future president stood in the shadows beside Eisenhower?

8 What links vice presidents Hannibal Hamlin, Garret Hobart, Henry Wallace, and Spiro Agnew?

9 Who said, "The vice presidency isn't worth a pitcher of warm spit"?

Presidential Firsts

All presidents are first-timers: first time elected, first term in office, and so on. But they experienced other firsts as well. Who was...

1 The first president to die in office?

2 The first (and only) president reelected after being voted out?

3 The first president to appear on a postage stamp?

4 The first president born in a hospital?

5 The first president to speak over the radio?

6 The first president not born a British subject?

7 The first president to have been a Rhodes Scholar?

8 The first (and only) president to name a son George Washington?

9 The first president to use electricity in the White House?

10 The first president to appear on television?

11 The first president to ride a train?

12 The first president to use a telephone in the White House?

13 The first president to have been divorced?

14 The first president to resign his office?

15 The first president to fly in an airplane?

16 The first (and only) bachelor president?

17 The first president sworn in by a woman?

18 The first president to hold a press conference?

19 The first president to wear a beard in office?

20 The first president to serve on the Supreme Court?

Friends and Relations

Forget the friends; let's concentrate on the relatives. How much do you know about these ties that bind?

1 How are John Adams and John Quincy Adams related?

2 How are Franklin D. Roosevelt and Theodore Roosevelt related?

3 How are Eleanor Roosevelt and Franklin Roosevelt related, other than as husband and wife?

4 How are George W. Bush and George H. W. Bush related?

5 How are the 67th Secretary of State and the 42nd President of the United States related?

Name That Lady!

Behind every successful man is a good woman. Give the first name of each president's first lady.

George Washington_____	**A** Abigail
John Adams_____	**B** Bess
Thomas Jefferson_____	**C** Dolley
James Madison_____	**D** Edith
James Buchanan_____	**E** Eleanor
Abraham Lincoln_____	**F** Mamie
Theodore Roosevelt_____	**G** Martha
Franklin D. Roosevelt_____	**H** Martha
Harry S. Truman_____	**I** Mary Todd
Dwight D. Eisenhower_____	**J** None; he was a bachelor

Details, Details

You know the details of your life; do you know the details of theirs?

1 Who was the only president to belong to no official political party?

2 Which 20th-century president was 73 years old when elected for his second term?

3 John Tyler had 15 of them, more than any other president. What were they?

4 Whose presidential library is in Little Rock, Arkansas?

5 Which president took the oath of office on board an aircraft in 1963?

6 Which president was the first to travel overseas as president?

7 Which uniquely long-serving president was the last to die in office of natural causes?

8 Who was the only president to hold office without being elected to either the presidency or vice presidency?

9 Which two presidents have been impeached?

Untimely Ends

Where were you when you heard that John F. Kennedy had been shot? You'll probably never forget. But do you remember the details of what happened in other presidential assassinations— or attempted assassinations?

1 Who said: "Honey, I forgot to duck," after a failed assassination attempt in March 1981?

2 In addition to Lincoln and Kennedy, two other presidents have been assassinated. Name one of them.

3 Who assassinated John F. Kennedy in Dallas, Texas, in 1963?

4 What was the name of the play Abraham Lincoln was watching when he was assassinated?

5 Who was the first president to be assassinated in the 20th century?

6 Who survived two assassination attempts in less than three weeks?

7 Who escaped an attempted assassination by Puerto Rican nationalists?

8 Who survived an assassination attempt at a Congressional funeral?

Winners

Presidents win the Oval Office when they're elected; some have won other big prizes as well. Name two of the three U.S. presidents who have won a Nobel Peace Prize.

Dopey Details

Are these trivial questions about presidents and parties true or false?

1 Bill Clinton plays the trumpet.　　　　　　　　　　　　　　　　TRUE ○　FALSE ○

2 Eleven years after the assassination of Lincoln, a group of counterfeiters plotted to steal his body and hold it for ransom.　　　　　　　　　　TRUE ○　FALSE ○

3 Abraham Lincoln was the tallest president.　　　　　　　　　　TRUE ○　FALSE ○

4 Woodrow Wilson was the first president to throw out the first pitch on baseball's opening day.　　　　　　　　　　　　　　　　　　TRUE ○　FALSE ○

5 Barack Obama was born outside the continental United States.　TRUE ○　FALSE ○

6 The Republican Party is older than the Democratic Party.　　　TRUE ○　FALSE ○

Take the Money and Run

You spend money, but do you ever really look at it? Without opening your wallet, name the president on each of the following.

1 Penny

2 Nickel

3 Dime

4 Quarter

5 Half dollar

6 One dollar bill

7 Two dollar bill

8 Five dollar bill

9 10 dollar bill

10 20 dollar bill

11 50 dollar bill

12 100 dollar bill

Isn't That Cute?

Match the nickname with the proper president.

Father of His Country_____

Red Fox_____

Father of the Constitution_____

Old Hickory_____

Old Tippecanoe_____

Old Rough and Ready_____

Big Bill_____

Man from Independence_____

Dutch_____

Poppy_____

A Ronald Reagan

B Thomas Jefferson

C William Henry Harrison

D Harry S. Truman

E George H. W. Bush

F George Washington

G Zachary Taylor

H Andrew Jackson

I William Howard Taft

J James Madison

Figureheads

They may not be talking heads, but they're still pretty amazing. Name the presidents found at Mount Rushmore.

Culture

America may be baseball and apple pie, but it's also football (the Super Bowl!), music (Elvis!), movies (*Titanic*!), books (*Gone with the Wind*!), and more. Exactly how American are you? Test your knowledge of American culture with these wide-ranging, challenging questions.

Batter Up!

How well do you know your sports?

1 Which baseball team plays at Wrigley Field?

2 Name the two hockey teams that play in New York.

3 What sport is Michelle Kwan best known for?

4 Which basketball player achieved the highest scoring average in the 20th century?

5 LaDainian Tomlinson holds the record for the most number of points scored in an NFL season, with 186. For which team does he play?

6 The Denver Broncos lost by a record of 45 points to which team in the 1990 Super Bowl?

7 Which basketball team plays in the Palace of Auburn Hills?

8 Name the U.S. soccer team that includes British superstar David Beckham.

9 What sport did Tony Dorsett play?

10 Who was nicknamed the "Yankee Clipper" and "Joltin' Joe"?

Oscar Winners

Match the movie with the year it won the Academy Award for Best Motion Picture.

*All About Eve*_____   **A** 1928

*All the King's Men*_____   **B** 1938

*Amadeus*_____   **C** 1943

*Annie Hall*_____   **D** 1949

*Casablanca*_____   **E** 1950

*Crash*_____   **F** 1954

*Dances with Wolves*_____   **G** 1965

*Gandhi*_____   **H** 1969

*Gladiator*_____   **I** 1972

*The Godfather*_____   **J** 1977

*Midnight Cowboy*_____   **K** 1982

*On the Waterfront*_____   **L** 1984

*The Sound of Music*_____   **M** 1990

*Titanic*_____   **N** 1997

*Wings*_____   **O** 2000

*You Can't Take It with You*_____   **P** 2005

First Choices

Americans love to be first. Will you be first to answer all these questions right?

1 In 1969, the *Mariner* beamed back to Earth the first pictures of which planet?

2 In 1934, the first-ever what was opened in Forth Worth, Texas. Was it a Laundromat, a library, or a disco?

3 Who was the first African-American secretary of state?

4 In 1885, Dr. Williams West Grant of Iowa performed the first-ever what?

5 In 1892, the first recorded game of which sport took place in Massachusetts?

6 Who was the first person to fly solo across the Atlantic Ocean?

7 Which Dodger became the first African-American to hit his way into what had been an all-white game, in 1947?

8 What cost five cents and was issued for the first time in 1847?

9 Which city lays claim to the first subway in America?

10 What was Ed White the first American astronaut to do?

Play Ball!

Are you a true baseball fan? Name five American League stadiums and five National League stadiums.

Talking Boxes

The Muppet Show, The George Burns and Gracie Allen Show, M*A*S*H*—they're all classics. Can you answer these questions about other classic TV and radio shows?

1 Who created Kermit the Frog?

2 At the beginning of every show, who sang, "Won't You Be My Neighbor"?

3 Name all the hosts of *Jeopardy!*

4 In what city did *Friends* take place?

5 Which *New Year's Rockin' Eve* host also counted down weekly music hits on the radio?

6 Who was the first host of *The Tonight Show*?

7 Who knows what evil lurks in the hearts of men?

8 Who directed *When Harry Met Sally* and starred on TV as "Meathead"?

9 Which radio host describes himself as "The most dangerous man in America"?

10 Who was the first actress to appear pregnant on TV?

Olympic Dreams

Do you dream of gold medals? Can you hum the Olympic theme? Then try to win this contest about America's Olympic sites.

1 Name the three places in the United States where the Summer Olympics have taken place.

2 Name the three places in the United States where the Winter Olympics have taken place.

Higher Learning

Are these statements about U.S. colleges and universities true or false?

1 Miami University at Oxford is located in Florida. TRUE ○ FALSE ○

2 Princeton University awards the Pulitzer Prizes. TRUE ○ FALSE ○

3 The University of Pennsylvania claims the oldest medical school. TRUE ○ FALSE ○

4 *Good Will Hunting* takes place at Boston College. TRUE ○ FALSE ○

5 Barnard College is affiliated with Columbia University. TRUE ○ FALSE ○

6 Carnegie Mellon University is located in Cleveland. TRUE ○ FALSE ○

7 You find the secret society called "Skull and Bones" at Yale. TRUE ○ FALSE ○

8 Harvard was originally known as King's College. TRUE ○ FALSE ○

9 Duke University is located in Durham, North Carolina. TRUE ○ FALSE ○

10 The College of William & Mary is the second oldest college in the nation. TRUE ○ FALSE ○

11 Robert E. Lee and his horse are buried on the campus of Washington and Lee University. TRUE ○ FALSE ○

Just Call Me Author

Sometimes writers become better known than the characters they create. Who are these famous authors?

1 What is Dr. Seuss's real name?

2 Who wrote *Gone with the Wind*?

3 O. Henry was found guilty of what crime?

4 Who is considered the inventor of the detective-fiction genre?

5 What children's book author edited and updated *The Elements of Style*?

6 Who, at 86, spoke and read his poetry at the inauguration of John F. Kennedy?

7 Who is the author of *The Andromeda Strain* and creator of the TV series *ER*?

8 Who wrote for both the Nancy Drew and Hardy Boys series?

9 Which poet wrote "The New Colossus," engraved in the pedestal of the Statue of Liberty?

10 Which science fiction writer has had books published in nine of the 10 major categories of the Dewey Decimal System?

American Ivy

American ivy may not be as well known in the plant kingdom as English ivy, but the universities that make up the Ivy League are known throughout the world. Name the eight Ivy League schools.

Novel Ideas

These books are distinctly American. Can you name the novels?

1 Which 1961 satirical novel created a new catch phrase for circular logic?

2 Name one of four sequels to *A Wrinkle in Time.*

3 Meg, Jo, Beth, and Amy March appear in what novel published as a single volume in 1880?

4 Which novel takes place in West Egg and East Egg?

5 Which novella tells the tragic story of George Milton and Lennie Small?

6 What is the name of the only novel Ralph Ellison published during his lifetime?

7 What is considered the first novel to be published in America?

8 The working title of what Sinclair Lewis novel, published in 1922, was *Pumphrey*?

9 What is the name of the 1996 serial novel written by Stephen King?

10 Which novel features Captain Ahab?

And the Award Goes to...

Americans love to hand out awards. Maybe you'll get an award for naming the award given to or for the following!

1 The Major League's pitchers of the year

2 The top college football player

3 Excellence in television

4 Excellence in music

5 Best in film and television

6 Excellence in the film industry

7 Excellence in television and/or radio broadcasting

8 Excellence in Broadway productions and performances

9 Excellence in Off-Broadway and Off-Off-Broadway productions and performances

Halls of Fame

Earn a place in the trivia hall of fame by locating these hallowed halls. Where is the...

1 Rock and Roll Hall of Fame?

2 Basketball Hall of Fame?

3 Baseball Hall of Fame?

4 Pro Football Hall of Fame?

5 International Tennis Hall of Fame?

6 Country Music Hall of Fame?

7 College Football Hall of Fame?

8 Volleyball Hall of Fame?

9 International Swimming Hall of Fame?

A Song in My Heart

From the March King to the Queen of Soul, American musicians have taken the world by storm. Can you name these kings and queens of music?

1 Who wrote "The Star Spangled Banner"?

2 Who is known as "The March King"?

3 Who is "The Queen of Soul"?

4 Who was known for playing the cornet as well as the trumpet?

5 Who wanted a bicycle or rifle for his 11th birthday, but instead got a guitar?

6 Which country music star owns a theme park in Pigeon Forge, Tennessee?

7 What comedian is well-known for his banjo playing?

8 Whose real name is Frances Gumm?

9 The movie *Walk the Line* detailed which country singer's life?

10 Which singer and actor, born in 1903, has three stars on the Hollywood Walk of Fame?

Cities and States

Are you from Celebration, Florida? Boring, Maryland? Or Last Chance, Colorado? Maybe not, but you probably know a lot about your city and state (even if they don't have crazy names). How much do you know about the other states and cities across the nation? Find out here!

Cityscapes

From singing and dancing cities to space needles and beyond, our cities, towns, and villages offer us unique places to live. How much do you know about these sites?

1 Which city was the capital of the United States before Washington, D.C.?

2 Which city in South Carolina gave its name to a type of dance?

3 In which city was the Motown record label founded?

4 What is the capital of Arizona?

5 Which is the only American city to be named after a British Prime Minister?

6 Which city is known as the home of country and western music?

7 In 1947, what allegedly crashed near Roswell, New Mexico?

8 Where is the Space Needle?

9 Which city is considered the capital of Silicon Valley?

10 From which city in the contiguous United States can you go south to Canada?

A State of Mind

Fifty stars, fifty states—thousands of trivia questions! Can you answer the state questions below?

1 What is the smallest state?

2 Which state joined the Union on January 3, 1959?

3 With which European nation did America conclude the Louisiana Purchase by buying over 800,000 square miles of land for $15 million?

4 In which state did Davy Crockett, Colonel Travis, and Jim Bowie perish while defending the Alamo?

5 In which state is the John F. Kennedy Space Center?

6 Which is the only state that begins with "A", but does not end in "A"?

7 Which state, founded in 1907, became the title of a movie musical in 1955?

8 Which state is known as the "Breadbasket of America"?

9 What became the 50th state?

10 In which state will you find the geographic center of the contiguous United States?

Americana

Going to Extremes

The highest, the lowest, the most, the least:
Which state lays claim to these extremes?

1 Which state grows the most wheat?
a. Oklahoma
b. Montana
c. Kansas

2 Which state had the lowest temperature recorded in U.S. history?
a. North Dakota
b. Alaska
c. Minnesota

3 Which state has the most lakes?
a. Alaska
b. Minnesota
c. Michigan

4 Which state has the largest living tree?
a. California
b. Washington
c. Maine

5 Which state had the biggest gold rush?
a. Colorado
b. Washington
c. California

6 Which contiguous state lies the farthest east?
a. Florida
b. Maine
c. Massachusetts

7 Which state raises the most cattle?
a. Texas
b. Oklahoma
c. Wyoming

8 Which state is the farthest south?
a. Arizona
b. Hawaii
c. Florida

9 Which state grows one-third of the potatoes in the United States?
a. Tennessee
b. Idaho
c. Maine

10 Which state has the most shoreline along the Atlantic Ocean?
a. Massachusetts
b. Virginia
c. Florida

Start a List

Some states have more in common than you think! Can you name...

1 The two states that start with "North"

2 The four states that start with "W"

3 The four states that start with "New"

4 The four states that start with "A"

5 Both states that start with "V"

6 The three states that start with "C"

7 The three states that start with "O"

8 Both states that start with "S"

9 Both states that start with "T"

10 The only state that starts with "L"

Six States, One Region

They've been around a long time: can you name the six states of New England?

A Capital Idea

Can you name the 50 states? If so, can you name the capitals of the states below?

1	Alabama	**11**	Mississippi
2	Alaska	**12**	Missouri
3	California	**13**	Montana
4	Delaware	**14**	Nevada
5	Florida	**15**	North Dakota
6	Kentucky	**16**	Oregon
7	Louisiana	**17**	Pennsylvania
8	Maine	**18**	Vermont
9	Maryland	**19**	Washington
10	Michigan	**20**	West Virginia

Nicknames

Which state is also known as...

The Peace Garden State_____	**A** Idaho
The Lone Star State_____	**B** Kansas
The Pine Tree State_____	**C** Maine
The Sunflower State_____	**D** Maryland
The Volunteer State_____	**E** Michigan
The Gem State_____	**F** Montana
The Treasure State_____	**G** North Dakota
The Great Lakes State_____	**H** Tennessee
The Beehive State_____	**I** Texas
The Old Line State_____	**J** Utah

Border States

Lakes, states, imaginary lines: they all serve as borders between states and nations. See if you can identify the borders below.

1 What two Great Lakes does Wisconsin have a shoreline on?

2 How many states border Alaska?

3 What body of water separates Russia from Alaska?

4 Which state has a border with both Maine and Vermont?

5 Which state shares a border with Washington and Montana?

6 Name the four states that share a border with Mexico.

7 Which circle of latitude is used as part of the border between the United States and Canada?

8 The United States borders which three oceans?

9 What body of water acts as a border between San Francisco and Oakland?

10 Name the two states that share a border with Florida.

11 Which state in New England does not border the ocean?

City-States

No, we're not talking about Ancient Greece. Instead, name four state capitals that include the word "city."

Geography

National parks, landmarks, forts: Geography in America is about so much more than north, south, east, and west. Test your knowledge about mountains and valleys, rivers and bays, and so much more in this mini GeoBee.

Parks for Grown-ups

Maybe you've visited some of these parks; maybe you haven't. Can you still identify them?

1 North America's highest mountain is located in which national park?

2 Which national park in Kentucky contains the world's largest known cave?

3 Which park served as an internment camp in World War II?

4 What does the Golden Spike National Historic Site in Utah commemorate?

5 In which park do alligators and crocodiles exist side by side?

6 In which state can you find Smokey Bear Historical State Park?

7 The Women's Rights National Historic Park marks the site of the first women's rights convention. Where is it?

8 Cadillac Mountain and Mount Desert Island call which park home?

9 What is the most visited national park?

10 In which state would you find Petrified Forest National Park?

11 Where is Canyonlands National Park located?

12 Which state is home to the Appomattox Court House National Historical Park?

13 In which state would you find Guadalupe Mountains National Park?

14 The majority of Yellowstone National Park lies in which state?

Home, Sweet Home

Do you really know where you are when you visit Yellowstone National Park? Name the three states that play host to it.

Extreme Behavior

Can you identify the country's highest, lowest, oldest, largest? See how you do here.

1 What is the lowest point of land in the United States?

2 Where are the country's tallest sand dunes?

3 The largest body of fresh water in the world is one of the Great Lakes. Which one is it?

4 What is the oldest city in the country?

5 What was the country's first national park?

6 In what state will you find the snowiest city?

7 Which state lies the farthest west?

8 What state recorded the highest temperature in the United States?

9 Where is the largest Chinatown outside Asia?

10 What is the United States' largest island?

A Place to Serve

They're not classified military secrets: Where are these military institutions?

1 United States Military Academy

2 United States Naval Academy

3 United States Coast Guard Academy

4 United States Merchant Marine Academy

5 United States Air Force Academy

Landmark Status

Sports stadiums and forts and aquariums—they're all U.S. landmarks. Can you match the landmark with its location?

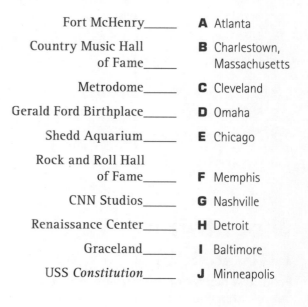

Fort McHenry_____	**A** Atlanta
Country Music Hall of Fame_____	**B** Charlestown, Massachusetts
Metrodome_____	**C** Cleveland
Gerald Ford Birthplace_____	**D** Omaha
Shedd Aquarium_____	**E** Chicago
Rock and Roll Hall of Fame_____	**F** Memphis
CNN Studios_____	**G** Nashville
Renaissance Center_____	**H** Detroit
Graceland_____	**I** Baltimore
USS *Constitution*_____	**J** Minneapolis

Where in the World?

In what city and state can you find each of the Ivy League colleges?

1 Yale

2 Harvard

3 Princeton

4 Columbia

5 Cornell

6 Brown

7 University of Pennsylvania

8 Dartmouth

Fort Nonsense?

Some of these statements about forts seem too silly to be true. But are they true? Or false?

1 Fort Dearborn became Detroit.	TRUE ○	FALSE ○
2 New Jersey has a Fort Nonsense.	TRUE ○	FALSE ○
3 Fort Ticonderoga was used in the Revolutionary War and in the French and Indian War.	TRUE ○	FALSE ○
4 Fort Putnam at the U.S. Military Academy at West Point overlooks Boston.	TRUE ○	FALSE ○
5 Fort McHenry was built to protect Washington.	TRUE ○	FALSE ○
6 Abraham Lincoln had a fort named after him in North Dakota.	TRUE ○	FALSE ○
7 Fort Worth, Texas, has never been a fort.	TRUE ○	FALSE ○
8 Fort King George is located in Georgia.	TRUE ○	FALSE ○

Mountains and Valleys

From the highs of mountains to the lows of valleys, this round of questions is sure to test your range of knowledge.

1 In what state are the majority of the Sierra Nevada Mountains?

2 Which state lays claim to Mount Whitney, the highest U.S. mountain outside Alaska?

3 Which mountains are higher: the Rockies or the Appalachians?

4 In which state is the Shenandoah Valley located?

5 In which national park is El Capitan, one of the most popular rock climbing destinations in the world?

6 Mount Saint Helens made news in 1980: why?

7 Mount Rushmore is located in which state?

8 In which state is the Santa Clara Valley located?

9 The White Mountains are part of what mountain chain?

10 Where are the Blue Ridge Mountains?

Water Wonderland

Rivers, canals, dams, bays: They're all here. Can you swim through these questions like a pro?

1 Lake Mead is located near which large city?

2 Which lake is the largest found completely in the United States?

3 What is the name of the bay that the Potomac River empties into?

4 Name one of the rivers that the Red River empties into.

5 Which bay is home to Alcatraz Island?

6 What narrow sea passage separates Alaska from Russia?

7 Memphis is located on the Mississippi River: true or false?

8 Which state is called the "Land of 10,000 Lakes"?

9 What dam created Lake Mead?

10 Which state lays claim to the mouth of the Mississippi River?

11 Which Great Lake is missing from this list: Ontario, Michigan, Erie, Superior?

12 Which canal opened for business in 1825?

Major American Events

From explorers to the Gold Rush to wars that shaped our country, this round focuses on everything from the discovery of Florida to the devastation of Hurricane Katrina. See how much you know about the events that changed our world.

Wonder About War?

Do you know the wars? The generals? What happened when? Test your war IQ in this round.

1 What is General MacArthur's first name?

2 In which war did General John J. Pershing command American troops?

3 In which war is *M*A*S*H* set?

4 Where did the Case-Church Amendment in 1973 prohibit further U.S. military intervention?

5 Which U.S. war was also known as the "Second War of Independence"?

6 American soldiers liberated the Philippine Islands in which war?

7 Other than Vietnam, where was the Vietnam War fought?

8 Hiroshima and what other city were targets of an atomic bomb in World War II?

9 In which war did the United States fight Canada?

10 In which war was the Battle of Midway fought?

11 Which war saw the Battle of Palo Alto?

12 In which war did American troops use trench warfare extensively?

13 What is the contemporary name for Armistice Day?

14 American soldiers invaded Cuba at the beginning of which war?

15 In 1949, the United States became a member of which military alliance?

And the Award Goes to...

Not the Academy Award: Name the highest military award bestowed by the U.S. government.

War, Part II

A range of wars, a range of questions: How well will you do?

1 In which war was the image of Uncle Sam first used?
   a. War of 1812
   b. Civil War
   c. World War I
   d. World War II

2 What killed the most soldiers during the Civil War?
   a. Hunger
   b. Disease
   c. Bullets
   d. Exposure

3 Which state was not a Confederate state?
   a. Kansas
   b. Florida
   c. Texas
   d. Louisiana

4 The United States declared war against which country in 1812?
   a. France
   b. Germany
   c. Britain
   d. Mexico

5 Which war saw the introduction of the income tax?
   a. Revolutionary War
   b. Civil War
   c. World War I
   d. World War II

6 In which century was the Mexican War?
   a. 17th
   b. 18th
   c. 19th
   d. 20th

7 Under which U.S. president were the last American troops withdrawn from Vietnam?
   a. Lyndon Johnson
   b. Richard Nixon
   c. Gerald Ford
   d. Ronald Reagan

8 What country did Iraq invade that led to the Persian Gulf War?
   a. Iran
   b. Afghanistan
   c. Israel
   d. Kuwait

9 During the Civil War, which side drafted soldiers?
   a. The Union
   b. The Confederacy
   c. Both
   d. Neither

10 About 50,000 soldiers were killed in which Civil War battle?
   a. Battle of Gettysburg
   b. Battle of Bull Run
   c. Battle of Fredericksburg
   d. Battle of Burgess' Mill

They Said That?

These military people are famous, and so are their statements.

1 What general proclaimed, "I shall return," when leaving the Philippines in World War II?

2 What naval commander said, "We have met the enemy, and they are ours"?

3 Which other naval commander said, "I have not yet begun to fight"?

4 Which naval hero said, "Don't give up the ship," during the War of 1812?

5 Who said, "Give me liberty or give me death"?

6 Which Alamo hero said, "Be sure you're right, then go ahead"?

The Civil War

Battles, generals, and surrender: they're all here in this quick quiz about the Civil War.

1 What is another name for the Battle of Pittsburgh Landing?

2 What was General Grant's birth name?

3 What surprising garment was Jefferson Davis wearing when he was captured?

4 Which Confederate state was the first to vote to secede from the Union?

5 What is a more popular name for the Battle of First Manassas?

6 What was the capital for most of the Confederacy?

7 The majority of Union troops wore what color uniform?

8 What was Stonewall Jackson's real name?

9 Only one Confederate was executed for war crimes. Who was it?

10 Who surrendered at Appomattox Court House?

11 Which Union general accepted the surrender at Appomattox Court House?

It's a Grand Old Flag

Every heart beats true for the red, white, and blue. But what's red and what's white? Is the statement below true or false?

There are seven white stripes and six red stripes on the American flag.

Wagons West

There's gold in them thar hills! Can you strike gold with your answers?

1 What kind of vehicle was a Conestoga?

2 By what popular name was the gunman James Butler Hickok known?

3 On the trail or on a cattle drive, what did the wrangler look after?

4 Which famous wagon trail that began in Independence, Missouri, wound all the way to the northwest?

5 What did the settlers do with a bit of jerky?

6 In western towns, what was a circuit rider?

7 Which hills in South Dakota were thick with gold hunters in 1874?

8 What popular name was given to the mail service between St. Joseph, Missouri, and San Francisco, California, from April 1860 to November 1861?

9 In which town did the Gunfight at the O. K. Corral take place?

10 What was a longhorn?

11 How was William Bonney better known?

12 Which animal is associated with William Frederick Cody?

The Numbers Game

Do you know both historical facts and figures? Test your number knowledge here.

1 In what year did Prohibition come into force?
a. 1914
b. 1919
c. 1926
d. 1929

2 In which century did slavery start in the South?
a. 15th century
b. 16th century
c. 17th century
d. 18th century

3 In which decade was the first transcontinental railroad finished?
a. 1830s
b. 1860s
c. 1890s
d. 1920s

4 What year was the Emancipation Proclamation enacted?
a. 1776
b. 1789
c. 1812
d. 1863

5 What year was NASA founded?
a. 1945
b. 1950
c. 1958
d. 1961

6 How many years are U.S. senators elected for?
a. Two
b. Four
c. Six
d. Eight

7 What year did Hurricane Katrina devastate New Orleans?
a. 2005
b. 2004
c. 2003
d. 2002

8 What year did the Hindenburg crash over New Jersey?
a. 1937
b. 1939
c. 1943
d. 1945

9 The severe drought in the Midwest, often called the "Dust Bowl," occurred in which decade?
a. 1910s
b. 1920s
c. 1930s
d. 1940s

What Does It All Mean?

They're very familiar acronyms. But what do the initials actually stand for?

1 CIA

2 USS (as in USS *Constitution*)

3 USDA

4 NASA

5 MASH

6 NASCAR

7 B&O Railroad

8 ASPCA

9 NYSE

10 GOP

11 POW

12 FBI

13 DEA

14 EPA

What Did They Find?

They came, they saw, they conquered. Who are they and what did they do?

1 Vitus Bering explored what region?

2 Daniel Boone explored the Kentucky wilderness: true or false?

3 Which city did Antoine de Cadillac found?

4 What is the name of the Indian guide and interpreter who accompanied Lewis and Clark?

5 Who was the first European to set foot in Florida?

6 The Hudson River is named after whom?

7 Louis Joliet and Father Jacques Marquette found which river in 1673?

8 Who bought the island of Manhattan in 1626 for $24?

9 Who lead the first expedition to the North Pole?

10 In Colorado, what is named after Zebulon M. Pike?

11 Captain James Cook was killed in Hawaii in 1779: true or false?

Name the Decade

In which decade of the 20th century did the following happen?

1 The famous "Monkey Trial" took place in Dayton, Tennessee.

2 Ronald Reagan starred in *Bedtime for Bonzo*.

3 Jimmy Hoffa disappeared.

4 The ill-fated 18th amendment became law.

5 Oliver North had his Iran-Contra convictions overturned.

6 Pearl Harbor was attacked by the Japanese.

7 Barney Clark was the first person to receive an artificial heart.

8 George Wallace ran for the presidency.

9 *Gone with the Wind* appeared in movie theaters.

10 The Vietnam War ended.

Words That Built a Nation

Actions may speak louder than words, but words helped build this country. From the opening of the Declaration of Independence to more recent state mottoes that proclaim their intentions, our documents and sayings transmit the nation's beliefs in liberty and justice for all. How familiar are you with these words?

Famous Words

See these questions about important words? Document your answers here!

1 What document starts with: "We the people of the United States, in order to form a more perfect Union"?

2 Who gave the first inaugural address?

3 Twelve amendments were originally proposed for the Bill of Rights; how many were ratified?

4 The Emancipation Proclamation ended slavery: true or false?

5 Which speech began with "Four score and seven years ago..."?

6 What did the 19th amendment grant?

7 What is the Economic Recovery Act of 1948 better known as?

8 Where did Executive Order 10730, signed by President Eisenhower on September 23, 1957, send federal troops?

9 What speech includes the following famous phrase: "Ask not what your country can do for you—ask what you can do for your country"?

The Constitution

You don't need a strong constitution to answer these questions about that famous document. What you do need is a good memory!

1 What year was the Constitution adopted?

2 When were women granted the right to vote?

3 The Constitution defines the three main branches of government: What are they?

4 What are the first 10 amendments known as?

5 How many times has the Constitution been amended?

6 In what city was the Constitution adopted?

7 What did the 13th amendment do?

8 Which amendment repealed the 18th amendment (regarding alcoholic beverages)?

9 What does the 22nd amendment limit?

10 Over 10,000 Constitutional amendments have been introduced in Congress since 1789: true or false?

American Documents, Part II

Here are more weighty words. Which do you recall?

1 What year was the Mayflower Compact signed?

2 What year was the Bill of Rights ratified?

3 For what occasion did Lincoln give the Gettysburg Address?

4 Lincoln's Gettysburg Address was about two minutes in length: true or false?

5 Which country signed the Louisiana Purchase Treaty with the United States?

6 The Treaty of Ghent ended which war?

7 What did President Lincoln issue on January 1, 1863?

8 The Monroe Doctrine warned which nations that the United States would not tolerate further colonization?

9 Which Supreme Court decision ended the "separate but equal" principle in education?

10 Which president signed into law the Civil Rights Act of 1964?

It's Official!

You may know your state's motto, but do you know your country's? Name the official motto of the United States.

State Sayings

Match the motto to the state, choosing from the list below.

In God We Trust_____   **A** Wyoming

Hope_____   **B** Texas

Equality Before the Law_____   **C** California

Eureka_____   **D** Wisconsin

North to the Future_____   **E** Delaware

Friendship_____   **F** Rhode Island

Equal Rights_____   **G** Florida

Forward_____   **H** Alaska

The Crossroads of America_____   **I** Indiana

Liberty and Independence_____   **J** Nebraska

In the Beginning

They may be oldies, but they're goodies. What do you know about these documents?

1 Who wrote the pamphlet *Common Sense*, which was published in 1776?

2 How many people signed the Declaration of Independence: 24, 37, or 56?

3 Where is the original Declaration of Independence today?

4 Who was the primary author of the Declaration of Independence?

5 Who was King of England when the Declaration of Independence was signed?

6 Who was the first person to sign the Declaration of Independence?

7 How many future presidents signed the Declaration of Independence?

8 Which piece of American currency shows the signing of the Declaration of Independence?

Famous Americans

Inventors, astronauts, politicians, athletes—and a bank robber and a pirate for good measure—show up in this section devoted to famous and infamous Americans. How much do you know about your fellow citizens?

Who Said It?

Famous words, famous speakers. Can you figure out who uttered the following statements?

1 "I only regret that I have but one life to lose for my country!"

2 "Let me assert my firm belief that the only thing we have to fear is fear itself...."

3 "There are no second acts in American lives."

4 "Nobody ever went broke underestimating the taste of the American public."

5 "These are the times that try men's souls."

6 "Senator, you're no Jack Kennedy."

7 "Sic semper tyrannis!"

8 "The British are coming!"

9 "When you come to a fork in the road, take it."

10 "Genius is 1 percent inspiration and 99 percent perspiration."

11 "Everyone wants to be Cary Grant. Even I want to be Cary Grant."

12 "Remember that time is money."

13 "A house divided against itself cannot stand."

14 "Man is the only animal that blushes. Or needs to."

15 "Take my wife, please."

16 "That's one small step for (a) man, one giant leap for mankind."

Fact or Fiction?

Are these American icons real people or fictional characters?

1 Daniel Boone

2 Pocohantas

3 Rip Van Winkle

4 Paul Bunyon

5 Johnny Appleseed

6 Pecos Bill

Who Are You?

Tinker, tailor, soldier, sailor: how well do you know these famous Americans?

1 Which letter of the alphabet did Malcolm Little adopt as his last name in 1952?

2 Which child actress of the 1930s became the American ambassador to Ghana?

3 Who was the second man to walk on the moon?

4 John D. Rockefeller made his fortune in which industry?

5 Thomas Edison held over 1,000 U.S. patents: true or false?

6 Who doesn't belong in this group: Billy the Kid, Buffalo Bill, Jesse James?

7 What was John Glenn the first American to do?

8 Who discovered a vaccine for polio?

9 Who was the first woman to run for president?

By Any Other Name

What's the more popular name for the following Americans?

1 John Chapman

2 Marion Michael Morrison

3 Cassius Clay

4 Old Brown of Osawatomie

5 Mary Anne Evans

6 Charles Lutwidge Dodgson

7 Allen Stewart Konigsberg

8 Joseph Louis Barrow

9 Frederick Austerlitz

10 Ralph Lifshitz

What's My Line?

Each person here is known for a particular "occupation." How does history remember them? Choose from the list below.

Jean Lafitte_____	**A** Astronaut
Shoeless Joe Jackson_____	**B** Bank robber
Kit Carson_____	**C** Baseball player
T. S. Eliot_____	**D** Deep Throat
George Marshall_____	**E** Figure skater
John Dillinger_____	**F** Frontiersman
Mark Felt_____	**G** Military commander
Cecil B. DeMille_____	**H** Movie director
Sally Ride_____	**I** Pirate
Michelle Kwan_____	**J** Poet
Carrie Chapman Catt_____	**K** Suffrage movement leader
Eddie Rickenbacker_____	**L** World War I pilot

Say What?

Some of these statements ring true; others don't. Which are true and which are false?

1 Albert Einstein was born in Germany.	TRUE ○	FALSE ○
2 Amelia Earhart named her first plane *Canary*.	TRUE ○	FALSE ○
3 Amelia Earhart was looking for Tahiti on her last flight.	TRUE ○	FALSE ○
4 John Glenn earned his pilot's license in the Air Force.	TRUE ○	FALSE ○
5 Susan B. Anthony was originally a teacher.	TRUE ○	FALSE ○
6 In 1928, Mickey Mouse appeared for the first time in *Steamboat Willie*.	TRUE ○	FALSE ○
7 Bill Gates dropped out of Yale.	TRUE ○	FALSE ○
8 In 1957, Martin Luther King Jr. founded the Southern Christian Leadership Conference.	TRUE ○	FALSE ○
9 Jesse Owens's real name is James Cleveland Owens.	TRUE ○	FALSE ○
10 Rosa Parks was 22 when she refused to give up her seat to a white man on a bus.	TRUE ○	FALSE ○

Who Thunk It?

Call them crazy, call them brilliant; these minds came up with some of our most famous inventions. Can you match the inventor to his or her invention? Choose from the list below.

John Moses Browning_____

Willis Carrier_____

Samuel Colt_____

Charles Goodyear_____

Cyrus McCormick_____

Edwin Binney and Harold Smith_____

Richard G. Drew_____

Mary Anderson_____

Dr. John Stith Pemberton_____

Lewis E. Waterman_____

A Coca-Cola

B Windshield wiper

C Air-conditioning

D Fountain pen

E Revolver

F Semiautomatic shotgun

G Vulcanized rubber

H Crayons

I Mechanical reaper

J Adhesive tape

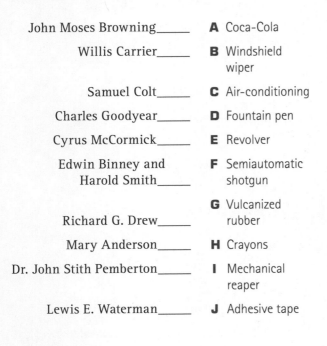

Twist My Arm

Name a musical Armstrong, an astronaut Armstrong, and an athlete Armstrong.

PAGE 9

Life in the Colonies

1 Jamestown
2 Georgia
3 People accused of witchcraft
4 Plymouth
5 Harvard
6 The Boston Massacre
7 Georgia
8 It was America's first continuously published newspaper
9 The mouth of the Hudson River
10 Tobacco

Early Americans

1 French
2 90 percent
3 West Coast
4 No
5 1621
6 Shawnee

Lucky 13

New Hampshire, Massachusetts, Rhode Island, Connecticut, New York, New Jersey, Pennsylvania, Delaware, Maryland, Virginia, North Carolina, South Carolina, Georgia

PAGE 10

War and Peace

1 c. April 19, 1775
2 a. Israel Putnam
3 d. The Treaty of Paris
4 c. December 16, 1773
5 a. John Nixon
6 b. The French
7 d. Snake
8 a. One
9 c. Molly Pitcher
10 b. Fool

PAGE 11

Names to Know

1 False
2 True
3 False
4 True
5 True
6 False
7 True
8 True
9 True
10 False

Who Founded What?*

1 Thomas Hooker
2 Peter Minuit and New Sweden Company
3 James Oglethorpe
4 Lord Baltimore
5 Puritans
6 John Wheelwright
7 Lord Berkeley and Sir George Carteret
8 Duke of York
9 Virginians
10 William Penn
11 Roger Williams
12 Eight English nobles
13 London Company

First, Last, and In-Between

1 Delaware
2 Delaware
3 Pennsylvania
4 Rhode Island
5 Virginia
6 North Carolina
7 Virginia Dare
8 North Carolina

PAGE 12

Mr. President!

1 John Adams
2 Thomas Jefferson
3 Calvin Coolidge
4 John F. Kennedy
5 Jefferson Davis
6 Herbert Hoover
7 George Washington, who approved the act that led to its construction
8 Franklin D. Roosevelt
9 Speaker of the House of Representatives
10 Franklin D. Roosevelt

Second in Line

1 They are all the official residences of vice presidents: Indonesia, Taiwan, and the United States, respectively
2 They have all won the Nobel Prize for Peace
3 No one; the office was vacant
4 Martin van Buren
5 They were all once vice presidents nominated for president—and then lost the election
6 Geraldine Ferraro
7 Richard Nixon
8 They were vice presidents that missed out on becoming president because they died, were replaced, or resigned from office
9 John Nance Garner, 32nd vice president

PAGE 13

Presidential Firsts

1 William Henry Harrison
2 Grover Cleveland
3 George Washington
4 Jimmy Carter
5 Warren Harding
6 Martin Van Buren
7 Bill Clinton
8 John Quincy Adams
9 Benjamin Harrison
10 Franklin D. Roosevelt
11 Andrew Jackson
12 Rutherford B. Hayes
13 Ronald Reagan
14 Richard Nixon
15 Theodore Roosevelt
16 James Buchanan
17 Lyndon B. Johnson
18 Woodrow Wilson
19 Abraham Lincoln
20 William Howard Taft

*Note: In all the Answer Keys throughout this book, the matching quizzes only contain the correct answer in order of the questions due to space constraints.

Answers

Friends and Relations

1 They are father and son
2 They are fifth cousins
3 They are fifth cousins
4 They are son and father
5 They are husband and wife

Name That Lady!

1 Martha
2 Abigail
3 Martha
4 Dolley
5 None; he was a bachelor
6 Mary Todd
7 Edith
8 Eleanor
9 Bess
10 Mamie

Details, Details

1 George Washington
2 Ronald Reagan
3 Children
4 Bill Clinton
5 Lyndon Johnson
6 Theodore Roosevelt
7 Franklin D. Roosevelt
8 Gerald Ford
9 Andrew Johnson and Bill Clinton

Untimely Ends

1 Ronald Reagan
2 James Garfield or William McKinley
3 Lee Harvey Oswald
4 *Our American Cousin*
5 William McKinley
6 Gerald Ford
7 Harry S. Truman
8 Andrew Jackson

Winners

Theodore Roosevelt, Woodrow Wilson, Jimmy Carter

Dopey Details

1 False; he plays the saxophone
2 True
3 True
4 False; Taft threw out the first pitch
5 True
6 False

Take the Money and Run

1 Abraham Lincoln
2 Thomas Jefferson
3 Franklin D. Roosevelt
4 George Washington
5 John F. Kennedy
6 George Washington
7 Thomas Jefferson
8 Abraham Lincoln
9 None—Alexander Hamilton
10 Andrew Jackson
11 Ulysses S. Grant
12 None—Benjamin Franklin

Isn't That Cute?

1 George Washington
2 Thomas Jefferson
3 James Madison
4 Andrew Jackson
5 William Henry Harrison
6 Zachary Taylor
7 William Howard Taft
8 Harry S. Truman
9 Ronald Reagan
10 George H. W. Bush

Figureheads

George Washington, Thomas Jefferson, Abraham Lincoln, Theodore Roosevelt

Batter Up!

1 Chicago Cubs
2 New York Islanders and New York Rangers
3 Figure skating
4 Michael Jordan
5 San Diego Chargers
6 San Francisco 49ers
7 Detroit Pistons
8 Los Angeles Galaxy
9 Football
10 Joe DiMaggio

Oscar Winners

1 1950
2 1949
3 1984
4 1977
5 1943
6 2005
7 1990
8 1982
9 2000
10 1972
11 1969
12 1954
13 1965
14 1997
15 1927/1928
16 1938

First Choices

1 Mars
2 Laundromat
3 Colin Powell
4 Appendix operation
5 Basketball
6 Charles Lindbergh
7 Jackie Robinson
8 The first U.S. postage stamp
9 Boston
10 Walk in space

Talking Boxes

1 Jim Henson
2 Fred Rogers
3 Art Fleming, Alex Trebek
4 New York City
5 Dick Clark
6 Steve Allen
7 The Shadow
8 Rob Reiner
9 Rush Limbaugh
10 Mary Kay Stearns in *Mary Kay and Johnny*

Olympic Dreams

1 Summer: St. Louis, Missouri; Los Angeles, California (twice); Atlanta, Georgia
2 Winter: Lake Placid, New York (twice); Squaw Valley, California; Salt Lake City, Utah

PAGE 18

Higher Learning

1 False; it's in Ohio
2 False; Columbia University awards the Pulitzers
3 True
4 False; it takes place at Massachusetts Institute of Technology
5 True
6 False; it's in Pittsburgh
7 True
8 False; Columbia University is correct
9 True
10 True
11 True

Just Call Me Author

1 Theodor Seuss Geisel
2 Margaret Mitchell
3 Embezzlement
4 Edgar Allan Poe
5 E. B. White
6 Robert Frost
7 Michael Crichton
8 Edward Stratemeyer
9 Emma Lazarus
10 Isaac Asimov

American Ivy

Brown, Columbia, Cornell, Dartmouth, Harvard, Princeton, University of Pennsylvania, Yale

PAGE 19

Novel Ideas

1 *Catch-22*
2 *A Wind in the Door, A Swiftly Tilting Planet, Many Waters,* and *An Acceptable Time*
3 *Little Women*
4 *The Great Gatsby*
5 *Of Mice and Men*

6 *Invisible Man*
7 *The Power of Sympathy* by William Hill Brown (1789)
8 *Babbitt*
9 *The Green Mile*
10 *Moby Dick*

And the Award Goes to...

1 Cy Young Award
2 Heisman Trophy
3 Emmy Awards
4 Grammy Awards
5 Golden Globe Awards
6 Academy Awards (or Oscars)
7 Peabody Awards
8 Tony Awards
9 Obie Awards

Halls of Fame

1 Cleveland, Ohio
2 Springfield, Massachusetts
3 Cooperstown, New York
4 Canton, Ohio
5 Newport, Rhode Island
6 Nashville, Tennessee
7 South Bend, Indiana
8 Holyoke, Massachusetts
9 Ft. Lauderdale, Florida

PAGE 20

A Song in My Heart

1 Francis Scott Key
2 John Philip Sousa
3 Aretha Franklin
4 Louis Armstrong
5 Elvis Presley
6 Dolly Parton
7 Steve Martin
8 Judy Garland
9 Johnny Cash
10 Bing Crosby

PAGE 21

Cityscapes

1 Philadelphia (New York was the first capital)
2 Charleston
3 Detroit, Michigan
4 Phoenix

5 Pittsburgh, named after William Pitt
6 Nashville, Tennessee
7 A UFO
8 Seattle, Washington
9 San Jose, California
10 Detroit, Michigan

A State of Mind

1 Rhode Island
2 Alaska
3 France
4 Texas
5 Florida
6 Arkansas
7 Oklahoma
8 Kansas
9 Hawaii
10 Kansas

PAGE 22

Going to Extremes

1 c. Kansas
2 b. Alaska
3 a. Alaska
4 a. California
5 c. California
6 b. Maine
7 a. Texas
8 b. Hawaii
9 b. Idaho
10 c. Florida

Six States, One Region

Connecticut, Maine, Massachusetts, New Hampshire, Rhode Island, and Vermont comprise the states of New England.

Start a List

1 North Carolina and North Dakota
2 Washington, West Virginia, Wisconsin, Wyoming
3 New Hampshire, New Jersey, New Mexico, New York
4 Alabama, Alaska, Arizona, Arkansas
5 Vermont and Virginia
6 California, Colorado, Connecticut
7 Ohio, Oklahoma, Oregon
8 South Carolina and South Dakota
9 Tennessee and Texas
10 Louisiana

Answers

PAGE 23

A Capital Idea

1 Montgomery
2 Juneau
3 Sacramento
4 Dover
5 Tallahassee
6 Frankfort
7 Baton Rouge
8 Augusta
9 Annapolis
10 Lansing
11 Jackson
12 Jefferson City
13 Helena
14 Carson City
15 Bismarck
16 Salem
17 Harrisburg
18 Montpelier
19 Olympia
20 Charleston

Nicknames

1 North Dakota
2 Texas
3 Maine
4 Kansas
5 Tennessee
6 Idaho
7 Montana
8 Michigan
9 Utah
10 Maryland

Border States

1 Lakes Superior and Michigan
2 None
3 The Bering Strait
4 New Hampshire
5 Idaho
6 California, Arizona, New Mexico, and Texas
7 The 49th parallel
8 The Atlantic, Pacific, and Arctic Oceans
9 San Francisco Bay
10 Alabama and Georgia
11 Vermont

City-States

Carson City, Jefferson City, Oklahoma City, Salt Lake City

PAGE 24

Parks for Grown-ups

1 Denali National Park and Preserve
2 Mammoth Cave National Park
3 Manzanar National Historic Site
4 The completion of the transcontinental railroad
5 Everglades National Park
6 New Mexico
7 Seneca Falls, New York
8 Acadia National Park
9 Great Smoky Mountains National Park
10 Arizona
11 Utah
12 Virginia
13 Texas
14 Wyoming

Home, Sweet Home

Wyoming, Montana, and Idaho

PAGE 25

Extreme Behavior

1 Death Valley in California
2 In the Great Sand Dunes National Park and Preserve in Colorado
3 Lake Superior
4 St. Augustine, Florida
5 Yellowstone
6 California (Blue Canyon)
7 Alaska
8 California
9 San Francisco
10 Hawaii

A Place to Serve

1 West Point, New York
2 Annapolis, Maryland
3 New London, Connecticut
4 Kings Point, New York
5 Colorado Springs, Colorado

Landmark Status

1 Baltimore
2 Nashville
3 Minneapolis
4 Omaha
5 Chicago
6 Cleveland
7 Atlanta
8 Detroit
9 Memphis
10 Charlestown, Massachusetts

Where in the World?

1 New Haven, Connecticut
2 Cambridge, Massachusetts
3 Princeton, New Jersey
4 New York, New York
5 Ithaca, New York
6 Providence, Rhode Island
7 Philadelphia, Pennsylvania
8 Hanover, New Hampshire

PAGE 26

Fort Nonsense?

1 False
2 True
3 True
4 False
5 False
6 True
7 True
8 True

Mountains and Valleys

1 California
2 California
3 Rocky Mountains
4 Virginia
5 Yosemite
6 It erupted
7 South Dakota
8 California
9 Appalachian Mountains
10 Georgia to Pennsylvania

Water Wonderland

1 Las Vegas
2 Lake Michigan
3 Chesapeake Bay
4 Mississippi River and Atchafalaya River
5 San Francisco Bay
6 The Bering Strait
7 True
8 Minnesota
9 Hoover Dam
10 Louisiana
11 Huron
12 Erie Canal

PAGE 27

Wonder About War?

1 Douglas
2 World War I
3 Korean War
4 Southeast Asia
5 War of 1812
6 World War II
7 Laos and Cambodia
8 Nagasaki
9 The War of 1812
10 World War II
11 Mexican-American War
12 World War I
13 Veterans Day
14 Spanish-American War
15 NATO

And the Award Goes to...

The Medal of Honor

PAGE 28

War, Part II

1 a. War of 1812
2 b. Disease
3 a. Kansas
4 c. Britain
5 b. Civil War
6 c. 19th
7 c. Gerald Ford
8 d. Kuwait
9 c. Both
10 a. Battle of Gettysburg

They Said That?

1 Douglas MacArthur
2 Commodore Oliver Hazard Perry
3 John Paul Jones
4 James Lawrence
5 Patrick Henry
6 Davy Crockett

PAGE 29

The Civil War

1 Shiloh
2 Hiram Ulysses Grant
3 His wife's coat
4 South Carolina
5 The First Battle of Bull Run
6 Richmond, Virginia
7 Blue
8 Thomas Jonathan Jackson
9 Henry Wirz
10 General Robert E. Lee
11 Ulysses S. Grant

It's a Grand Old Flag

False: There are six white stripes and seven red stripes.

Wagons West

1 It was a covered wagon, named after a valley in Pennsylvania
2 Wild Bill Hickok
3 Horses
4 The Oregon Trail
5 They chewed it—it was dried meat
6 A traveling preacher
7 The Black Hills
8 Pony Express
9 Tombstone, Arizona
10 Tough, half-wild cattle, roaming the unfenced ranches
11 Billy the Kid
12 Buffalo; his nickname was Buffalo Bill

PAGE 30

The Numbers Game

1 b. 1919
2 c. 17th century
3 b. 1860s
4 d. 1863
5 c. 1958
6 c. Six
7 a. 2005
8 a. 1937
9 c. 1930s

What Does It All Mean?

1 Central Intelligence Agency
2 United States ship
3 United States Department of Agriculture
4 National Aeronautics and Space Administration
5 Mobile Army Surgical Hospital
6 National Association for Stock Car Auto Racing
7 Baltimore and Ohio Railroad
8 American Society for the Prevention of Cruelty to Animals
9 New York Stock Exchange
10 Grand Old Party
11 Prisoner of War
12 Federal Bureau of Investigation
13 Drug Enforcement Administration
14 Environmental Protection Agency

PAGE 31

What Did They Find?

1 Coast of Alaska
2 True
3 Detroit
4 Sacagawea
5 Ponce de Leon
6 Henry Hudson
7 Mississippi River
8 Peter Minuit
9 Robert Peary
10 Pike's Peak
11 True

Answers

PAGE 31 (CONT.)

Name the Decade

1 1920s
2 1950s
3 1970s
4 1910s
5 1990s
6 1940s
7 1980s
8 1960s
9 1930s
10 1970s

PAGE 32

Famous Words

1 The Constitution
2 George Washington
3 10
4 False
5 Lincoln's Gettysburg Address
6 Women the right to vote
7 The Marshall Plan
8 Little Rock, Arkansas, to maintain order and peace while the integration of Central High School took place
9 John F. Kennedy's 1961 inaugural address

The Constitution

1 1787
2 1920
3 Legislative, judicial, and executive
4 The Bill of Rights
5 27
6 Philadelphia
7 Abolish slavery and grant Congress power to enforce abolition
8 The 21st amendment
9 A president to two terms
10 True

PAGE 33

American Documents, Part II

1 1620
2 1791
3 The dedication for the cemetery for the Union war dead
4 True
5 France
6 The War of 1812
7 The Emancipation Proclamation
8 European
9 Brown v. Board of Education
10 Lyndon Johnson

It's Official!

In God We Trust

State Sayings

1 Florida
2 Rhode Island
3 Nebraska
4 California
5 Alaska
6 Texas
7 Wyoming
8 Wisconsin
9 Indiana
10 Delaware

In the Beginning

1 Thomas Paine
2 56
3 National Archives in Washington, D.C.
4 Thomas Jefferson
5 George III
6 John Hancock
7 Two
8 The $2 bill

PAGE 34

Who Said It?

1 Nathan Hale
2 Franklin D. Roosevelt
3 F. Scott Fitzgerald
4 H. L. Mencken

5 Thomas Paine
6 Lloyd Bentsen
7 John Wilkes Booth
8 Paul Revere
9 Yogi Berra
10 Thomas Edison
11 Cary Grant
12 Benjamin Franklin
13 Abraham Lincoln
14 Mark Twain
15 Henny Youngman
16 Neil Armstrong

PAGE 35

Fact or Fiction?

1 Real
2 Real
3 Fictional
4 Fictional
5 Real
6 Fictional

Who Are You?

1 X
2 Shirley Temple
3 Edwin "Buzz" Aldrin Jr.
4 Oil
5 True
6 Buffalo Bill
7 Orbit the earth
8 Jonas Salk
9 Victoria Woodhull

By Any Other Name

1 Johnny Appleseed
2 John Wayne
3 Muhammad Ali
4 John Brown
5 George Eliot
6 Lewis Carroll
7 Woody Allen
8 Joe Louis
9 Fred Astaire
10 Ralph Lauren

What's My Line?

1 Pirate
2 Baseball player
3 Frontiersman
4 Poet
5 Military commander
6 Bank robber
7 Deep Throat
8 Movie director
9 Astronaut
10 Figure skater
11 Suffrage movement leader
12 World War I pilot

PAGE 36

Say What?

1 True
2 True
3 False
4 False
5 True
6 True
7 False
8 True
9 True
10 False

Who Thunk It?

1 Semiautomatic shotgun
2 Air-conditioning
3 Revolver
4 Vulcanized rubber
5 Mechanical reaper
6 Crayons
7 Adhesive tape
8 Windshield wiper
9 Coca-Cola
10 Fountain pen

Twist My Arm

Louis, Neil, Lance

2 Entertainment

The actors' faces, the suspenseful stories, the clever dialogue, the toe-tapping tunes you can't get out of your head—all of these and more make movies, television, music, theater, and other entertainment an indelible part of life. Ready for an entertaining challenge?

Screens Big and Small

Flicks, films, movies, "talkies"—whatever you call them, they play a powerful role in our culture. Thanks, Hollywood, for the memories. (Hey, we'll always have Paris.) Lights, camera, action!

Trivia in Technicolor

Here are some colorful questions about the big screen to get us started.

1 During which war was the 1968 film *The Green Berets* set?

2 Which Quentin Tarantino film features the characters Mr. Orange, Mr. Pink, and Mr. White?

3 In which 1990 film did Sean Connery play a defecting Soviet submarine commander?

4 Oprah Winfrey made her big-screen debut in which award-winning dramatic film?

5 Which film introduced Peter Sellers as the bumbling Inspector Clouseau?

6 In which 1968 animated film were the villains called the Blue Meanies?

7 Which 1986 film features Eddie Murphy as the bodyguard to a child with supernatural powers?

8 Which 1939 epic was the first color film to win a Best Picture Oscar?

9 What 1967 Swedish film caused a stir because of its sexual frankness?

10 In which 1997 film do Tommy Lee Jones and Will Smith attempt to keep the hidden population of aliens under control in New York City?

Making Connections

Identify the missing link in each of these questions.

1 What connects the films *Enter the Dragon*, *The Curse of Frankenstein*, and *Malcolm X*?

2 Peter Sellers, Alan Arkin, and Roberto Benigni are connected by which film role?

3 Who connects the films *The Doors*, *JFK*, and *Natural Born Killers*?

4 The films *Private Benjamin*, *Bird on a Wire*, and *The First Wives Club* are connected by whom?

5 Who connects *The Professional (aka Léon)* to *Star Wars Episode I: The Phantom Menace*?

6 What connects Olive Oyl to the film *The French Connection*?

7 Which 1963 film connects James Garner, James Coburn, and Charles Bronson?

8 What connects a female deer with a drink with jam and bread?

9 What surname connects the thespians Gordon, Glenda, and Samuel L.?

10 Who connects *T.J. Hooker* and *Star Trek*?

The Name Is James

Answer true or false.

1 *James and the Giant Peach* was a 1996 film adaptation of a book by Maurice Sendak.   TRUE ○   FALSE ○

2 Santino "Sonny" Corleone was played by James Caan in the movie *The Godfather*.   TRUE ○   FALSE ○

3 In 1950, Jimmy Stewart played a down-and-out character with an invisible rabbit named Harvey for a friend.   TRUE ○   FALSE ○

4 Who stars in the 1996 Brian De Palma film *Mission: Impossible*?   TRUE ○   FALSE ○

5 In the movie *Angels with Dirty Faces*, James Cagney costarred with Abbott & Costello.   TRUE ○   FALSE ○

6 Stewart Granger had to change his birth name, James Stewart, because another actor was using it.   TRUE ○   FALSE ○

7 On *Star Trek*, the middle initial of Captain James T. Kirk, commander of the *Starship Enterprise*, stood for Thomas.   TRUE ○   FALSE ○

8 British actor James Mason died in 1984 shortly after starring in the film *The Shooting Party*.   TRUE ○   FALSE ○

9 Roger Moore portrayed James Bond only four times.   TRUE ○   FALSE ○

10 James Leary played the title role in the TV Western *The Virginian*.   TRUE ○   FALSE ○

11 For his role as an oil tycoon in *Giant*, James Dean died his hair gray and shaved his scalp to create a receding hairline.   TRUE ○   FALSE ○

Film Buff Special

If you're passionate about the art of cinema, this round is for you.

1 Who was the star of the 1953 French comedy *Mr. Hulot's Holiday*?

2 Who directed the classic film of the French New Wave, *À Bout de Souffle*?

3 Which Japanese film, directed by Akira Kurosawa, was the inspiration for *The Magnificent Seven*?

4 Who directed the Australian film *Picnic at Hanging Rock*?

5 In which 1957 film does Henry Fonda play the sole juror to stand against a guilty verdict at a trial?

6 Who directed the 1980 film of Stephen King's horror novel *The Shining*?

7 Who directed the 2001 film *Moulin Rouge!*?

8 D. W. Griffith's *The Birth of a Nation* was accused of reviving which organization?

9 Who made the Apu trilogy of films, the first of which was *Pather Panchali*?

10 Which Ingmar Bergman film features the theatrical Ekdahl family in early 20-century Sweden?

Call Him Duke

John Wayne made over 200 films during the course of his career. Can you name 20 of them?

Famous and Oh, So Young

Check out these facts about the kids we see growing up on screen. Answer true or false.

1 Child actor Bart Carey, married eight times, once said, "I was a 14-year-old boy for 30 years."   TRUE ○   FALSE ○

2 Kevin McCallister was left home alone in New York City in a 1992 film.   TRUE ○   FALSE ○

3 Shirley Temple was the youngest person ever to receive an Oscar in the 20th century.   TRUE ○   FALSE ○

4 Drew Barrymore played Elliott's sister in *ET: The Extra-Terrestrial*.   TRUE ○   FALSE ○

5 Evin Cosby costarred with her father, Bill, in the film *Nickelodeon*.   TRUE ○   FALSE ○

6 Mark Lester played the Dickens character Tiny Tim in a 1968 film.   TRUE ○   FALSE ○

7 Christina Ricci played the daughter, Wednesday, in *The Munsters*.   TRUE ○   FALSE ○

8 Natalie Wood first came to light in the 1947 film *Miracle on 34th Street*.   TRUE ○   FALSE ○

9 Child film star Shirley Temple became the U.S. ambassador to Morocco in the 1970s.   TRUE ○   FALSE ○

Screen Test: Even More Connections

These brain-teasers may require a little research—got your remote ready?

1 Which role connects Audrey Hepburn in a 1976 film and Mary Elizabeth Mastrantonio in a 1991 film?

2 What is the connection between the films *Easy Rider*, *The China Syndrome*, and *My Darling Clementine*?

3 What is the connection between the TV show *ER* and the films *Jurassic Park* and *Congo*?

4 Who connects the films *El Cid*, *Major Dundee*, and *The Omega Man*?

5 What is the connection between the films *Ghost*, *Octopussy*, and *10*?

6 What connects the films *The Forbidden Planet*, *West Side Story*, and *Kiss Me Kate*?

7 What is the connection between Rita Coolidge, Nancy Sinatra, and Sheryl Crow?

8 What is the connection between the films *Three Men and a Baby*, *Natural Born Killers*, and *Look Who's Talking*?

9 What was the name of the cruise ship in the TV series *The Love Boat*?

10 *Dead Men Don't Wear Plaid*, *Against All Odds*, *The Umbrella Woman*, and *The Thorn Birds* are all connected by which actress?

11 Who is Enrique Claudin, played on film by Herbert Lom, Claude Rains, and Lon Chaney?

12 Who is the only actor to be nominated for Oscars in the 1950s, '60s, '70s, and '80s?

13 Which film opens with the line "No man's life can be encompassed in one telling"?

14 Her real name is Tula Finklea, and she costarred with Fred Astaire in the 1953 film *The Band Wagon*. What is her stage name?

Heaven and Hell

Here's a celestial, sometimes devilish, round of questions.

1 In which 1978 high school film does Frankie Avalon descend from heaven to sing "Beauty School Dropout"?

2 At the end of which 1990 film did Patrick Swayze ascend to heaven?

3 Who was Ronald Reagan's leading lady in the 1957 film *Hellcats of the Navy*?

4 In which TV series did Michael Landon play an angel on Earth?

5 In Frank Capra's 1946 film *It's a Wonderful Life*, how does an angel earn its wings?

6 Which series of horror flicks features a fearsome-looking character called Pinhead?

7 Which 1978 film featured Warren Beatty as a wrongfully killed quarterback?

8 Which Rodgers and Hammerstein musical features a man returning from heaven?

9 In the 1999 film *Dogma*, which supreme role was played by Alanis Morissette?

10 In *High Plains Drifter*, Clint Eastwood painted the town red and signposted it what?

Hey, Good-Looking!

Here are some beautiful questions to worry your pretty head with.

1 Who played pretty woman Vivian Ward on film?

2 In the Disney version of *Beauty and the Beast*, what was Beauty's name?

3 Which famous actress won the Miss Hungary title in 1936?

4 The song "I Feel Pretty" features in which musical?

5 Which former national beauty queen appeared in *Swordfish* alongside John Travolta and won an Oscar for her performance in *Monster's Ball*?

6 What rating of beauty was given to Bo Derek in a 1979 Blake Edwards film starring Dudley Moore?

7 In a 1986 film, which color was the actress Molly Ringwald pretty in?

8 Who won a best actor Oscar for his role in the 1999 film *American Beauty*?

9 Which French sex symbol married the film director Roger Vadim?

10 Which Disney film featured the song "Once Upon a Dream"?

Titles and Entitlement

Find out how well you know princes, kings, and the trappings of royalty.

1 Who made a fleeting appearance as King Richard at the end of the film *Robin Hood: Prince of Thieves*?

2 Which actor played CIA deputy director James Greer in adaptations of Tom Clancy novels?

3 When Robert De Niro played the monster, which actor played Baron Victor Frankenstein?

4 Who played the lead in the 1991 film *King Ralph*?

5 Who wrote the novel on which Stanley Kubrick's 1980 film *The Shining* was based?

6 Which actor played Tom Wingo, who fell in love with Barbra Streisand's Susan Lowenstein, in the 1991 film *The Prince of Tides*?

7 Peter O'Toole played which English king in the films *Becket* and *The Lion in Winter*?

8 Who provides the adult Simba's voice in the Disney animated film *The Lion King*?

Driving Tests

Hop in and take these questions for a spin!

1 Which actress drove a bus with a bomb on board in the film *Speed*?
   a. Sandra Bullock   b. Jodi Foster
   c. Meryl Streep   d. Cher

2 In which 1968 film did Steve McQueen drive a Ford Mustang?
   a. *Cannonball Run*   b. *Taxi Driver*
   c. *Bullitt*   d. *Easy Rider*

3 What was the name of the 1984 film in which Eddie Murphy drove a tank?
   a. *A Bridge Too Far* b. *Best Defense*
   c. *Tank Girl*   d. *Dead Men Don't Wear Plaid*

4 What was the 1993 film in which Michael Douglas played a motorist stuck in a traffic jam who eventually cracked under the pressure?
   a. *Falling Down*   b. *Die Hard*
   c. *Young Guns*   d. *Crack-Up*

5 Which 1969 film featured Dennis Hopper driving a chopper motorcycle?
   a. *Easy Rider*   b. *Gone in 60 Seconds*
   c. *Thunder Road*   d. *Grease*

6 In which 1971 film did Steve McQueen compete in a famous 24-hour race?
   a. *Marathon Man*   b. *The Road Warrior*
   c. *Papillon*   d. *Le Mans*

7 Which 1965 film, costarring Jack Lemmon and Tony Curtis, was set in 1908?
   a. *The Great Race*   b. *The Time Machine*
   c. *It's a Mad, Mad, Mad World*   d. *Gentlemen Prefer Blondes*

8 At the end of which 1991 film did Geena Davis drive a car into a canyon?
   a. *The Blues Brothers* b. *Vertigo*
   c. *Thelma and Louise*   d. *Ghost*

9 Name the actor who played the chauffeur in the film *Driving Miss Daisy*.
   a. Morgan Freeman   b. Donald Pleasance
   c. Wesley Snipes   d. Clarence Williams III

10 Which 1971 Steven Spielberg film featured a traveler terrorized by an evil truck driver?
   a. *The Hitcher*   b. *Duel*
   c. *American Graffiti* d. *Christine*

Maybe Baby

Try these very childish questions.

1 In which 1968 film did Mia Farrow give birth to the son of Satan?

2 Which *Star Trek* actor directed the film *Three Men and a Baby*?

3 What sort of animal was Baby in the film *Bringing Up Baby*, starring Cary Grant?

4 Name the 1987 film in which Diane Keaton played an executive who acquires a baby.

5 Which actor-director named his son Satchel?

6 The life of which sporting legend was chronicled in the 1992 film *The Babe*?

7 What was the title of the 1998 sequel to the 1995 film *Babe*?

8 Who starred alongside Holly Hunter in the 1987 film *Raising Arizona*?

9 Which comedy duo assisted Santa Claus in the 1934 film *Babes in Toyland*?

10 In which film sequel did Rick Moranis inadvertently expose his two-year-old son to a ray that made him grow excessively?

A Robotic Question

The late 1950s produced dozens of B movies about space aliens. Can you name 10 of them?

Spooks and Specters

Here's a round to chill your bones! Answer true or false.

1 Haley Joel Osment played Cole Sear, the boy who could see dead people, in *The Sixth Sense*. TRUE ○ FALSE ○

2 Tobe Hooper directed the 1982 film *Poltergeist*. TRUE ○ FALSE ○

3 Marie Osmond played the possessed child in *The Exorcist*. TRUE ○ FALSE ○

4 *The Ghost and Mrs. Robinson* was a 1947 film starring Rex Harrison that told the story of a widow's love for a ghost. TRUE ○ FALSE ○

5 Jack Nicholson started his career in the 1960s horror films *The Raven*, *The Terror*, and *The Little Shop of Horrors*. TRUE ○ FALSE ○

6 Demi Moore's character in the film *Ghost* was named Molly. TRUE ○ FALSE ○

7 The 1983 film *Christine*, based on a Stephen King novel, told the story of a demented librarian. TRUE ○ FALSE ○

8 In the 1989 Steven Spielberg film *Always*, Richard Dreyfuss plays a ghost watching over his girlfriend. TRUE ○ FALSE ○

9 Alfred Hitchcock directed the 1973 supernatural thriller *Don't Look Now*, starring Donald Sutherland and Julie Christie. TRUE ○ FALSE ○

10 The film *Blithe Spirit* was based on a play written by Noel Coward. TRUE ○ FALSE ○

11 In the 1981 movie *Ghost Story*, Fred Astaire plays a New England lawyer haunted by the demise of a long-dead love interest. TRUE ○ FALSE ○

Action!

Which films open with the following memorable lines? Match your answers from the list below.

"I never knew the old Vienna before the war, with its Strauss music, its glamour, and easy charm."_____

A *Monty Python and the Holy Grail*

"Saigon..."_____

B *Strangers on a Train*

"Henslowe, do you know what happens to a man who doesn't pay his debts? His boots catch fire!"_____

C *Shakespeare in Love*

"I beg your pardon, but aren't you Guy Haines?"_____

D *The Godfather*

"Last night, I dreamt I went to Manderley again."_____

E *Rebecca*

"So this is the world, and there are almost six billion people on it. When I was a kid, there were three. It's hard to keep up."_____

F *Apocalypse Now*

"The white zone is for immediate loading and unloading of passengers only."_____

G *Airplane!*

"It is I, Arthur, son of Uther Pendragon from the castle of Camelot. King of the Britons, defeater of the Saxons, Sovereign of all England!"_____

H *Jerry Maguire*

"Chapter One. He adored New York City. He idolized it out of all proportion."_____

I *The Third Man*

"I believe in America. America has made my fortune."_____

J *Manhattan*

Science Fiction Facts

Do you know your way around space, aliens, and other far-out matters?

1 Who plays the part of Ripley in the *Alien* films?

2 Which 1995 film starring Tom Hanks told the true story of a failed moon mission?

3 In which 1977 film did Richard Dreyfuss attempt to mold a sculpture from mashed potatoes?

4 Which cult sci-fi film starring Harrison Ford was based on the novel *Do Androids Dream of Electric Sheep?*

5 Which ex-Monty Python member directed the 1995 film *Twelve Monkeys*, starring Bruce Willis?

6 Which 1927 film directed by Fritz Lang is regarded as the first great science-fiction film?

7 Who wrote the book from which Stanley Kubrick made the film *2001: A Space Odyssey?*

8 In which sequel did Arnold Schwarzenegger appear as a destructor in 1991?

9 Which film, made in 1956 with Kevin McCarthy, was remade in 1978 starring Donald Sutherland?

10 In the film *Mars Attacks!*, who played the president of the United States?

11 In *2001: A Space Odyssey*, what does Hal the computer do as its intelligence drains away?

Metallic Movies

Steel yourself for these heavy-metal questions.

1 Who played Private Joker in the 1987 film *Full Metal Jacket?*

2 In which 1989 film did Julia Roberts suffer from diabetes?

3 For which film did Jeremy Irons win a best actor Oscar for his portrayal of Claus von Bülow?

4 In *Pushing Tin*, the 1999 comedy starring John Cusack, to what does the title refer?

5 Name the actor famous for playing Tarzan on TV and who played *Doc Savage, The Man of Bronze* on film.

6 In which 1976 film did Gene Wilder witness a murder on a transcontinental train?

7 Which 1998 version of an Alexandre Dumas novel starred Leonardo DiCaprio?

8 Name the 1987 film in which Richard Dreyfuss and Danny DeVito played two feuding salesmen.

9 The 1999 animated film *The Iron Giant* was based on a book by which English poet?

10 In the 1980s TV series *Remington Steele*, Pierce Brosnan's title character is a ruse. What's the purpose?

On the Beach

Life is a beach (and so are these questions)! Answer them true or false.

1 *The Sandpiper* was a 1953 film in which Burt Lancaster embraced Deborah Kerr on the beach. TRUE ◯ FALSE ◯

2 The full name of the character played by David Hasselhoff in *Baywatch* was Mitch Buchannon. TRUE ◯ FALSE ◯

3 The beaches of Amity Island were terrorized by a shark in the *Amityville Horror* series of films. TRUE ◯ FALSE ◯

4 The first 20 minutes of the 1998 box office smash *Saving Private Ryan* depict the bloody storming of Omaha Beach in the Second World War. TRUE ◯ FALSE ◯

5 Bette Midler starred in the 1988 film *Beaches*. TRUE ◯ FALSE ◯

6 In the 1962 film *Goldfinger*, we see Ursula Andress walking from the sea onto the beach in a white bikini. TRUE ◯ FALSE ◯

7 The film *Quadrophenia* depicts a seaside battle at the British resort Brighton. TRUE ◯ FALSE ◯

8 In *Planet of the Apes* (1968), Charlton Heston sinks to his knees upon discovering the Statue of Liberty buried in the sand. TRUE ◯ FALSE ◯

9 Alex Garland's *The Beach* is set in Thailand. TRUE ◯ FALSE ◯

10 Gregory Peck plays the male lead in the film version of Nevil Shute's novel *On the Beach*. TRUE ◯ FALSE ◯

Big Screen Quotes

From which films are the following lines taken? Match the right quote to the right movie.

"I'm sorry, honey, but you know…toys don't last forever."_____   **A** *The Graduate*

"Chuck! Chuck! It's Marvin, your cousin, Marvin Berry. You know that new sound you're looking for? Well, listen to this!"_____   **B** *Notting Hill*

"It's from the Talmud. It says, 'Whoever saves one life, saves the world entire.'"_____   **C** *The Usual Suspects*

"The greatest trick the devil ever pulled was to convince the world he didn't exist."_____   **D** *Back to the Future*

"I love the smell of Napalm in the morning."_____   **E** *Toy Story 2*

"Prison life consists of routine, and then more routine."_____   **F** *Apocalypse Now*

"For God's sake, Mrs. Robinson, here we are, you got me into your house… and tell me your husband won't be home for hours…."_____   **G** *The Shawshank Redemption*

"I've watched you your whole life…I know you better than you know yourself…."_____   **H** *Schindler's List*

"I enjoyed the movie very much….Did you ever consider having more horses in it?"_____   **I** *Duck Soup*

"I could dance with you till the cows come home."_____   **J** *The Matrix*

Robotic Riddles

Run these puzzlers through your circuits, and see what computes.

1 Which *Star Wars* character made C-3PO?

2 What is the name of the robot in the 1956 film *Forbidden Planet*?

3 Which 1976 film was set in a hotel resort staffed by robots?

4 In which 1974 film did apparently ideal spouses turn out to be robots?

5 Who played the title role in the 1987 film *Robocop*?

6 Which ex-member of the Monkees produced the TV series *Metal Mickey*?

7 What is the name of the android played by Brent Spiner in *Star Trek: The Next Generation*?

8 In which 1999 film did Robin Williams play a domestic android?

9 Which character, played on film by Linda Hamilton, was the Terminator trying to kill?

10 Which 2001 film by Steven Spielberg stars Haley Joel Osment as a child android?

11 In 1979's *Alien*, a surprise android emerges mid-film. Where does it come from?

Big Screen Birds

Here are a few questions to ruffle your feathers.

1 Which brothers starred in the film *Duck Soup*?

2 What sort of bird accompanied a cat in the title of a 1939 Bob Hope film?

3 What was the name of the parrot that taught Doctor Dolittle to talk to the animals?

4 In which 1978 film did Richard Burton lead a troop of mercenaries?

5 Which 1969 film, starring Clint Eastwood, was based on a novel by Alistair MacLean?

6 What was the name of the character played by John Wayne in the film *True Grit*?

7 Which 1970 Robert Altman film, named after its main character, had that character searching for the secret of flight?

8 On whose poem was the 1963 horror film *The Raven* based?

9 In which film did Kris Kristofferson play Rubber Duck?

10 What was Anthony Edwards's call-in sign in the 1986 film *Top Gun*?

11 In what 1976 film, based on a Jack Higgins novel of the same name, do the Nazis consider kidnapping Winston Churchill during the Second World War?

12 Brandon Lee, son of martial arts legend Bruce Lee, was accidentally killed during the filming of what 1993 movie?

Man to Man

Here are some questions—or answers—that include the word "man."

1 Which explosive 1993 film starred Sylvester Stallone pitted against Wesley Snipes?

2 What was the title of the 1976 film featuring Sir Laurence Olivier as a vicious Nazi dentist?

3 Who played the title role in the 1960s TV drama *Danger Man*?

4 In which 1980 film did Peter O'Toole play a manic film director?

5 Which film first featured the song "Que Sera Sera"?

6 In what 1997 comedy film is Bill Murray mistaken for a spy and drawn into an international assassination conspiracy?

7 Which TV hero worked for the Office of Scientific Intelligence?

8 Who played Liberty Valance in the film *The Man Who Shot Liberty Valance*?

9 What was Mark Harris's underwater alter ego?

10 Who played the title role in the 1992 film *The Lawnmower Man*?

11 Which musical features the song "76 Trombones"?

Blue Movies

It's not what you think! All of these flicks involve the color blue.

1 Which 1990 film comedy costarred Steve Martin and Rick Moranis?

2 In which 1990 film did Jamie Lee Curtis play a rookie cop hunting a serial killer?

3 What was *Blue Thunder* in a 1983 film?

4 Angela Lansbury played the mother of Elvis Presley in which 1961 film?

5 Which 1986 film shared its title with a hit record by Bobby Vinton?

6 Which 1949 film starred Jean Simmons in a role that was reprised by Brooke Shields in a 1980 remake?

7 Which film told the story of the jazz legend Billie Holiday?

8 Which film featured the songs "Sweet Home Chicago" and "Minnie the Moocher"?

9 What was the title of the 1988 film in which Matthew Broderick played a raw army recruit?

10 What was the Blue Angel in the 1930 film of the same name starring Marlene Dietrich?

11 In which 1990 Spike Lee film does Denzel Washington play a struggling jazz trumpeter?

B Movies

All of the answers in this quiz are films that start with the letter *B*.

1 In which 1956 film did Marilyn Monroe play a café singer?

2 In which 1955 classic did Sidney Poitier play a teacher in an inner-city school?

3 In which 1998 Disney/Pixar film did Kevin Spacey provide the voice for Hopper?

4 What was the title of the 1975 film in which John Wayne played a Chicago policeman sent to London to arrest a gangster?

5 Which 1987 film, directed by Blake Edwards, costarred Bruce Willis and Kim Basinger?

6 The song "Be Our Guest" was sung by a candlestick in which Disney film?

7 Which Oscar-winning film of 1995 told the story of William Wallace?

8 Which 1968 film starring Jane Fonda and set in the 41st century featured a blind angel?

9 Which 1976 film, set among New York gangsters in 1929, starred a teenage Jodie Foster?

10 In which 1992 film costarring Sharon Stone did Michael Douglas investigate a murder?

Days Like These

It's just one of those days.

1 Which film saw Arnold Schwarzenegger battling against Satan in the shape of Gabriel Byrne?

2 In which film did the Marx Brothers assist a young girl who owned a sanatorium and a racehorse?

3 In which 1990 film did Tom Cruise play a stock car driver?

4 Which 1962 film is based on John Wyndham's book about giant plants taking over the world?

5 Which 1973 film shared its title with a 1957 hit for Buddy Holly and the Crickets?

6 In which 1969 film did Richard Burton play Henry VIII in pursuit of his second wife?

7 What was the 1998 film in which Harrison Ford crash-landed a plane on a deserted island?

8 George Clooney fell in love with Michelle Pfeiffer in which 1996 film?

9 In which film did Sir Anthony Hopkins play a butler called Stevens?

10 In which 1996 film does Will Smith play a U.S. Air Force pilot battling against alien invaders?

11 In which 1993 film comedy does Bill Murray play a TV weatherman who is doomed to live the same day over again and again?

12 In what book does Mitch Albom chronicle life lessons learned from a dying professor?

What's Up, Doc?

Just what the doctor ordered—a group of medical movie questions.

1 In which film did Harrison Ford play Dr. Richard Kimble?

2 Which Bond villain was played by Joseph Wiseman in a 1962 film?

3 Who played Dr. Who on film in 1965 and 1966?

4 In which film about John Merrick did Sir Anthony Hopkins play Dr. Frederick Treves?

5 Jack Nicholson played a patient in a mental institute in which 1975 film?

6 In the 1978 film *The Boys from Brazil*, Gregory Peck plays which infamous Nazi?

7 Who wrote the novel on which the 1965 film *Dr. Zhivago* was based?

8 The films *Coma* and *Black Rain* starred which famous second-generation actor?

9 In which film did Robin Williams play a psychiatrist who treated a coma patient played by Robert De Niro?

10 Dr. Hunter Campbell "Patch" Adams is renowned for mixing humor with his medicine. Who portrayed him in a 1998 film?

Movie Tunes

Can you identify which films these hit songs came from in the '80s or '90s?

"Eye of the Tiger," Survivor (1982)_____   A *Cocktail*

"Up Where We Belong," Joe Cocker and Jennifer Warnes (1982)_____   B *Top Gun*

"All Time High," Rita Coolidge (1983)_____   C *Octopussy*

"We Don't Need Another Hero," Tina Turner (1985)_____   D *Robin Hood, Prince of Thieves*

"Separate Lives," Phil Collins and Marilyn Martin (1985)_____   E *An Officer and a Gentleman*

"Take My Breath Away," Berlin (1986)_____   F *Mad Max: Beyond Thunderdome*

"(I've Had) The Time of My Life," Bill Medley and Jennifer Warnes (1987)_____   G *The Lion King*

"Kokomo," The Beach Boys (1988)_____   H *Dirty Dancing*

"(Everything I Do) I Do It for You," Bryan Adams (1991)_____   I *White Nights*

"Can You Feel the Love Tonight," Elton John (1994)_____   J *Rocky III*

Stage and Screen

Select the correct option from the four possible answers about the movie biz.

1   Which series of films stars Robbie Coltrane?
    a. *Mission Impossible*
    b. *The Lord of the Rings*
    c. *Harry Potter*
    d. *Star Wars*

2   When were the first film studios founded in Hollywood?
    a. 1911
    b. 1921
    c. 1929
    d. 1934

3   What nationality was screen idol Errol Flynn?
    a. American
    b. English
    c. Irish
    d. Australian

4   Which musical holds the world record for the highest box-office takings worldwide?
    a. *The Phantom of the Opera*
    b. *Les Misérables*
    c. *Cats*
    d. *Chicago*

5   Which of these was *not* a film starring Meryl Streep?
    a. *Kramer vs. Kramer*
    b. *Sophie's Choice*
    c. *Out of Africa*
    d. *Indecent Proposal*

6   Who directed the 1962 film *Jules et Jim*?
    a. Eric Rohmer
    b. Jean-Luc Godard
    c. François Truffaut
    d. Patrice Leconte

7   Vivien Leigh was married to which of these actors?
    a. Clark Gable
    b. Humphrey Bogart
    c. Laurence Olivier
    d. James Mason

8   What nationality was the ballerina Alicia Markova?
    a. Russian
    b. Polish
    c. British
    d. French

9   *The Endless Summer* is a film about what sport?
    a. Sailing
    b. Cricket
    c. Swimming
    d. Surfing

Body of Knowledge

Wring your hands, purse your lips, and knit your brow with concentration as you answer these questions.

1   Which Gothic horror film features Johnny Depp hunting a headless horseman?

2   Which spy was played by Michael Caine in the film *Billion Dollar Brain*?

3   What was Major Hoolihan's nickname in *M*A*S*H*?

4   In which film did Shirley Temple sing "On the Good Ship Lollipop"?

5   Which 1946 horror film featured a demonic severed hand?

6   Who was nicknamed the Man of a Thousand Faces?

7   Which actress was known as "The Girl With the Million-Dollar Legs"?

8   Who played the creator of Edward Scissorhands?

9   Which pop group starred in a 1968 film called *Head*?

10 Of what did Steve Martin have two in the title of a 1983 film?

Television

Now let's narrow down our focus from the wide screen to the television screen in your living room. Sitcoms, dramas, music—you'll be astounded that so much information comes from such a little box!

On the Box
Channel-hop your way through these TV teasers.

1 Fox and Dana were the lead characters on what long-running series?

2 Which of the TV detectives in *Cagney & Lacey* was married?

3 What is the name of Homer Simpson's only son?

4 Who created *Thunderbirds*, a popular British series from the mid-1960s that featured marionettes?

5 Who became an international superstar after landing the role of J. R. Ewing?

6 Hannibal Smith was the leader of what gang of renegade soldiers on a popular series in the mid-1980s?

7 Who made his name playing the scruffy detective Colombo?

8 In which city is the medical drama *ER* set?

9 Who played Bret Maverick in the TV series *Maverick* and later starred in the film *Divine Secrets of the Ya-Ya Sisterhood*?

10 Which city was policed by Sonny Crockett and Ricardo Tubbs?

Universally Challenging
Don't look away from this set of real screen gems.

1 Which of the Teletubbies has a triangular antenna?

2 On whose novel was the drama series *Brideshead Revisited* based?

3 Which Joe Cocker recording was used as the theme for the TV series *The Wonder Years*?

4 Who portrayed Taggart in the Scottish TV series of the same name?

5 Ed Asner played the editor of the fictional *Los Angeles Tribune* in which TV series?

6 On which singer's TV show did the Osmond Brothers make their debut?

7 What is the name of Frasier Crane's brother?

8 Which TV series featured a Pontiac Trans Am car?

9 What was the name of Lee Majors's character in the TV series *The Six Million Dollar Man*?

10 Sabrina Duncan, Jill Munroe, and Kelly Garrett were the original characters in which TV series?

Street Smarts

Explore this round of questions about streets and addresses—don't get lost in the multiple choice quiz.

1 Who played Captain Frank Furillo in *Hill Street Blues*?
   a. Telly Savalas   b. Buddy Ebsen
   c. Daniel Travanti   d. Donny Osmond

2 Which family lived at 698 Sycamore Road, San Pueblo, California?
   a. The Partridge Family   b. The Brady Bunch
   c. The Douglas Family   d. The Bradford Family

3 Who played Lieutenant Mike Stone in *The Streets of San Francisco*?
   a. Sammy Davis Jr.   b. Dean Martin
   c. Karl Malden   d. Dick Van Dyke

4 Della Street was which TV character's secretary?
   a. Joe Mannix   b. Perry Mason
   c. Kojack   d. Tom Bradford

5 Which TV family lived on Crestview Drive?
   a. The Clampetts   b. The Addams Family
   c. The Nelsons   d. The Stones

6 Who played the character Kookie in the TV series *77 Sunset Strip* and charted with such hits as "Kookie Lend Me Your Comb"?
   a. Frankie Avalon   b. Fabian
   c. Edd Byrnes   d. Micky Dolenz

7 Which family lived on Mockingbird Lane?
   a. The Ricardos   b. The Cleavers
   c. The Andersons   d. The Munsters

8 On which Bedrock thoroughfare did the Flintstones live?
   a. Brontosaurus Boulevard b. Stone Cave Road
   c. Triceratops Way   d. Stegosaurus Street

Watching the Detectives

Try this arresting group of questions.

1 Who played Detective Dave Starsky's partner, Ben "Hutch" Hutchinson, in the 1970s series *Starsky and Hutch*?

2 Sean Connery investigated a series of killings in a 14th-century abbey in which film?

3 Which opera lover was assisted by Sergeant Lewis?

4 Who played Hercule Poirot in the 1974 film *Murder on the Orient Express*?

5 Which detective has been played by both Richard Roundtree and Samuel L. Jackson?

6 Who played Sherlock Holmes on film to Nigel Bruce's Dr. Watson?

7 Which TV detective played by James Garner lived in a trailer park?

8 Which 2000 film was a comedy about an FBI agent working undercover at a beauty pageant?

9 Who wrote the TV drama series *The Singing Detective*?

Classic TV

See if you can answer this quiz about shows from an earlier time.

1 In which 1960s prime-time soap did Ryan O'Neal play Rodney Harrington?

2 Who sang the theme for the TV Western *Rawhide*?

3 In the 1970s, William Conrad played which portly private investigator?

4 Which actor first stepped out of the TARDIS in *Doctor Who*?

5 The TV company Desilu was formed by a husband and wife team. Desi Arnaz was the husband. Who was the wife?

6 Which member of The Monkees starred in the TV series *Circus Boy* as a child actor?

7 In which 1970s series did Roger Moore play Lord Brett Sinclair?

8 In which city was *Hawaii Five-O* set?

9 What piece of classical music was used for the theme for *The Lone Ranger*?

Spin-offs

Don't let your head spin as you sort out the new programs that came in the wake of classics.

1 Which spin-off from *Buffy the Vampire Slayer* features a vampire cursed with a conscience?

2 *The Men from Shiloh* was a spin-off from which TV Western?

3 *Laverne & Shirley*, *Mork & Mindy*, and *Joanie Loves Chachi* were spin-offs from which TV show?

4 What was the title of the spin-off from *The Cosby Show* that told of the college life of Denise Huxtable?

5 Which *Star Trek* features Captain Kathryn Janeway as a ship's commander?

6 Edith Bunker's outspoken cousin in *All in the Family* was given her own show. What was it?

7 Name one of the spin-offs from the police show *Law & Order*.

8 The title character in Frasier originally appeared in which 1980s comedy series?

9 *The Bionic Woman* was a spin-off from what show?

10 What is the connection between the TV shows *Rhoda*, *Lou Grant*, and *Phyllis*?

Beasts on the Box

Answer this savage quiz about famous TV animals.

1 Which TV drama from the 1960s featured Clarence the cross-eyed lion?

2 Who described himself as "the fastest mouse in Mexico"?

3 What was the name of Manuel's pet rat in *Fawlty Towers*?

4 Hollywood had a talking horse called Francis, and TV had a talking horse called...?

5 What was the name of Doctor Who's robotic dog?

6 Trigger was the horse of which screen cowboy?

7 Who played Robin to Adam West's Batman?

8 What is the name of Martin Crane's dog in *Frasier*?

9 Which dolphin was the best friend of Sandy and Bud Ricks?

10 What sort of creature was Aristotle, the Addams family's pet?

Television Tunes

How well do you remember these musical moments from TV?

1 Which U.S. sitcom used the song "Love and Marriage" sung by Frank Sinatra as its theme?

2 Who sang the theme to *The Love Boat*?

3 The Rembrandts recorded the song "I'll Be There for You" as the theme for which hit TV series?

4 Al Jarreau had a hit with the TV theme for which 1980s TV series?

5 Which real-life rocker appeared in *Happy Days* as the character Leather Tuscadero?

6 Which singer played Sonny Crockett's wife in *Miami Vice*?

7 What is the name of the saxophonist in the *Muppet Show* band?

8 Which singer provided the theme and some of the incidental music for *Ally McBeal*?

Theater

So many of our greatest entertainers got their start on the "boards"—some of them in classical theater, some through opera, and still others through vaudeville. Understanding details of their lives gives us an intriguing glimpse of our culture. How deep is your knowledge of theater? Step to the center of the stage, please, and project your voice.

All the World's a Stage

Can you identify the stage musicals that featured the following songs? Match the correct musical with the right song, from the list below.

"On the Street
Where You Live"_____   A *La Cage aux Folles*

"All I Ask of You"_____   B *Annie*

"The Movie in My Mind"_____   C *Phantom of
                                    the Opera*

"I Don't Know How
to Love Him"_____   D *No, No, Nanette*

"I Am What I Am"_____   E *Porgy and Bess*

"It Ain't Necessarily So"_____   F *Miss Saigon*

"Getting to Know You"_____   G *Fiddler on the Roof*

"Aquarius"_____   H *High Society*

"Day by Day"_____   I *How to Succeed in
                                    Business Without
                                    Really Trying*

"It's a Hard Knock Life"_____   J *The King and I*

"Sunrise, Sunset"_____   K *The Pajama Game*

"Love from a
Heart of Gold"_____   L *Jesus Christ
                                    Superstar*

"Let's Misbehave"_____   M *Hair*

"I Want to Be Happy"_____   N *My Fair Lady*

"Steam Heat"_____   O *Godspell*

A Night at the Opera

Test your knowledge of the great opera story lines.

1 Which opera character was stabbed to death by Don José?

2 Don Alfonso was a character in which Mozart opera?

3 Mimi, Marcello, and Musetta are all characters from which opera?

4 Which pop singer took his name from the man who composed the opera *Hansel and Gretel*?

5 What is the name of the barber of Seville?

6 The highwayman Macheath is the hero of which opera?

7 Which opera was based on the Alexandre Dumas novel *The Lady of the Camellias*?

8 Lieutenant Pinkerton is a character from which opera?

9 In Wagner's *Tristan and Isolde*, what nationality is Isolde?

10 Baron Scarpia is a character from which Puccini opera?

Treading the Boards

Start with a set of questions about classic plays and theater.

1 Which Shakespearean comedy has a heroine called Rosalind who seeks refuge in the Forest of Arden?

2 Who wrote the original play *Who's Afraid of Virginia Woolf*?

3 Which acting technique is associated with the Russian director Konstantin Stanislavsky?

4 *Mourning Becomes Electra* by Eugene O'Neill is based on *The Oresteia*, a trilogy by what ancient Athenian dramatist?

5 Which play by Oliver Goldsmith features the comic character Tony Lumpkin?

6 Which dramatist is associated with the technique of deliberately distancing the audience from the action?

7 Which fellow dramatist wrote of Shakespeare: "He was not of an age, but for all time"?

8 Which stage musical has the subtitle "The American Tribal Love-Rock Musical"?

9 By what name is the dramatist Jean-Baptiste Poquelin better known?

10 Which play inspired the name Angry Young Men for a group of British playwrights and writers of the 1950s?

Class Acts of Vaudeville

Test your knowledge of the entertainment pioneers who emerged from the live variety-show industry.

1 Why did New York vaudeville promoters advertise "clean" shows and curtail the sale of alcohol in their theaters in the 1880s?

2 Joe Keaton and Myra Edith Cutler were vaudeville performers whose child went on to become a motion picture pioneer. By what name is Joseph Frank Keaton better known?

3 As a youth, Hungarian-born Ehrich Weiss had early success as a cross-country runner and a trapeze artist. In the early 20th century, he gained greater fame—for what and under what name?

4 When Gummo left the Marx Brothers to serve in the First World War, who replaced him?

5 His parents hoped that Chicago-born Benjamin Kubelsky would become a classical violinist. But that instrument became his trademark in another kind of success—as a comedian. By what name is he better known?

6 In the November 1940 presidential election, some votes went to comedienne Gracie Allen. Why?

Ed Sullivan's Really Big Shoe

Test your memory about the great talent announcer with the distinctive nasal voice.

1 What early career path placed Ed Sullivan in a powerful position within the entertainment industry?

2 CBS's Studio 50 in New York City was renamed what in 1967?

3 What nighttime talk show eventually occupied the same studio?

4 How did the rock group The Doors get banned from the Ed Sullivan Show?

5 Why did Ed Sullivan miss the September 8, 1956, appearance of Elvis Presley on his show?

6 On February 9, 1964, Sullivan pulled off a "really big coup" and earned a record-breaking audience with one guest act. Who was the act?

7 In what 1963 movie did Sullivan play himself?

What Makes Us Laugh

If indeed laughter is the best medicine, then drugstores should stock up on such heart-lifting amusements as the funny pages, sitcoms, and, of course those brave souls who dare to stand up and tell us jokes from the stage.

Laurel and Hardy

Here's another fine mess of questions.

1 Let's get the partners in comedy straight— which one was the skinny British guy and which the larger American fellow?

2 In 1912, British vaudeville performer Stanley Jefferson moved to the United States, but why did the comedian switch to the name Stan Laurel?

3 While working in British comedy shows, Stan Laurel became an understudy for which famous-but-quirky comedian?

4 Describe the typical on-screen costumes (hats, ties, and jackets) worn by Laurel and Hardy.

5 In what 1934 movie did Laurel and Hardy star alongside Little Bo Peep?

6 Who played Colonel Gregor McGregor in the 1935 movie *Bonnie Scotland*?

7 In what 1917 movie did Stan Laurel make his debut appearance?

8 What was Oliver Hardy's real first name?

9 What was Oliver Hardy's nickname?

Situation Comedies

Take a look at the comedy TV shows that keep us smiling.

1 Who played Sybil Fawlty in *Fawlty Towers*?

2 In which city is *Frasier* set?

3 What is the name of the manservant in *The Addams Family*?

4 In which series did Michael J. Fox play the deputy mayor of New York?

5 Which comedy series was introduced with the words: "These are the Tates. And these are the Campbells"?

6 Who plays Dan Connor in *Roseanne*?

7 In which city was *Happy Days* set?

8 What's the name of Jerry's next-door neighbor in *Seinfeld*?

9 What series was originally called *These Friends of Mine* before being changed to the name of the main character?

10 How are Dorothy, Blanche, Rose, and Sophia collectively known?

Abbot and Costello

Play along with Bud Abbott and Lou Costello, partners in the "field" of comedy.

1 In their famous "Who's on First" comedy routine, which comedian is explaining where the baseball players are on the field, and which comedian is trying to understand?

2 According to the classic Abbott and Costello "Who's on First" routine, tell which of the oddly named baseball players are at each of these positions:

First base
Second base
Third base
Pitcher
Catcher
Left field
Center field
Shortstop

3 In the 1940s and 1950s, movies with titles like *Abbott and Costello Meet Frankenstein* became a staple. Who else, according to the movie story lines, did the comedic duo "meet"?

4 In 1945, Abbott and Costello had a short-lived rift. What caused the ill feelings?

5 In their movie, *Buck Privates*, what female singing group sang "The Boogie Woogie Bugle Boy"?

6 In what Abbott and Costello movie did Ella Fitzgerald sing "A-Tisket, A-Tasket"?

7 What famous radio personality did Abbott and Costello stand in for in 1940?

8 In *Pardon My Sarong*, what future television star played a detective?

9 Who played Count Dracula in *Abbott and Costello Meet Frankenstein*?

See Ya in the Funny Pages

Match the name of the long-running strip with its creator, listed below.

*Nancy*_____	**A**	Walt Kelly
*Dennis the Menace*_____	**B**	Bil Keane
*Li'l Abner*_____	**C**	Ernie Bushmiller
*Peanuts*_____	**D**	Al Capp
*Calvin and Hobbes*_____	**E**	Mort Walker
*Pogo*_____	**F**	Charles Schulz
*Beetle Bailey*_____	**G**	Jim Davis
*Andy Capp*_____	**H**	Reg Smythe
*Garfield*_____	**I**	Bill Watterson
*Family Circus*_____	**J**	Hank Ketcham

Disney Delights

Draw on your knowledge of the great animator.

1 Which was the first Disney film to be nominated for a best picture Oscar?

2 Name the whale in *Pinocchio*.

3 Which was the first Disney film to be made with a stereo soundtrack?

4 Which Disney film featured a character called Thomas O'Malley?

5 What were the names of the canine parents in *101 Dalmations*?

6 In the Disney animation *Robin Hood*, what sort of animal was Little John?

7 What is the name of the skunk in *Bambi*?

8 Which was the first animated Disney film to tell the story of a real person?

9 Which 1994 Disney film has a soundtrack by Tim Rice and Elton John?

Will Rogers

This cowboy humorist was loved by one and all.

1 What was Will Rogers's ethnic heritage?
a. German
b. Lithuanian
c. Native American
d. Bolivian

2 An accomplished cowboy, Will Rogers was known for incorporating what into his stand-up act?
a. Showy western clothing
b. Calf wrestling
c. A lariat
d. Quick-draw and shooting pistols

3 Rogers County, Oklahoma, was named after whom?
a. Will Rogers
b. Betty Rogers, Will's wife
c. Will Rogers Jr., Will's oldest child
d. Clement Vann Rogers, Will's father and a delegate to the Oklahoma Constitutional Convention

4 What New York City incident brought Will Rogers valuable early publicity?
a. He roped a wild steer that was climbing the stands in Madison Square Garden
b. He persuaded a distraught woman not to jump off a building in Times Square
c. He lassoed an armed robber in the middle of Broadway
d. He lassoed an infant

5 In the 1930s, his radio show was billed as "Will Rogers and His Famous Alarm Clock." Why did he need an alarm clock on the show?
a. Its ticking provided a "passage of time" sound effect
b. To keep track of the time limit on his broadcasts
c. As a running joke, he smashed 17 clocks on air
d. To prevent other guests from talking too long

6 Will Rogers was listed in the *Guinness Book of World Records* for throwing three lariats at once and roping what three targets?
a. A horse's neck, the horse's rider, and the horse's legs
b. A pig, a steer, and a horse
c. Three horses at once
d. Three spectators

7 Audiences became familiar with Will Rogers's endearing drawl primarily through his films, but he also made many silent films. Which one of these was a "talkie"?
a. *The Strange Boarder*
b. *Boys Will Be Boys*
c. *The Ropin' Fool*
d. *Life Begins at Forty*

8 Will Rogers insisted that his Cherokee ancestors were waiting in America to meet:
a. The *Nina, Pinta*, and *Santa Maria*
b. The *Mayflower*
c. Vasco de Gama
d. The USS *Maine*

9 Which of the following is *not* a Will Rogers quote:
a. "I don't belong to any organized party. I'm a Democrat."
b. "A humorist entertains, and a lecturer annoys."
c. "Before I refuse to take your questions, I have an opening statement."
d. "Never miss a good chance to shut up."

10 Will Rogers was often mentioned as a successor to Mark Twain, and he had a professional connection to the literary great. What was it?
a. They shared an editor
b. They shared a publishing house
c. They both won Great American Comic awards
d. Rogers appeared in a film of a Twain novel

The Truth About 'Toons

Catch us stretching the truth about cartoons. Answer the following questions true or false.

1 Barney Rubble has a wife named Wilma.   TRUE ○   FALSE ○

2 Felix the Cat has frequent run-ins with Officer Dibble.   TRUE ○   FALSE ○

3 Deputy Dawg is continually harassed by Musky Muskrat.   TRUE ○   FALSE ○

4 Betty Boop was once censored for immorality.   TRUE ○   FALSE ○

5 Disc jockey Wolfman Jack provides the voice for Shaggy, Scooby-Doo's best friend.   TRUE ○   FALSE ○

6 The red-bearded, pistol-packing Yosemite Sam appears frequently to bedevil Daffy Duck.   TRUE ○   FALSE ○

7 Soul singer Isaac Hayes provides the voice for Chef in the animated series *South Park*.   TRUE ○   FALSE ○

Name That Comedian

Match the funny-person's name below to the action or role described.

Trying desperately to keep up with a candy factory's conveyor belt_____   **A** Lucille Ball

Joe the Bartender, who dips his finger in a frothy glass of beer_____   **B** Charlie Chaplin

A bumpkin named Clem Kadiddlehopper_____   **C** Jackie Gleason

A laugh that goes "nyuk, nyuk, nyuk"_____   **D** Curly Howard

A "tramp" with an uncomfortable walk due to ill-fitting clothes_____   **E** Red Skelton

The Circus

Prancing horses, elephants, tigers, trapeze artists, and clowns—what's not to like about the circus? It's such a fundamental part of our entertainment industry that we find traces of it everywhere we turn.

Under the Big Top

Crack your whip at this round of questions about life when the circus comes to town.

1 What nickname did the showman William Cody acquire for supplying the Kansas Pacific Railroad with bison meat?

2 What crack shot and circus performer shot ash from a cigarette held by Crown Prince Wilhelm of Germany?

3 By what name was the illusionist and showman Ehrich Weiss better known?

4 What type of performer were Lou Jacobs, Grock, Coco, and Bozo?

5 What famous company has shows called Saltimbanco, Quidam, "O," and La Nouba?

6 What is the name of the musical by Irving Berlin that is loosely based on the life of the sharpshooter Annie Oakley?

7 What illusionist spent 44 days suspended in a glass box beside the River Thames in London in 2003?

8 What is the name of the white-faced, clown-like character invented by the famous mime Marcel Marceau?

9 The tightrope walker Charles Blondin cooked an omelet while high on a wire halfway across what spectacular natural tourist attraction?

10 What name links a man born David Seth Kotkin with Charles Dickens?

Name That Circus

Of the many circuses that have won fame around the United States and the world, name at least two.

P. T. Barnum

Entertain yourself with intriguing facts about the ultimate showman.

1 What do the P and T stand for?
a. Pontius Theodore
b. Phineas Taylor
c. Paul Tyler

2 Barnum was an innovator in the transportation of traveling circuses. How so?
a. He used elephants to pull equipment carts
b. He was the first to move his own circus by train
c. He devised sideshow tents from lightweight cardboard and paper

3 Hours before his death in 1891, P. T. Barnum showed that business was never far from his mind. In what way?
a. He sold one of his mansions
b. He bought three lions, four tigers, and two elephants to add to his circus
c. He asked how ticket sales were going for the day in the box office

4 Which book was not written by P. T. Barnum?
a. *Life of P. T. Barnum*
b. *There's a Sucker Born Every Minute*
c. *Art of Money Getting*

The Pachyderm Pack

Here's a round of really big questions.

1 Who played the Elephant Man in the 1980 film of the same name?

2 Who collaborated with Paul McCartney on the song "Ebony and Ivory"?

3 What name is given to a male elephant?

4 What is the name of the rodent who is Dumbo's best friend?

5 Which *H* word is the name given to a seat on the back of an elephant or camel?

6 Which literary elephant married his cousin Celeste?

7 What is the name of the elephant that was the major attraction at Barnum & Bailey's Circus?

8 Who wrote the *Just So* story "The Elephant's Child," which told how the elephant got its long trunk?

9 The Order of the Elephant is the name of the highest honor that can be awarded to a person in which European country?

A Family of Daredevils on High

Try this set of puzzlers about the Flying Wallendas.

1 The Wallendas debuted with the Ringling Bros. and Barnum & Bailey Circus at Madison Square Garden in 1928. But something was missing. What?
a. Founder Karl Wallenda was lost backstage
b. The Wallendas' luggage was lost, so they performed without costumes, in their underwear
c. The Wallendas' safety net was lost in transit

2 Founder Karl Wallenda lived to age 73. How did he die?
a. From a heart attack
b. From a high-wire fall during a promotional walk in Puerto Rico
c. From lung cancer

3 Karl Wallenda learned his trade as a teen when he answered an ad for:
a. "A hand balancer with courage"
b. "A part-time wire walker"
c. "A daredevil with a head for heights"

4 What's the source of the "flying" part of the act's name?
a. In early circus acts, they were typically shot out of a cannon into a net
b. They once performed with miniature wings on their shoulders
c. The name stuck after a press description of an accident

Popular Music

We take our popular music very personally. A song we haven't heard for decades can still evoke emotions that are as strong as when we first heard the tune. Every song that gets your toes tapping is part of a soundtrack for your life.

Ol' Blue Eyes

Take an up-close look at Frank Sinatra.

1 The band of entertainers that included Frank Sinatra, Dean Martin, and Sammy Davis Jr. was known as:
a. The Blind Mice
b. The Three Kings
c. The Rat Pack

2 Which Sinatra song has been covered by Dorothy Squires, Elvis Presley, Shane MacGowan, and the Sex Pistols?
a. "My Way"
b. "The Best Is Yet to Come"
c. "Call Me Irresponsible"

3 Which Illinois town did Sinatra sing of in 1957?
a. Chicago
b. Springfield
c. East St. Louis

4 Which Sinatra daughter had a No. 1 duet with him in 1967?
a. Nancy
b. Tina
c. Elizabeth

5 In what year did Sinatra die?
a. 1991
b. 1998
c. 2001

6 Which actress released a version of the Sinatra song "Something Stupid" with Robbie Williams?
a. Doris Day
b. Nicole Kidman
c. Cher

7 Which Irish rock singer performed a duet, "I've Got You Under My Skin," with Sinatra?
a. Van Morrison
b. Bono
c. Sinéad O'Connor

8 In which 1988 animated film did Sinatra provide the voice for a singing sword picked up by Bob Hoskins?
a. *Who Framed Roger Rabbit*
b. *The Little Mermaid*
c. *Fantasia 2000*

9 Sinatra was married four times. To which wife was he married for the shortest time?
a. Nancy Barbato
b. Ava Gardner
c. Mia Farrow

10 In which 1956 film did Sinatra star alongside Bing Crosby and Grace Kelly?
a. *High Society*
b. *Carousel*
c. *Anything Goes*

Elvis Lives!

Pull on your blue suede shoes and test your knowledge.

1 Elvis Presley was born:
   a. A twin
   b. Covered in hair
   c. Left-handed
   d. Holding a guitar

2 Elvis's tyrannical manager was:
   a. Jed Clampett
   b. Colonel Harland Sanders
   c. Colonel Tom Parker
   d. Major Sinclair Yeates

3 In which film did Elvis sing "Return to Sender"?
   a. *The Postman Always Rings Twice*
   b. *Girls! Girls! Girls!*
   c. *Girl Happy*
   d. *Blue Hawaii*

4 What was the name of the record label on which Elvis first recorded in 1954?
   a. Nashville's Best
   b. Apple Records
   c. Sun Records
   d. South Star

5 What song did Elvis sing to the tune of "O Sole Mio"?
   a. "It's Now or Never"
   b. "All Shook Up"
   c. "Big Love, Big Heartache"
   d. "Blueberry Hill"

6 Which country and pop star of the day wrote Elvis's 1970 hit "Kentucky Rain"?
   a. Merle Haggard
   b. Eddie Rabbitt
   c. Dolly Parton
   d. Mel Tillis

7 In which state was Elvis born?
   a. Mississippi
   b. Louisiana
   c. Tennessee
   d. Kentucky

8 Elvis joined the U.S. Army in 1968 as private 53310761. What rank was he when he left in 1960?
   a. Still a private
   b. Sergeant
   c. Master sergeant
   d. Lieutenant

9 What was the title of the first film in which Elvis starred?
   a. *Loving You*
   b. *Love Me Tender*
   c. *Jailhouse Rock*
   d. *G.I. Blues*

10 In which two films did Elvis portray a Native American?
   a. *Charro*
   b. *Flaming Star*
   c. *Wild in the Country*
   d. *Stay Away, Joe*

The Beatles

How fabulous is your knowledge of the Fab Four?

1 What was the Beatles' first UK No. 1 hit, in April 1963?
a. "All My Loving"
b. "Ask Me Why"
c. "Can't Buy Me Love"
d. "From Me to You"

2 Name the three grandchildren mentioned in the song "When I'm 64."
a. Alan
b. Chuck
c. Dave
d. Vera

3 What song was a double A-side single with "Strawberry Fields Forever"?
a. "Penny Lane"
b. "With a Little Help from My Friends"
c. "Sgt. Pepper's Lonely Hearts Club Band"
d. "All You Need Is Love"

4 What was the name of the record label set up by the band?
a. Orange
b. Pear
c. Apple
d. Grape

5 What was the Beatles' first film called?
a. *A Hard Day's Night*
b. *Help!*
c. *Magical Mystery Tour*
d. *Gimme Shelter*

6 Which track from *Magical Mystery Tour* had the line, "There's nothing you can do that can't be done, nothing you can sing that can't be sung"?
a. "All You Need Is Love"
b. "A Day in the Life"
c. "And Your Bird Can Sing"
d. "Baby You're a Rich Man"

7 Which ex-Beatles' debut album was *All Things Must Pass*?
a. Paul McCartney
b. John Lennon
c. George Harrison
d. Ringo Starr

8 Richard Starkey is the real name of which one of the Fab Four?
a. Ringo Starr
b. John Lennon
c. Paul McCartney
d. None of them—it's a pseudonym used by Ringo

9 How many times was "Sgt. Pepper's Lonely Hearts Club Band" performed live by the band?
a. Twice—while touring India
b. Just once, in New York City
c. Never
d. At every show

Musical Moments

This round will get you humming—if you can deduce the answers.

1 Which 1968 Mel Brooks film was about a musical that featured the song "Springtime for Hitler"?

2 How many Von Trapp children were there in *The Sound of Music*?

3 Who played the title role in the 1974 film version of *Mame*?

4 Which song from *Doctor Dolittle* won a best song Oscar in 1968?

5 On which George Bernard Shaw play was the musical *My Fair Lady* based?

6 In which 1956 film did Grace Kelly play Tracy Samantha Lord?

7 In the 1983 film *Flashdance*, which actress was a welder by day and a dancer by night?

8 Alan Parker directed which famous pop star in the title role of the 1996 film *Evita*?

9 In which 1952 film did Gene Kelly sing "What a glorious feeling, I'm happy again"?

10 What song did John Travolta sing while leaping off a car in a 1978 film?

The Rolling Stones

The ultimate '60s-era rock band delivers plenty of satisfaction.

1 Which of the following musicians was not in the original Rolling Stones lineup?
a. Mick Jagger
b. Ronnie Wood
c. Ian Stewart
d. Brian Jones

2 A song by what musician inspired the name of the Rolling Stones?
a. Buddy Holly
b. Little Richard
c. Elvis Presley
d. Muddy Waters

3 What is meant by the "British Invasion"? Pick one explanation:
a. A 1960s boom in the production of World War II movies starring British actors and plots
b. The extreme popularity in the United States and Canada of British rock bands (such as the Beatles and the Rolling Stones), as well as other British culture, during the mid-1960s
c. Domination of the U.S. luxury cruise market by British companies taking passengers to the Caribbean
d. An ill-considered British incursion into Canada in the 1930s

4 Which song is not on the 1971 Rolling Stones album *Sticky Fingers*?
a. "Brown Sugar"
b. "Wild Horses"
c. "(I Can't Get No) Satisfaction"
d. "Can't You Hear Me Knocking"

5 Four people died, one from a beating, at the notorious 1969 Altamont Speedway concert outside San Francisco, headlined by the Rolling Stones. What organization was reputed to have been hired for security?
a. The Pinkerton Agency
b. The California Highway Patrol
c. The San Francisco Police Department
d. Hell's Angels

Strike Up the Band

Here's a round of teasers about great musicals.

1 Which was the first musical to win 10 Oscars?

2 Which Oscar-winning 1972 musical film was set in prewar Berlin at the Kit Kat Club?

3 In which musical did we first meet the character of Fanny Brice?

4 Which 1969 musical had Clint Eastwood singing "They Call the Wind Mariah"?

5 What were Rodgers's and Hammerstein's first names?

6 Where, according to the title of the 1944 musical starring Judy Garland, were you to meet?

7 Which actress was *Dirty Dancing* with Patrick Swayze in 1987?

8 Judy Garland and James Mason both won Oscar nominations for their roles in which 1954 musical directed by George Cukor?

9 With which cartoon character did Gene Kelly dance in the film *Anchors Aweigh*?

10 Where was American citizen Gene Kelly living, according to the title of the 1951 film directed by Vincente Minnelli?

A Musical Medley

Feel free to whistle while you select the correct answer from four possible ones.

1 Which of these was *not* one of the Three Tenors?
a. Luciano Pavarotti
b. Carlo Bergonzi
c. Plácido Domingo
d. José Carreras

2 In which year were both Michael Jackson and Madonna born?
a. 1955
b. 1958
c. 1962
d. 1965

3 What kind of musical instrument is a serpent?
a. Percussion
b. Wind
c. Electronic
d. String

4 "We skipped the light fandango," sang Procol Harem in "A Whiter Shade of Pale." What is a fandango?
a. A spicy Creole dish
b. A Mexican candelabra
c. A form of flamenco
d. A gymnastic floor exercise

5 What kind of musical instrument is a kit?
a. A set of castanets
b. A one-stringed harp
c. A pocket-sized violin
d. A conch-shell trumpet

6 In which year were Cream's *Fresh Cream* and Bob Dylan's *Blonde on Blonde* released?
a. 1965
b. 1966
c. 1967
d. 1968

7 What is the predominant sound in John Cage's *4'33"*?
a. Strings
b. Singing
c. Silence
d. Synthesizer

8 What is one of the principal instruments in a gamelan orchestra?
a. Trombones
b. Bugles
c. Guitars
d. Xylophones

9 What kind of music is associated with the British performers Ewan MacColl and Sandy Denny?
a. Classical
b. Heavy metal
c. Folk
d. Opera

10 What is a djembe?
a. An Iranian harp
b. A Caribbean harp
c. An African drum
d. An Indian guitar

PAGE 45

Trivia in Technicolor

1 The Vietnam War
2 *Reservoir Dogs*
3 *The Hunt for Red October*
4 *The Color Purple*
5 *The Pink Panther*
6 *Yellow Submarine*
7 *The Golden Child*
8 *Gone with the Wind*
9 *I Am Curious (Yellow)*
10 *Men in Black*

Making Connections

1 The surname Lee (Christopher Lee played Frankenstein's monster, Bruce Lee starred in *Enter the Dragon*, and Spike Lee directed *Malcolm X*.)
2 All played Inspector Clouseau
3 All were directed by Oliver Stone
4 Goldie Hawn
5 The actress Natalie Portman, who played the part of 12-year-old Mathilda in *The Professional* and Queen Amidala in *The Phantom Menace*
6 Popeye, Olive Oyl's boyfriend, and the first name of Popeye Doyle, the detective in *The French Connection* played by Gene Hackman
7 *The Great Escape*
8 The song "Do-Re-Mi" from *The Sound of Music*
9 Jackson
10 William Shatner

PAGE 46

The Name Is James

1 False; the author was Roald Dahl
2 True
3 True
4 False; the character was named Jim Phelps
5 False; he costarred with The Dead End Kids
6 True
7 False; it stood for Tiberius
8 True
9 False; he played James Bond seven times
10 False; it was James Drury
11 True

Film Buff Special

1 Jacques Tati
2 Jean-Luc Godard
3 *The Seven Samurai*
4 Peter Weir
5 *12 Angry Men*
6 Stanley Kubrick
7 Baz Luhrmann
8 The Ku Klux Klan
9 Satyajit Ray
10 *Fanny and Alexander*

PAGE 47

Famous and Oh, So Young

1 False; Mickey Rooney said it
2 True
3 True; it was a special award given to her in 1934 at the age of 6
4 True
5 False; Tatum O'Neal starred with her father Ryan in that movie
6 False; he played Oliver Twist that year
7 False; she played Wednesday in *The Addams Family* film
8 True
9 False; she was ambassador to Ghana

Screen Test: Even More Connections

1 Maid Marian
2 All starred members of the Fonda family
3 Michael Crichton
4 Charlton Heston, who starred in them all
5 The name Moore. The films starred, respectively, Demi, Roger, and Dudley Moore.
6 They are all based on Shakespeare plays (*The Tempest, Romeo and Juliet*, and *The Taming of the Shrew*).
7 Each performed a Bond theme song: Coolidge for *Octopussy*, Sinatra for *You Only Live Twice*, and Crow for *Tomorrow Never Dies*.
8 All featured stars of *Cheers*: Ted Danson in *Three Men and a Baby*, Woody Harrelson in *Natural Born Killers*, and Kirstie Alley in *Look Who's Talking*.
9 *Pacific Princess*

10 Rachel Ward
11 The Phantom of the Opera
12 Jack Lemmon
13 *Gandhi*
14 Cyd Charisse

PAGE 48

Heaven and Hell

1 *Grease*
2 *Ghost*
3 Nancy Davis, who became his wife
4 *Highway to Heaven*
5 A bell must ring
6 *Hellraiser*
7 *Heaven Can Wait*
8 *Carousel*
9 God
10 "Hell"

Titles and Entitlement

1 Sean Connery
2 James Earl Jones
3 Kenneth Branagh
4 John Goodman
5 Stephen King
6 Nick Nolte
7 Henry II
8 Matthew Broderick

Hey, Good-Looking!

1 Julia Roberts
2 Belle
3 Zsa Zsa Gabor
4 *West Side Story*
5 Halle Berry
6 10 (out of 10)
7 Pink (*Pretty in Pink*)
8 Kevin Spacey
9 Brigitte Bardot
10 *Sleeping Beauty*

Answers

PAGE 49

Driving Tests

1 a. Sandra Bullock
2 c. *Bullitt*
3 b. *Best Defense*
4 a. *Falling Down*
5 a. *Easy Rider*
6 d. *Le Mans*
7 a. *The Great Race*
8 c. *Thelma and Louise*
9 a. Morgan Freeman
10 b. *Duel*

Maybe Baby

1 *Rosemary's Baby*
2 Leonard Nimoy
3 A leopard
4 *Baby Boom*
5 Woody Allen (He named his son as a tribute to Louis Armstrong, who was nicknamed Satchmo, which is short for "Satchel Mouth.")
6 Babe Ruth
7 *Babe: Pig in the City*
8 Nicholas Cage
9 Laurel and Hardy
10 *Honey, I Blew Up the Kid*

PAGE 50

Spooks and Specters

1 True
2 True
3 False; it was Linda Blair
4 False; the title was *The Ghost and Mrs. Muir*
5 True
6 True
7 False; it told the story of a haunted car
8 True
9 False; Nicolas Roeg directed the film
10 True
11 True

Action!

1 *The Third Man*
2 *Apocalypse Now*
3 *Shakespeare in Love*
4 *Strangers on a Train*
5 *Rebecca*
6 *Jerry Maguire*
7 *Airplane!*
8 *Monty Python and the Holy Grail*
9 *Manhattan*
10 *The Godfather*

PAGE 51

Science Fiction Facts

1 Sigourney Weaver
2 *Apollo 13*
3 *Close Encounters of the Third Kind*
4 *Blade Runner*
5 Terry Gilliam
6 *Metropolis*
7 Arthur C. Clarke
8 *Terminator 2: Judgment Day*
9 *Invasion of the Body Snatchers*
10 Jack Nicholson
11 It sings "Bicycle Built for Two" ("Daisy, Daisy")

Metallic Movies

1 Matthew Modine
2 *Steel Magnolias*
3 *Reversal of Fortune*
4 "Pushing tin" is a slang term for air traffic control
5 Ron Ely
6 *Silver Streak*
7 *The Man in the Iron Mask*
8 *Tin Men*
9 Ted Hughes
10 Afraid that customers wouldn't hire a female detective, Stephanie Zimbalist invents a male boss

PAGE 52

On the Beach

1 False; the film was *From Here to Eternity*
2 True
3 False; that describes the *Jaws* movies
4 True
5 True
6 False; that was another Bond film, *Dr. No*
7 True
8 True
9 True
10 True

Big Screen Quotes

1 *Toy Story 2*
2 *Back to the Future*
3 *Schindler's List*
4 *The Usual Suspects*
5 *Apocalypse Now*
6 *The Shawshank Redemption*
7 *The Graduate*
8 *The Matrix*
9 *Notting Hill*
10 *Duck Soup*

PAGE 53

Robotic Riddles

1 Anakin Skywalker
2 Robby the Robot
3 *Futureworld*
4 *The Stepford Wives*
5 Peter Weller
6 Micky Dolenz
7 Data
8 *Bicentennial Man*
9 Sarah Connor
10 *A.I. Artificial Intelligence*
11 Unknown to the crew of the spaceship *Nostromo*, science officer Ash, played by Ian Holm, is actually an android planted on the mission by the company they all work for

Big Screen Birds

1 The Marx Brothers
2 *The Cat and the Canary*
3 Polynesia
4 *The Wild Geese*
5 *Where Eagles Dare*
6 Reuben J. "Rooster" Cogburn
7 *Brewster McCloud*
8 Edgar Allan Poe
9 *Convoy*
10 Goose
11 *The Eagle Has Landed*
12 *The Crow*

PAGE 54

Man to Man

1 *Demolition Man*
2 *Marathon Man*
3 Patrick McGoohan
4 *The Stunt Man*
5 *The Man Who Knew Too Much*
6 *The Man Who Knew Too Little*
7 The Six Million Dollar Man
8 Lee Marvin
9 The Man from Atlantis, played by Patrick Duffy
10 Jeff Fahey
11 *The Music Man*

Blue Movies

1 *My Blue Heaven*
2 *Blue Steel*
3 A high-tech police helicopter
4 *Blue Hawaii*
5 *Blue Velvet*
6 *The Blue Lagoon*
7 *Lady Sings the Blues*
8 *The Blues Brothers*
9 *Biloxi Blues*
10 The name of a nightclub
11 *Mo' Better Blues*

PAGE 55

B Movies

1 *Bus Stop*
2 *Blackboard Jungle*
3 *A Bug's Life*
4 *Brannigan*
5 *Blind Date*
6 *Beauty and the Beast*
7 *Braveheart*
8 *Barbarella*
9 *Bugsy Malone*
10 *Basic Instinct*

Days Like These

1 *End of Days*
2 *A Day at the Races*
3 *Days of Thunder*
4 *The Day of the Triffids*
5 *That'll Be the Day*
6 *Anne of the Thousand Days*
7 *Six Days, Seven Nights*
8 *One Fine Day*
9 *The Remains of the Day*
10 *Independence Day*
11 *Groundhog Day*
12 *Tuesdays With Morrie*, which became a 1999 television movie

PAGE 56

What's Up, Doc?

1 *The Fugitive*
2 Dr. No
3 Peter Cushing
4 *The Elephant Man*
5 *One Flew Over the Cuckoo's Nest*
6 Dr. Josef Mengele
7 Boris Pasternak
8 Michael Douglas
9 *Awakenings*
10 Robin Williams

Movie Tunes

1 *Rocky III*
2 *An Officer and a Gentleman*
3 *Octopussy*
4 *Mad Max: Beyond Thunderdome*
5 *White Nights*
6 *Top Gun*
7 *Dirty Dancing*

8 *Cocktail*
9 *Robin Hood, Prince of Thieves*
10 *The Lion King*

PAGE 57

Stage and Screen

1 c. *Harry Potter*
2 a. 1911
3 d. Australian
4 a. *The Phantom of the Opera*
5 d. *Indecent Proposal*
6 c. François Truffaut
7 c. Laurence Olivier
8 c. British
9 d. Surfing

Body of Knowledge

1 *Sleepy Hollow*
2 Harry Palmer
3 Hot Lips
4 *Bright Eyes*
5 *The Beast with Five Fingers*
6 Lon Chaney
7 Betty Grable
8 Vincent Price
9 The Monkees
10 Brains (in *The Man with Two Brains*)

PAGE 58

On the Box

1 *The X-Files*
2 Mary Beth Lacey, played by Tyne Daly, was married to Harvey
3 Bart
4 Gerry Anderson
5 Larry Hagman
6 The A-Team
7 Peter Falk
8 Chicago
9 James Garner
10 Miami in *Miami Vice*

Answers

Universally Challenging

1 Tinky Winky
2 Evelyn Waugh
3 "With a Little Help from My Friends"
4 Mark McManus
5 *Lou Grant* (and originally on *The Mary Tyler Moore Show*)
6 Andy Williams's
7 Niles
8 *Knight Rider*
9 Steve Austin
10 *Charlie's Angels*

Street Smarts

1 c. Daniel Travanti
2 a. The Partridge family
3 c. Karl Malden
4 b. Perry Mason
5 a. The Clampetts in *The Beverly Hillbillies*
6 c. Edd Byrnes
7 d. The Munsters
8 b. Stone Cave Road

Watching the Detectives

1 David Soul
2 *The Name of the Rose*
3 Inspector Morse
4 Albert Finney
5 Shaft
6 Basil Rathbone
7 Jim Rockford in *The Rockford Files*
8 *Miss Congeniality*
9 Dennis Potter

Classic TV

1 *Peyton Place*
2 Frankie Laine
3 Frank Cannon
4 William Hartnell
5 Lucille Ball
6 Micky Dolenz
7 *The Persuaders*
8 Honolulu
9 "The William Tell Overture"

Spin-offs

1 *Angel*
2 *The Virginian*
3 *Happy Days*
4 *A Different World*
5 *Star Trek: Voyager*
6 *Maude*
7 *Law & Order: Special Victims Unit* or *Law & Order: Criminal Intent* (also *Crime & Punishment, Law & Order: Trial by Jury*, and *Conviction*)
8 *Cheers*
9 *The Six Million Dollar Man*
10 They were all spin-offs from *The Mary Tyler Moore Show*

Beasts on the Box

1 *Daktari*
2 Speedy Gonzalez
3 Basil
4 Mr. Ed
5 K-9
6 Roy Rogers
7 Burt Ward
8 Eddie
9 Flipper
10 An octopus

Television Tunes

1 *Married...With Children*
2 Jack Jones
3 *Friends*
4 *Moonlighting*
5 Suzi Quatro
6 Sheena Easton
7 Zoot
8 Vonda Shepard

All the World's a Stage

1 *My Fair Lady*
2 *Phantom of the Opera*
3 *Miss Saigon*
4 *Jesus Christ Superstar*
5 *La Cage aux Folles*
6 *Porgy and Bess*
7 *The King and I*
8 *Hair*
9 *Godspell*
10 *Annie*
11 *Fiddler on the Roof*
12 *How to Succeed in Business Without Really Trying*
13 *High Society*
14 *No, No, Nanette*
15 *The Pajama Game*

A Night at the Opera

1 *Carmen*
2 *Cosi fan tutte*
3 *La Bohème*
4 Engelbert Humperdinck
5 Figaro
6 *The Beggar's Opera*
7 *La Traviata*
8 *Madame Butterfly*
9 Irish
10 *Tosca*

Treading the Boards

1 *As You Like It*
2 Edward Albee
3 Method acting
4 Aeschylus
5 *She Stoops to Conquer*
6 Bertolt Brecht
7 Ben Jonson
8 *Hair*
9 Molière
10 *Look Back in Anger*

Class Acts of Vaudeville

1 To attract women
2 Buster Keaton
3 Magician and escape artist Harry Houdini
4 Zeppo, the youngest Marx brother
5 Jack Benny
6 As a publicity stunt, she had announced she was running for president on the Surprise Party ticket

Ed Sullivan's Really Big Shoe

1 He was a theater writer for New York City newspapers
2 The Ed Sullivan Theater
3 *Late Night with David Letterman*
4 In the song "Light My Fire," they were asked to delete the phrase "girl, we couldn't get much higher." CBS censors read that as a drug reference, but the band sang the line anyway.
5 Sullivan was on medical leave after a car accident
6 The Beatles, in their first live American appearance
7 *Bye Bye Birdie*

PAGE 64

Laurel and Hardy

1 Stan Laurel was the thin British one, and Georgia-born Oliver Hardy the portly one
2 He thought the shorter name would fit better on movie posters
3 Charlie Chaplin
4 Both wore derby hats. Stan Laurel wore a bow tie and a loose double-breasted jacket. Oliver Hardy wore a long tie and a tight-fitting jacket.
5 *Babes in Toyland* (also released as *March of the Wooden Soldiers*)
6 Vernon Steele
7 *Nuts in May*
8 Norvell
9 Babe

Situation Comedies

1 Prunella Scales
2 Seattle
3 Lurch
4 *Spin City*
5 *Soap*
6 John Goodman
7 Milwaukee
8 Kramer
9 *Ellen*
10 The Golden Girls

PAGE 65

Abbot and Costello

1 Straight man Abbott does the explaining and by the end of the routine, the frustrated and befuddled Costello appears to finally get the positions straight
2 First base: Who
Second base: What
Third base: I don't know
Pitcher: Tomorrow
Catcher: Today
Left field: Why
Center field: Because
Shortstop: I don't give a darn
3 The Killer, Boris Karloff
The Invisible Man
Captain Kidd
Dr. Jekyll and Mr. Hyde
The Keystone Kops
The Mummy
4 Costello was upset because Abbott hired a house servant that Costello had fired
5 The Andrews Sisters
6 *Ride 'Em Cowboy*
7 Fred Allen
8 William Demarest, who later went on to star in *My Three Sons*, as Uncle Charlie
9 Bela Lugosi

See Ya in the Funny Pages

1 Ernie Bushmiller
2 Hank Ketcham
3 Al Capp
4 Charles Schulz
5 Bill Watterson
6 Walt Kelly
7 Mort Walker
8 Reg Smythe
9 Jim Davis
10 Bil Keane

Disney Delights

1 *Beauty and the Beast*
2 Monstro
3 *Fantasia*
4 *The Aristocats*
5 Pongo and Perdita
6 A bear
7 Flower
8 *Pocahontas*
9 *The Lion King*

PAGE 66

Will Rogers

1 c. Native American
2 c. A lariat
3 d. Clement Vann Rogers, Will's father and a delegate to the Oklahoma Constitutional Convention
4 a. He roped a wild steer that was climbing the stands in Madison Square Garden
5 b. To keep track of the time limit on his broadcasts
6 a. A horse's neck, the horse's rider, and the horse's legs
7 d. *Life Begins at Forty*
8 b. The *Mayflower*
9 c. "Before I refuse to take your questions, I have an opening statement."
10 d. Rogers appeared in a film of a Twain novel.

PAGE 67

The Truth About 'Toons

1 False; Wilma is the name of Fred Flintstone's wife
2 False; Officer Dibble rides herd on Top Cat and his gang
3 True
4 True; the boop-oop-a-doop girl was censored in the 1930s for her racy clothing
5 False; Shaggy is voiced by another radio personality, Casey Kasem
6 False; Yosemite Sam was created as an archenemy for Bugs Bunny
7 True

Answers

Name That Comedian

1 Lucille Ball
2 Jackie Gleason
3 Red Skelton
4 Curly Howard
5 Charlie Chaplin

Under the Big Top

1 Buffalo Bill
2 Annie Oakley, performing with Buffalo Bill's Wild West Show
3 Harry Houdini
4 Clowns
5 Cirque du Soleil
6 *Annie Get Your Gun*
7 David Blaine
8 Bip
9 Niagara Falls
10 David Copperfield

Name That Circus

Barnum & Bailey, Ringling Bros., Cirque du Soleil, Big Apple Circus, Circus Royale, Circus Krone, Circus Circus

P. T. Barnum

1 b. Phineas Taylor
2 b. He was the first to move his own circus by train
3 c. He asked how ticket sales were going for the day in the box office
4 b. *There's a Sucker Born Every Minute*

The Pachyderm Pack

1 John Hurt
2 Stevie Wonder
3 Bull
4 Timothy
5 Howdah
6 Babar the Elephant
7 Jumbo
8 Rudyard Kipling
9 Denmark

A Family of Daredevils on High

1 c. The Wallendas' safety net was lost in transit
2 b. From a high-wire fall during a promotional walk in Puerto Rico
3 a. "A hand balancer with courage"
4 c. The name stuck after a press description of an accident

Ol' Blue Eyes

1 c. The Rat Pack
2 a. "My Way"
3 a. Chicago
4 a. Nancy
5 b. 1998
6 b. Nicole Kidman
7 b. Bono
8 a. *Who Framed Roger Rabbit*
9 c. Mia Farrow
10 a. *High Society*

Elvis Lives!

1 a. A twin (Elvis's twin, Jesse, was stillborn)
2 c. Colonel Tom Parker
3 b. *Girls! Girls! Girls!*
4 c. Sun Records
5 a. "It's Now or Never"
6 b. Eddie Rabbitt
7 a. Mississippi
8 b. Sergeant
9 b. *Love Me Tender*
10 b. and d. *Flaming Star* and *Stay Away, Joe*

The Beatles

1 d. "From Me to You"
2 b. Chuck, c. Dave, and d. Vera
3 a. "Penny Lane"
4 c. Apple
5 a. *A Hard Day's Night* (1964)
6 a. "All You Need Is Love"
7 c. George Harrison
8 a. Ringo Starr
9 c. Never

Musical Moments

1 *The Producers*
2 Seven
3 Lucille Ball
4 "Talk to the Animals"
5 *Pygmalion*
6 *High Society*
7 Jennifer Beals
8 Madonna
9 *Singin' in the Rain*
10 "Greased Lightning"

PAGE 73

The Rolling Stones

1 b. Ronnie Wood
2 d. Muddy Waters (his tune "Rollin' Stone" provided the inspiration)
3 b. The extreme popularity in the United States and Canada of British rock bands during the mid-1960s
4 c. "(I Can't Get No) Satisfaction"
5 d. Hell's Angels

Strike Up the Band

1 *West Side Story*
2 *Cabaret*
3 *Funny Girl*
4 *Paint Your Wagon*
5 Richard and Oscar
6 *Meet Me in St. Louis*
7 Jennifer Grey
8 *A Star Is Born*
9 Jerry from *Tom and Jerry*
10 In Paris (*An American in Paris*)

PAGE 74

A Musical Medley

1 b. Carlo Bergonzi
2 b. 1958
3 b. Wind
4 c. A form of flamenco
5 c. A pocket-sized violin
6 b. 1966
7 c. Silence
8 d. Xylophones
9 c. Folk
10 c. An African drum

3 | Sports

Whether you're an athlete who enjoys firsthand the thrill of competition or an armchair observer who has memorized their favorite team statistics for the past 20 years, no trivia challenge would be complete without a slew of quizzes designed to test the avid sports enthusiast.

The Competitive Arena

Let's start this section with a series of questions about the greatest international event, for which many athletes train their whole lives. We're talking Olympics. After that you'll find a few more colorful quizzes that are extremely interesting.

Olympic Events

With so many sports and countries represented, it can be a challenge keeping up with the details. How well do you know the following events?

1 What is always the final event in a decathlon?

2 How many events are there in a pentathlon?

3 Which is the only swimming event to have been held in every Olympics?

4 Which sport was featured only once, at the 1900 Olympics in a match between France and Britain?

5 Which member of the British royal family competed in three-day events at the 1976 Olympics?

6 In which summer event have American athletes enjoyed the most success?

7 Which of the following were once Olympic events: tug-of-war, rugby, polo, lacrosse, or golf?

8 How many events were held at the 2008 Summer Games: 188, 276, or 302?

9 In which two summer events did men not compete in the 2008 games?

10 The 1896 Olympics featured which event that was said to follow the legendary route of Pheidippides?

Which Came First?

Can you spot which sport was first introduced to the modern Olympic roster?

1 Gymnastics or football?

2 Table tennis or handball?

3 Modern pentathlon or triathlon?

4 Field hockey or ice hockey?

5 Bobsleigh or luge?

6 Shooting or archery?

7 Taekwondo or judo?

8 Skating or skiing?

9 Badminton or volleyball?

10 Equestrian or cycling?

Ahhh...I see!

What was seven gold-medal–winner Mark Spitz's day job reputed to be?

Olympic Traditions

Perhaps no other international event is steeped in as much tradition as the Olympics. Are you in the know about all of the history involved?

1 How many rings are depicted on the Olympic flag, and what do they represent?

2 Traditionally, which country leads the parade at the opening ceremony of the Olympics?

3 What is significant about the gold medals awarded in 1912?

4 What color of medal was presented to the winners in the first modern Olympics in 1896?

5 In which decade were the games first televised?

6 Why were women forbidden from watching the ancient Olympic Games?

7 According to tradition, when is the Olympic flame extinguished?

8 What does the official Olympic motto—*Citius, Altius, Fortius*—mean in English?

9 What is the official second language of the Olympics?

10 At the traditional closing ceremony of the Games, the mayor of the current host city presents the flag to whom?

Olympic Host Cities

Every four years cities across the world compete to see who will host the next Olympics. For those that do, the rewards are rich because they become a part of the history books.

1 Other than Munich, what is the only other German city to host the Summer Olympics in the 20th century?

2 In which country were the Olympic Games held in 776 BC?

3 Which Spanish city hosted the 1992 Summer Olympics?

4 What was the American venue of the 1996 Summer Olympics?

5 Which host city to the 1984 Winter Games was devastated by civil war in the 1990s?

6 How many Olympics of the 20th century were held in Africa?

7 Why did the United States boycott the 1980 Moscow Olympics?

8 The eruption of which mountain prevented the 1908 Olympics from being held in Rome?

9 How many Olympic Games have been missed due to war?

10 Which U.S. host city to the Winter Games was rocked by scandal and allegations of bribery?

Olympic History

If you have a knack for keeping track of landmark events, you'll have no problem sailing through this mixed round of historic questions.

1 Which member of the British royal family opened the 1956 Melbourne Olympics?

2 Which member of the royal family is a representative on the International Olympic Committee?

3 To what position in the Olympic hierarchy was Juan Antonio Samaranch elected in 1980?

4 In which year did Japan first compete in the Summer Olympics: 1912, 1952, or 1972?

5 What kind of sporting projectile was thrown by Geoff Capes in the Olympic Games?

6 In which year were Israeli Olympic athletes murdered by terrorists?

7 What record did the Soviet gymnast Nikolai Adrianov achieve between 1972 and 1980?

Winning Colors

Most sports are not for the color-blind. Here's a warm-up round that requires you to consider all the color details an athlete should know.

1 In which sport do red and yellow balls oppose black and blue balls?
a. Croquet
b. Polo
c. Table pool

2 In which Canadian city do the Blue Jays play their home baseball games?
a. Montreal
b. Vancouver
c. Toronto

3 Which English soccer team is nicknamed the Black Cats and plays its home games at the Stadium of Light?
a. Sunderland
b. Newcastle United
c. Norwich City

4 What color belt does a first Dan wear in judo?
a. Yellow
b. Black
c. Purple

5 What color is the center of an archery target?
a. Black
b. Red
c. Gold

6 Which color is representative of the most difficult ski runs?
a. Red
b. Black
c. Orange

7 Which colorful horse won the 2001 Grand National?
a. Red Marauder
b. Blue Angel
c. Midnight Hero

8 What color shirts are worn by the French national rugby team?
a. Blue
b. Red
c. Black

9 Which color is associated with the baseball teams of Boston and Cincinnati?
a. Blue
b. Red
c. White

10 What color jersey did soccer goalkeeper Lev Yashin always wear when playing for Russia?
a. Black
b. Red
c. Yellow

11 What color flag indicates a foul throw in a javelin competition?
a. Yellow
b. White
c. Red

12 What color cap does a goalkeeper wear in water polo?
a. Red
b. White
c. Orange

Extreme Sports

The sports featured here typically fall outside the mainstream and are celebrated for their adrenaline-pumping thrills. Just make sure you don't wipe out if you decide to test yourself with this adventurous round.

1 Which television network is credited with creating the X Games?

2 Which two extreme sports debuted in the 1996 and 1998 Olympics?

3 What's the name of the U-shaped structure many extreme sports use to showcase their daring?

4 Who is credited with creating the Boom Boom HuckJam, a 30-city arena tour featuring some of the world's best extreme athletes?

5 Who was born September 3, 1986, in Carlsbad, California, and went on to win Olympic gold in snowboarding?

6 Which extreme sport most resembles motocross?

7 Which extreme sport is a cousin to both snowboarding and water skiing?

8 Which extreme sport involves using an airfoil or wing as participants descend a slope on either skis or a snowboard?

9 Which host city had to build a BMX track for the first ever Olympic competition in this sport?

10 How many wheels on a skateboard?

International Roundup

While cheering for the home team is easy to understand in any language, the following questions are designed to see how much you know about the sports around the world as well as your own backyard. Good luck!

1 What is the Gaelic word for *pole*, the type that is thrown in the Highland Games?

2 What are Canada's national sports?

3 In which country did the sport of sumo wrestling originate?

4 Which sport is played by the Philadelphia Flyers?

5 Alongside Norway, which country pioneered orienteering?

6 What is the national sport of Malaysia?

7 Which American sport was invented by Abner Doubleday?

8 In which country was croquet invented?

9 In sumo wrestling, what name is given to a wrestler who has attained the rank of grand champion?

10 What is the most popular sport in Bulgaria?

11 How many players form a Gaelic soccer team?

To the Finish Line!

Can you answer this grab bag of sporting questions?

1 What is a more common name for a natatorium?
a. Gymnasium
b. Indoor swimming pool
c. Young referee

2 Octopush is an underwater version of which sport?
a. Tug-of-war
b. Wrestling
c. Hockey

3 The Hawaii Ironman competition, first held at Waikiki Beach in 1978, is what type of event?
a. Triathlon
b. Marathon
c. Decathlon

4 The basic equipment of what competition includes cross-country skis, poles, boots, and a bolt-action (nonautomatic) rifle?
a. Ironman
b. Id'tarod
c. Biathlon

5 In which sport do competitors attempt to win the Giro D'Italia?
a. Triathlon
b. Bicycling
c. Formula 1

6 A water polo ball is the same size as what other ball?
a. Soccer ball
b. Baseball
c. Basketball

7 Men's water polo was introduced to the Olympics in 1900. How many years until the women's event was added?
a. 20 years
b. 64 years
c. 100 years

8 What Olympic team sport allows substitutions between players without stopping play?
a. Hockey
b. Curling
c. Badminton

9 Which event ranks behind the Super Bowl as the largest single-day sporting event in the world in terms of press credentials issued for on-site media coverage?
a. Indianapolis 500
b. Boston Marathon
c. Kentucky Derby

10 How many soccer World Cups were held in the 1940s?
a. None
b. Two
c. Five

11 Which country has won soccer's World Cup five times?
a. Brazil
b. Argentina
c. England

The Winter Games

For the past 50 years these events are especially cool to watch on television because you can do so from the warm comfort of your own living room. Match the host city to its respective year.

1956____	A	Albertville, France
1960____	B	Calgary, Canada
1964____	C	Cortina d'Ampezzo, Italy
1968____	D	Grenoble, France
1972____	E	Innsbruck, Austria
1976____	F	Lake Placid, New York, United States
1980____	G	Lillehammer, Norway
1984____	H	Nagano, Japan
1988____	I	Salt Lake City, Utah, United States
1992____	J	Sapporo, Japan
1994____	K	Sarajevo, Yugoslavia (now Bosnia and Herzegovina)
1998____	L	Squaw Valley, California, United States
2002____	M	Vancouver, Canada
2006____	N	Turin (Torino), Italy
2010____		

At the Races

This section covers a lot of ground with all kinds of amazing races. From NASCAR to horses, from the Tour de France to the Boston Marathon, you'll be sure to get a good workout from working on these mental pursuits.

Horse Sense

Pony up and tell the truth. How well do you know the terminology you'd need to know around a horse track?

1 A race in which horses finish so close that no clear winner is apparent is called a:
a. Blanket finish
b. Tie
c. Naked finish

2 The mother of a horse with a specially bred bloodline is called a:
a. Mare
b. Dam
c. Nag

3 A race for female horses is called a:
a. Bell race
b. Mareathon
c. Distaff

4 The physical barriers placed near the inner rail during rainy weather to prevent horses being trained from messing up the track are called:
a. Dogs
b. Mutts
c. Clubs

5 A horse that is labeled a poor starter and hesitates at the start of a race is called a:
a. Par
b. Dwelt
c. Dud

6 A blacksmith who makes iron shoes for horses' hooves is called a:
a. Farrier
b. Shoe-fitter
c. Stabler

7 During menstruation, when a female horse is most likely to conceive, she is said to be:
a. Houseable
b. Horsing
c. Hovering

8 A race for three-year-old fillies is called an:
a. Oats Race
b. Owners' Race
c. Oaks

9 The ridge between a horse's shoulder bones is known as the:
a. Withers
b. Mount
c. Cliff

10 The obedience section of an equestrian event is called:
a. Corsage
b. Dressage
c. Fromage

NASCAR Flags

Drivers depend on a special series of flags to alert them to any changes that can affect their safety and the outcome of the race. Match the right color to its meaning.

One lap left in the race_____	**A** Black
Signals the start of the race and any restarts_____	**B** Black with white cross
Stops the race because of major accidents or weather issues_____	**C** Blue with yellow stripe
Laps are no longer scored until car reports to the pits_____	**D** Checkered
Race is over_____	**E** Green
Return to the pits because of mechanical failure or rules infraction_____	**F** Red
Check your mirrors because faster traffic is approaching_____	**G** White
Signals caution due to an accident, debris, or weather_____	**H** Yellow

Built for Speed

Buckle up! This round is going to go so fast your head will spin. Just hold tight through the curves and you'll be fine.

1 What is the nationality of racing driver Jacques Villeneuve?

2 How many people work in a NASCAR pit crew?

3 Which famous car rally is held annually in Monaco?

4 Which driver set a record of 51 Grand Prix wins in 1993?

5 What was considered the drink of champions after Louis Meyer, the winner of the 1936 Indianapolis 500, was photographed gulping it down?

6 What does the acronym NASCAR stand for?

7 In which country was the first modern speedway built in 1906?

8 How many times has a member of the Unser family won the Indianapolis 500?

9 The Italian driver Enzo Ferrari raced for what other company?

10 Which Food TV Network superstar penned a cookbook about NASCAR cooking?

11 In case it becomes smeared or dirty, what part of a race car is covered with three thin layers of plastic that can be torn off during a pit stop?

Walk, Trot, Canter...

Can you name the gaits for a five-gaited and a seven-gaited horse?

Horse Play

Place your bets. It's time for a day at the races. All of the following questions require a true-false answer, so your odds are even.

1 In 1996, Cigar won the Dubai World Cup, a super-rich horse race in its inaugural year. TRUE ◯ FALSE ◯

2 The U.S. Triple Crown, Preakness, and Kentucky Derby form the Belmont Stakes. TRUE ◯ FALSE ◯

3 Janet Guthrie was the first woman to train a Grand National winner. TRUE ◯ FALSE ◯

4 Yankees, Canadians, and Trixies are kinds of accumulator bets. TRUE ◯ FALSE ◯

5 Willie Carson is a famous jockey with the middle names of Fisher Hunter. TRUE ◯ FALSE ◯

6 Party Politics was the winning horse in the Grand National in the 1992 election year. TRUE ◯ FALSE ◯

7 The Kentucky Derby is a longer race than the French Derby, the Irish Derby, or the Epsom Derby. TRUE ◯ FALSE ◯

8 If a horse races a distance of three kilometers, it travels nine furlongs. TRUE ◯ FALSE ◯

9 Picador is the name given to a matador on horseback. TRUE ◯ FALSE ◯

10 The Prix de l'Arc de Triomphe is run on the Longchamp course. TRUE ◯ FALSE ◯

Speed Machines

Bicycle racing has a variety of events with a near infinite number of variations. Can you match the right event with its proper description?

Known as the tag-team relay of track racing_____ **A** Criterium

Riders start together and sprint against each other on specified laps throughout the race to earn points_____ **B** Cyclocross

Two teams of three riders start on opposite sides of the track; after the first lap, teammates begin to pull off the track so that the third rider completes the final lap of the race solo_____ **C** Dual Slalom

Two riders or two four-person teams begin from a standing start at opposite sides of the track_____ **D** Madison Relay

Track riders jockey for position as they try to outwit each other before the final dash to the line_____ **E** Match Sprint

The cyclist starts from a standing start and races one kilometer alone against the clock_____ **F** Olympic Sprint

Conducted on a short course with varied terrain, this race involves high speeds and many obstacles that require running dismounts_____ **G** Points Race

A short road race on a circuit, usually city streets_____ **H** Pursuit

Any race that combines some or all road events, such as the Tour de France_____ **I** Stage Race

Two off-road competitors race head-to-head down parallel courses; riders face each other twice, once on each side of the course_____ **J** Time Trial

Vive la France

Following the Tour de France, one of the greatest racing events in the world, requires a general familiarity with a few French words. Take this matching quiz to see how well you can keep up.

The sag wagon, or broom wagon, that sweeps the back of the field and picks up riders who abandon the course_____   **A** Alpe d'Huez

The last rider in the race field_____   **B** Derailleur

A lever-activated mechanism that changes the gear ratio by pushing the chain off of one sprocket and onto another_____   **C** Echelon

The most famous climb in the Tour, it's the most prestigious stage (21 switchbacks!) for any climber to win_____   **D** Hors catégorie

A pace line in which following riders angle away from the leader to get maximum crosswind draft_____   **E** Lanterne rouge

A rating reserved for the toughest climbs, such as the Col du Galibier_____   **F** Maillot jaune

The person who takes care of all nonmanagement, nonmechanical details for a team of riders, from finalizing hotel arrangements to assembling the day's feed bags_____   **G** Soigneur

The race leader's jersey_____   **H** Voiture balai

Getting the Runaround

Do you know the most direct route for this round? If you're passionate about running you will!

1 In 1975, which New Zealand athlete became the first man to run the mile in under 3 minutes 50 seconds?

2 In 1999, who smashed the men's 100-meter world record at a meet in Athens?

3 Which 1927 invention enabled sprinters to start faster?

4 In a 110-meter hurdles race, how many hurdles are negotiated?

5 Which well-known American won his second Olympic title in the 400-meter hurdles in 1984?

6 How many laps of the track are run for a 400-meter outdoor race in the Olympics?

7 Who won an Olympic gold medal for the 100 meters in 1924 and was portrayed in the film *Chariots of Fire*?

8 In what year were women's track and field events added to the Summer Olympics?

9 What distance is the longest track event in the women's heptathlon?

10 How many lanes are there on an Olympic running track?

11 Who claimed nine Olympic gold medals by winning the long jump in Atlanta?

12 Which American gold-medal winner of 1968 gave his name to a style of high jumping?

13 Which American gold-medal winner in the 1960 Olympics suffered from polio and wore leg braces until she was nine?

14 What company did Phil Knight and Bill Bowerman form in 1964 to market a lighter and more comfortable shoe?

Formula 1 Facts

These cars are capable of pulling in excess of 5G forces in some curves. Can you keep up with the fastest sport on earth?

1 Which famous track hosted the British Grand Prix in 1985?

2 The tires of which company have been used for the majority of world championship cars?

3 Which son of a Brazilian diplomat won the first of his three world titles in 1981?

4 Who was the first Frenchman to become Formula I Champion?

5 Which famous name in the world of Grand Prix racing became confined to a wheelchair after a road crash in 1986?

6 Who was Damon Hill's father?

7 Which Grand Prix is held in the streets of Monte Carlo?

8 What nationality is Keke Rosberg?

9 In which year was the 300th motor racing Grand Prix staged: 1968, 1978, or 1988?

10 Which horse-racing course staged five British Grand Prix races?

11 What was the nationality of Grand Prix driver Jack Brabham?

Marathon Man

Tighten your laces to see if you can go the distance with these running-related questions. Perhaps you'll score a personal best.

1 In which year was the first London Marathon held?

2 What is the world's oldest marathon?

3 In which park does the New York Marathon finish?

4 Who wore the No. 1 bib at the 2003 London Marathon?

5 In what city does the Marine Corps Marathon begin every year?

6 From what country was Ibrahim Hussein, the first African to win the Boston Marathon?

7 Which Tour de France winner finished 496th in the 2008 Boston Marathon?

8 What were Snickers candy bars called in England in the 1980s?

9 Who wrote the novel *The Loneliness of the Long Distance Runner*?

10 In 1975, which major marathon became the first to include a wheelchair division?

11 The Boston Marathon traditionally takes place on the third Monday of what month?

12 A marathon is run over 26 miles (42 kilometers) and how many yards?

13 How many people entered the first New York Marathon in 1970?

Water Sports

Water, hands down, is the most important nutrient on the planet. The average human body is about 65 percent water. Perhaps that explains our attraction to sports that rely on the wet stuff for their playing field. Whether you swim like a fish or just prefer to catch them for the sport of it, tread carefully because this section will test your abilities to the limit.

A Quick Dip

How well do you know your pool lingo? Can you enter into this round with nary a splash, or do you prefer to do cannonballs?

1 What name is given to the final swimmer in a relay race?
a. Anchor
b. Alternate
c. Steamer

2 The starting spot behind each lane is known as what?
a. Slab
b. Chop
c. Block

3 The area along the edge of the pool where water overflows and recirculates is called:
a. Lane
b. Gutter
c. Alley

4 The wave created in front of the swimmer's head as they move through the water is called a:
a. Bow wave
b. Hurdle wave
c. Crest wave

5 Which competitive stroke incorporates a dolphin kick?
a. Freestyle
b. Breaststroke
c. Butterfly

6 What term describes a race or event held in a lake or ocean?
a. Long-distance swimming
b. Cross-channel swimming
c. Open-body swimming

7 What term describes a swimmer who is swimming facedown on his or her stomach?
a. Deft
b. Prone
c. Agile

8 Once their qualifying times are determined, in which lanes are the fastest swimmers placed in a pool?
a. Outside lanes
b. Center lanes
c. They're positioned right-to-left

9 What is it called when a swimmer kicks the legs independently of each other, not in unison, in an up-and-down motion?
a. Spring kick
b. Flutter kick
c. Dolphin kick

10 The resistance the water causes swimmers as they move through the water is known as:
a. Draw
b. Heave
c. Drag

Splish Splash

Don't just stand there dipping your toe into the side of the pool. Let's start off by jumping into the deep end with this mixed round of questions.

1 Name the actor, famous for playing Tarzan, who was the first man to swim 100 meters in under a minute.

2 What is the second-fastest swimming stroke?

3 Which swimming stroke begins the first leg of a 4 x 100-meter medley relay?

4 What is the longest distance among swimming events held at the Olympic Games?

5 Captain Matthew Webb, the first man to swim the English Channel without a life jacket, later died trying to swim the rapids of which waterfall?

6 In 1979, Diana Nyad became the first person to swim to Florida from which Caribbean island?

7 What massive land mammal can swim 20 miles a day?

8 What great American inventor is credited with inventing swim fins?

9 What bodily fluid does the average human produce enough of in a lifetime to fill two swimming pools?

10 The earliest known goggle artifacts, estimated to have been made in the 1300s, were crafted from what type of polished shell?

Swimmingly Superb Stumpers

Can you name 10 swimming terms that begin with the letter *S*? We'll give you 10, and you can probably name more!

Take the Plunge!

Diving is an exciting water sport that involves many complicated tumbles, twists, and other acrobatic maneuvers. Can you score a perfect 10 before you have to hit the water?

1 In the 1984 Olympics, who was the first male diver in 56 years to win the platform and springboard events?

2 Ernst Bransten, widely recognized as the "father of diving in the United States," came to America from which European country shortly before 1920?

3 There are six basic groups of dives, including the inward, twisting, and arm-stand. Can you name the three others?

4 What type of diving is done from a flexible aluminum or steel plank, measuring 16 feet long and 20 inches wide?

5 All divers strive to be rigid and vertical when they enter the water to minimize what?

6 What type of diving became part of the Olympic program in 2000?

7 Cliff diving was said to have originated on which island in the South Pacific?

8 During the Cliff Diving World Championship's opening ceremony in 1998, Frederic Weill performed a spectacular dive from a height of 86 feet using what piece of transportation equipment as a platform?

9 What is the wheel called along the side of a diving board that can be used to adjust its stability and stiffness?

10 About how fast would your body be traveling when it hits the water after diving from a 10-meter platform: 20 mph, 31 mph, or 52 mph?

Reel Them In!

Do you have what it takes to land a big one? See how well you know your fish species with this watery round of true and false questions.

1 Walleyes are known for their marble-like eyes, which let them see well in dim light.   TRUE ○   FALSE ○

2 Trout are the only fish with an adipose fin (the small fin on the back just in front of the tail).   TRUE ○   FALSE ○

3 White and striped bass are members of the temperate bass family, as opposed to black bass, which belong to the sunfish family.   TRUE ○   FALSE ○

4 Flatheads are more apt to eat dead fish than any other catfish species.   TRUE ○   FALSE ○

5 Pike lose their teeth in the summer and don't bite.   TRUE ○   FALSE ○

6 The white sturgeon, which is found in rivers along the Pacific Coast, will reach a weight of almost a ton.   TRUE ○   FALSE ○

7 Like pike, muskies feed actively throughout the year and are a popular target of ice fishermen.   TRUE ○   FALSE ○

8 Leeches are one of the top baits for walleyes.   TRUE ○   FALSE ○

9 Research has shown that a sudden decrease in light level triggers walleyes to bite.   TRUE ○   FALSE ○

10 The fry of all bass turn coal black within a few days after they hatch, but only the smallmouth bass stay that way, which is why they're referred to as black bass.   TRUE ○   FALSE ○

Fish Tales!

Sure you've heard plenty about the one that got away, but how well can you reel in the tricky details these questions pose?

1 What zodiac sign is traditionally depicted as two fish?

2 In what type of water would you use a fly rod?

3 The international record for largest catch (a 2,664-pound white shark) was landed off the coast of which continent?

4 The best time of year to catch a trophy walleye is five to seven weeks after what event?

5 What freshwater fish found in North America makes the longest spawning migration?

6 According to researchers, what color is most visible to walleyes?

7 What prehistoric fish has scales so abrasive that they're sold as nail files in the shops of Manaus, Brazil?

8 What Peter Benchley best seller left people afraid to go in the water when it was published in 1975?

9 What North American freshwater fish is covered with hard, diamond-shaped scales and has long jaws with needlelike teeth?

10 Koi, the brightly colored fish often found in ornamental ponds, is actually a member of which fish family?

Land Ho!

Have you ever been sailing? If so, try testing your sea legs with a round of these spirited queries.

1 What three-letter word is the name for a forward sail on a yacht?

2 How many sailing hulls does a trimaran have?

3 What Olympic yachting class calls for a crew of three people?

4 In sailing, how many masts does a sloop have: one, two, or three?

5 What is the name of the annual yachting festival that is held on the Isle of Wight?

6 What name is given to the lines on a sailboat for hoisting the sails?

7 According to the history books, what game was played by the crew on board the *Mayflower*: darts, polo, or table tennis?

8 In yachting, what shape is a spinnaker?

9 Although sailing for transportation predates written history, which European country is credited with modern sport sailing?

10 Founded in 1906 as the first ocean race for amateur sailors in normal boats, this race begins in Newport, Rhode Island, and finishes in which Caribbean island?

Splash Goes the Sailor

Can you name the one water sport that celebrates victory by tossing one of its team members into the water? What's that teammate called?

Row, Row, Row the Boat

The term crew is used in American schools and colleges to designate the sport of rowing, such as Yale Crew or St. Andrew's Crew. When outside of the academic sphere, the sport is simply known as rowing. Would you be up the creek without a paddle with this round?

1 Until about 50 years ago, women's rowing was considered to be only "recreational" and few clubs or colleges offered it, but which institution of higher education has had women rowers as part of its history since 1877?

2 What is the name given to the person who steers the boat?

3 How many boats race at a time during a Henley race, named after the famous Henley Royal Regatta held on the River Thames in England?

4 What is the Olympic distance for rowing: 2,000 meters, 4,000 meters, or 6,000 meters?

5 What is the distance of The Harvard–Yale Boat Race, begun in 1852?

6 What direction does the boat usually travel?

7 The trailing end of the boat is called the stern. What is the forward end called?

8 When sitting in the coxswain's position, what are the left and right sides of the boat called?

9 What do you call a person who rows with two oars, one in each hand?

10 Before the days of motorized boats, a heavily built boat called a cutter would row along following a race. Who would typically sit in the passenger seat?

Ice and Snow Sports

Here's the irony about this section. Though the athletes must sometimes compete in subzero conditions, winter sports are actually hot because they're full of speed and excitement. So grab an extra pair of socks if you'll need them, but make no mistake: these quizzes are sure to leave you sweating in the end.

The Slush Pile

Watch your step with this mixed assortment of chilly questions.

1 In which sport do competitors change lanes after every lap?

2 Which was the first Asian country to host the Winter Olympics?

3 Which famous Austrian skier was World Downhill Champion four times in the 1970s?

4 Which country won 29 gold medals at the 1998 Winter Olympics?

5 Which city hosted the 1998 Winter Olympics?

6 What nationality is alpine skier Ingemar Stenmark: Finnish, Norwegian, or Swedish?

7 What piece of equipment takes its name from the Norwegian word for snowshoe?

8 Which East German skater received a special Olympic award from the IOC president in 1988?

9 Who composed "Bolero," to which Jayne Torvill and Christopher Dean skated and won a gold medal?

10 In mountaineering, what *C* word is the name of the metal plates with spikes that are fixed to the feet when climbing on ice?

11 Which winter sport is named after the French word for "sled"?

You're Getting Colder...

In which winter event has Bjorn Daehlie won more medals than the legendary Carl Lewis, Mark Spitz, Eric Heiden, or Sonja Henie?

Downhill Daring

Racing down snow-covered hills at top speed has never been a sport for the timid. Whether you're a master of the steep slopes or prefer the bunny hills instead, strap on your skis and see how fast you can make your way to the bottom of this round of riddles.

1 What name is given to a skier's quilted trousers?

2 What nickname was given to the British ski jumper Eddie Edwards?

3 Name the three alpine events in which skiers accumulate points during World Cup competition.

4 Which mountain range includes the highest peak in the contiguous United States?

5 What equipment was first built for the Sun Valley Lodge ski resort near Ketchum, Idaho?

6 What process did Milton Pierce patent in 1951?

7 What California event prompted Norwegian skiers to bring their specialized snow shoes to the area in 1849, thus introducing downhill skiing to the American West?

8 What happened most recently in the mid-1800s on Mount Hood in Oregon?

9 In 1973 Rick Sylvester ski-jumped off which mountain in Yosemite National Park and then parachuted to the base of the cliff?

10 What World Cup champion American skier uses a unicycle to train in the off-season?

Slap Shot!

How well do you know your hockey trivia? Take your turn at this round of questions and remember to whack them as hard as you can!

1 In which British town was the National Hockey Stadium built, which was used by England Hockey as its national stadium from 1995 to 2003?

2 In 1996, which legendary ice-hockey player moved from the St. Louis Blues to play for the New York Rangers?

3 What does the letter *C* signify on a hockey shirt?

4 What shirt number was worn by Edmonton Oiler's star player Wayne Gretzky?

5 What's the maximum number of players a team is allowed to have on the ice at any time?

6 What material is used to safeguard spectators during a game and prevent the puck from sailing off the ice?

7 When does a face-off occur?

8 What happens when players "change on the fly"?

9 How many points are earned when the puck goes in the goal?

10 What trophy is awarded annually by the NHL to its playoff championship team?

Sizing Up the Competition

Can you match these Winter Olympic athletes with their respective events?

Picabo Street_____ **A** Alpine skiing

Bonnie Blair_____ **B** Figure skating

Michelle Kwan_____ **C** Freestyle skiing

Jonny Moseley_____ **D** Hockey

Bode Miller_____ **E** Ski jumping

Mike Eruzione _____ **F** Speed skating

Apolo Ohno_____

Eddie Edwards_____

Kristi Yamaguchi_____

Eric Heiden_____

Crazy for Curling

It's been described as "chess on ice," but essentially curling is a team sport that depends on strategy, not speed, to get stones into prime position on the ice. Try your hand at lining up some of the terminology of curling—all of the words begin with the letter *B*.

A curling competition or tournament_____   **A** Backline

The line across the ice at the back of the house; stones over this line
are removed from play_____   **B** Biter

An end in which no points have been scored_____   **C** Blank end

A stone in motion touched by a member of either team or any part of their equipment
Such stones are removed from play_____   **D** Board weight

The circle at the center of the house_____   **E** Bonspiel

A stone that just touches the outer edge of the circles_____   **F** Brush

A device used to sweep the ice in the path of a moving stone_____   **G** Burned stone

To curl in behind a guard_____   **H** Bury a stone

A stone thrown with sufficient momentum or force to reach the back boards
of the curling sheet_____   **I** Button

The Cutting Edge

Speed skaters rely on super-sharp blades and amazingly strong thighs to secure their wins. Are you well-honed and ready for this round?

1 Who produced the greatest single feat in Winter Olympic history when he won all five long track events at the 1980 Lake Placid Olympics?

2 Clap skates feature a spring-loaded front hinge, which allow skaters to do what?

3 What type of speed skating was introduced in the 1992 Winter Olympics?

4 Which is longer: a hockey skate or a speed skate?

5 Which parts of a speed skater's body should almost be touching when in proper racing position?

6 What do speed skaters wear for identification on the track?

7 A foul in speed skating is usually called when skaters do what when they try to pass the competition?

8 When skaters follow closely behind their competition, what are they doing?

9 Which female Olympic speed skater also made waves as a member of the 1989 Sundance Fruit Juicer Cycling Tour?

10 It's often assumed that this short track racer was named after the Greek god of sunlight and prophecy, but such is not the case. What's his full name?

Figure 8s

These are the skating details that every figure skater and true enthusiast must know. Can you spot the right answer to the following questions?

1 In this jump, the takeoff is on a forward outside edge, and then the skater makes one and a half revolutions in the air and lands on the other foot on a back outside edge. Name that jump.
a. Axel jump
b. Lutz
c. Salchow

2 Name the jump in which the skater stops briefly with one foot extended behind, then swings that leg forward and around with a wide scooping motion, before landing backward on the foot and leg that performed the scooping motion.
a. An axel jump
b. Lutz
c. Salchow

3 This star of the 1976 Olympics also had a hairstyle that was copied by young girls everywhere.
a. Dorothy Hamill
b. Peggy Fleming
c. Michelle Kwan

4 Skating is believed to have originated in Scandinavia around 1000 BC. The earliest known skates were strapped to the bottom of the foot and used what material for the blade?
a. Metal
b. Bone
c. Stone

5 When did the International Skating Union eliminate from competition the compulsory section, in which prescribed figures were traced?
a. 1970
b. 1950
c. 1990

6 In Olympic figure skating, what type of music are skaters not allowed to use in their routine?
a. Rock music
b. Music with vocals
c. Jazz

7 In what sport did Tanya Harding, the infamous skater banned from the skating world for arranging an attack on Nancy Kerrigan, compete in a televised match?
a. Golf
b. Poker
c. Boxing

8 Where was American world champion Sonja Henie born?
a. Oslo, Norway
b. Oswego, New York
c. Ottawa, Canada

9 What happened to the U.S. figure skating team in 1961?
a. They were involved in a doping scandal
b. They were killed in a plane crash
c. They won every event in which they competed

10 For which country did Katarina Witt compete?
a. East Germany
b. Austria
c. United States

Taking a Spin

Who was the only U.S. woman in the 1968 Winter Olympics to win a gold medal and in what sport?

It's All Luge to Me

The Olympic luge competition is another sport that requires turning a blind eye to danger since a wipeout at top speed can have disastrous consequences. Play it safe and see how well you do picking the right answer from the following choices.

1 Luge is the only sliding sport measured to this increment:
  a. The single tenth of a second
  b. The single hundredth of a second
  c. The single thousandth of a second

2 Speeds in luge can exceed how many mph?
  a. 75
  b. 90
  c. 115

3 Having no formal luge program at the time of the 1964 Winter Games, the United States' first Olympic luge team consisted mainly of:
  a. College students
  b. American soldiers stationed in Europe
  c. Seminarians living abroad

4 The average luge run has a vertical drop that's equivalent to:
  a. 10 stories (100 feet)
  b. 20 stories (200 feet)
  c. 30 stories (300 feet)

5 What was built in 1979 for the 1980 Olympic Winter Games in Lake Placid that had a major effect on the sport of luge?
  a. The nation's first refrigerated luge run
  b. A sled factory just outside the city
  c. Numerous billboards and signs to celebrate the talents of the American team

6 The cream used to reduce friction between the sled runners and the ice contains microscopic particles of which substance:
  a. Salt
  b. Diamonds
  c. Wax

7 What equipment do luge racers wear to help them withstand the vibrations of their sleds during a run?
  a. Mouth guards
  b. Neck straps
  c. Padded leggings

8 What is embedded in the racers gloves' to help them paddle faster at the start of a race?
  a. Metal spikes
  b. Sandpaper
  c. Brass tacks

9 What is credited with holding the sled and athlete on the wall of a banked curve?
  a. Ice
  b. The blades of the sled
  c. Gravitational force

10 The combination of small curves on a luge track with few or no straight stretches between them is called a:
  a. Kreisel
  b. Labyrinth
  c. Death loop

On the Open Green

If you like to watch invigorating competition outside, then this section is for you. All the major sports are here, including golf, football, baseball, and soccer, as well as a few surprises. So take your pick and have some fun. That's what it's all about, after all.

Golf on the Fairway

How long have you been puttering around with your clubs? Dust them off and see how well you fare on this fairway.

1 Is a spoon, a knife, or a fork a type of golf club?

2 Which Australian golfer carried the Olympic torch over Sydney Harbour Bridge at the opening ceremony of the 2000 Olympics?

3 Who won more Ryder Cups in the 20th century: the United States or Europe?

4 In golf, which *B* word is the name given to a score of one over par on a hole?

5 What name is given to a score of three under par on a golf hole?

6 Name the royal and ancient club that is known as the "home of golf."

7 How many strokes over par are taken if a golfer makes a snowman?

8 In 1997, who became the youngest-ever golfer to win the U.S. Masters?

9 What name is given to a shot that misses the ball completely but counts as a shot?

10 In 1981, what type of golf ball did the USGA refuse to sanction?

A Round of Golf

Are you up for playing with the pros? Before you step on the green, see if you can unravel this golfing terminology.

1 What nickname is given to the clubhouse on a golf course?

2 How many shots under par is a birdie?

3 On a golf course, what do the initials GUR stand for?

4 What name is given to the closely mown section of a golf hole between the green and the tee?

5 What is the American term for what the British call a bunker?

6 What is happening to a golfer who is suffering from "the yips"?

7 What is the alternative name for a No. 3 wood?

8 Which form of golf is based on holes won, lost, and halved, as opposed to the total strokes taken?

9 What do you call the person who carries a golfer's clubs?

10 Which playing card is the alternative name for a hole in one?

The Eye of the Tiger

See if you can sort out what's true about the legendary Tiger Woods in the following statements.

1 Tiger's average clubhead speed is 125 mph, while an average person's speed is 84 mph. TRUE ○ FALSE ○

2 It took 11 strokes for Tiger to hole his very first par four when he was only 18 months old. TRUE ○ FALSE ○

3 Tiger was three years old when he scored his first hole-in-one. TRUE ○ FALSE ○

4 When Tiger was two years old, he putted against Bob Hope on *The Mike Douglas Show*. TRUE ○ FALSE ○

5 Tiger's fourth-place tie in the 2004 EDS Byron Nelson Championship marked his 500th Top 10 finish on the PGA Tour. TRUE ○ FALSE ○

6 Tiger Woods holds the record for the most wins by any player in his 20s. TRUE ○ FALSE ○

7 Tiger shot 48 for nine holes at age three and was featured in *Golf Digest* at age five. TRUE ○ FALSE ○

8 Tiger received the nickname "Tiger" after his childhood love for the famous cornflakes mascot. TRUE ○ FALSE ○

9 In 1999 Tiger Woods became the first person to win four consecutive PGA events. TRUE ○ FALSE ○

10 Tiger Woods won 28 of the first 100 PGA Tour events he entered. TRUE ○ FALSE ○

Soccer World Cup

Perhaps no other international championship playoff draws more crowds from around the world. Everyone, it seems, is eager to see their favorite team win. Who is rooting for you with this round?

1 Which Frenchman gave his name to the original World Cup trophy?

2 In 1982, which nation became the second to win the World Cup for the third time?

3 Gerd Muller was the leading scorer in the 1970 World Cup finals. Which country did he represent?

4 Which nation lost consecutive World Cup finals in 1974 and 1978?

5 How many years separated the third and fourth World Cups?

6 Who scored the first-ever hat trick in a World Cup final?

7 Which nation qualified for the 2002 World Cup as holders?

8 What was the nickname of Zaire, the first African nation to qualify for the World Cup?

9 What sort of animal was World Cup Willie, England's 1966 mascot?

10 Which country won the World Cup in 1986?

Gridiron to White House

Can you name the man who played Knute Rockne on the silver screen and eventually sat in the Oval Office?

Home Turf

How many teams in the NFL do you follow? Match the right team to its respective playing field to see if you know them as well as you think.

Arizona Cardinals_____   **A** Arrowhead Stadium

Atlanta Falcons_____   **B** Bank of America Stadium

Carolina Panthers_____   **C** Edward Jones Dome

Chicago Bears_____   **D** FedEx Field

Detroit Lions_____   **E** Ford Field

Green Bay Packers_____   **F** Georgia Dome

Minnesota Vikings_____   **G** Gillette Stadium

New Orleans Saints_____   **H** Heinz Field

Philadelphia Eagles_____   **I** Lambeau Field

Tennessee Titans_____   **J** Lincoln Financial Field

Seattle Seahawks_____   **J** LP Field

St. Louis Rams_____   **L** Lucas Oil Stadium

Tampa Bay Buccaneers_____   **M** Metrodome

Washington Redskins_____   **N** Paul Brown Stadium

Buffalo Bills_____   **O** Qwest Field

Cincinnati Bengals_____   **P** Ralph Wilson Stadium

Indianapolis Colts_____   **Q** Raymond James Stadium

Kansas City Chiefs_____   **R** Soldier Field

New England Patriots_____   **S** Superdome

Pittsburgh Steelers_____   **T** University of Phoenix Stadium

Pigskin Roundup

Here's a collection of football facts that's not for the faint of heart. How well can you plow through these tough questions?

1 What term describes a game in which one team prevents another from scoring?

2 What kind of pass was legalized in 1906 to revolutionize the game of football?

3 The Denver Broncos lost to which team in the 1990 Super Bowl by a record 45 points?

4 What artificial surface is used in place of grass on many football fields?

5 Who lost the 1991 Super Bowl when the New York Giants beat them 20–19?

6 What must be scored before a two-point conversion can take place?

7 What is the area called between the defense's 20-yard line and its goal line?

8 What is it called when the defensive team rushes toward the line of scrimmage as soon as the ball is snapped to try to sack the quarterback?

9 Who was defeated 34–7 by the Baltimore Ravens in Super Bowl XXXV in 2001?

10 Whose wardrobe malfunction before an estimated 140 million viewers during the halftime show of Super Bowl XXXVIII resulted in fines levied by the FCC?

Play Ball!

Think fast. You'll need to make sure you can cover all the bases with this lightning round of true and false questions.

1 Only wooden bats are allowed in professional baseball.	TRUE ○	FALSE ○
2 The batting order can change after every inning.	TRUE ○	FALSE ○
3 The bull pen is the part of the field reserved for visiting press and photographers to observe the game.	TRUE ○	FALSE ○
4 A catch doesn't count if a player uses his hat or any other part of his uniform to catch the ball.	TRUE ○	FALSE ○
5 If a batter is said to "choke up" at the plate, he is afraid to swing.	TRUE ○	FALSE ○
6 When a pitcher throws a fastball near the batter, it's called a "brushback."	TRUE ○	FALSE ○
7 A grounder is a ball that is no longer in play.	TRUE ○	FALSE ○
8 A fork ball is a pitch that is thrown so that once it reaches home plate it drops very quickly and unexpectedly.	TRUE ○	FALSE ○
9 A "frozen rope" is used to help pitchers warm up before play.	TRUE ○	FALSE ○
10 A knuckleball is a type of fastball that's very difficult to throw.	TRUE ○	FALSE ○

World Series Matchup

The record books always make it easy to remember who won the World Series, but can you match the winners in the list below with the correct opponents? Hint: the Atlanta Braves, Cleveland Indians, and the New York Yankees appear twice.

1995 Atlanta Braves_____	**A** Atlanta Braves
1996 NewYork Yankees_____	**B** Cleveland Indians
1997 Florida Marlins_____	**C** Colorado Rockies
1998 New York Yankees_____	**D** Detroit Tigers
1999 New York Yankees_____	**E** Houston Astros
2000 New York Yankees_____	**F** New York Mets
2001 Arizona Diamondbacks_____	**G** New York Yankees
2002 Anaheim Angels_____	**H** San Diego Padres
2003 Florida Marlins_____	**I** San Francisco Giants
2004 Boston Red Sox_____	**J** St. Louis Cardinals
2005 Chicago White Sox_____	**K** Tampa Bay Rays
2006 St. Louis Cardinals_____	
2007 Boston Red Sox_____	
2008 Philadelphia Phillies_____	

Football Greats

These masters of the gridiron all got their start playing college football. Do you know them well enough to trace each player back to his early beginnings?

1 Which quarterback for the Pittsburgh Steelers started his college career for Louisiana Tech?
 a. Roger Staubach   b. Ken Stabler
 c. Terry Bradshaw   d. Joe Namath

2 Which infamous running back for the Buffalo Bills played for the University of Southern California?
 a. Earl Campbell   b. O. J. Simpson
 c. Franco Harris   d. Walter Payton

3 Which tight end for the Oakland Raiders played for Notre Dame?
 a. Dave Casper   b. Charlie Sanders
 c. Jim Langer   d. Mike Webster

4 Which linebacker for the Chicago Bears first played for Illinois?
 a. Jack Lambert   b. Dick Butkus
 c. Bobby Bell   d. Jack Ham

5 Which defensive tackle for the Los Angeles Rams first played for Utah State?
 a. Merlin Olsen   b. Alan Page
 c. Bobby Lilly   d. Joe Greene

6 Which cornerback for the San Francisco 49ers first played for UCLA?
 a. Jimmy Johnson   b. Roger Wehrli
 c. Louis Wright   d. Willie Brown

7 Which fleet-footed running back for the Arizona Cardinals started his career playing college football for Miami?
 a. Edgerrin James   b. Tim Castille
 c. Tim Hightower   d. Joe Namath

8 Which Colts quarterback played college football for Tennessee?
 a. Jeff George   b. Jim Harbaugh
 c. Peyton Manning   d. Charlie Daniels

9 Which quarterback from the Philadelphia Eagles first soared in his college days at Syracuse?
 a. A. J. Feeley   b. Kevin Kolb
 c. Donovan McNabb   d. Boomer Esiason

10 Which Tampa Bay quarterback first played for San Jose State?
 a. Bruce Gradkowski   b. Jeff Garcia
 c. Brad Johnson   d. Jerry Garcia

The National Pastime

How much do you know about one of America's favorite sports? Will you hit a home run with this round?

1 About how large in acres is the average baseball field?

2 What is the minimum number of players on a college softball team?

3 In baseball, what do the initials NL stand for?

4 Which was the first non-American team to win the World Series in baseball?

5 With which baseball team did Babe Ruth begin his Major League career?

6 Which stadium is known as "The House that Ruth Built"?

7 Which baseball star was nicknamed "The Yankee Clipper"?

8 In baseball, what's a "dinger"?

9 In what year was the World Series not held because the players' strike shortened the season?

10 How many sides to a home plate?

11 Who pitched his 2,000th strikeout to Danny Tartabull of the New York Yankees on August 11, 1993?

Heroes and Legends

How much do you love baseball? This multiple choice round has a few curveballs thrown in, so do your best to stay in the game.

1 The 1989 World Series was interrupted by what natural event?
a. Earthquake
b. Tornado
c. Hurricane

2 Which team was said to suffer the "Curse of the Bambino" for trading Babe Ruth in 1920?
a. Baltimore Orioles
b. Boston Red Sox
c. New York Yankees

3 What position was Mickey Mantle best known for playing?
a. Center field
b. Catcher
c. Third base

4 In how many consecutive games did New York Yankee Joe DiMaggio hit during his legendary 1941 streak?
a. 36
b. 46
c. 56

5 Where was Babe Ruth born?
a. Brooklyn, New York
b. Baltimore, Maryland
c. Boston, Massachusetts

6 Who wrote "Casey at the Bat"?
a. Dylan Thomas
b. Edgar Allan Poe
c. Ernest L. Thayer

7 Which Hall of Fame pitcher is credited with inventing the curveball?
a. Candy Cummings
b. Addie Joss
c. Red Faber

8 Whose career total of 714 home runs stood as a major league record until 1974, when Hank Aaron of the Atlanta Braves topped it?
a. Babe Ruth's
b. Ty Cobb's
c. Joe DiMaggio's

9 Who developed the Knickerbocker Rules—the first published rules of modern baseball—in 1845?
a. Abner Doubleday
b. Alexander Cartwright
c. Milton Bradley

10 What is Babe Ruth alleged to have worn under has cap while playing baseball?
a. Cornstarch
b. Mink oil
c. A cabbage leaf

Court Sports

Do you enjoy having courtside seats so you can see all the action up close and personal? If so, you'll love this section because you'll be the star of the show. Just put on your game face and get ready to cover everything from basketball to badminton, with a few rounds of tennis in between!

Hoops to Hollywood

For the most part, the following questions pertain to basketball stories that made it to the big screen. Do you know enough to make all your answers slam dunks?

1 Which Oscar-winning cartoon character co-starred with Michael Jordan in the 1996 film *Space Jam*?

2 Jimmy Chitwood was the name of the fictional star player for the Hickory High School basketball team in what 1986 film?

3 Jamal Wallace is an inner-city kid from the Bronx who has an aptness at basketball and a genius at writing in which Gus Van Sant movie?

4 Josh Baskin wakes to finds himself in an adult body literally overnight in what 1988 movie?

5 Ken Reeves is a white professional basketball player who takes a job as basketball coach at Carver High School in this Emmy Award–winning television show.

6 This movie was inspired by the true story of Texas Western Coach Don Haskins, who led the first all-black starting lineup team to win the NCAA national basketball championship in 1966.

7 A 14-year-old orphan finds a pair of sneakers once owned by Michael Jordan and suddenly discovers his own amazing basketball prowess.

8 Two basketball hustlers each think they're the best in town, and when they join forces there's nothing that can stop them—well, almost nothing.

9 Nick Nolte plays a college basketball coach who breaks the rules to get the players he needs to stay on top.

10 Ray Allen plays Jesus Shuttlesworth, the most sought-after high school basketball prospect in the nation whose father must convince him to go to college.

Billie and Bobby

In 1973, Billie Jean King and Bobby Riggs played a tennis match known as The Battle of the Sexes. Where was it played, and who won?

Hoop Dreams

Are you fast with a layup? How about your record making three-point shots? Whatever condition your game is in, you're sure to get a good workout with this round of basketball questions.

1 The Harlem Globetrotters basketball team was founded in which city?

2 Under NBA rules, a basketball player is removed from the game after committing how many fouls?

3 What old-fashioned article of clothing is associated with New York's basketball team?

4 What is the official playing time in an NBA basketball game?

5 Which basketball player achieved the highest points average in the 20th century?

6 Whose difficulty at the free-throw line led to the term "Hack-a-Shaq"?

7 What name was Magic Johnson born with?

8 In which African country was the seven-foot center and NBA superstar Hakeem Olajuwon born?

9 Who was the 1960–61 NBA Rookie of the Year nicknamed the "'Big O"?

10 Which Los Angeles Laker was decorated as a six-time NBA MVP and a member of the NBAs 35th and 50th Anniversary All-Time Teams?

Court Terminology

Would you need a referee to help you sort out the following words that relate to court sports? Here's a hint that will help you—all of them begin with the letter *T*.

1 Tennis elbow is a form of this inflammation.

2 A two-syllable synonym for tournament.

3 Rotational force exerts this on the hand every time a tennis ball is hit.

4 At a championship level, this type of competition is held at Flushing Meadows, New York.

5 In 1992 she became the youngest person inducted into the International Tennis Hall of Fame.

6 This team is better known as the Aggies.

7 Take too many steps without dribbling the ball and this is what you'll be doing.

8 A group of players working together toward a common goal.

9 The motion that causes a tennis ball to rotate forward in the direction it is traveling.

10 A foul most commonly associated with unsportsmanlike, noncontact behavior.

Big Ten Legends

Many NBA players start out playing college ball in the famous Big Ten conference. See how many athletes you can match to their alma maters.

John Wooden_____	**A** Indiana
Isiah Thomas_____	**B** Iowa
Earvin "Magic" Johnson_____	**C** Michigan State
Kelvin Ransey_____	**D** Minnesota
Ronnie Lester_____	**E** Northwestern
Kevin McHale_____	**F** Ohio State
Billy McKinney_____	**G** Purdue

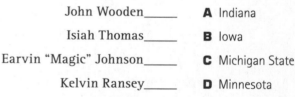

Serve This Up!

What 1980s tennis player was nicknamed "Peanut"?

Volleyball Madness

Volleyball is a fun sport to watch because it's fast-paced and requires so much teamwork. How well would you fare on the court? See how many of the following true or false statements you can spike to find out.

1 Two players make up a beach volleyball team.   TRUE ○ FALSE ○

2 Volleyball was invented in 1916 by William G. Morgan at the University of North Carolina as an alternative to basketball.   TRUE ○ FALSE ○

3 Volleyball originated as an intercollegiate sport.   TRUE ○ FALSE ○

4 In the early 1920s, Bulgaria became the first country in the world with a governing body of volleyball.   TRUE ○ FALSE ○

5 A maximum of 10 players are on the court during an indoor volleyball game.   TRUE ○ FALSE ○

6 The forearm pass became a part of the game in the 1940s.   TRUE ○ FALSE ○

7 Since 2000, beach volleyball players have worn sports sandals as required by Olympic regulations.   TRUE ○ FALSE ○

8 Games are determined by the best of six sets.   TRUE ○ FALSE ○

9 With each point, the team that is serving rotates clockwise.   TRUE ○ FALSE ○

10 Only front-row players are allowed to block shots.   TRUE ○ FALSE ○

Mad for Badminton

Don't let the quaint terms fool you. Badminton can be an aggressive and fast-paced sport to watch. For this round, try to match the following phrases.

The exchange of shots that decides each point_____   **A** Balk

A four-letter word for what the players hit_____   **B** Bird

A fast, downward shot that cannot be returned_____   **C** Carry

An illegal shot where the shuttle is caught and held on the racket, then slung_____   **D** Drop

Any deceptive move that throws the opponent off before or during the serve_____   **E** Forecourt

Another name for the bird_____   **F** Kill

Hitting the base of the shuttle with the racket frame (illegal until 1963)_____   **G** Let

A minor violation that results in a replay_____   **H** Rally

The front third of the court_____   **I** Shuttlecock

A soft shot that falls rapidly_____   **J** Wood shot

Game, Set, Match

Tennis is a popular spectator sport worldwide, but it doesn't hurt to be fast on your feet if you want to stay abreast of the game. How well would you be able to keep up with the competition?

1 What is the score in games when a set tie-breaker comes into play?

2 Which female tennis player married fellow player Roger Cawley in 1975?

3 What nationality is tennis player Michael Stich?

4 What is the name of Venus Williams's tennis-playing sister?

5 In which country was tennis star Anna Kournikova born?

6 In which country was tennis star Greg Rusedski born?

7 Which is the only Grand Slam tennis title that Bjorn Borg did not win?

8 In 1997, who became the youngest woman to win a Grand Slam tennis title?

9 In 1993, which tennis player was stabbed on court by Günter Parche?

10 In which South American country was Gabriella Sabatini born?

11 Which is the only Grand Slam tennis tournament played in the Southern Hemisphere?

12 Which famous tennis star died of an AIDS-related illness on February 6, 1993?

13 Which tennis player got engaged to Jimmy Connors in 1974?

The World of Wimbledon

Since 1877, Wimbledon has grown from its roots as a garden-party tournament to one of the largest tennis events in the world. Just how much do you know about these history-making courts?

1 Which German tennis star won his first Wimbledon singles title in 1985?

2 Which American won the most men's singles titles at Wimbledon in the 20th century?

3 Who partnered with Billie Jean King for doubles in 1979, when she won her 20th Wimbledon title?

4 Who was John McEnroe's doubles partner in four of his five Wimbledon doubles titles?

5 How many Wimbledon singles titles did Martina Navratilova win?

6 When Arthur Ashe won his only Wimbledon singles title, which fellow American did he beat in the final?

7 What's the name of the watch company that adorns the scoreboard of Wimbledon's center court?

8 Who won the 1980 Wimbledon mixed doubles title with her brother John Austin?

9 How old was Boris Becker when he won his first Wimbledon title?

10 Which king officially opened Wimbledon in 1922?

11 What color balls were used at Wimbledon for the first time in 1986?

Inside Sports

It may seem that boxing and gymnastics have little in common, but they both require an athlete who isn't afraid of a little pain. And martial arts, fencing, and archery fans may not travel in the same circles, but all these sports trace their roots to military training, some dating back centuries. So go ahead and test your own limits with this varied collection of quizzes.

Combat Clues

There are many traditional forms of martial arts. Can you defend your know-how by matching the following descriptions with the correct form?

Introduced in 1820, it's primarily used for healing and longevity_____ **A** Aikido

A loose translation of this Korean style means "the way of the foot and the fist"_____ **B** Bando thaing

This physical art form was founded in Japan in the early 1900s by O-Sensei ("Great Teacher") Morihei Ueshiba_____ **C** Capoeira

This relatively new Japanese martial art translates to mean "sword fighter"_____ **D** Chanbara

This form of hand-to-hand combat system was originally used to train the Russian military_____ **E** Gatka

Introduced in post–Word War II, the first instructor of this Burmese combat-style martial art in the United States was Dr. Maung Gyi_____ **F** Haidong Gumdo

This Japanese martial art was originally used for espionage_____ **G** Judo

This Indian martial art focuses on fighting techniques that use swords and other weapons. It is associated with Sikhism_____ **H** Kandoshin

Now considered a sport by many, it was introduced in Okinawa as a self-defense art_____ **I** Karate

Started in Brazil by African slaves during the colonial period, this martial art translates to "fight dances" and involves music_____ **J** Krav maga

A Japanese martial art founded in the 1800s by Kano Jigoro, it became an Olympic sport in 1964_____ **K** Ninjitsu

This freestyle form founded in 1975 by Nigerian Soke Happy John Uvwiefenigwere combines many Asian fighting techniques_____ **L** Sambo

This Korean martial art dates back to 371–384 AD and uses only the sword and focuses on a balanced mental state_____ **M** Taekwondo

This Israeli martial art involves hand-to-hand combat killing techniques and is taught to military personnel, law officers, and some civilians_____ **N** Tai chi

The practice of this ancient Indian martial art is commonly referred to as "Indra's fist"_____ **O** Vajra Mukti

The Knockout Knack

See if you could qualify as a Golden Glove with this round of multiple-choice questions.

1 At which boxing weight did Floyd Patterson win an Olympic gold medal in 1952?
a. Middleweight
b. Heavyweight
c. Welterweight
d. Light welterweight

2 Who was the first boxer to beat Sugar Ray Leonard professionally?
a. Mike Tyson
b. Muhammad Ali
c. Roberto Duran
d. Sugar Ray Robinson

3 In 1986, who became the youngest-ever World Heavyweight Boxing Champion?
a. Mike Tyson
b. Evander Holyfield
c. Lennox Lewis
d. Michael Spinks

4 In 1990, which boxer was charged with the attempted murder of promoter Frank Warren, a charge he was later acquitted of?
a. Alessandro Scapecchi
b. Terry Marsh
c. Joe Manley
d. Terrance Farthington

5 Who won the heavyweight boxing gold medal at the 1964 Olympics?
a. Buster Mathis
b. Manuel Ramos
c. Joe Frazier
d. Muhammad Ali

6 At the 1992 Olympics, which country won seven gold medals in boxing?
a. Cuba
b. Philippines
c. France
d. Italy

7 Which female boxer is nicknamed "the Fleetwood Assassin"?
a. Laila Ali
b. Jane Couch
c. Tanya Harding
d. Joan Frazier

8 What is the name of the premier U.S. boxing tournament for amateur boxers?
a. Juniors World Championships
b. Golden Gloves
c. Future Stars National Tournament
d. Golden Amateurs

9 Who did Rocky Marciano beat to become World Heavyweight Boxing Champion?
a. Joe Louis
b. Joe Frazier
c. Jersey Joe Walcott
d. George Foreman

10 How long is the interval between boxing rounds?
a. One minute
b. 90 seconds
c. Two minutes
d. Five minutes

Robin the Hood

Can you guess how many times Errol Flynn battled with his sword in the movie in which he played Robin Hood?

Fencing Facts

How much do you know about this most ancient combat sport? To see for yourself, try to determine which of these statements are true.

1 Baron Pierre de Coubertin, founder of the modern Olympic Games, wrote a rule that permitted professional fencers called "masters" to compete in the first two Games while the other sports remained strictly amateur. TRUE ○ FALSE ○

2 In 1575, Queen Elizabeth I of England promised punishment to anyone caught teaching sword skills. TRUE ○ FALSE ○

3 In foil and saber, one fencer is on offense and the other on defense in what is termed "right of way." The initiator of an attack scores the point if both fencers record touches simultaneously. TRUE ○ FALSE ○

4 Foil is based on light swords that nobility used to train for duels, and points may be scored only when the tip of the sword hits an opponent's torso. TRUE ○ FALSE ○

5 A competitor in the individual fencing events at the Olympics wins by being first to score nine touches. TRUE ○ FALSE ○

6 Olympic fencing switched to electronic scoring with the foil in 1936. TRUE ○ FALSE ○

7 Touches once were recorded by covering the sword's tip with a blood-soaked cloth and counting the marks it made. TRUE ○ FALSE ○

8 In Tokyo's 1964 Olympics, Ildiko Ujlaki-Rejto of Hungary, a fencer who was born deaf and learned fencing from written instructions, won gold in the women's individual and team foil. TRUE ○ FALSE ○

9 In Athen's 2004 Olympics, Mariel Zagunis won a gold medal in the women's saber and became the first American to win a gold medal in fencing since the St. Louis Games in 1904. TRUE ○ FALSE ○

10 American fencer Peter Westbrook competed in the saber in every Summer Olympics from 1976 to 1996, except for the 1980 Olympics, which the United States boycotted. TRUE ○ FALSE ○

Into the Ring

Remember to stay light on your toes so you don't get caught against the ropes with this quick round—it will be over before you know it!

1 In which European country was the boxer Joe Bugner born?

2 What *P* word is the name given to the prize money for a boxing bout?

3 How many consecutive fights did Rocky Marciano win, 43 by knockouts: 49, 50, or 51?

4 Which former World Heavyweight Boxing Champion was nicknamed "the Easton Assassin"?

5 Including intervals, what would be the full duration of a 12-round boxing bout?

6 Which British boxer lost his world heavyweight title to Hasim Rahman in 2001?

7 Who died on April 12, 1981, after having been boxing champion between 1937 and 1948?

8 What is the name of Leon Spinx's boxing brother?

9 Who claimed he could "float like a butterfly, sting like a bee"?

10 Who is the regal-named promoter who has advanced the careers of Muhammad Ali, George Foreman, and Mike Tyson?

PAGE 83

Olympic Events

1 1,500 meters
2 Five
3 1,500-meter freestyle
4 Cricket
5 Princess Anne
6 Diving
7 All of them
8 302
9 Softball and synchronized swimming
10 Marathon

Which Came First?

1 Gymnastics (1896)
2 Handball (1936)
3 Pentathlon (1912)
4 Field hockey (1908)
5 Bobsleigh (1924)
6 Shooting (1896)
7 Judo (1964)
8 Skating (1908)
9 Volleyball (1964)
10 Cycling (1896)

PAGE 84

Olympic Traditions

1 Five rings representing the continents of the world
2 Greece, where the Olympics originated
3 They were the last Olympic medals that were made entirely of gold
4 A silver medal was awarded to winning athletes in the first modern Olympics, and they also received a certificate and an olive branch
5 1960s (the 1960 Rome games)
6 Because the male athletes competed naked
7 At the close of the games during the closing ceremony
8 Swifter, Higher, Stronger
9 French
10 The mayor of the next host city

Olympic Host Cities

1 Berlin
2 Greece
3 Barcelona
4 Atlanta
5 Sarajevo
6 None
7 In protest at the Soviet Union's invasion of Afghanistan
8 Vesuvius
9 Five
10 Salt Lake City

Olympic History

1 The Duke of Edinburgh, Prince Philip
2 Princess Anne
3 President of the International Olympic Committee
4 1912
5 A shot in shot-putting
6 1972
7 Greatest number of medals (15) by a male Olympian, a record since broken by Michael Phelps

PAGE 85

Winning Colors

1 a. Croquet
2 c. Toronto
3 a. Sunderland
4 b. Black
5 c. Gold
6 b. Black
7 a. Red Marauder
8 a. Blue
9 b. Red
10 a. Black
11 c. Red
12 a. Red

PAGE 86

Extreme Sports

1 ESPN
2 Mountain biking and snowboarding
3 Half-pipes
4 Tony Hawk
5 Shaun White
6 BMX
7 Wakeboarding
8 Woopy jumping
9 Beijing
10 Four

International Roundup

1 Caber
2 Ice hockey for winter and lacrosse for summer
3 Japan
4 Ice hockey
5 Sweden
6 Sepak takraw, a type of "kick volleyball" that's played on a badminton court
7 Baseball
8 France
9 Yokozuna
10 Soccer (known there as football)
11 15

PAGE 87

To the Finish Line!

1 b. Indoor swimming pool
2 c. Hockey
3 a. Triathlon
4 c. Biathlon
5 b. Bicycling
6 a. Soccer ball
7 c. 100 years
8 a. Hockey
9 b. Boston Marathon
10 a. None
11 a. Brazil

Answers

The Winter Games

1 Cortina d'Ampezzo, Italy, 1956
2 Squaw Valley, California, United States, 1960
3 Innsbruck, Austria, 1964
4 Grenoble, France, 1968
5 Sapporo, Japan, 1972
6 Innsbruck, Austria, 1976
7 Lake Placid, New York, United States, 1980
8 Sarajevo, Yugoslavia (now Bosnia and Herzegovina), 1984
9 Calgary, Canada, 1988
10 Albertville, France, 1992
11 Lillehammer, Norway, 1994
12 Nagano, Japan, 1998
13 Salt Lake City, Utah, United States, 2002
14 Turin (Torino), Italy, 2006
15 Vancouver, Canada, 2010

Horse Sense

1 a. Blanket finish
2 b. Dam
3 c. Distaff
4 a. Dogs
5 b. Dwelt
6 a. Farrier
7 b. Horsing
8 c. Oaks
9 a. Withers
10 b. Dressage

NASCAR Flags

1 White
2 Green
3 Red
4 Black with white cross
5 Checkered
6 Black
7 Blue with yellow stripe
8 Yellow

Built for Speed

1 Canadian
2 Seven
3 Monte Carlo Rally
4 Alain Prost
5 A bottle of milk
6 National Association for Stock Car Auto Racing
7 England
8 Nine
9 Alpha Romeo
10 Mario Batali
11 The windshield

Horse Play

1 True
2 True
3 False; it was Jenny Pitman
4 True
5 True
6 True
7 False
8 False; it travels 16 furlongs
9 True
10 True

Speed Machines

1 Madison relay
2 Points race
3 Olympic sprint
4 Pursuit
5 Match sprint
6 Time trial
7 Cyclocross
8 Criterium
9 Stage race
10 Dual slalom

Vive la France

1 Voiture balai
2 Lanterne rouge
3 Derailleur
4 Alpe d'Huez
5 Echelon
6 Hors catégorie
7 Soigneur
8 Maillot jaune

Getting the Runaround

1 John Walker
2 Maurice Greene
3 Starting blocks
4 10
5 Ed Moses
6 One
7 Eric Henry Liddell
8 1928
9 800 meters
10 Eight
11 Carl Lewis
12 Dick Fosbury
13 Wilma Rudolph
14 Nike

Formula 1 Facts

1 Silverstone
2 Goodyear
3 Nelson Piquet
4 Alain Prost
5 Frank Williams
6 Graham Hill
7 Monaco Grand Prix
8 Finnish
9 1978
10 Aintree
11 Australian

Marathon Man

1 1981
2 Boston Marathon
3 Central Park
4 Gezahegne Abera
5 Arlington, Virginia
6 Kenya
7 Lance Armstrong
8 Marathon Bars
9 Alan Sillitoe
10 Boston Marathon
11 April
12 385
13 123

PAGE 93

A Quick Dip

1 a. Anchor
2 c. Block
3 b. Gutter
4 a. Bow wave
5 c. Butterfly
6 a. Long-distance swimming
7 b. Prone
8 b. Center lanes
9 b. Flutter kick
10 c. Drag

PAGE 94

Splish Splash

1 Johnny Weissmuller
2 Butterfly
3 Backstroke
4 1,500 meters
5 Niagara Falls
6 The Bahamas
7 Elephants; they use their trunks as snorkels
8 Benjamin Franklin
9 Spit—approximately 25,000 quarts of it
10 Tortoise shell

Swimmingly Superb Stumpers

1 Strokes
2 Speedo
3 Seconds
4 Sprint
5 Sidestroke
6 Springboard
7 Scissors kick
8 Synchronized
9 Somersault
10 Shallow

Take the Plunge!

1 Greg Louganis
2 Sweden
3 Forward, backward, and reverse
4 Springboard diving
5 Splash
6 Synchronized diving
7 The Hawaiian island of Lana'i
8 A helicopter
9 Fulcrum
10 31 mph

PAGE 95

Reel Them In!

1 True
2 False
3 True
4 False
5 False
6 True
7 False
8 True
9 True
10 False

Fish Tales!

1 Pisces
2 A running stream
3 Australia
4 Spawning
5 American eel
6 Orange
7 Pirarucu
8 *Jaws*
9 Gar (also known as garfish and garpike)
10 Carp

PAGE 96

Land Ho!

1 Jib
2 Three
3 Soling
4 One
5 Cowes
6 Halyards
7 Darts
8 Triangular
9 Holland
10 Bermuda

Row, Row, Row the Boat

1 Wellesley College
2 Coxswain
3 Two
4 2,000 meters
5 Four miles
6 Forward
7 Bow
8 Port (left side); starboard (right side)
9 Sculler
10 The umpire

Splash Goes the Sailor

The sport is called crew. The teammate is the coxswain.

PAGE 97

The Slush Pile

1 Speed skating
2 Japan
3 Franz Klammer
4 Germany
5 Nagano, Japan
6 Swedish
7 Ski
8 Katarina Witt
9 Ravel
10 Crampons
11 Luge

You're Getting Colder...

Cross-country skiing

PAGE 98

Downhill Daring

1 Shin pads
2 Eddie the Eagle
3 Downhill, slalom, and giant slalom
4 The Sierra Nevada range in California and Nevada
5 The chairlift
6 Artificial snow making
7 The California Gold Rush
8 A volcanic eruption
9 El Capitan
10 Bode Miller

Answers

PAGE 98 (CONT.)

Slap Shot!

1 Milton Keynes
2 Wayne Gretzky
3 Captain
4 99
5 Six
6 Plexiglas
7 At the start of each game and beginning of each period
8 A substitution is made
9 One
10 The Stanley Cup

Sizing Up the Competition

1 Alpine skiing
2 Speed skating
3 Figure skating
4 Freestyle skiing
5 Alpine skiing
6 Hockey
7 Speed skating
8 Ski jumping
9 Figure skating
10 Speed skating

PAGE 99

Crazy for Curling

1 Bonspiel
2 Backline
3 Blank end
4 Burned stone
5 Button
6 Biter
7 Brush
8 Bury a stone
9 Board weight

The Cutting Edge

1 Eric Heiden
2 Raise their heels off the blade, allowing for a longer extension and stride
3 Short track
4 Speed skate
5 Stomach and thighs
6 Armbands
7 Touching as they pass on the inside

8 Drafting to lessen their wind resistance
9 Bonnie Blair
10 Apolo Anton Ohno

PAGE 100

Figure 8s

1 a. Axel jump
2 c. Salchow
3 a. Dorothy Hamill
4 b. Bone
5 c. 1990
6 b. Music with vocals
7 c. Boxing
8 a. Oslo, Norway
9 b. They were killed in a plane crash
10 a. East Germany

Taking a Spin

Peggy Fleming in figure skating

PAGE 101

It's All Luge to Me

1 c. The single thousandth of a second
2 b. 90
3 b. American soldiers stationed in Europe
4 c. 30 stories (300 feet)
5 a. The nation's first refrigerated luge run
6 b. Diamonds
7 a. Mouth guards
8 a. Metal spikes
9 c. Gravitational force
10 b. Labyrinth

PAGE 102

Golf on the Fairway

1 Spoon
2 Greg Norman
3 United States, which won it 24 times
4 Bogey
5 Albatross
6 St. Andrews
7 Three strokes
8 Tiger Woods
9 Air shot
10 Asymmetrical

A Round of Golf

1 The 19th hole
2 One under par
3 Ground under repair
4 Fairway
5 Sand trap
6 The golfer has an acquired problem of tremors, freezing, or jerking while putting
7 A spoon
8 Match play
9 Air shot
10 Ace

PAGE 103

The Eye of the Tiger

1 True
2 True
3 False
4 True
5 False
6 True
7 True
8 False
9 False
10 True

Soccer World Cup

1 Jules Rimet
2 Italy
3 West Germany
4 Netherlands
5 12 years, the third was held in 1938 and the fourth delayed to 1950 because of World War II
6 Geoff Hurst
7 France
8 The Leopards
9 Lion
10 Argentina

Gridiron to White House

Ronald Reagan

PAGE 104

Home Turf

1 University of Phoenix Stadium
2 Georgia Dome
3 Bank of America Stadium
4 Soldier Field
5 Ford Field
6 Lambeau Field
7 Metrodome
8 Superdome
9 Lincoln Financial Field
10 LP Field
11 Qwest Field
12 Edward Jones Dome
13 Raymond James Stadium
14 FedEx Field
15 Ralph Wilson Stadium
16 Paul Brown Stadium
17 Lucas Oil Stadium
18 Arrowhead Stadium
19 Gillette Stadium
20 Heinz Field

Pigskin Roundup

1 Shutout
2 Forward pass
3 San Francisco 49ers
4 AstroTurf
5 Buffalo Bills
6 Touchdown
7 Red zone
8 Blitz
9 New York Giants
10 Janet Jackson

PAGE 105

Play Ball!

1 True
2 False
3 False; it's where pitchers warm up
4 True
5 False
6 True
7 False; it's a baseball that bounds or rolls along the ground when hit
8 True
9 False; it's another name for a line drive
10 False; a knuckleball is a slow-moving pitch, which is difficult to throw

World Series Matchup

1 Cleveland Indians 4–2
2 Atlanta Braves 4–2
3 Cleveland Indians 4–3
4 San Diego Padres 4–0
5 Atlanta Braves 4–0
6 New York Mets 4–1
7 New York Yankees 4–3
8 San Francisco Giants 4–3
9 New York Yankees 4–2
10 St. Louis Cardinals 4–0
11 Houston Astros 4–0
12 Detroit Tigers 4–1
13 Colorado Rockies 4–0
14 Tampa Bay Rays 4–1

PAGE 106

Football Greats

1 c. Terry Bradshaw
2 b. O. J. Simpson
3 a. Dave Casper
4 b. Dick Butkus
5 a. Merlin Olsen
6 a. Jimmy Johnson
7 a. Edgerrin James
8 c. Peyton Manning
9 c. Donovan McNabb
10 b. Jeff Garcia

The National Pastime

1 Two acres
2 Nine
3 National League
4 Toronto Blue Jays
5 Boston Red Sox
6 Yankee Stadium
7 Joe DiMaggio
8 A home run
9 1994
10 Five
11 Red Sox's Roger Clemens

PAGE 107

Heroes and Legends

1 a. Earthquake
2 b. Boston Red Sox
3 a. Center field
4 c. 56
5 b. Baltimore, Maryland
6 c. Ernest L. Thayer
7 a. Candy Cummings
8 a. Babe Ruth's
9 b. Alexander Cartwright
10 c. A cabbage leaf

PAGE 108

Hoops to Hollywood

1 Bugs Bunny
2 Hoosiers
3 Finding Forrester
4 Big
5 The White Shadow
6 Glory Road
7 Like Mike
8 White Men Can't Jump
9 Blue Chips
10 He Got Game

Billie and Bobby

Billie Jean King won in the Houston Astrodome

PAGE 109

Hoop Dreams

1 New York
2 Six
3 Knickerbockers, for the Knicks
4 48 minutes of playing time
5 Michael Jordan
6 Shaquille O'Neil
7 Earvin Effay Johnson
8 Nigeria
9 Oscar Robertson
10 Kareem Abdul-Jabbar

Answers

Court Terminology

1 Tendonitis
2 Tourney
3 Torque
4 Tournament
5 Tracey Austin
6 Texas A&M
7 Traveling
8 Team
9 Topspin
10 Technical foul

Big Ten Legends

1 Purdue
2 Indiana
3 Michigan State
4 Ohio State
5 Iowa
6 Minnesota
7 Northwestern

Serve This Up!

Maureen "Peanut" Louie Harper

Volleyball Madness

1 True
2 False; it was invented in 1895 at the Holyoke, Massachusetts, YMCA
3 False; it was a recreational activity for businessmen on lunch break
4 True
5 False; there are six players per team
6 True
7 False; they play barefoot
8 False; it's best of five
9 True
10 True

Mad for Badminton

1 Rally
2 Bird
3 Kill
4 Carry
5 Balk
6 Shuttlecock
7 Wood shot
8 Let
9 Forecourt
10 Drop

Game, Set, Match

1 6–6
2 Evonne Goolagong
3 German
4 Serena
5 Russia
6 Canada
7 U.S. Open
8 Martina Hingis
9 Monica Seles
10 Argentina
11 Australian Open
12 Arthur Ashe
13 Chris Evert

The World of Wimbledon

1 Boris Becker
2 Pete Sampras
3 Martina Navratilova
4 Peter Fleming
5 Nine
6 Jimmy Connors
7 Rolex
8 Tracy Austin
9 17
10 George V
11 Yellow balls

Combat Clues

1 Tai chi
2 Taekwondo
3 Aikido
4 Chanbara
5 Sambo
6 Bando thaing
7 Ninjitsu
8 Gatka
9 Karate
10 Capoeira
11 Judo
12 Kandoshin
13 Haidong Gumdo
14 Krav maga
15 Vajra Mukti

The Knockout Knack

1 a. Middleweight
2 c. Roberto Duran
3 a. Mike Tyson
4 b. Terry Marsh
5 c. Joe Frazier
6 a. Cuba
7 b. Jane Couch
8 b. Golden Gloves
9 c. Jersey Joe Walcott
10 a. One minute

Fencing Facts

1 True
2 False; it was King Edward I in 1286
3 True
4 True
5 False; it's 15 touches or the most points at the end of the third three-minute period
6 True
7 False; a dye-soaked cloth was used
8 True
9 True
10 True

Into the Ring

1 Hungary
2 Purse
3 49
4 Larry Holmes
5 47 minutes
6 Lennox Lewis
7 Joe Louis
8 Michael Spinx
9 Muhammad Ali
10 Don King

4 Food and Drink

Of course you know all about food—after all, you eat it every day. But do you know exactly what a Chinese gooseberry is or the flavoring in *slivovitz*? How about what's behind the most expensive coffee in the world? Put down your fork and pick up your pencil! It's time to dig into the vast and extremely delicious banquet that is the world of food and drink.

Soft Drinks

In bartenders' terms, anything that's not alcoholic falls under the heading of soft drinks. And while you won't find milk or milk-shakes in most bars, you will find them here, along with questions about a vast range of beverages throughout history. Quench your thirst for knowledge with these puzzlers!

Drinks of History

Potent and fragrant brews infuse the history of mankind. Take a slurp of these.

1 The Incas of the Andes used maize to make a drink called *chichi*. What was it?

2 What drink was first served in Venice after 1682, with the opening of the Caffè Florian?

3 What did medieval diners do with the wassail bowl?

4 In 18th-century London, the wits and writers met daily at what kind of places to talk, catch up on news, and partake of refreshment?

5 The ancient Maya made a bitter chocolate drink by beating cacao beans with spices, water, and what grain?

6 British naval ships in the mid-1700s mixed what type of juice with their water and rum to prevent scurvy?

7 Name the frothy drink of beaten egg, milk, and sugar, sometimes fortified with wine or brandy, that was enjoyed by American colonials.

Mixed Drinks

It's a mixed bag (or perhaps cup) of beverage questions here, so stay on your toes!

1 What fruits flavor the liqueur Southern Comfort?

2 What three-letter word is Chinese for tea?

3 Who was the composer of *The Water Music*?

4 Vinho Verde is a white wine from what European country?

5 What was the name of the bar in the film *Casablanca*?

6 Who wrote the novel *The Cider House Rules*?

7 What 1977 album by The Little River Band was named after a drink made with rum and an emu egg?

8 From what country does tequila originate?

9 From what fruit is the lightly alcoholic drink "perry" made?

10 What is the title of the poem that contains the line "Water, water, every where, nor any drop to drink"?

A Cup of Joe

Think you know your (black) stuff? See if you're wide awake enough to pick the right answers about coffee.

1 *Espresso* literally means:
a. Speed it up
b. To go
c. Forced out
d. Black and intense

2 Forty percent of the world's coffee is produced by:
a. Africa
b. Columbia and Brazil
c. Turkey
d. Southeast Asia

3 An *ibrik* is:
a. A South American tool for grinding coffee beans
b. The Turkish word for *barista*
c. A Middle Eastern coffeehouse
d. A long-handled copper pot for making Turkish coffee

4 Kopi Luwak, the world's most expensive coffee (up to $600 per pound), is:
a. Processed during a full moon
b. Brewed only with solid gold pots
c. Made from coffee beans eaten and excreted by a Sumatran wildcat
d. Grown at a higher altitude than any other bean

5 The name *cappuccino* comes from:
a. The drink's resemblance to the brown cowls worn by Capuchin monks
b. The similarity in color to the fur of Capuchin monkeys
c. The Italian *puccino*, meaning "light brown one"
d. The size of the cup in which it's commonly served

6 Most coffees are a blend of:
a. Light and dark roasts
b. Caffeine and essential oils
c. Arabica and robusta beans
d. African and South American beans

7 Arabica varieties such as Java and Mocha are named after:
a. The plantations where they're grown
b. The coffee grower who developed that variety
c. Their predominant flavorings
d. Their ports of origin

8 Coffee beans grow on:
a. A low, spreading vine
b. A bush
c. A tree
d. The roots of a coffee plant

9 Coffee was the first food to be:
a. Shipped from Europe to the New World
b. Freeze-dried
c. Used in Aztec religious ceremonies
d. Roasted and ground for drinking

10 Sixteenth-century Muslim rulers banned coffee because of:
a. Its stimulating effects
b. The gambling that took place in coffeehouses
c. The black market that sprang up in the coffee trade
d. Sufi mystics who wanted coffee limited to spiritual ceremonies

Name That Plant!

All tea, whether green, white, black, Earl Grey, Indian, or Chinese, is made from the same plant. The differences come from region of growth, how the leaves are harvested, and how they're processed. Give the Latin name for this plant that Carl Linnaeus bestowed in honor of a Czech-born Jesuit priest, Rev. Georg Kamel.

A Quiz About the Cup That Soothes...

Tea occupies a place of prominence in many cultures, whether it's figuring in age-old rituals or stewing all day on the back of the stove. See if you've got the mind of a tea-taster in this true or false quiz.

1 Russian samovars were designed to both heat and brew tea.   TRUE ○   FALSE ○

2 The first recorded mention of tea drinking was in southwest China in 200 BC.   TRUE ○   FALSE ○

3 French traders roaming the world in search of fur and spices first brought tea from China back to Europe.   TRUE ○   FALSE ○

4 The Hundred Rules of the traditional Japanese tea ceremony, formalized in print in the 16th century and still practiced today, are meant to teach strict attention to duty and formal structure.   TRUE ○   FALSE ○

5 Tea was considered such a valuable commodity that early English tea caddies were equipped with locks.   TRUE ○   FALSE ○

6 Earl Grey tea is perfumed by the essence of orange blossoms.   TRUE ○   FALSE ○

7 The Irish are the world's biggest consumers of tea at an average of four cups per person per day.   TRUE ○   FALSE ○

8 Since prehistoric times, mankind has drunk teas made of infusions of herbs in boiling water.   TRUE ○   FALSE ○

9 When the British first discovered tea, bricks of it were used as currency.   TRUE ○   FALSE ○

10 In China, tea is traditionally drunk without additional flavorings such as milk or lemon.   TRUE ○   FALSE ○

A Bountiful Cup of...Yogurt

Mankind has been eating yogurt as long as there has been recorded history and probably longer. See if you've got the goods on this ancient food.

1 Immigrants from what country brought yogurt to America as early as 1784?

2 In what century did yogurt gain popularity as a "health food" when a Russian bacteriologist noted that Bulgarians who ate it regularly lived an average of 87 years?

3 In addition to its nutrients, the health benefit of yogurt primarily comes from populating the intestinal system with what?

4 In 1947, what fledgling company added strawberry jam to yogurt and marketed it as "sundae-style"?

5 Nomadic herdsmen of the Neolithic era found that milk carried in what kind of bags curdled naturally into yogurt?

6 After these nomadic tribes discovered yogurt accidentally, they realized it was an easy way to do what?

7 In which country do they ferment mare's milk to make a yogurt-like drink called coumis?

8 In 1542, what French king was treated for depression by a healer from Constantinople who fed him sheep's milk yogurt?

9 What is the name of the thin, slightly fizzy yogurt drink made in Russia and the Caucasus?

10 What is the name of the cooling yogurt-based salad served in India that often includes cucumber, onions, and seasonings such as mint, cumin, parsley, or dill?

Cream of the Crop

Match the cream or milk product with its description.

Clotted cream_____   A   A thick, creamy low-salt, un-aged cheese, widely used in Europe

*Fromage frais*_____   B   Clarified butter widely used in Indian cuisine

Quark_____   C   Thick, spreadable cream with a mottled surface and a fat content of 55 percent

Paneer_____   D   A kind of Swedish yogurt similar to buttermilk

Crème fraiche_____   E   A cooling Indian drink made by mixing yogurt with spices or rosewater

Filmjölk_____   F   A fresh French cheese, like a thick sour cream, made of blending curds and whey

Lassi _____   G   Milk that has been slightly curdled, but with the curds and whey mixed together

Ghee_____   H   A soft, fresh curd cheese used in Indian cooking

---

Sparkling Soda

From its roots as a slightly medicinal beverage (there's a reason soda jerks could be found at drug-stores!), soda pop and soft drinks have pervaded American culture. But how much do you really know about it?

1 What soft drink was created when a pharmacist mixed fruit syrups at a soda fountain in Waco, Texas, in 1885?

2 Although early versions of Coca-Cola contained only an infinitesimal amount of the chemical used to make cocaine, what year did the drink truly become totally "cocaine-free"?

3 Soda is also known in various regions of the United States as pop or tonic, while Australians say "fizzy drinks." What do the British and Irish call it?

4 What soda was originally formulated to contain lithium as a mood stabilizer?

5 Who is the world's largest purchaser of vanilla extract?

6 What was the first cola product sold by Royal Crown Cola when it was founded by a young pharmacist in Georgia?

7 What chocolate soda claims that its steam sterilization process offers a nearly unlimited shelf life?

8 What wine-colored, cherry-flavored cola was invented in Salisbury, North Carolina, in 1917?

9 Dr. John Pemberton invented Coke in 1886 in what Southern town, now home to a huge Coke museum?

10 What is the popular Scottish soda with the tough-guy image, sold with the slogan, "Made in Scotland from girders"?

Animal Planet

Name four types of animals whose milk is consumed or used to make butter, yogurt, cheese, or other products.

Beer, Wine, and Spirits

In this section you'll find an exhilarating cocktail of quizzes about beers, wines, liquors, and spirits. If you know all about Château d'Yquem and what part of New Zealand grows the best sauvignon blanc, then these questions are for you. Think these questions are the hard stuff? That's the point!

On Wine

You don't have to be a highly specialized expert on wine to enjoy a glass, or to answer most of the questions below.

1 Which South American wine country is known for its good-value red wine?

2 In the process of wine making, what is *marc*?

3 On the TV show *Absolutely Fabulous*, what was Patsy and Edina's favorite tipple?

4 Which veteran British TV cook was known for swigging a glass of wine while he was cooking?

5 For which French wine is there an annual race?

6 Which famous auction house is known for its wine course?

7 What South Australian valley is especially famous for its wineries?

8 Where is the pinotage grape most commonly grown?

9 In the 1980s, sauvignon blanc from which part of New Zealand began to attract considerable acclaim?

10 Chardonnay made in California typically has a strong flavor of what wood?

Size Counts

Some wine bottles are bigger than others. Match the term for the different bottle sizes with the amount of standard 750 ml bottles it contains.

Rehoboam_____	A	16 standard bottles
Salmanzar_____	B	2 standard bottles
Magnum_____	C	8 standard bottles
Methusaleh/Imperiale_____	D	3 standard bottles
Melchior_____	E	24 standard bottles
Marie-Jeanne_____	F	12 standard bottles
Nebuchadnezzar_____	G	4 standard bottles
Double-Magnum_____	H	6 standard bottles
Balthazar_____	I	20 standard bottles

Are You a Pi-not It All?

What kind of French wine is traditionally made from the pinot noir grape?

In Vino Veritas

The wise old saying holds that under the influence can be the place to find out the real story. See if you can sort out true from false, with or without a glass of vino.

1 Only one glass of Château d'Yquem, a dessert wine from Bordeaux, is produced by each vine because only the perfect grapes are used.   TRUE ○   FALSE ○

2 The best champagnes are known as *cuvées superieures*.   TRUE ○   FALSE ○

3 The term for winemaking is *viniculture*.   TRUE ○   FALSE ○

4 The tasting term *toastiness* is a reference to smokiness in the wine's scent.   TRUE ○   FALSE ○

5 Most Champagne is a blend of chardonnay, pinot meunier, and pinot noir grapes.   TRUE ○   FALSE ○

6 Red wine is made from red grapes, and white wine is made from white grapes.   TRUE ○   FALSE ○

7 Fortified wines are those that have been distilled to have a greater alcohol content.   TRUE ○   FALSE ○

8 Port comes from Portugal.   TRUE ○   FALSE ○

9 Tempranillo is the main grape used to make Spanish Rioja.   TRUE ○   FALSE ○

10 Tokaji (pronounced toe-KI) is a world-class dessert wine from Japan.   TRUE ○   FALSE ○

Ancient History

Alcoholic drinks have a long and venerable history, from the beer of the ancient Egyptians to the many monasteries throughout the ages that made proprietary brews.

1 What alcoholic drink made from the fermented maguey agave plant was produced by Mesoamericans as long ago as 8000 BC?

2 What ancient people first cultivated hops?

3 What movement began in Preston, Lancashire, in North West England in 1835?

4 What drink was created at France's Fécamp Abbey in the early 16th century?

5 What was Dom Perignon's occupation when he invented Champagne?

6 What liqueur of whiskey mixed with honey and herbs was said to have been invented by Bonnie Prince Charlie?

7 Ninkasi was the Mesopotamian goddess of what?

The Tricky Grape

There are countless grape varietals grown in vineyards around the world, offering their own distinctive varietal character along with the character of the soil and the region where they're grown. Some names depend on where the grape is grown, such as French *syrah* and Australian *shiraz*—same grape, different country. Name the grape varietals used to make the following wines.

1 Chardonnay

2 Pinot grigio

3 Cabernet sauvignon

4 Riesling

5 Zinfandel

6 Merlot

Know Your (Hard) Stuff

Can you answer these questions about spirits?

1 In past centuries, a tot of what drink was given to British sailors each day they were at sea?

2 What *G* word is a spirit made with juniper berries?

3 What liqueur has given its name to a bright greenish-yellow color?

4 Which world-famous French wine-making region ends with an *X*?

5 What was the popular drink among the aristocracy and the rich of Russia in the 19th century?

6 What fruit is used to flavor Cointreau?

7 In which century was California's first vineyard planted?

8 Still today, German beer is protected by the purity law of 1516 which states that beer may only contain three ingredients. What are they?

9 In France, what is a *crú?*

10 Alsace is a winemaking region in what country?

11 What term denotes the driest champagne: brut or extra-dry?

12 Which is the better quality wine in France: *vin de table* or *vin de pays*?

What Was Her Name?

Can you name the child actress of the 1930s and '40s who had a nonalcoholic drink named after her?

A Spirited Matchup

Almost any ingredient that contains starch or sugar can be distilled into an alcoholic drink. See if you can pair the final product with its base or primary flavoring below.

Rum_____	A Rice
Kirsch_____	B Sugar cane or molasses
Ouzo_____	C Juniper berries
Tequila_____	D Apples
Whiskey_____	E Pepper
Calvados_____	F Cherries
Cachaça_____	G Plums
Grappa_____	H Grapes, flavored with star anise
Gin_____	I Grape skins
Sake_____	J Sugar cane
Pertsovka_____	K Maguey (agave) plant
Slivovitz_____	L Barley or rye

Cheers!

Hope you're still thirsty for more questions about wine, beer, and spirits.

1 What word doesn't belong in this group and why? Chardonnay, semillon, merlot, riesling

2 Which Portuguese river valley in the northern part of the country is the home of port?

3 In which city is the world's largest beer festival held each October?

4 About how many wine-producing châteaux are there in France's Bordeaux region: 7,000, 1,700, or 700?

5 In Scotland, the whiskey industry provides about 1 in 54 jobs: true or false?

6 Which countries are the world's first- and second-largest exporters of wine?

7 What is special about the makers of Belgium's Chimay and Westvleteren beer?

8 Vougeot, Meursault, and Pouilly-Fuissé are all from which French wine region?

9 What are the ingredients of a gimlet cocktail?

10 With what country is the pinotage grape chiefly associated?

I'll Have a Cold One!

Beer is the most popular drink in the world. What's your brew?

1 The German beer glass known as a *mass krug* holds how much beer?

2 Kriek is brewed with what type of fruit?

3 Stout or porter such as Guinness gets its dark, thick characteristics because what is done to the barley malt?

4 The ale style known as IPA came about because British brewers realized that the strongly hopped ale would better survive the long transit to where?

5 What's the name of the Belgian style of beer that is naturally fermented using wild yeasts?

6 What country drinks the most beer per capita?

7 Why is some beer preferably drunk at room temperature rather than chilled?

8 In general, ales tend to have fruity, more complex aromas while lagers taste smoother and crisper. What makes the difference between them?

To Your Health

Most toasts before drinking wish the drinkers health and luck. Match the toast with the country where it's traditional.

Cheers_____	A Turkey
Sláinte (health)_____	B Sweden
Santé (health)_____	C Britain
Skål (health)_____	D Russia
Na zdorovye (health)_____	E Romania
Noroc (luck)_____	F Spain
Genatsoot (life)_____	G Israel
L'chaim (life)_____	H Armenia
Şerefe (honor)_____	I Scotland and Ireland
Salud (health)_____	J France

Water of Life

Vodka is an easy mixer, so it's no surprise that it's the most popular spirit there is when it comes to cocktails. It embraces any flavor and happily absorbs anything you care to infuse it with. Name four classic vodka cocktails.

Core Foods: Bread and Meat, Fruits and Veggies

The human diet has always been made up of some variation on the major groups of grains, proteins, fruits, and vegetables. But how well do you really know the facts about the foods you eat every day? Now's the time to find out!

Mixed Veggies

It won't be hard to get your daily dose of vegetables with these tempting questions.

1 Yosemite Sam is the arch-enemy of what carrot-munching cartoon character?

2 Which explorer is credited with introducing the potato to Europe?

3 According to the saying, what butters no parsnips?

4 Which of these is not a vegetable: cabbage, cucumber, cauliflower?

5 What was Baldrick's favorite vegetable in the TV series *Blackadder*?

6 Which vegetable is the main ingredient of the Russian soup borscht?

7 Which best-selling dolls of the 1980s came with their own adoption papers?

8 Which 1995 animated film brought to life the character of Mr. Potato Head?

9 Broad, green, and butter are all types of what?

10 What is the botanical name for a pepper?

11 What drink, made from a pepper root, is very popular in Fiji?

12 What is said to be used, along with a stick, to encourage a donkey?

13 What name is more commonly used for an aubergine?

14 What foul-smelling fruit from Malaysia is regarded as a delicacy?

15 What do Americans call the vegetable usually known in Britain as a courgette?

You Say It This Way, I Say It That Way

What famous red orb is considered by many to be a vegetable, but is actually a fruit?

Fruity Facts

Try these fruity questions and branch out from the ordinary.

1 Which fruit is grown in a vineyard?

2 What kind of fruit did Little Jack Horner pull out of a pie?

3 Which Israeli port is also the name of a variety of orange?

4 On which record label did The Beatles record "Hey Jude"?

5 Who wrote the novel *Oranges Are Not the Only Fruit*?

6 Cantaloupe and honeydew are varieties of which type of fruit?

7 The great Southern cook Edna Lewis found that raspberries could be preserved in the refrigerator for a year simply by mixing them with an equal amount of what?

8 Apricots were first grown more than 4,000 years ago in what country?

Know Your Onions

Get your daily dose of vitamins with this test of your knowledge of fruits and vegetables.

1 To what fruit family does the kumquat belong?

2 A raspberry is made up of tiny round pieces called what?

3 What is the alternative name for a Chinese gooseberry?

4 What state is nicknamed "The Potato State"?

5 Who wrote the play *The Cherry Orchard*?

6 Which common vegetable has the highest sugar content?

7 Which fruity song is the flip side of The Beatles hit "Penny Lane"?

8 What artist created the painting titled *The Potato Eaters*?

9 Name the famous film producer whose ancestors crossed cauliflower with rabe to create the vegetable that carries his family name.

10 What variety of berry was named after an American judge?

Fruit Salad

This sweet round of questions has a decidedly fruity flavor.

1 Apart from sugar cane, what is the main plant used as a source of table sugar?

2 What is the primary ingredient of guacamole?

3 What fruit shares its name with a high-ranking Chinese civil servant?

4 The juice of what fruit is mixed with coconut and rum to make a piña colada?

5 Royal Gala and Cox's Orange Pippin are varieties of what fruit?

6 Of what type of fruit is a plantain a variety?

7 What alcoholic drink is made from the leftovers of sugar refining?

8 Morello is a variety of what type of fruit?

9 What kind of fruit is a greengage?

10 The name of what fruit is used to mean an unwelcome third on a romantic occasion for two?

Catch and Release

Dip your line in the water and see how much you know about the fish and seafood we consume. Answer these questions true or false.

1. Drift-netting, with enormous nets dangled in the ocean, is indiscriminately harmful to marine life, entangling many other creatures besides the fish it's intended to catch. TRUE ○ FALSE ○

2. The United Nations has banned drift nets larger than one mile in length. TRUE ○ FALSE ○

3. In the second half of the 20th century, stocks of cod in the northern Atlantic declined by 65 percent. TRUE ○ FALSE ○

4. As a country, Iceland consumes the most fish per capita, at a rate of more than 200 pounds per person annually. TRUE ○ FALSE ○

5. The next highest consumer of fish is the British, who eat 100 pounds per person annually. TRUE ○ FALSE ○

6. Americans eat 25 pounds of seafood per person annually. TRUE ○ FALSE ○

7. Fifty percent of seafood production in the United States comes from Maine. TRUE ○ FALSE ○

8. It takes four to seven years for a lobster to grow to one pound in size. TRUE ○ FALSE ○

9. Fishing was one of the first commercial industries in the United States. TRUE ○ FALSE ○

10. Squid, octopus, clams, and oysters are all mollusks. TRUE ○ FALSE ○

Garden Variety

In general, a fruit is any sweet and edible part of a plant. A vegetable is a plant that has an edible part, be it leaf, stem, root, or otherwise. A question about either is one of the things below.

1. What color is a banana before it ripens?

2. A Calville Blanc, a Fuji, a Pink Lady, and a Honeycrisp are all what fruit?

3. What spear-shaped vegetable appears in spring?

4. What vegetable has a variety called "purple sprouting"?

5. The tree of what very common fruit is botanically not a tree but an herb?

6. In the high Andes, *chuño* is what vegetable left out at night to freeze-dry?

7. Is a sea cucumber a vegetable?

8. *Mermelada*, the original version of marmalade made in Portugal, was made with what fruit?

9. In what century did a French chef figure out a way to can food in jars?

10. Early records of pickling date back to 2500 BC in India. What was the vegetable pickled?

The Big One

Since the 1860s, farmers in South Africa have been raising animals whose meat is low in fat, high in protein. It is red meat and can taste like beef or veal depending on the animal's age when slaughtered. What is this creature?

Herbal Remedy

Don't get caught confusing your pesto with your pasta on these multiple choice questions.

1 What herb is most commonly used to make pesto?
a. Oregano   b. Basil
c. Chives   d. Garlic

2 What part of the ginseng plant is used in herbalism?
a. Root   b. Leaves
c. Seeds   d. Scent

3 Pennyroyal is what type of herb?
a. Flowering   b. Medicinal
c. Mint   d. Nonedible

4 What herb is commonly mixed with onion in stuffing?
a. Sage   b. Rosemary
c. Fenugreek   d. Tarragon

5 What herb is used in the making of the salmon dish gravlax?
a. Anise   b. Fennel fronds
c. Pollen dust   d. Dill

6 "Parsley, sage, rosemary, and thyme" is a line from which song by Simon and Garfunkel?
a. "I Am an Island"   b. "Scarborough Fair"
c. "Mrs. Robinson"   d. "The Boxer"

7 The lacy outer covering of the nutmeg is used to make what spice?
a. Bitters   b. Cinnamon
c. Allspice   d. Mace

8 A clove is a spice, but what aromatic vegetable grows in sections called cloves?
a. Onions   b. Garlic
c. Rutabagas   d. Fennel

9 What herb, frequently used as a garnish, comes in flat-leaved and curly forms?
a. Parsley   b. Chives
c. Peppermint   d. Sage

10 What pungent plant allegedly keeps vampires away?
a. Onions   b. Leeks
c. Peppermint   d. Garlic

Who's Coming to Dinner?

Match the scientific name for the types of eaters below with their description.

Granivore_____   **A** Obtains its energy from sunlight

Detritivore_____   **B** Eats seeds

   C Feeds on animals but doesn't kill them

Herbivore_____

   D Eats dead and decomposing organic material

Graminivore_____

Omnivore_____   **E** Feeds on meat

Piscivore_____   **F** Feeds on grass

   G A plant that feeds on decaying matter

Phototroph_____

Carnivore_____   **H** Eats fish

   I "Eats everything," referring to an animal with a broad diet

Saprophyte_____

Parasite_____   **J** Eats plants

Eat Your Greens

Here's a bounteous harvest of questions straight from the local farmers' market.

1 Are green and red bell peppers botanically the same?

2 What vegetable has a variety called mizuna?

3 Globe, Jerusalem, and Chinese are all types of what vegetable?

4 What is fermented to make sauerkraut?

5 What vegetable is associated with the last day of October?

6 Of what is King Edward a variety?

7 What vegetable was said to give fighter pilots better night vision during World War II?

8 Lima, French, and runner are all types of what?

9 *Actinidia chinensis* is said to have originated in China. By what name do Americans know it better?

10 What's the primary ingredient in hummus?

Name That Loaf

Match the breadstuff with its country or region of origin.

Pita_____   A Middle East

Tortilla_____   B Russia

Lavash_____   C Italy

Baguette_____   D Sweden

Kulich_____   E Greece

Panettone_____   F Mexico

Limpa_____   G Germany

Dinkel_____   H France

Make Mine Meat

If you prefer your steak on the rare side, then you might also prefer these questions about the meatier side of the dinner table.

1 What is the meat of a deer called?

2 The French eat the fattened livers of what two waterfowl?

3 From what country does kielbasa sausage originate?

4 Despite being banned in some cultures, what is the most popular meat in the world, making up more than 43 percent of all meat eaten?

5 What meat originally was used to make the Swedish sausage falukorv?

6 The Italian dish *osso bucco* is made with tomatoes, wine, and what kind of meat?

7 What is the most commonly eaten bird in the Western world?

8 What dark-coated cattle are one of the world's most popular breeds?

9 Where did the popular sausage merguez originate?

10 The United States is the biggest beef producer (though we consume most of what we produce). What country is the largest beef exporter?

Squeaky and Delicious

What notoriously squeaking cheese can be grilled without it melting?

The Staff of Life

Wheat and other grains have been cultivated for millennia. Nibble at these staples of life in the questions below.

1 What two rivers bounded the Fertile Crescent where grains were first cultivated?

2 Rice cultivation is thought to have started by what Chinese river?

3 Unpolished rice with only the husks removed is what kind of rice?

4 In which modern country was maize first domesticated?

5 What is the name of the waterlogged fields where rice is grown?

6 The Central Plains of the United States, where the majority of the nation's wheat is cultivated, is known as what?

7 What technology that aided in grinding grains was developed around 200 BC?

8 What protein in wheat provides the stickiness to trap the air bubbles of the fermenting yeast, allowing the bread to rise?

9 Centuries before Marco Polo was said to have brought noodles back from China, who was already making pasta of flour and water?

10 Pearl millet was first cultivated in what country?

Bread and Cheese

Bread is perhaps the most universal food on the planet. And where grains grow well, it's usually ideal land for cattle grazing. Hence, cheese making tends to thrive where diets rely on bread. Make a meal of these bread-and-cheese questions.

1 Caerphilly cheese hails from where?

2 What type of chewy bread is woven into a curly twist and often topped with salt?

3 Chèvre is made from the milk of what animal?

4 Roti and puri are breads from what country?

5 What country produces Manchego cheese?

6 Where does halloumi cheese come from?

7 What Italian bread derives its name from its slipper-like shape?

8 Paneer is a type of cheese from where?

9 What famous French blue cheese is matured in caves?

10 Where would you most likely get a farl?

The Sweeter Side of Life

Babies are born with a taste for sugar. Sweet is a taste that stays with many of us the rest of our lives—after all, we speak of people having a "sweet tooth," not a "meat tooth." Holidays and special occasions bring out the best in sweets and special treats, so here's a round of challenging questions with sugar on top!

Just Desserts

Put down your spoon and pick up your pencil to see if your brain is as sharp as your sweet tooth on these dessert questions.

1 Which type of fruit is a Jonathan?

2 What is the literal meaning of the Italian dessert *tiramisu*?

3 Who inspired the naming of the dessert Peach Melba?

4 A loganberry is a cross between a raspberry and what?

5 Apart from milk, cream, and sugar, what is the main ingredient of crème caramel?

6 What type of pastry is used to make cream puffs?

7 The founding family of Cadbury Chocolates belonged to what religious group?

8 The leaf of what shrub is sweet enough to be used in place of sugar?

9 What dessert of meringue, fruit, and whipped cream was named after a Russian ballerina?

10 What are the three main elements of Baked Alaska?

Sugar and Spice

These questions are all things nice.

1 Which band had a 1963 hit with the song "Sugar and Spice"?

2 Who left the band The Sugarcubes to forge a successful solo career?

3 What rocker played a bus driver in the Spice Girls' movie *Spice World*?

4 What clean-cut singer had a 1959 hit called "Wang Dang Taffy-Apple Tango"?

5 Who composed "The Dance of the Sugarplum Fairies" in *The Nutcracker*?

6 Anthony Kiedis is the lead singer of what band?

7 What cartoon group topped the charts with the song "Sugar, Sugar" in 1969?

8 How are rappers Cheryl James and Sandra Denton otherwise known?

9 The phrase "Sugar pie, honey bunch" is part of the chorus of what classic soul hit from the 1960s?

10 What song opens with the line, "I'm just mad about Saffron"?

Food of the Gods

Think you're the greatest chocolate lover of all time? See if you can separate the truth from the falsehoods about your favorite obsession.

1 Chocolate is made from the fermented and roasted beans of the cacao plant, plus some form of fat (such as cocoa butter or oil), and often sugar and vanilla. TRUE ○ FALSE ○

2 Hershey's is the largest producer of chocolate in the entire world. TRUE ○ FALSE ○

3 The typical 1.55-ounce milk-chocolate Hershey's bar is Hershey's most famous product. TRUE ○ FALSE ○

4 In 1942, production of Hershey's Kisses was halted to save foil for the war effort. TRUE ○ FALSE ○

5 It takes about 75 Hershey's Kisses to equal a pound of chocolate. TRUE ○ FALSE ○

6 Eating chocolate stimulates the body to release endorphins, the pleasure hormone. TRUE ○ FALSE ○

7 The chocolate that fine chocolate candy makers use as the base for all their exquisite fillings is called *couverture*. TRUE ○ FALSE ○

8 White chocolate contains no cocoa butter. TRUE ○ FALSE ○

9 In 1960, Alfred Hitchcock used chocolate syrup to simulate blood while filming the shower scene in *Psycho*. TRUE ○ FALSE ○

10 Americans annually eat far more chocolate per capita than Europeans. TRUE ○ FALSE ○

Satisfy a Sweet Tooth

Match the classic cakes and sweets from around the world with their description.

Battenburg_____   A A Japanese brown-sugar cake

Black Forest_____   B The classic French wedding cake of a towering mound of cream puffs stuck together with caramel syrup

Dundee_____   C A crumbly fudge of sesame-seed paste or semolina

Genoese_____   D Gelatinous cubes flavored with rosewater and dusted with powdered sugar, also known as Turkish Delight

Croquembouche_____ E A highly distinctive black licorice tablet from a Yorkshire town in England

Pontefract_____   F Marzipan-encased cake with a checkerboard of white and pink batters

Karumetou_____   G A rich, almond-topped fruitcake

Eccles_____   H A nougat typically made with honey and almonds or other nuts

Lokum_____   I A buttery, sugar-topped currant cake

Halva_____   J A buttery sponge cake

Turrón_____   K A sweet phyllo pastry filled with custard

Galaktoboureko_____ L A cake made with chocolate, cherries, and cream

A Special Occasion

Each holiday brings its own distinctive food to the table, from America's Thanksgiving pumpkin pies to the plum puddings that define a British Christmas. Enjoy a seasonal taste of these holiday-specific foods from around the world.

1 What time of year do Spanish people traditionally eat the honey and almond delicacy called *turrón*?

2 What's the Swedish word for a laden table of special-occasion foods?

3 What noble cheese, made with the same mold as French Roquefort, is considered a necessity for the British Christmas season?

4 Heart-shaped cookies made of what are sold at fairs throughout Germany in the autumn?

5 Why is Britain's classic Christmas pudding called "plum" when there are no actual plums in it?

6 Hanukkah is often celebrated with potato latkes and jelly doughnuts fried in oil. What's the significance of the oil used in cooking?

7 Following Ramadan, the fasting season in the Muslim calendar, there is a celebratory feast called Eid ul-Fitr. For how many days do people feast?

8 During what season do Orthodox Russians consume a sweet cheesecake-like dessert called *paska* or *pashka*?

9 During Diwali, the Hindu holy festival of lights, a celebration that falls in October or November each year, families make and share great quantities of what type of food?

10 Why should you not cut the noodles in the dish before serving them during Chinese New Year?

The Cold Stuff

Ice cream in various forms is a staple dessert in many cultures. See if you can eat your way around the world in cold sweetness.

1 What do the British call an ice cream cone with a flaky chocolate bar stuck in it?

2 What's ice cream called in India?

3 If you were in Italy, where would you go to buy a scoop of their intensely flavored ice creams?

4 From what country does the ice-cream brand Häagen-Dazs come?

5 Soft-serve ice cream was invented in Britain in the 1950s. Name one of the chemists who worked on the process before later moving on to a prominent political career.

6 What is the most popular flavor of ice cream in Argentina?

7 Name the country in Europe that annually eats the most ice cream per capita.

8 Is Italian gelato lower or higher in fat than traditional ice cream?

9 If you order *matcha* ice cream in Japan, what will the flavoring be?

10 What kind of milk is the base of *dondurma*, the ice cream that is most popular in Turkey?

Chocolate Worship

What's the two-word botanical name that reflects the divine status accorded to chocolate by many of its worshipful devotees?

Cookie Monster

Test your cookie knowledge with the questions below.

1 A Belgian *spekuloos* is:
a. A lens for a microscope
b. A question
c. A spicy hard gingerbread biscuit
d. A chocolate cookie with frosting

2 In Britain, a digestive is:
a. A tablet to settle your stomach
b. A wholemeal cookie, sometimes dipped in chocolate
c. A "breakfast biscuit" with barley in it
d. A drink after dinner

3 The Italian word *biscotti* literally means:
a. Cut in two
b. Double-sugar
c. Hard as baked clay
d. Twice-baked

4 Dijon's baked specialty, *pain d'epices*, is:
a. A spicy gingerbread
b. A sweet white bread bought in slabs at the grocer's
c. A black-pepper and chocolate cookie
d. A chewy anise-flavored candy

5 America's word *cookie* is from:
a. The African *koonky,* meaning snack
b. The Dutch *koekje,* meaning little cake
c. The German *kunkle,* meaning rest break
d. The Irish Gaelic *comhke,* meaning sweet

6 Hermits are typically:
a. A large spice cookie with raisins
b. A small, hard ginger-flavored biscuit
c. A long-keeping spicy cookie with no butter
d. An eggless cookie with lots of ginger

7 Snickerdoodles are:
a. A large, flat chocolate cookie without a lot of sugar
b. Crisp wafers with a pink and brown layer
c. A soft cinnamon-spiced cookie with a crackled surface
d. Chewy cookies with chopped peanuts

8 Pfefferneüse, or "peppernuts," are a German cookie:
a. That's dipped in chocolate
b. That's flavored with lots of ground caraway
c. That were created for traveling since they can be stored all winter long
d. Spiced, baked in balls, and rolled in powdered sugar

9 The English word "marchpane" has been superseded by:
a. Frangipane
b. Eccles cakes
c. Marzipan
d. Crème fraiche

Having Your Cake and Eating It Too

If you like sweets, you won't get caught out on any of these flavorful questions.

1 What was the name of the 1999 novel by Joanne Harris about a young woman who opens a candy making shop in a small French village?

2 What large British baking company shares its name with a famous writer and poet and is advertised as making "exceedingly good cakes"?

3 What candy bar has a layer of peanut butter nougat topped by a layer of peanuts and caramel, the whole enrobed in chocolate?

4 Who wrote the novel *Charlie and the Chocolate Factory*?

5 Who makes an ice cream with the flavor Chubby Hubby?

6 What popular chocolate and hazelnut spread started life in post-war Italy as Pasta Gianduja?

7 What is the literal meaning in English of crème brûlée?

8 What syrup is liberally dripped over the flaky Greek and Turkish pastry *baklava*?

Food Around the World

Food can be one of the most distinctive characteristics of a culture, one that's easily recognized—and easily shared. The tastes of another country and people help us to come closer. Whether you're an ace Asian cook, a connoisseur of fusion cuisine, or just someone who enjoys the occasional taco, see how much you know about food around the world.

International Cuisine

Take 10 on tasty treats from food around the globe.

1 Pizza and pasta are the best known exports of what nation's cuisine?

2 *Moules-frites* are a specialty of what country?

3 Which nation gave rise to the doner kebab?

4 In which country are lunches packed into bento boxes?

5 Which country invented the dip guacamole?

6 In which country are steamed rice rolls named *banh cuon* popular at breakfast?

7 *Masala dosa* is a vegetarian dish from the south of what country?

8 In which country are tapas a staple part of most people's diet?

9 What is the name of the type of German bread made from malted rye?

10 Which Southeast Asian nation is the home of gado-gado?

Potluck

This quiz will get your taste buds tingling.

1 Chaumes, reblochon, and chevrotin are all types of what?

2 Which country shares its name with a type of poultry?

3 What type of dessert wine was described by Louis XIV as "the Wine of Kings, and the King of Wines"?

4 *Matambre* is a beef dish from what South American country?

5 In which Asian nation might you order meat dumplings called *momos*?

6 Chicken Kiev is named after which country's capital?

7 Which region of the world does couscous come from?

8 With what country is tequila usually associated?

9 Which country's cuisine includes *tum yam* soup and *banh chung*?

10 Where might you be served a dish of mealie-meal porridge?

The Truth About Food

See if you can separate the truth from the chaff in the statements below as you hopscotch across the map.

1 Argentina is the second largest beef producer in South America.   TRUE ○   FALSE ○

2 The name of Hungary's national dish, goulash, comes from an old Hungarian word *gulyashus*, which means "meat dish prepared by milkmaids."   TRUE ○   FALSE ○

3 Agriculture employs more than a quarter of Poland's population, but it generates less than 4 percent of the gross domestic product.   TRUE ○   FALSE ○

4 Belgium has an area of less than 12,000 square miles and contains more than 2,000 chocolate shops.   TRUE ○   FALSE ○

5 Pilsner beer was first brewed in 1842 in the Hungarian town of Pizen (Pilsen), by a Bavarian brewer who took advantage of the town's unusually soft water to create a clear golden beer.   TRUE ○   FALSE ○

6 Germany has more than 300 types of bread and more than 1,500 types of sausage.   TRUE ○   FALSE ○

7 France produces at least 800 types of cheese.   TRUE ○   FALSE ○

8 One of the remaining reminders of French rule in Vietnam (from 1887–1954) is the fact that baguettes (French-style bread) are still widely available and used for sandwiches.   TRUE ○   FALSE ○

9 The Singapore Sling, the famous cocktail invented in Singapore's Raffles Hotel, was meant to appeal to ladies with its pinkish color.   TRUE ○   FALSE ○

10 Coffee represents 10 percent of export revenue for many Central American countries.   TRUE ○   FALSE ○

National Dish

Match the typical example cuisine with the nation that consumes it.

Sushi_____   A Brazil
Calentita_____   B Jamaica
Biltong_____   C Gibraltar
Borscht_____   D Spain
Feijoada_____   E Russia
Ackee and saltfish_____   F South Africa
Kimchee_____   G Korea
Gravlax_____   H Sweden
Rösti_____   I Switzerland
Paella_____   J Japan

The Little Dishes

In Greece, a *meze* is a small dish that is often served to accompany drinks, such as the classic anise-flavored Greek *ouzo*. Name three typical mezes that would likely appear on the Greek table (it's okay if you don't know the exact Greek name for everything!).

Dish It Up

It doesn't matter where it's from; international foods all have one thing in common: They're beloved. See if you can answer these international culinary questions.

1 What's the name of the rounded clay oven where Indian cooks roast meat or bake bread?

2 A typical Greek moussaka has meat sauce, béchamel, and what vegetable?

3 At a seder, Jewish families eat a meal that includes matzos, and what dish of chopped apples, nuts, and cinnamon mixed with wine?

4 The hearty Mexican stew posole has pork, chiles, and other seasonings, and what ingredient made of corn?

5 What national chain of doughnut restaurants can be found throughout much of Canada?

6 If you were having a Thursday night supper of yellow pea soup followed by pancakes, where might you be?

7 Each October, around 6 million visitors flock to which German town to drink beer and eat traditional German foods?

8 Many Portuguese dishes incorporate a dried fish known as *bacalhau*—what fish is this?

9 In Israel, many restaurants are devoted to what food, made fresh throughout the day and often served warm, garnished with a hard-boiled egg?

10 *Ful medames*, a dish of partially mashed fava beans served with garnishes, is popular in what countries?

Flat as a Pancake

Can you name 10 of the most common flat-breads that are eaten almost every day?

Food Science

There's more to food than just cooking and eating. The chemical makeup of food, from fat to fiber and sugar to starch, is nearly as important. How much do you know about what's in the food you eat and how the digestive process works? Here's the place to find out.

The Body Knows

We're so inundated with dietary info these days that it's hard to keep it all straight. See if you can sort out the truth from the statements below.

1 The body will manufacture all the fat it needs so there is no need to consume fat in the diet.   TRUE ◯   FALSE ◯

2 White bread contains no fiber.   TRUE ◯   FALSE ◯

3 A zinc deficiency leads to night blindness.   TRUE ◯   FALSE ◯

4 A petite woman with a sedentary lifestyle consumes less energy in 24 hours than a 100-watt bulb.   TRUE ◯   FALSE ◯

5 Your tongue has millions of taste buds on its surface.   TRUE ◯   FALSE ◯

6 Fruit juice is a good source of fiber.   TRUE ◯   FALSE ◯

7 The initials MSG stand for monosodium gluconate.   TRUE ◯   FALSE ◯

Food and Fitness

You know you are what you eat, but you may have to digest awhile to get the answers to these.

1 What process, beginning in your mouth, is finally completed in your colon?

2 Cows have four and humans have one. What?

3 Apart from bones, what other part of the human body uses most of the calcium in your diet?

4 What causes the uncomfortable condition of a "stitch in the side" during exercise?

5 What mineral is the main constituent of red blood cells?

6 The illegal use of what type of banned substance caused Ben Johnson to be stripped of his 1988 Olympic gold medal?

7 Which brown-green secretion helps you digest fat?

8 The eating of what vegetable was used as a cover story to hide the development of radar during World War II?

9 Rickets is caused by a lack of what vitamin?

In the Know with Nutrition

Do you understand what's what with all those fats, carbs, sugars, and more in your food? This healthy checklist of questions may help you pinpoint any weak spots.

1 In terms of protein content, how do beans differ from fish, meat, and eggs?

2 A diet rich in saturated fats raises the levels of what in your blood?

3 What are the common names of lactose and fructose?

4 Does a gram of fat give you more, less, or about the same energy as a gram of carbohydrate?

5 What vital fluid has no nutritional value whatsoever?

6 What's a good source of monounsaturated fat: smoked salmon or olive oil?

7 What is the name of the scientific study of food and diet?

8 What are the chemical components of protein?

9 What substance found in wheat and rye must be avoided by people with celiac disease?

10 What is the only macronutrient whose lack can lead to a deficiency disease?

Nutrition and Health

Some nutrients and minerals are so essential that just a trace can be the difference between health or illness.

1 What organ regulates imbalances between sodium and potassium?

2 Which nationality was the first known to use citrus fruits to counter scurvy at sea?

3 The lack of what leads to the swollen thyroid condition called goiter?

4 The yolk of eggs are rich in what mineral?

5 In 1918, a British physician cured rickets with what simple supplement?

6 A lack of what vital element can cause nerves to stop transmitting signals or make the heart beat irregularly or stop?

7 What orange substance, found in carrots, is turned by the body into Vitamin A?

8 Iron is more easily absorbed by the body if you eat it with what vitamin?

9 What vitamin is created by the body from sunlight on the skin?

10 Available in eggs, nuts, and wheat germ, what vitamin acts as a disease-fighting antioxidant and may help slow aging in cell?

You're Soaking in It

Name the amount of water that one human being will consume over the average lifetime. Is it 10,000 gallons, 15,000 gallons, 50,000 gallons, or 100,000 gallons?

Tossed Salad

Not quite satisfied? Brain still full of fun and useful facts, such as how many blackbirds were baked in that pie? Think of this mixed grill of questions as a savory cheese course or a soothing digestif to round off your appetite.

Mix and Match

Look back—way, way back—to choose the right responses below.

1 Which of these foods did the ancient Romans not eat:
a. Cilantro   b. Pomegranates
c. Runner beans   d. Lentils

2 Which of these foods did early Americans eat?
a. Chicken   b. Turkey
c. Oats   d. Cheese

3 From what language does the word "sugar" derive?
a. Sanskrit   b. Amharic (Ethiopian)
c. Greek   d. Chinese

4 Which of the foods below did not originate in Mesoamerica?
a. Cocoa   b. Turkeys
c. Vanilla   d. Rice

5 Wine and beer were first produced in:
a. Greece   b. Italy
c. Mesopotamia   d. China

6 At least 6,000 years ago, the Sumerians were making which:
a. Gin   b. Cheese
c. Peanut butter   d. Rum

7 In AD 408, the Visigoth leader Alaric demanded a ransom from Rome that included 3,000 pounds of:
a. Pepper   b. Gold coins
c. Honey   d. Lead

8 The most widely used sweetener in the ancient world was:
a. Maple syrup   b. Sugar cane
c. Sugar beets   d. Honey

9 The ancient Greek and Latin words for "olive" are the basis of which modern word:
a. Origin   b. Oil
c. Ovoid   d. Oval

10 When Europeans first arrived in the Americas in the late 15th century, which food did they *not* find:
a. Potatoes   b. Avocados
c. Okra   d. Tomatoes

Food On-Screen

Food can make a powerful statement on the big screen and the small, serving to deepen our understanding of a character or provide comic relief. Check your (taste) memory for these memorable flavors.

1 In the title of the classic 1968 film starring Doris Day, *With Six You Get...* what?

2 In which series is a coffee bar called Central Perk a favorite meeting place?

3 What is the name of the toddler in the *Popeye* cartoons?

4 What is the favorite food of the *Teenage Mutant Ninja Turtles*?

5 Which New York-based TV detective had a penchant for lollipops?

6 In the 1970s, Bingo and Snork were members of what fruit-flavored TV singing quartet?

7 Michael Jackson was filming a commercial for what soft drink company when his hair caught fire?

8 On *The Andy Griffith Show*, silent toddler Leon (played by Ron Howard's baby brother) was always offering grownups a taste of what type of sandwich?

9 In what 1987 film does a down-on-her-luck housekeeper spend all her lottery winnings on creating a dinner reminiscent of her days as a famous chef?

10 Arnold's Drive-In was a meeting place on which long-running TV series?

Television Cooks

Match the celebrity chef with his or her most celebrated catchphrase or notable characteristic.

Rachael Ray_____   A Orange clogs

Martha Stewart_____   B Minimax cooking

Emeril Lagasse_____   C Being "naked"

Julia Child_____   D "Hey, y'all!"

Two Fat Ladies_____   E "Bam!"

Nigella Lawson_____   F Riding on a motor-cycle and sidecar

Jamie Oliver_____   G "Yum-o!"

Mario Batali_____   H "It's a good thing."

The Galloping Gourmet_____ I Licking her fingers

Paula Deen_____   J "Bon appétit!"

Tightening the Belt

Feeling a little overstuffed? Match the popular diet with its primary characteristic.

Atkins_____

Weight Watchers_____

Master Cleanse_____

South Beach_____

Jenny Craig_____

A A fast where the dieter drinks only water with lemon, cayenne, and maple syrup

B A diet based initially on premade, prepackaged food

C A diet that completely eliminates carbohydrates

D A diet based on counting points that estimate the day's caloric intake

E A diet focusing on consuming mainly lean protein and vegetables

Pie Posers

There's more to pie than apples and pastry. Roll out your best effort here.

1 Which comic strip strongman eats cow pie in Cactusville?

2 What kind of bird is the cartoon character Tweetie Pie?

3 With which 1971 hit did Madonna top the charts in 2000?

4 What is the Italian word for pie?

5 Which nursery rhyme character meets a pieman?

6 In clothing terms, what is a pork pie?

7 Jason Biggs was the star of what 1999 hit comedy movie?

8 Who wrote the poem "The Pied Piper of Hamelin"?

Puddings and Pies

Puddings and pies—and questions about them—can be both sweet and savory.

1 What kind of pie is traditionally eaten on Thanksgiving Day in America?

2 From which country did the savory tart Quiche Lorraine originate?

3 What fruit is the main ingredient of Eve's Pudding?

4 In the nursery rhyme, how many blackbirds were baked in a pie?

5 What amphibious name is given to a Yorkshire pudding containing sausages?

6 Which farm animal's blood is dried to make black pudding?

Tasty Trivia

Hopscotch through the world of food in the questions here.

1 What type of pasta literally means "little tongues" in Italian?

2 A savoy is which type of vegetable?

3 With which period in the Christian calendar are simnel cakes associated?

4 What color is cayenne pepper?

5 In which country did chutney originate?

6 What vitamin is not present in eggs?

Call It Macaroni

Can you name 20 "styles" of Italian pasta?

PAGE 123

Drinks of History

1 A type of beer
2 Coffee
3 Drank toasts from it
4 Coffeehouses
5 Cornmeal
6 Lime or lemon
7 Syllabub

Mixed Drinks

1 Peaches and oranges
2 Cha
3 Handel
4 Portugal
5 Rick's Café
6 John Irving
7 Diamantina Cocktail
8 Mexico
9 Pears
10 *The Rime of the Ancient Mariner* by Coleridge

PAGE 124

A Cup of Joe

1 c. Forced out
2 b. Columbia and Brazil
3 d. A long-handled copper pot for making Turkish coffee
4 c. Made from coffee beans eaten and excreted by a Sumatran wild cat
5 a. The drink's resemblance to the brown cowls worn by Capuchin monks
6 c. Arabica and robusta beans
7 d. Their ports of origin
8 b. A bush
9 b. Freeze-dried
10 a. Its stimulating effects

Name That Plant!

Camellia sinensis

PAGE 125

A Quiz About the Cup that Soothes...

1 True
2 True
3 False; it was the Dutch who introduced it
4 False; it's meant to offer serenity and reflectiveness
5 True
6 False; it's the essence of bergamot
7 True
8 True
9 False; but brick tea *was* used as currency in Russia and China
10 True

A Bountiful Cup of...Yogurt

1 Turkey
2 20th century
3 Good bacteria
4 Dannon
5 Animal skin
6 Preserve milk
7 Mongolia
8 King Francois I
9 Kefir
10 Raita

PAGE 126

Cream of the Crop

1 c. Thick, spreadable cream with a mottled surface and a fat content of 55 percent
2 f. A fresh French cheese, like a thick sour cream, made of blending curds and whey
3 a. A thick, creamy low-salt, un-aged cheese, widely used in Europe
4 h. A soft, fresh curd cheese used in Indian cooking
5 g. Milk that has been slightly curdled, but with the curds and whey mixed together
6 d. A kind of Swedish yogurt similar to buttermilk
7 e. A cooling Indian drink made by mixing yogurt with spices or rosewater
8 b. Clarified butter widely used in Indian cuisine

Sparkling Soda

1 Dr Pepper
2 1929
3 Minerals
4 7UP
5 The Coca-Cola Company
6 Chero-Cola
7 Yoo-hoo
8 Cheerwine
9 Atlanta
10 Irn-Bru

Animal Planet

Cows, goats, sheep, water buffalo, yaks, horses (Mongolian mares' milk)

PAGE 127

On Wine

1 Chile
2 Fruit residue
3 Bollinger Champagne
4 Keith Floyd
5 Beaujolais Nouveau
6 Sotheby's
7 Barossa Valley
8 South Africa
9 Marlborough
10 Oak

Size Counts

1 6 standard bottles
2 12 standard bottles
3 2 standard bottles
4 8 standard bottles
5 24 standard sodes
6 3 standard bottles
7 20 standard bottles
8 4 standard bottles
9 16 standard bottles

Are You a Pi-not It All?

Burgundy or pinot noir

Answers

In Vino Veritas

1 True
2 False; they are known as *de luxe cuvées*
3 False; viniculture is growing grapes; winemaking is vinification
4 False; it's the buttery flavor that comes from oak barrels
5 True
6 False; red wine comes from allowing the grape skins to ferment with the juice. For white wine, the skins are removed before fermentation
7 False; fortified wines have had brandy or another spirit added to them
8 True
9 True
10 False; it's from Hungary

Ancient History

1 Pulque
2 The Babylonians
3 The temperance movement
4 Benedictine
5 He was a monk
6 Drambuie
7 Beer

The Tricky Grape

1 Chardonnay
2 Pinot grigio
3 Cabernet sauvignon
4 Riesling
5 Zinfandel
6 Merlot

Know Your (Hard) Stuff

1 Rum
2 Gin
3 Chartreuse
4 Bordeaux
5 Champagne
6 Oranges
7 The 18th century
8 Water, hops, barley malt
9 A vineyard
10 France
11 Brut (literally, raw or rough)
12 *Vin de pays*

What Was Her Name?

Shirley Temple

A Spirited Matchup

1 Sugar cane or molasses
2 Cherries
3 Grapes, flavored with star anise
4 Maguey (agave) plant
5 Barley or rye
6 Apples
7 Sugar cane
8 Grape skins
9 Juniper berries
10 Rice
11 Pepper
12 Plums

Cheers!

1 Merlot; it's a red wine grape
2 The Douro Valley
3 Munich (the Oktoberfest)
4 7,000
5 True
6 France and Italy
7 They're Trappist monks
8 Burgundy
9 Gin or vodka and lime juice
10 South Africa (the grape is a cross of pinot noir and cinsault)

I'll Have a Cold One!

1 One liter
2 Cherries
3 It's roasted
4 India (India Pale Ale)
5 Lambic
6 The Czechs, followed by the Irish and the Germans
7 Not chilling beer reveals a wider range of flavors
8 The yeast used in brewing

To Your Health

1 Britain
2 Scotland and Ireland
3 France
4 Sweden
5 Russia
6 Romania
7 Armenia
8 Israel
9 Turkey
10 Spain

Water of Life

Bloody Mary, Cosmopolitan, Martini, Gimlet, Gibson, Long Island Iced Tea, Cape Cod, Vodka Tonic, Screwdriver, Harvey Wallbanger, White Russian

Mixed Veggies

1 Bugs Bunny
2 Sir Walter Raleigh
3 Fine words
4 Cucumber
5 Turnips
6 Beets
7 Cabbage Patch Kids
8 *Toy Story*
9 Bean
10 Capsicum
11 Kava
12 A carrot
13 Eggplant
14 Durian
15 Zucchini

You Say It This Way, I Say It That Way

Tomato

PAGE 132

Fruity Facts

1 Grapes
2 Plum
3 Jaffa
4 Apple
5 Jeanette Winterson
6 Melons
7 Sugar
8 China

Know Your Onions

1 Citrus
2 Drupes
3 Kiwi fruit
4 Idaho
5 Anton Chekhov
6 Taro
7 "Strawberry Fields Forever"
8 Vincent Van Gogh
9 Albert R. "Cubby" Broccoli, best known for the James Bond series of films
10 Loganberries

Fruit Salad

1 Sugar beet
2 Avocado
3 Mandarin
4 Pineapple (*piña* is Spanish for pineapple)
5 Apple
6 Banana
7 Rum
8 Cherry
9 Plum
10 Gooseberry

PAGE 133

Catch and Release

1 True
2 False; the United Nations has banned nets longer than 1 1/2 miles
3 True
4 True
5 False; second are the Japanese, who consume about 150 pounds per person annually
6 False; we eat about 15 pounds a person annually
7 False; it comes from Alaska
8 True
9 True
10 True

Garden Variety

1 Green
2 Apples
3 Asparagus
4 Broccoli
5 A banana tree
6 Potatoes
7 No, it's a marine animal, sometimes called a sea slug; it's edible but not a plant
8 Quinces (*marmelos*)
9 In the 18th century, in 1795, Nicholas Appert figures out how to heat food in jars for preservation
10 Cucumbers

The Big One

The ostrich

PAGE 134

Herbal Remedy

1 b. Basil
2 a. Root
3 c. Mint
4 a. Sage
5 d. Dill
6 b. "Scarborough Fair"
7 d. Mace
8 b. Garlic
9 a. Parsley
10 d. Garlic

Who's Coming to Dinner?

1 Eats seeds
2 Eats dead and decomposing organic material
3 Eats plants
4 Feeds on grass
5 "Eats everything," referring to an animal with a broad diet
6 Eats fish
7 Obtains its energy from sunlight
8 Feeds on meat
9 A plant that feeds on decaying matter
10 Feeds on animals but doesn't kill them

PAGE 135

Eat Your Greens

1 Yes
2 Greens
3 Artichoke
4 Cabbage
5 Pumpkin
6 Potato
7 Carrot
8 Bean
9 Kiwi fruit
10 Chickpeas

Name That Loaf

1 Greece
2 Mexico
3 Middle East
4 France
5 Russia
6 Italy
7 Sweden
8 Germany

Make Mine Meat

1 Venison
2 Geese and ducks
3 Poland
4 Pork
5 Ox meat
6 Veal
7 Chicken
8 Angus
9 North Africa
10 Brazil

Answers

Squeaky and Delicious

Halloumi

The Staff of Life

1 The Tigris and Euphrates
2 The Yangtze
3 Brown
4 Mexico
5 Paddies
6 The Breadbasket
7 The water mill
8 Gluten
9 The Romans
10 Africa

Bread and Cheese

1 Wales
2 A pretzel
3 A goat
4 India
5 Spain
6 Cyprus
7 Ciabatta
8 India
9 Roquefort
10 Scotland or Ireland (a "farl" is a small cake or bread, either baked or cut into a triangular shape)

Just Desserts

1 Apple
2 "Pick me up"
3 Opera singer Dame Nellie Melba
4 Blackberry
5 Eggs
6 Choux
7 Quakers
8 Stevia
9 Pavlova
10 Ice cream, meringue, and cake

Sugar and Spice

1 The Searchers
2 Björk
3 Meat Loaf
4 Pat Boone
5 Tchaikovsky
6 Red Hot Chili Peppers
7 The Archies
8 Salt-n-Pepa
9 "I Can't Help Myself"
10 "Mellow Yellow"

Food of the Gods

1 True
2 True
3 False; Kisses are Hershey's top seller
4 True
5 False; it takes about 95
6 True
7 False; *couverture* is usually used for the exterior coating
8 False; white chocolate contains no cocoa solids, but good versions do have cocoa butter
9 True
10 False; Americans average about 12 pounds per person a year, while the Swiss, Europe's top chocolate consumers, eat nearly double that amount

Satisfy a Sweet Tooth

1 Marzipan-encased cake with a checkerboard of white and pink batters
2 A cake made with chocolate, cherries, and cream
3 A rich, almond-topped fruitcake
4 A buttery sponge cake
5 The classic French wedding cake of a towering mound of cream puffs stuck together with caramel syrup
6 A highly distinctive black licorice tablet from a Yorkshire town in England
7 A Japanese brown-sugar cake
8 A buttery, sugar-topped currant cake

9 d. Gelatinous cubes flavored with rosewater and dusted with powdered sugar, also known as Turkish Delight
10 c. A crumbly fudge of sesame-seed paste or semolina
11 h. A nougat typically made with honey and almonds or other nuts
12 k. A sweet phyllo pastry filled with custard

A Special Occasion

1 Christmas
2 Smörgåsbord
3 Stilton
4 Gingerbread
5 "Plum" is an Old English word for dried fruit
6 The oil celebrates the Hanukkah miracle of the one-day supply of oil that lasted for eight days
7 Three days
8 Easter
9 Sweets
10 Leaving the noodles long signifies a long and happy life

The Cold Stuff

1 A "99"
2 *Kulfi*
3 A *gelateria*
4 The United States—the European-sounding name was intended as a marketing tool
5 Margaret Thatcher
6 *Dulce de leche*
7 Finland, at nearly 14 liters per person (though U.S. residents eat an average of 23 liters per person)
8 Lower—despite the rich flavor, gelato typically has 7 percent to 8 percent fat, compared to the average 10 percent fat in American ice cream
9 Powdered green tea
10 Goat's milk

Chocolate Worship

Theobroma cacao, or "food of the gods."

PAGE 140

Cookie Monster

1 c. A spicy hard gingerbread biscuit
2 b. A wholemeal cookie, sometimes dipped in chocolate
3 d. Twice-baked
4 a. A spicy gingerbread
5 b. The Dutch *koekje*, meaning little cake
6 a. A large spice cookie with raisins
7 c. A soft cinnamon-spiced cookie with a crackled surface
8 d. Spiced, baked in balls, and rolled in powdered sugar
9 c. Marzipan

Having Your Cake and Eating It Too

1 *Chocolat*
2 Mr. Kipling
3 Snickers
4 Roald Dahl
5 Ben and Jerry's
6 Nutella
7 "Scorched cream"
8 Honey

PAGE 141

International Cuisine

1 Italy
2 Belgium
3 Turkey
4 Japan
5 Mexico
6 Vietnam
7 India
8 Spain
9 Pumpernickel
10 Indonesia

Potluck

1 Cheese
2 Turkey
3 Tokaji
4 Argentina
5 Nepal
6 Ukraine
7 North Africa
8 Mexico
9 Thailand
10 Burundi

PAGE 142

The Truth About Food

1 False; they're the largest
2 False; it means "meat dish prepared by herdsman"
3 True
4 True
5 True
6 True
7 False; but they do produce at least 500
8 True
9 True
10 False; it represents nearly 25 percent

National Dish

1 Japan
2 Gibraltar
3 South Africa
4 Russia
5 Brazil
6 Jamaica
7 Korea
8 Sweden
9 Switzerland
10 Spain

The Little Dishes

Taramasalata (roe spread), tzatziki (cucumber and yogurt blend), skordalia (potato and garlic spread), melitzanosalata (eggplant spread), dolmades (stuffed vine leaves), Greek salad, spanakopita (spinach in phyllo), tyropita (cheese in phyllo), saganaki (fried cheese), olives

PAGE 143

Dish It Up

1 Tandoor
2 Eggplant
3 Haroset
4 Hominy
5 Tim Hortons
6 Sweden
7 Munich
8 Cod
9 Hummus
10 Egypt and Sudan

PAGE 144

The Body Knows

1 False
2 False
3 False; it dulls the sense of taste
4 True
5 False; the average adult has about 3,000 taste buds
6 False; fruit is a good source of fiber. Juicing it removes much of the roughage
7 False; it's monosodium glutamate

Food and Fitness

1 Digestion
2 Stomachs
3 Teeth
4 A cramp of the diaphragm muscle
5 Iron
6 Steroids
7 Bile
8 Carrots, the British let it be known that their pilots' night vision had improved from eating carrots when in fact their nighttime successes against the Germans were due to radar
9 Vitamin D

In the Know with Nutrition

1 Beans are not a complete protein
2 Cholesterol
3 Milk sugar and fruit sugar
4 More
5 Water
6 Olive oil
7 Nutrition
8 Amino acids
9 Gluten
10 Protein

Nutrition and Health

1 The kidneys
2 The Chinese
3 Iodine
4 Iron
5 Cod liver oil
6 Potassium
7 Carotene
8 Vitamin C
9 Vitamin D
10 Vitamin E

You're Soaking In It

About 15,000 gallons

Mix and Match

1 c. Runner beans
2 b. Turkey
3 a. Sanskrit
4 d. Rice
5 c. Mesopotamia
6 b. Cheese
7 a. Pepper
8 d. Honey
9 b. Oil
10 c. Okra

PAGE 147

Food On-Screen

1 Eggroll
2 *Friends*
3 Sweet Pea
4 Pizza
5 Kojak
6 Banana Splits
7 Pepsi-Cola
8 Peanut butter and jelly ("No thanks, Leon.")
9 *Babette's Feast*
10 *Happy Days*

Television Cooks

1 "Yum-o!"
2 "It's a good thing."
3 "Bam!"
4 "Bon appétit!"
5 Riding on a motorcycle and sidecar
6 Licking her fingers
7 Being "naked"
8 Orange clogs
9 Minimax cooking
10 "Hey, y'all!"

Tightening the Belt

1 A diet that completely eliminates carbohydrates
2 A diet based on counting points that estimate the day's caloric intake
3 A fast where the dieter drinks only water with lemon, cayenne, and maple syrup
4 A diet focusing on consuming mainly lean protein and vegetables
5 A diet based initially on premade, prepackaged food

PAGE 148

Pie Posers

1 Desperate Dan
2 Canary
3 "American Pie"
4 Torta
5 Simple Simon
6 A type of hat
7 *American Pie*
8 Robert Browning

Puddings and Pies

1 Pumpkin
2 France
3 Apple
4 24
5 Toad in the Hole
6 Pig

Tasty Trivia

1 Linguine
2 Cabbage
3 Lent
4 Red
5 India
6 Vitamin C

5 | Around the World

Look up the term *worldly-wise*, and you'll find such definitions as "sophisticated," "possessing broad knowledge," and "well-informed about human affairs." So sharpen your pencil and let's find out how worldly-wise you actually are.

Countries Today

Let's set aside ancient history for the moment, and consider where we are—and how we got there.

Far-flung Facts

Who knows where these questions will take you?

1 What is the full, official name of Luxembourg?

2 Which U.S. city is known colloquially as "The Big Easy"?

3 Which city, which is also a country, has the lowest birth rate in the world?

4 New Zealand is in the South Pacific, but where is Zealand?

5 How many Emirates are there in the United Arab Emirates?

6 Which waterfall is the world's highest?

7 Bruce Chatwin and Paul Theroux both wrote books about which remote part of South America?

8 What is the name of the largest pyramid in Egypt?

9 In which city was Graham Green's famous Asian novel *The Quiet American* set?

Capital Punishment

Choose from the list of countries below to match the appropriate capital city.

Zagreb_____	**A** Cambodia
Santiago_____	**B** Cameroon
Bogatá_____	**C** Canada
San José_____	**D** Chile
N'Djamena_____	**E** Colombia
Ottawa_____	**F** Costa Rica
Havana_____	**G** Croatia
Nicosia_____	**H** Cuba
Phnom Penh_____	**I** Cypress
Yaoundé_____	**J** Republic of Chad

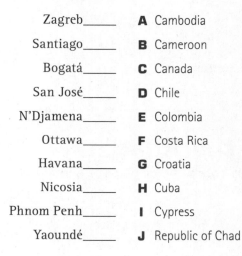

Can You Name It?

Which African country was formed from the former Gold Coast and British Togoland?

New National Identities

What are the following countries or cities now known as?

1 Ceylon

2 Rhodesia

3 The Friendly Islands

4 New Holland

5 Constantinople

6 Batavia

7 Edo

8 Formosa

9 South West Africa

10 Palmerston

Hit the Road

Stops all 'round the globe pose some tough questions....

1 What is the official language of Lichtenstein?

2 In which cemetery in Buenos Aires is Eva Peron buried?

3 In South America, which country is located between Guyana and French Guiana?

4 The lowest city in the world, at about 800 feet below sea level, is in the Middle East. What's its name?

5 Which U.S. state has a flag that features a Union Jack in one corner?

6 Which two countries, both bordering the Mediterranean, have cities called Tripoli?

7 Which city is served by Marco Polo Airport?

8 In which country is the source of the River Rhine?

9 What is the name of the body of water in Alaska where the *Exxon Valdez* oil spill occurred?

10 If you landed at Don Muang Airport, in which city would you be?

Going Globe-trotting

Got your bags packed? You're on your way!

1 What is the southernmost point of the continental United States?

2 The legendary land of vampires, Transylvania, is a part of which country?

3 Which river flows through China, Burma, Laos, Thailand, Cambodia, and Vietnam?

4 What is Israel's unit of currency?

5 What does the name Tierra del Fuego mean in English?

6 What is the modern name of the Chinese city formerly known as Canton?

7 Good King Wenceslas has a famous square named after him. Where?

8 Where would you find the Sha Tin and Happy Valley racetracks?

9 The language known as Tagalog is spoken primarily in which country?

10 Of which country is Tirol a province?

End of Empire

Here's a round of questions about former colonies.

Which country ruled Guyana before its independence?_____   **A** Brunei

Which colony did Portugal return to China in 1999?_____   **B** Cambodia

From which country did the Philippines gain independence in 1946?_____   **C** Cuba

Which modern country was once known as German South West Africa?_____   **D** Goa

Which former Portuguese colony is now an Indian state?_____   **E** Indonesia

Which three modern countries once comprised French Indochina?_____   **F** Laos

Kalimantan Timur is a province of which country?_____   **G** Macau

Which sultanate gained independence from Britain in 1984?_____   **H** Namibia

Which Caribbean state was U.S.-ruled from 1899 to 1902?_____   **I** United Kingdom

    J United States

    K Vietnam

Headlines of the Past

How's your memory for front-page news of the 1970s? Choose your answers from the list below.

On January 27, 1973, where were the peace talks that finally ended the Vietnam War?_____   **A** Jimmy Carter

What were Ling-Ling and Hsing-Hsing, presents from China to the United States in 1972?_____   **B** Spiro Agnew

Which ruling figure first stepped outside his imperial islands as head of state in 1971?_____   **C** The Shah of Iran, Mohammed Reza Pahlavi

Where did Carl Bernstein and Bob Woodward work while uncovering the Watergate scandal?_____   **D** Emperor Hirohito of Japan (also known as Emperor Shōwa)

Which U.S. president wobbled at the knees, having run too far in Maryland in 1979?_____   **E** Patrick White

Who fled Iran on January 16, 1979?_____   **F** Pakistan

Which Australian novelist received the Nobel Prize for Literature in 1973?_____   **G** In space

Of which country did Zulfikar Ali Bhutto become president in 1971?_____   **H** Paris

Where did Deke move from one craft to shake hands with Alexei in another in 1975?_____   **I** Giant pandas

The visit of which U.S. vice president to New Zealand in 1970 provoked public protests?_____   **J** *The Washington Post*

The Year 2000

Try this round about international events at the turn of the millennium.

1 Which former leader of Yugoslavia appeared at the UN International Tribunal charged with war crimes?
a. Radovan Karazic
b. Slobodan Milosevic
c. Hermann Göring
d. Bela Lugosi

2 Which German city hosted the Expo 2000 World's Fair?
a. Hanover
b. Frankfurt
c. Berlin
d. Dusseldorf

3 Whose running mate was Joseph Lieberman?
a. British Prime Minister Tony Blair
b. Failed U.S. presidential hopeful John Kerry
c. Failed U.S. presidential hopeful Al Gore
d. Secretary of State Condoleezza Rice

4 Of what did General Joseph Ralston take command?
a. NATO, as supreme commander
b. Belize, as president
c. United States Marine Corps
d. Monte Carlo, as mayor

5 Which type of plane crashed in July in France, leading to a cancellation of further flights?
a. Single-passenger ultralights built in Paris
b. The space shuttle
c. The *Concorde*
d. F-16 fighter jets

6 Who was the creator of the comic strip *Peanuts*, who died in 2000?
a. Charles Schulz
b. Hank Ketchum
c. Bill Keane
d. Bill Melendez

7 What was the Steel Dragon, which opened in Japan in August 2000 and was the tallest, fastest, and longest of its kind at the time?
a. An elevated bullet train
b. A shopping mall escalator
c. A roller coaster
d. An elevator in a skyscraper

8 What took off for the 100th time in October 2000?
a. The *Spruce Goose*
b. The space shuttle
c. A globe-circling balloon
d. *Air Force One*

9 Which country decided to bring back its old anthem, but with new words?
a. Russia
b. Mexico
c. France
d. Canada

10 Which aerospace consortium announced plans for a super-jumbo, able to seat 555 passengers?
a. NASA
b. Airbus Industries
c. The International Space Station
d. Air Travel America

Let's Hear It for the Parrot Heads!

What pop singer makes his home (and his living) in the southernmost town in the United States?

The Year 1900

The turn of the 20th century was a momentous time for the world. Answer these questions true or false.

1 Brigham Roberts was barred from taking a seat in the U.S. House of Representatives because he was a polygamous Mormon. TRUE ○ FALSE ○

2 A future world leader, by the name of Theodore Roosevelt, published an adventure novel called *Savrola*. TRUE ○ FALSE ○

3 King Umberto was assassinated by an anarchist in Monza, Italy. TRUE ○ FALSE ○

4 In January, the bubonic plague broke out in Sydney, Australia. TRUE ○ FALSE ○

5 A violent anti-Christian, anti-foreign movement called the Qing Rebellion broke out in China. TRUE ○ FALSE ○

6 A decorative architectural feature called the "cakewalk" became all the rage among American homebuilders. TRUE ○ FALSE ○

7 Huge British celebrations were held upon the failure of the Boer siege of the town of Mafeking. TRUE ○ FALSE ○

8 A German aviation innovation called the *Zeppelin* had its maiden voyage. TRUE ○ FALSE ○

9 Nationalist leader John Redmond called upon the people of Ireland to rise up against the British. TRUE ○ FALSE ○

10 A train called *The Deutchland* was setting new speed records between Paris and Berlin. TRUE ○ FALSE ○

It's a Date

Test your knowledge of what happened when in the world. Choose answers from the list below.

In which year was Hong Kong returned from Britain to China?_____   **A** 1788

In which year did the Berlin Wall fall?_____   **B** 1948

U.S. Independence Day celebrates the Declaration of Independence adopted on July 4 of which year?_____   **C** 1946

In which year was the Dutch right-wing politician Pim Fortuyn assassinated?_____   **D** 1989

In which decade of the 19th century was Singapore founded?_____   **E** 1997

In which year did India achieve independence?_____   **F** 1991

When did Japan's emperor lose the status of god?_____   **G** 1947

In which year was Israel declared an independent state?_____   **H** 1810s

Australia Day commemorates the arrival of the British First Fleet in what year?_____   **I** 2002

In which year did the government repeal apartheid laws in South Africa?_____   **J** 1776

Famous Firsts

Can you finish this round first? Get ready, get set, go!

1 In which country was the motorcar invented?
a. Germany
b. United States
c. Italy
d. France

2 Which country played host to the first modern Olympic Games in 1896?
a. Greece
b. Switzerland
c. Spain
d. Great Britain

3 What notable achievement did Sir Edmund Hillary make in 1953?
a. The first person to reach the South Pole
b. The first person to reach the summit of Mount Everest
c. The first person to swim the English Channel
d. The first person to circumnavigate the globe in a row boat

4 What breakfast food was served at the Battle Creek Sanatorium, Michigan, in 1894?
a. Tang
b. Biscuits and gravy
c. Cornflakes
d. Bacon and eggs

5 Who was the first monarch to live at Buckingham Palace?
a. Queen Victoria
b. William IV
c. George II
d. Queen Elizabeth, the Queen Mother

6 What ancient building project is alleged to have killed a million construction workers?
a. The Suez Canal
b. The Great Wall of China
c. The Sphinx
d. The Pyramids of Giza

7 In which country did women gain the right to vote in 1893?
a. New Zealand
b. Austria
c. France
d. United States

8 Which game, according to legend, came into being when William Webb Ellis picked up the ball and ran with it in 1823?
a. Rugby
b. American football
c. Table tennis
d. Squash

9 Who packed off his first tourists to Paris in 1961, starting a holiday revolution?
a. Anthony Eden
b. Thomas Cook
c. Harold Macmillan
d. John Cheever

10 What was the nickname of Ivan, the first czar?
a. "The Terrible"
b. "The Beneficent"
c. "The Garlic Eater"
d. "The Decrepit"

Long Live the Queen

Can you name the year when the Victorian era officially came to an end?

Monumental Task

These monuments were built for the moment, but made to last forever.

1 In which country is Yad Vashem, a memorial to the six million Jews killed during the Holocaust?

2 Which arch in Paris bears the names of 386 of Napoleon's generals?

3 Who is commemorated by the statue at the top of the column in London's Trafalgar Square?

4 In which country do the Colossi of Memnon stand as reminders of the pharaohs?

5 In which American city is the Lincoln Memorial?

6 Which mountain in the United States is carved with 59-foot high likenesses of Washington, Jefferson, Lincoln, and Roosevelt?

7 In which country was a monument to Lord Nelson destroyed by a bomb in 1966?

8 In which Australian city is the Tomb of the Unknown Soldier located?

9 The Menin Gate, where Belgian firefighters sound the *"Last Post"* every night, is a monument to the fallen of which war?

10 What incendiary event does the Monument, in London, commemorate?

Russian Roulette

Take a spin through this set of brainteasers about Russia.

1 To which Scandinavian raiders did Rurik, the legendary name provider of Russia, belong?

2 In 1773, which Russian ruler crushed a revolt led by Pugachev?

3 Who was the last leader of the USSR?

4 Which 16th-century czar of Russia married five wives in nine years and killed his oldest son?

5 What was the family name of Michael, first of his line, who became czar of Russia in 1613?

6 How many states were formed on the breakup of the USSR in 1991?

7 During which 19th-century war did Russian troops fire on the British?

8 Which Russian ruler became czar in 1598 and later had an opera by Mussogorsky written about him?

9 Which Russian city was renamed Petrograd in 1914 and Leningrad in 1924?

10 Which Soviet leader got so angry he banged his shoe on the desk while addressing the United Nations?

Europe

The New World (North and South America) owes much of its exploration and development to Europeans. Time marches on, but let's check on how things have been going "back home."

Vive la France

Can you answer these brain teasers about this lovely country?

1 Which French heroine was burned at the stake in Rouen?

2 What is the common name of the oldest university in France?

3 Which Parisian nightclub became famous for its cancan?

4 In which building is the famed Hall of Mirrors?

5 Which singer was "Lost in France" in 1976?

6 Who captained France to victory in the 1998 soccer World Cup?

7 Which city provided "the French connection" in the film of the same name?

8 What name is given to the national flag of France?

9 During the Second World War, Marshal Philippe Pétain ruled over unoccupied France. By what name was his regime known?

10 Which mountain range separates France from Spain?

When in Rome

Well, if you're *really* in Rome you'll have no trouble with these.

1 What kind of racing vehicles wheeled around the Circus Maximus in Rome?

2 What was the Roman name for ordinary working people?

3 Which town was buried by a volcanic eruption in AD 72?

4 To what new religion did Emperor Constantine subscribe in AD 312?

5 What was the main battle unit of the Roman army called?

6 In a Roman city, what was the basilica?

7 Who was the king of the Roman gods?

8 What kind of weapon was a ballista?

9 For what purpose did the Romans install a hypocaust in their houses?

10 The Pantheon in Rome was a unique building in its time. What shape was it?

French 202

If you mastered the first set of questions about this country, you should score well here, too! So here's an even deeper exploration of Western Europe's largest country.

1 What type of building did the Musée d'Orsay in Paris used to be?

2 Which great event in French history did Robespierre and Danton help bring about?

3 What is the name of the French national anthem?

4 What rank in the church did the 17th-century French leaders Richelieu and Mazarin each hold?

5 Which symbol of France later became the badge of the Scouts?

6 Which French city is the seat of the Council of Europe and the European Parliament?

7 Which French town was the last English possession in France?

8 What was the Maginot Line?

9 Which engineering project, first suggested in the 19th century, was dismissed because Britain feared an underground invasion from France?

10 In which senior position did Edith Cresson break a male monopoly in 1991?

It's Not Easy Being Green

Test your knowledge of Irish history with this set of brainteasers.

1 Which famous saint is supposed to have sent the snakes packing from Ireland?

2 The Parachute Regiment shooting of 13 people, in Derry in 1972, is known as what?

3 Name the Irish socialist who was executed by the British as he was sitting in a chair, suffering from battle wounds.

4 Who was the first woman to be elected president of the Irish Republic, in 1990?

5 Which little people were first mentioned in a 14th-century retelling of an old story?

6 Which 17th-century English leader laid waste to Ireland with his parliamentary army?

7 Which battle, fought on July 1, 1690, is still a cause of contention today?

8 Name the IRA hunger-striker who was elected MP for Fermanagh-South Tyrone in 1981.

9 Which university, founded in Dublin in 1592, is Ireland's oldest?

10 Who was the first Irish prime minister to be known officially as the Taoiseach, in 1937?

Let's Have a Party!

Can you name the item of traditional Greek "clothing" that spawned a kind of fraternity party far and wide in 1960s America?

It's All Greek to Me!

Do you know the answers to these questions about the founders of modern society?

1 Which ancient people were famous for training children for outdoor life from an early age?
a. Spartans
b. Oracles
c. Philosophers
d. Rabbis

2 Which king died a hero's death fighting the Persians at Thermopylae?
a. Theseus
b. Leonidas
c. Aegeus
d. Thor

3 Which Greek teacher lectured at the Academy in Athens?
a. Plato
b. Diogenes
c. Peisistratos
d. Socrates

4 What kind of architectural features did Greek builders design that are known as Doric, Ionian, or Corinthian?
a. Columns
b. Stairways
c. Friezes
d. Banisters

5 Who in ancient Greece would have carried a sarissa?
a. A foot soldier
b. A doctor
c. A teacher
d. A maid

6 In which city did Pericles hold the floor as leader?
a. Thebes
b. Corinth
c. Athens
d. Troy

7 Which author is known as both the father of history and the father of lies?
a. Herodotus
b. Xenophon
c. Siculus
d. Plato

8 Which Athenian general wrote the first definitive account of the Peloponnesian War?
a. Euclid
b. Alcibiades
c. Thucydides
d. Moses

9 Where was the most famous oracle in all of Greece?
a. Delphi
b. Dodonna
c. Athens
d. Peter the Great

10 Which Greek philosopher, accused of impiety, drank poison and killed himself?
a. Socrates
b. Pythagoras
c. Hippo
d. Epictitus

Asia

It's been several centuries since the Venetian named Marco Polo regaled us with tales of the riches and wonders to be found in the Far East. It's about time for an update, don't you think?

The World's Largest Continent

Yup, we have a lot of ground to cover, so fasten your rickshaw belts!

1 "Uncle Ho" was the revolutionary leader of which country?

2 Which Asian country fought against the Allies during the Second World War?

3 Who was the leader of Cambodia's Khmer Rouge, famous for its "killing fields"?

4 In which country did the Tamil Tigers start a guerrilla war in 1983?

5 In which country did the Cultural Revolution take place?

6 Which country was called Siam for most of its history?

7 In 1947, British India was divided into two countries, India and...?

8 Which militant religious group took over Afghanistan in 1996?

9 Which country was once led by shahs and is now led by ayatollahs?

The Land of the Rising Sun

How much do you know about Asia's island dynamo, Japan? Let's find out!

1 Which title was Yoritomo the first to assume in Japan in 1192?

2 Who was Jimmu Tenno?

3 In the 1500s, which European country's traders were allowed into Nagasaki but no further?

4 What religious sect released nerve gas into the Tokyo subway in March 1995?

5 Whose arrival in 1853 startled the Japanese, who had never seen such ships before?

6 Which emperor gave his name to the period of westernization that began in 1868?

7 Which fleet did the Japanese defeat at Tsushima in 1905?

8 Which neighboring Asian state did the Japanese conquer in 1931 and rename Manchukuo?

9 What natural disaster devastated Tokyo-Yokohama in 1923?

10 Which emperor succeeded Hirohito in 1989?

War in the Pacific

Try out this battle-worthy round about the fighting in the Eastern Hemisphere.

1 Which naval battle in 1942 was a turning point of the war in the Pacific?
a. Battle of Midway
b. Dolittle Raid
c. Siege of Singapore
d. Battle of the Somme

2 In what month of 1942 did Singapore fall?
a. June
b. February
c. December
d. November

3 Which important naval battle did the Allies win in May 1942?
a. Battle of Adak Island
b. Battle of Santa Cruz
c. Battle of the Coral Sea
d. Battle of Ikobee Bridge

4 What airborne weapons did the Japanese send to attack the United States in November 1944?
a. Bomb-carrying balloons
b. Pigeons with homing devices
c. One-person gliders
d. Helicopters

5 What American general declared at Melbourne in 1942: "I shall return"?
a. General Douglas MacArthur
b. General George Marshall
c. General George Patton
d. Vice General Stewart Fairbaugh

6 Which naval battle of October 1944 opened the way for the U.S. recapture of the Philippines?
a. Guadalcanal
b. Java Sea
c. Leyte Gulf
d. The Battle of the Marne

7 Where was there a mass breakout of Japanese prisoners in Australia in 1944?
a. Cowra, New South Wales
b. Port Macquarie, New South Wales
c. Canberra, New South Wales
d. Melbourne, New South Wales

8 Which Japanese island was taken by the Americans in June 1945 after 83 days of fighting?
a. Biak
b. Okinawa
c. Guam
d. Hokkaido

9 Which U.S. cruiser was sunk in the Philippines, its last mission having been to carry materials for the atomic bomb to the U.S. base at Guam?
a. USS *Indianapolis*
b. USS *Northampton*
c. USS *Quincy*
d. USS *Yorktown*

10 In which month in 1945 was an atom bomb dropped on Hiroshima?
a. January
b. August
c. December
d. June

A Strangely Delicious Fact

What favorite starchy dinner item was born in ancient Asia and now is most famously paired with meatballs?

Africa

Archaeologists tell us Africa is where all human civilization began. This round will check in with the motherland. We'll go right to the original source!

Out of Africa

Can you answer these questions about Africa during the last century?

1 The Oscar-winning film *Out of Africa* tells the story of which woman?

2 Which is the largest country in Africa?

3 In which country is Timbuktu?

4 Who wrote the novel *The African Queen*?

5 Which American pop group had a hit with a song titled "Africa" in 1983?

6 Which African country was invaded by Italy on October 3, 1935?

7 On which African island was Freddy Mercury born?

8 Name the most highly populated city in Africa?

9 In 1992, Abuja replaced Lagos as the capital of which country?

10 Which southern African country, beginning with B, was known as Bechuanaland before gaining independence from Britain in 1966?

Even *More* About Africa

If you passed the last test, you'll probably do great on this one, too!

1 Which country had Hastings Banda as its "president for life" until 1994?

2 Which capital's name translates as "elephant's trunk"?

3 In which country did Letsie III become king twice—first in 1990 and again in 1996?

4 Who led a coup that deposed Milton Obote in 1971?

5 In which ocean are the Cape Verdi Islands?

6 Which nation was the target of a planned coup, allegedly supported by Mark Thatcher?

7 In which African country is the mountainous region of Drakensberg?

8 How many African countries have Mediterranean shorelines?

9 Which country is sandwiched between Benin and Ghana?

African Matchup

Test your brain with these puzzlers about the continent's long and varied history. Choose answers from the list below.

What name did Nyasaland assume on gaining independence from Britain in 1964?_____   **A** Algeria

What name did the Gold Coast adopt on becoming independent in 1957?_____   **B** Ghana

Which ancient African kingdom, located south of Egypt, had its capital at Meroë?_____   **C** Kush

Which kingdom in West Africa became famous for its bronze casting, many pieces surviving from the 15th and 16th centuries?_____   **D** Zanzibar

In which country was the Sharpeville Massacre?_____   **E** Benin

Of which country did former schoolteacher Kenneth Kaunda become president in 1964?_____   **F** South Africa

Which European country seized colonies in Africa in the 19th century because it wanted "a place in the sun"?_____   **G** Zambia

Which state, founded in 1822, became known for registering oil tankers?_____   **H** Malawi

In which African country did the FLN fight the French for independence, achieved in 1962?_____   **I** Liberia

Which island joined mainland Tanganyika to form the independent state of Tanzania?_____   **J** Germany

From the African Plains

Africa is home to dozens of animals that roam the plains. Can you name 10 of them?

Way Down Under

The term *down under* is rarely used in the lands that qualify as down under (Australia and New Zealand). That stands to reason: From their point of view, a significant part of the developed world is *up north*.

Australian Prime Ministers

How well do you know Australian leaders?

1 Who was the first Australian prime minister?
a. Kevin Rudd
b. Edmund Barton
c. Malcolm Frazer

2 Which prime minister was known as "the little digger"?
a. William Morris Hughes
b. Frank Forde
c. Alfred Deakin

3 Who was the Australian prime minister at the outset of the Great Depression in 1930?
a. Woodrow Wilson
b. Rod Laver
c. James Henry Scullin

4 Which World War II prime minister died in office?
a. John Curtin
b. Harold Holt
c. Earle Page

5 What was the party of Robert Menzies when elected prime minister in 1949?
a. United Australia Party
b. Labor Party
c. Free Trade Party

6 Near which Victorian beach did Harold Holt disappear in 1967?
a. Bells Beach
b. Portsea
c. Cape Bridgewater

7 Which prime minister voted himself out of office?
a. John Grey Gorton
b. Ben Chifley
c. Paul Hogan

8 Who led the Australian Labor Party to success in 1972 with the slogan "It's time."
a. James Scullin
b. Orson Welles
c. Gough Whitlam

9 What are the middle names of Robert J. L. Hawke?
a. James Lee
b. Jacob Lacey
c. Jerome Lance

10 Which prime minister managed a rock-and-roll band in his youth?
a. Arthur Fadden
b. Paul Keating
c. Johnny O'Keefe

Aboriginal Australia

Let's start with some questions about the continent's indigenous peoples.

Which Aboriginal Australian was taken to England with Captain Arthur Phillip in 1792?_____	**A** 1970s
In what decade was the Myall Creek Massacre?_____	**B** 1830s
At what mission was painter Albert Namatjira born?_____	**C** Eddie Mabo
Who led the 1963 Aboriginal Freedom Rides?_____	**D** Neville Bonner
Which Aboriginal pastor later became a state governor?_____	**E** Canberra
Who was the first Aboriginal politician to be elected to the Federal Parliament, in 1971?_____	**F** Hermanns-burg
Where was an Aboriginal "tent embassy" set up in 1972?_____	**G** Bennelong
In what decade was the Aboriginal flag first flown?_____	**H** Charles Perkins
Who initiated the action that led to the 1992 High Court decision on native title?_____	**I** Sir Doug Nicholls

Australian Affairs

Put your thinking cap on, mate, and stretch your noggin with this quiz!

1 Which New Zealand prime minister died on board a ship returning from Australia in 1906?

2 What is the name of the defense treaty signed by Australia, New Zealand, and the United States in 1951?

3 In which year did Papua New Guinea gain full independence from Australia?

4 In what year did New Zealand formally become independent?

5 From 1839 to 1841, New Zealand was part of which Australian colony?

6 Name the first governor of New South Wales.

7 In which year did French agents blow up the Greenpeace vessel *Rainbow Warrior*?

8 Who became the first premier of New Zealand in 1856?

9 The writings of which theorist of "systematic colonization" shaped settlements in Adelaide, South Australia, and Canterbury, New Zealand?

10 In which year did Australia and New Zealand agree to send troops to Vietnam?

It's in the Bag!

Animals that carry their young in a pouch are called marsupials and are a frequent sighting in Australia. Can you name three that you might see if you were strolling through the Outback?

NZ PMs

Think you know New Zealand's leaders? Here's your chance to prove it. Choose from the list below.

Who was the longest-serving prime minister?_____	**A** Sir Robert Muldoon
Which prime minister was born in Derry, Ireland?_____	**B** Sir Keith Holyoake
Who became New Zealand's first Labour prime minister in 1935?_____	**C** Michael Moore
Which prime minister later became governor-general?_____	**D** William Massey
Which prime minister was an engine driver with limited education?_____	**E** David Lange
Which prime minister had the nickname "Piggy"?_____	**F** Jennifer Shipley
Which prime minister's father was a fellow of the Royal College of Surgeons?_____	**G** Norman Kirk
Who was prime minister for just three months in 1990?_____	**H** Michael Savage
Who became New Zealand's first female prime minister in 1997?_____	**I** Richard Seddon

Australia Emerges

Do you know the answers to these questions about the birth of this nation?

1 Who is described as the "father" of the Australian Federation?
a. Kevin Rudd
b. James Cook
c. Sir Henry Parkes

2 Which country, other than Australia, was represented at the 1890 Federation Conference?
a. New Zealand
b. United States
c. Indonesia

3 Which was the last colony (later a state) to join the Federation?
a. Australian Capital Territory
b. New South Wales
c. Western Australia

4 Where in Sydney was the Federation constitution proclaimed on January 1, 1902?
a. The Opera House
b. Centennial Park
c. The Harbor Bridge

5 Who was Australia's first governor-general?
a. Lord Hopetoun
b. Lord Tennyson
c. Michael Jeffrey

6 How many points does the Federation star have?
a. Seven
b. Eight
c. Five

7 Where did the Commonwealth Parliament first sit?
a. Sydney
b. Melbourne
c. Brisbane

8 In what year did the Commonwealth Parliament move to Canberra?
a. 1901
b. 1923
c. 1927

9 In which year was the Blue Ensign officially adopted as Australia's national flag?
a. 1923
b. 1945
c. 1953

Maori History

Now let's check in with New Zealand's native peoples.

1 What food plant did Maoris most value before European settlement?

2 Who is the Maori god of earthquakes?

3 In Maori mythology who fished up the land from the sea?

4 What was the European import initially rejected by the Maori and called *wai piro*, or "stinking water"?

5 What country did Chief Waikato visit in 1820?

6 What tribal elder was proclaimed the first Maori king in 1858?

7 The Treaty of Waitingi, signed in 1860, was a voluntary transfer of sovereign power from the Maori to whom?

8 In what year did a Maori rugby team first visit Australia?

9 In what decade was the Maori council established?

10 How many major tribal variants are there of the Maori language?

Fly Me

What cute and cuddly Australian animal was used in the famous Qantas commercials in the 1970s?

Heading South of the (U.S.) Border

Our neighbors to the south exert quite a cultural influence. Let's see how much you know about what's going in your own backyard.

Around South America

Test your knowledge of the southern Americas.

1 Which country was ruled by Bernardo O'Higgins in the early 19th century?

2 In 1999, parts of which South American country were devastated by mud landslides?

3 In which South American country is Dutch the official language?

4 Which capital city has a name meaning "I see the mountain"?

5 In which country was Che Guevara born?

6 In which city is the Maracana soccer stadium?

7 In which country is the Itaipu Dam?

8 Which Peruvian lake is the world's highest?

9 What is the main currency unit of Ecuador?

10 Which South American country is the supposed site of El Dorado, the lost city of gold?

Getting to Know the Ancient Mexicans

Try this round of questions about early native culture.

1 The Mexica, the Acolhua, and the Pepaneca tribes are known by what broader term?

2 Despite their tribal differences, what trait did the Aztec people share?

3 Where in the modern world would you find the ruins of the ancient Aztec city Tenochtitlan, built on an island in Lake Texcoco?

4 Spaniards such as Hernán Cortés, Bernal D'az del Costillo, and Francisco Pizarro were known collectively as what?

5 Beyond military advantages, what natural factor played a substantial role in the Spanish conquest of native American populations?

6 The 16th-century Laws of Burgos forbade the Spanish mistreatment of native Americans and encouraged what?

7 What two now-common domestic animals were unfamiliar to American natives when the Spanish invaders introduced them?

8 Who was the Aztec ruler in power at the time of the Spanish conquest?

Test Yourself with These Great Mexican Mind Benders

Here are some true-false questions about the United States' neighbor to the south.

1 With 109 million people, Mexico is the world's most populous Spanish-speaking country. TRUE ○ FALSE ○

2 Mexico's closest neighbors to the southeast are Honduras and El Salvador. TRUE ○ FALSE ○

3 Just prior to the Summer Olympics in 1968, 200 to 300 student demonstrators in Mexico City were slain by the military and other armed men. TRUE ○ FALSE ○

4 Mexico had a long succession of emperors in the 19th century. TRUE ○ FALSE ○

5 Mexico is one of the world's largest oil producers. TRUE ○ FALSE ○

6 About 30 percent of Mexicans are Indian. TRUE ○ FALSE ○

7 At least half of the Mexican population is Protestant. TRUE ○ FALSE ○

8 Mexico's people live primarily in rural areas and are largely dependent upon agriculture. TRUE ○ FALSE ○

Scattered Points South

These points are down Mexico way—and way beyond. Choose answers from the list below.

Which South American soldier-statesman became known as "the liberator" and has a country named after him?_____   **A** The Incas

Which people did Tupac Amaru lead in a revolt against their Spanish rulers in 1780?_____   **B** United States

On which island did Toussaint L'Ouverture try to imitate the French Revolution and create a new order among slaves?_____   **C** Brazil

Which country ruled Havana in 1899?_____   **D** Spain

In which modern country did the Chavin culture flourish some 2,500 years ago?_____   **E** Simon Bólivar

Which Caribbean island did England take from Spain in 1655 to create a buccaneers' haven?_____   **F** Chile

Which two countries agreed to share the New World between them in 1494?_____   **G** Nicaragua

Which country defeated Peru and Bolivia in the 1879 War of the Pacific?_____   **H** Peru

In which country did President Vargas take power in 1930?_____   **I** Portugal

Where was Somoza removed by the Sandinistas in 1979?_____   **J** Jamaica

   K Haiti

Government

Rulers, borders, forms of government, revolutions, and changes in leadership—we'll touch on all of that as we explore our knowledge of how we organize and govern ourselves.

Heads of State

Kings, presidents, and other rulers, far and wide...think you know all about them? Let's see!

1 Which country has the world's only Hindu monarchy?
a. Nepal
b. India
c. Indonesia

2 In which country was its former king elected prime minister in 2001?
a. Japan
b. Thailand
c. Bulgaria

3 Which modern country, other than Brunei, is ruled by a sultan?
a. Malaysia
b. Oman
c. Chad

4 Which nation reinstated its monarchy in 1975?
a. Japan
b. England
c. Spain

5 Which monarch is head of state in more countries than any other?
a. Queen Elizabeth II
b. The emperor of Japan
c. The standing president of the United Arab Emirates

6 In which country did a former ballet dancer succeed his father as king in 2004?
a. Thailand
b. Cambodia
c. Uzbekistan

7 Which country's head of state is traditionally elected by a Loya Jirga?
a. Afghanistan's
b. Iran's
c. Laos'

8 Who was the first president of the Republic of Colombia, which originally consisted of modern Colombia, Venezuela, Ecuador, and Panama?
a. Simón Bolivar
b. Francisco de Paula Santander
c. Domingo Caycedo

9 The Moro Naba is the king of the Mossi people, who mostly live in which African country?
a. Ghana
b. Burkina Faso
c. Niger

10 In which country did King Bhumibol ascend to the throne in 1946?
a. Thailand
b. New Zealand
c. Togo

Governing Bodies

How well versed are you in leadership issues? Take this test and find out!

1 In which ancient city did citizens practice ostracism, voting to expel politicians they disliked?
a. Athens
b. Rome
c. Carthage

2 Whose national parliament from 1906 to 1917 was known as the Duma?
a. Japan
b. Sweden
c. Russia

3 In which European country was there both a Long and a Rump parliament?
a. England
b. Portugal
c. Germany

4 Which country has Europe's oldest lawmaking body, dating from 930?
a. Iceland
b. Poland
c. Spain

5 Which Communist leader addressed the United Nations for over four hours in 1960?
a. Nikita Khrushchev of the Soviet Union
b. Mao Zedong of China
c. Fidel Castro of Cuba

6 Which two European nations have the longest continuous treaty of friendship, signed in 1373?
a. England and Portugal
b. England and Switzerland
c. Switzerland and Italy

Do You Have the Right?

Which European country granted women the right to vote in 1971?

7 Which Pacific kingdom claimed in 1976 to have the heaviest monarch at 463 pounds?
a. Tonga
b. Samoa
c. Fiji

8 Which country has the oldest still-functioning written constitution?
a. Greece
b. United States
c. Costa Rica

9 Which modern multinational executive body was headed by Jacques Delors until 1995?
a. Amnesty International
b. The European Commission
c. The United Nations

Taking a Royal Challenge

Here's a round of royal riddles—all about kings.

1 Who deposed the king of Libya in 1969?

2 What is the maiden name of Billie Jean King?

3 Kingston is the capital of which island?

4 Who acquired the nickname "the king of Hollywood"?

5 Who wrote the short story "The Man Who Would Be King"?

6 Which Shakespeare play features the ungrateful daughters Goneril and Regan?

7 Which blues guitarist called his instrument Lucille?

8 Which film earned Yul Brynner his only Oscar?

9 Who kidnapped Fay Wray?

10 Who was Britain's longest reigning king?

Titles and Entitlement

Royalty, lords, and ladies...can you answer these questions?

1 What is the favorite color of the pop star Prince?

2 What is the name given to the wife of a sultan?

3 Which Hollywood star known for his portrayal of Western characters was called "The Duke"?

4 Carrie Fisher played which royal character in the *Star Wars* films?

5 King Bhumibol, an accomplished musician, is the popular monarch of which Asian country?

6 In the British nobility, which is more senior—a viscount or a baron?

7 Which teenage Queen of the Nile became a character in a Shakespeare play?

8 What British aristocrat disappeared after he allegedly murdered his family's nanny?

9 Who won his only best actor Oscar for his role in the film *The African Queen*?

10 What have you joined if you have taken the King's shilling?

Risings and Revolutions

Test your brain by taking this quiz about significant movements in history.

1 A popular uprising across Eastern Europe led to what momentous event in Berlin in 1989?

2 Whose regime did Fidel Castro topple in 1959?

3 Which gladiator led a rising against Rome?

4 Which flag was first flown in 1777 aboard a ship leaving Portsmouth, New Hampshire?

5 In which European city was a violent student protest held in 1968?

6 In which city did the Easter Rising break out in 1916?

7 Who led the Communist takeover of China in 1949?

8 Which emperor took power after the French Revolution?

9 Who led the Iranian revolution of 1979?

10 Who led the 1917 Communist Revolution in Russia?

States and Provinces

How much do you know about regions *within* nations?

1 What is the capital of the Darfur region of Sudan?

2 Ulundi is the capital of which South African province?

3 Which is the smallest Canadian province?

4 Which is Mexico's westernmost state?

5 Zachodniopomorskie (West Pomerania) is a province of which country?

6 Mainland France's easternmost town, Lauterbourg, lies in which region?

7 Which Central American nation has a region called Petén?

8 What is the capital of British Columbia?

9 Kosovo is a province of which country?

10 Stuttgart is the capital of which German *land* (state)?

Getting the Vote

Check out these examples of people power through the ages. Do you have the power to answer these questions?

1 Which U.S. state kept American people guessing during the 2000 presidential election?
a. Florida
b. Minnesota
c. New Hampshire

2 Which country elected its first president on April 14, 2002?
a. Vietnam
b. Indonesia
c. East Timor

3 In 1988, who became the first woman to head an elected government in an Islamic state?
a. Shajarat ad-Durr, in Egypt
b. Khalida Zia, in Bangladesh
c. Benazir Bhutto, in Pakistan

4 Where did a bishop named Abel Muzorewa become his country's first black prime minister after an election in 1979?
a. New Zealand
b. South Africa
c. Rhodesia

5 Who was elected president of Haiti after the fall of dictator Jean-Claude Duvalier in 1990?
a. Jean-Bertrand Aristide
b. Rene Preval
c. Juan Bosch

6 Who campaigned for a "new deal" in the 1932 American election?
a. Franklin D. Roosevelt
b. Harry Truman
c. Woodrow Wilson

7 Who defeated George McGovern in a 1972 landslide victory to become U.S. president?
a. Jimmy Carter
b. Richard M. Nixon
c. Gerald Ford

8 Which Canadian prime minister won the long struggle for a Canadian native constitution?
a. Pierre Trudeau
b. Joe Clark
c. Brian Mulroney

9 In which country are the world's biggest democratic elections held?
a. India
b. United States
c. China

10 In which country did Corazon Aquino win the leadership in 1986?
a. Indonesia
b. The Philippines
c. India

Geography

There's no mountain high enough, no river wide enough to keep us from exploring our big wide planet and all of its beautiful geographical features.

Water, Water, Everywhere

Take this quiz, and go with the flow.

1 Which is the world's busiest ship canal?

2 Which literary villain disappeared over the Reichenbach Falls?

3 What is a tsunami?

4 What is the name of the waterfront sector of Shanghai where foreigners were once confined and banks built?

5 In which country is the River Kwai?

6 Which singer had a worldwide hit with "Orinoco Flow"?

7 Which is the world's least salty sea?

8 Which song by a famous duo starts with the line: "When you're weary, feeling small"?

9 Which is the longest river in Asia?

10 Of all the rivers in the world, which contains the greatest amount of water?

Peak Achievements

Climb every mountain or hill or gentle slope.

1 Which fictional character fell asleep in the Catskill Mountains for 20 years?

2 What is the highest mountain in North America?

3 Which peak is nicknamed "The Meanest Mountain on Earth"?

4 What was the only tune that "Tom, Tom, the Piper's Son" could play?

5 Which 1993 film sees Sylvester Stallone battling in the mountains against John Lithgow?

6 From which mountain did Moses descend with the Ten Commandments?

7 What is the highest point on Antarctica?

8 Near which city did Julie Andrews sing "The hills are alive with the sound of music"?

9 In which country are the Taurus Mountains?

10 According to Laurel and Hardy, where is the trail of the lonesome pine?

Pick the Biggest

Out of each list, from continents to counties, which is the largest?

1 Continents
- a. Africa
- b. Asia
- c. Australia
- d. Europe

2 Islands
- a. Sardinia
- b. Ibiza
- c. Minorca
- d. Corfu

3 World oceans
- a. Arctic Ocean
- b. Indian Ocean
- c. Pacific Ocean
- d. Atlantic Ocean

4 Former Soviet states
- a. Belarus
- b. Turkmenistan
- c. Ukraine
- d. Uzbekistan

5 African countries
- a. Nigeria
- b. Lesotho
- c. Rawanda
- d. Burundi

6 Cities
- a. London
- b. New York
- c. Paris
- d. Tokyo

7 Lakes
- a. Lake Toba
- b. Lake Garda
- c. Lake Windermere
- d. Lake Victoria

8 Eastern Europe
- a. Estonia
- b. Lithuania
- c. Latvia
- d. Poland

9 English counties
- a. Cumbria
- b. County Durham
- c. Lancashire
- d. Northumberland

Islands on the Screen

No man is an island, but all of these questions relate to one.

1 Who played Long John Silver in the 1950 film *Treasure Island*?

2 John Mills played the patriarch of which ship-wrecked family in a 1960 film?

3 Which 1963 film, based on a novel by William Golding, told the story of a group of school-boys stranded on a desert island?

4 In *Jason and the Argonauts*, to which island did Jason sail in his quest for the Golden Fleece?

5 In which TV series did Ricardo Montalban play the owner of an island where visitors paid $10,000 to make their dreams come true?

6 On which island are the film and the novel *Catch 22* set?

7 On which island was the actor Errol Flynn born?

8 The film *The Island of Dr. Moreau* was based on whose novel?

9 On which island is the film *Zorba the Greek* set?

10 Which Oscar-winning actor was born on Sakhalin Island?

Snowcapped and Steep

What mountain range stretches from China and Tibet into India?

Bodies of Water

Here are some great questions about lakes and lake people—let's dive right in!

1 According to legend, what did the Lady in the Lake give to King Arthur?

2 Which 1995 film about a monster, starring Ted Danson, was set in Scotland?

3 Which African lake was named after a British queen?

4 Which Hollywood actress was known for her distinctive hairstyle, which swept across one eye?

5 Which is the world's largest lake by surface area?

6 Which biblical sea is also known as Lake Tiberias?

7 Which family group had a 1968 hit with the song "Indian Lake"?

8 Toronto stands on which lake?

9 What event was held at Lake Placid in 1980?

10 What giant animal terrorized Bill Pullman and Bridget Fonda in the film *Lake Placid*?

I'm from Longuyland

Long Island is actually not an island at all. What is it?

Compass Points

How well do you know the map of the world? Let's find out!

1 Which is farther north: Kenya or Mali?

2 Which is closer to the Equator: Colombia or Uruguay?

3 What is the easternmost country on the African mainland: Mozambique or Somalia?

4 Which is farther east: Puerto Rico or Cuba?

5 Does Tonga lie north or south of the Equator?

6 Which is farther west: Zambia or Cameroon?

7 What is the world's most southerly continent?

8 Which is farther east: Iraq or Iran?

9 Does Egypt span the Tropic of Cancer or the Tropic of Capricorn?

10 What is Arabia's most southerly country?

Going with the Flow

How much do you know about the world's rivers? Answer true or false.

1 The Nile is the longest river in the world.   TRUE ○   FALSE ○

2 Rome stands by the Tiber River.   TRUE ○   FALSE ○

3 The Lena River flows through Finland.   TRUE ○   FALSE ○

4 The Loire is the longest river in France.   TRUE ○   FALSE ○

5 The Danube flows from Germany to the Black Sea.   TRUE ○   FALSE ○

6 The Mississippi River is longer than its tributary, the Missouri.   TRUE ○   FALSE ○

7 Baghdad is situated on the Tigris River.   TRUE ○   FALSE ○

8 The Rhine derives its name from the Celtic word *renos*, meaning "raging flow."   TRUE ○   FALSE ○

9 Africa's River Congo is also known as the Zaire.   TRUE ○   FALSE ○

10 The Yellow River is the world's second-longest river.   TRUE ○   FALSE ○

Informative Island Issues

Take this quiz all about places surrounded by water.

1 Rhodes is the largest of which group of Greek islands?

2 Which film told the story of the incarceration of Henri Charrière on Devil's Island?

3 Which British entrepreneur owns Neckar Island?

4 Fort de France is the capital of which island?

5 Name the singer who had a 1957 hit with "In the Middle of an Island."

6 Which popular island and holiday destination derives its name from the Portuguese for "bearded"?

7 Who wrote the novel *Coral Island*?

8 In October 1983, General Hudson Austin led forces to take control of which island?

9 Who founded Island Records?

10 Which song ends with the line, "and an island never cries"?

11 Which island, situated in the Pacific Ocean, is noted for its pines and penal history?

12 What Channel Island has the same name as a breed of cow?

13 The capital of what Indian Ocean island group is Male?

14 What Alaskan island gave its name to a sub-species of brown bear?

15 Both Paul Gauguin and Jacques Brel lived and worked on what island group in French Polynesia?

16 Where was singer Bjork born?

17 What South Pacific island is the site of giant, mysterious statues?

18 What huge island off the African coast is noted for its baobab trees?

19 What Mediterranean island is split into Greek and Turkish zones?

The Glory of Cultures

Culture...it's a broad term for all of the subtle ways we define ourselves as people: language, families, music, buildings, and belief systems, for instance. How about nicknames and secret societies? Sure, we've got that covered, too.

Lost Worlds

Here's a quick little quiz on famous ancient ruins and sites.

1 In which country is Machu Picchu?
a. Brazil
b. Peru
c. Mexico

2 On which island are the ruins of Borobudur?
a. Java
b. Easter Island
c. New Zealand (North Island)

3 In which modern country are the ruins of Troy?
a. Italy
b. Turkey
c. Egypt

4 In which country is Chichén Itzá?
a. Mexico
b. Bolivia
c. Ecuador

5 The ruins of Carthage stand near which Mediterranean capital?
a. Tunis
b. Rabat
c. Cairo

6 In which Southeast Asian country is Angkor Wat?
a. Vietnam
b. Cambodia
c. Thailand

7 Which city contains the ruins of the Parthenon?
a. Athens
b. Rome
c. Cairo

8 In which country is Antakya, once called Antioch?
a. Egypt
b. Turkey
c. United States

9 The ancient city of Tikal is in which modern country?
a. Guatemala
b. Rhodesia
c. Cambodia

10 Which island was known to the Romans as Hibernia?
a. Crete
b. England
c. Ireland

Around the World

A Tribal Gathering

From the four possibilities provided, pick the correct answer about world tribes.

1 In which country do the Yanomami people mostly live?
a. Scotland
b. Luxembourg
c. Denmark
d. Brazil

2 What country do the majority of Maoris call home?
a. Canada
b. South Africa
c. New Zealand
d. China

3 On which continent do the pygmy people live?
a. Africa
b. Asia
c. South America
d. Australia

4 Which of these groups campaigns for tribal peoples' rights?
a. Amnesty International
b. Survival
c. Médicins Sans Frontières
d. Friends of the Earth

5 Which river delta is the homeland of the Ogoni people?
a. Mekong Delta
b. Denube Delta
c. Niger Delta
d. Mississippi Delta

6 The Ogiek live in the Mau Forest of which country?
a. Kenya
b. Libya
c. Yemen
d. Iran

7 Which desert is home to the Tuareg?
a. Gobi Desert
b. Namib Desert
c. Sahara Desert
d. Atacama Desert

8 In which part of Africa do most Hutus and Tutsis live?
a. Horn of Africa
b. Central Africa
c. Western Africa
d. Madagascar

9 The Himba live in Namibia and which other country?
a. Angola
b. Somalia
c. Mauritania
d. Gabon

10 Which country is home to the Mursi, Bodi, and Konso tribes?
a. Morocco
b. Ethiopia
c. Argentina
d. Vietnam

Tongues and Places

Match the place with the language spoken there, choosing answers from the list below.

Tel Aviv_____	**A** Arabic
Lisbon_____	**B** Bengali
Budapest_____	**C** Flemish/Dutch
Brussels_____	**D** Hebrew
Zagreb and Belgrade_____	**E** Hungarian
Beirut_____	**F** Kurdish
Bangladesh_____	**G** Latvian
Northern Iraq_____	**H** Nepali
Riga_____	**I** Portuguese
Kathmandu_____	**J** Serbo-Croatian

Secret Societies

Answer true or false—but shhh! It's a secret.

1 Mithras is the name of the Eastern god that Roman soldiers worshipped in secretive cult ceremonies.   TRUE ○   FALSE ○

2 The Freemasons, with their first Grand Lodge founded in 1717, are said to be the biggest worldwide secret society.   TRUE ○   FALSE ○

3 The notorious Thugs of India, ruthless bands that robbed and murdered travelers, were suppressed by the British in the mid-19th century.   TRUE ○   FALSE ○

4 The secret criminal society known as the Mafia, also called the Cosa Nostra, traces its roots to northern Italy.   TRUE ○   FALSE ○

5 Japan's major criminal organization is known as the Yakuza.   TRUE ○   FALSE ○

6 The Carbonari was a secretive band of restaurant workers who instigated riots in the 1800s.   TRUE ○   FALSE ○

7 The Ku Klux Klan was a white supremacist organization that spread terror through the American South following the abolition of slavery.   TRUE ○   FALSE ○

8 Organized Chinese crime gangs are called triads.   TRUE ○   FALSE ○

9 *Die Fledermaus*, a Johann Strauss operetta, deals with the beliefs and rituals of the Masons.   TRUE ○   FALSE ○

10 The Fenians, an Irish nationalist society, derived its name from legendary warriors led by Finn MacCumhail.   TRUE ○   FALSE ○

Color My World...

Here is a rainbow of colorful questions....

1 Musically speaking, what color is the Danube River?

2 What is the equivalent of the Red Cross in Muslim countries?

3 In which country is the Yellow River?

4 What color belt is worn by the highest grades in judo and karate?

5 Which country's flag has a large yellow star on a red background?

6 What medal is awarded to those wounded or killed by enemy action while serving in the U.S. military?

7 What color is associated with death in Islam?

8 What color of haze did Jimi Hendrix find himself in?

9 What is the name, which translates as "gold," of the Tokyo street reputed to have the most expensive real estate on earth?

10 Violet Elizabeth Bott appeared in which series of books written by Richmal Crompton?

They're Not All Egyptian...

Can you name two other ancient peoples who erected pyramids?

What's in a Nickname?

By what other names are these people and places known?

1 Which Middle Eastern city is nicknamed the "Pearl of the Desert"?

2 What was the real name of the murderer who was nicknamed the "Boston Strangler"?

3 Which composer was nicknamed the "March King"?

4 Which boxer was nicknamed the "Manassa Mauler"?

5 Which American president was nicknamed "Old Hickory"?

6 Which pop star is nicknamed the "Groover from Vancouver"?

7 Which singer and actress was nicknamed the "Professional Virgin"?

8 Which legendary sports star was nicknamed the "Sultan of Swat"?

9 Which British king was known as the "Wisest Fool in Christendom"?

The World Is a Colorful Place

Can you name 20 international cities, villages, countries, or states that feature a color in their name?

Exploration and Discovery

Thank goodness for those brave souls among us who are willing to leave the serenity of home to explore unknown lands and cultures. Let's take a deeper look at those risk takers who advance our knowledge of the world around us.

Journeys and Destinations

Remember, getting there is half the fun, so take this quiz and see how you do!

1 What title is shared by a James Mason film, a Jules Verne novel, and a Rick Wakeman album?

2 Who played Columbus in the film *1492: Conquest of Paradise*?

3 Alex Winter costarred alongside whom in the film *Bill and Ted's Bogus Journey*?

4 What was the name of the submarine in the 1960s TV series *Voyage to the Bottom of the Sea*?

5 Which actress won an Academy Award for her role in the film *A Passage to India*?

6 What was the title of the last "road" film costarring Bob Hope and Bing Crosby?

7 Which 1971 action film starred Gene Hackman and a stunning chase sequence?

8 Where was the 2001 film *The Shipping News* set and filmed?

9 In which South American country were Butch Cassidy and the Sundance Kid tracked down?

Discoveries

Test your knowledge of those "Eureka!" moments.

1 In which Asian country did people first make paper and use it for money?

2 Who explored the Land of Punt in reed boats?

3 Which Nordic sailors traveled in longships to Iceland, Greenland, England, and North America?

4 Which explorer is credited as the first to take tobacco and potatoes from the New World?

5 Whose mission was "to explore strange new worlds, to seek out new life and new civilizations"?

6 Who was the first European to visit both Australia and New Zealand?

7 European sailors had to sail around which African cape to reach the Indian Ocean?

8 In 1858, which great lake in Africa did the explorer John Hanning Speke name after Britain's queen?

9 Which newly discovered continent was named after an Italian explorer called Amerigo Vespucci?

10 Who was the first explorer to circumnavigate the globe, proving it was not flat?

Captain Cook

Here's a round of questions on the exploits of one of the world's great explorers. Answer true or false.

1 Captain James Cook was born in 1728 in England's Yorkshire County.   TRUE ○   FALSE ○

2 Cook took four voyages of discovery to the South Pacific.   TRUE ○   FALSE ○

3 Cook's vessel for the first voyage was called *Endeavor*.   TRUE ○   FALSE ○

4 Cook sailed to Vanuatu to observe the transit of the planet Venus.   TRUE ○   FALSE ○

5 In 1769 Cook first sighted the North Island of New Zealand.   TRUE ○   FALSE ○

6 Cook first sighted the Australian mainland off the coast of the modern-day state of Queensland.   TRUE ○   FALSE ○

7 In 1770, Cook explored a large inlet called Botany Bay on the east coast of Australia.   TRUE ○   FALSE ○

8 In 1773, Cook returned to New Zealand for a second time aboard the *Resolution*.   TRUE ○   FALSE ○

9 An astronomer named Joseph Banks sailed with Cook on his first voyage.   TRUE ○   FALSE ○

10 In 1779 Cook and four marines with him were killed in a confrontation with Hawaiian natives.   TRUE ○   FALSE ○

Ages of Discovery

The journeys and achievements of great explorers are sometimes a great mystery. See how many of these you can answer.

1 What feat was Ferdinand Magellan the first to achieve?

2 Which member of royalty was known as "The Navigator"?

3 Which European explorer spent time in the court of Kublai Khan?

4 Who discovered the sea route from Europe to India in 1498?

5 Who was the first Englishman to circumnavigate the globe?

6 Who was the first European to round the Cape of Good Hope, in 1488?

7 Which famous explorer and naturalist sailed the world on the *Beagle*?

8 Which father and son sailed from England to Newfoundland and Nova Scotia in 1497?

9 Who led the colonization of Virginia in the 1580s?

10 Who claimed the Philippines for Spain in 1521?

Who Sailed The Dove?

In the 1960s, a teenage boy set out from California on a small sailboat. What was his name, and where did he travel?

The Polar Regions

You can't get any farther north, and you can't get any farther south. A few rugged souls live year-round in the planet's polar regions—some of them scientists and some of them indigenous people. Let's find out more about them.

All Iced Up

All answers in this round start with "ice." Can you answer them?

1 What name is given to a glacial period when ice sheets covered much of the Earth?

2 Name a North Atlantic island whose hot springs and volcanoes provide geothermal energy.

3 A mass of ice attached to land but projecting into the sea is called what?

4 What name is given to a large chunk of floating ice that's hazardous to ships?

5 What name is given to a steep part of a glacier, resembling a frozen waterfall?

6 What name is given to the yellow-white glare in the sky caused by reflection from an ice field?

7 A vessel with a reinforced bow for cutting a channel through ice is called what?

8 What is a thick mass of ice permanently covering the polar regions?

9 What name is given to a buildup of ice on rivers that raises the water level, causing floods?

10 Ice crystals in polar skies that cause haloes and coronas are called what?

Arctic Living

Test your skill by answering these questions about the folks who live way up north.

1 As a group, the Yupik, the Inupiat, the Aleuts, and the Kalaallit are more popularly known as what?

2 The Saami, once called Lapps, are inhabitants of the tundra of northern Norway. Traditionally, they herd what kind of animal?

3 What is the significance of Nunavut?

4 Native people have been using snowshoes for how long?

5 The Siberian village of Oymyakon holds what distinction?

6 What country lays claim to the most northerly village?

7 What kind of craft crossed the Arctic Ocean beneath the ice cap in 1958?

8 What did Ann Bancroft achieve in 1986?

The Truth About Antarctica

Let's explore some cold, hard facts about our southernmost continent. Answer them true or false.

1 Antarctica accounts for more than 9 percent of the Earth's land surface.   TRUE ○   FALSE ○

2 Antarctica consists of two massive blocks of ancient rock, which are separated by a deep channel.   TRUE ○   FALSE ○

3 Seventy-five percent of Antarctica is covered by ice.   TRUE ○   FALSE ○

4 Antarctica has always been a subzero zone at the bottom of the planet.   TRUE ○   FALSE ○

5 It's too cold for active volcanoes in Antarctica.   TRUE ○   FALSE ○

6 Among the continents, Antarctica ranks fifth in size, behind Asia, North America, South America, and Africa.   TRUE ○   FALSE ○

7 Despite its cold temperatures, Antarctica is considered a desert because it gets little annual precipitation.   TRUE ○   FALSE ○

8 The ice covering Antarctica averages about a mile in thickness.   TRUE ○   FALSE ○

The Cold Facts About Antarctica

It's cold, barren, and fascinating. Do you know the answers to these questions?

1 Who are the only people who inhabit Antarctica?
a. Scientists and support staff
b. Scores of roving explorers on dogsleds
c. No one but Australian and South African adventurers

2 The Antarctic Treaty is also known as what?
a. The Paris Resolutions
b. The Madrid Protocol
c. The Geneva Conventions

3 How does the Antarctic Treaty protect the continent?
a. Bans nuclear power
b. Bans additional weather stations
c. Bans mining, protects plant and animal life, and regulates waste disposal

4 How many countries agreed to the Antarctic Treaty, and when did it become law?
a. About 40 nations have signed—became law in 1998
b. No countries have signed—still under negotiation
c. Twelve countries have signed, but it has not yet become law

5 Where is the coldest place on Earth?
a. Vostok Research Station, East Antarctica
b. Japan's Showa Station, East Ongul Island
c. Scott Base, Ross Island

6 Who was the first explorer to circumnavigate Antarctica?
a. Ferdinand Magellan
b. Richard Byrd
c. James Cook

7 Why did Ernest Shackleton have to abandon his 1914–15 expedition?
a. His famished crew ran out of food
b. Ice crushed his ship
c. They were lost

8 Australian geologist Douglas Mawson accomplished what in 1909?
a. Discovered gold in the mountains of Antarctica
b. Discovered the South Magnetic Pole
c. Traveled Antarctica's entire coastline by dogsled

PAGE 157

Far-flung Facts

1 Grand Duchy of Luxembourg
2 New Orleans
3 Vatican City
4 In Denmark, that country's largest island
5 Seven
6 Angel Falls, Venezuela
7 Patagonia (Chatwin wrote *In Patagonia*, and Theroux wrote *The Old Patagonian Express*.)
8 The Great Pyramid of Cheops (also known as the Great Pyramid of Khufu and the Great Pyramid of Giza)
9 Saigon (now Ho Chi Minh City)

Capital Punishment

1 Croatia
2 Chile
3 Colombia
4 Costa Rica
5 Republic of Chad
6 Canada
7 Cuba
8 Cypress
9 Cambodia
10 Cameroon

Can You Name It?

Ghana

PAGE 158

New National Identities

1 Sri Lanka
2 Zimbabwe
3 Tonga
4 Australia
5 Istanbul
6 Jakarta
7 Tokyo
8 Taiwan
9 Namibia
10 Darwin

Hit the Road

1 German
2 Recoleta Cemetery
3 Suriname
4 Jericho

5 Hawaii
6 Libya and Lebanon
7 Venice, Italy
8 Switzerland
9 Prince William Sound
10 Bangkok, Thailand

Going Globe-trotting

1 Key West
2 Romania
3 Mekong
4 Shekel
5 Land of Fire
6 Guangzhou
7 Prague
8 Hong Kong
9 Philippines
10 Austria

PAGE 159

End of Empire

1 United Kingdom
2 Macau
3 United States
4 Namibia
5 Goa
6 Vietnam, Cambodia, and Laos
7 Indonesia
8 Brunei
9 Cuba

Headlines of the Past

1 Paris
2 Giant pandas
3 Emperor Hirohito of Japan (also known as Emperor Shōwa)
4 *The Washington Post*
5 Jimmy Carter, taken ill while running
6 The Shah of Iran, Mohammed Reza Pahlavi
7 Patrick White
8 Pakistan
9 In space. Astronauts Deke Slayton (USA) and Alexei Leonov (USSR) were taking part in the first joint Soviet-American space mission.
10 Spiro Agnew

PAGE 160

The Year 2000

1 b. Slobodan Milosevic
2 a. Hanover
3 c. Failed U.S. presidential hopeful Al Gore
4 a. NATO, as supreme commander
5 c. The *Concorde*
6 a. Charles Schulz
7 c. A roller coaster
8 b. The space shuttle
9 a. Russia, which voted to restore the old Soviet anthem
10 b. Airbus Industries

Let's Hear It for the Parrot Heads!

Jimmy Buffett

PAGE 161

The Year 1900

1 True
2 False; Winston Churchill is the future leader who wrote *Savrola*—to relieve the tedium of his military life in India
3 True
4 True
5 False; that describes the Boxer Rebellion
6 False; the "cakewalk" was a dance fad in America
7 True
8 True
9 True
10 False; *The Deutchland* was an ocean liner that set speed records for crossing the Atlantic

It's a Date

1 1997
2 1989
3 1776
4 2002
5 1810s
6 1947
7 1946
8 1948
9 1788
10 1991

Answers

PAGE 162

Famous Firsts

1 a. Germany, in 1885
2 a. Greece
3 b. The first person to reach the summit of Mount Everest
4 c. Cornflakes
5 a. Queen Victoria
6 b. The Great Wall of China
7 a. New Zealand
8 a. Rugby—he was a student at Rugby School in England
9 b. Thomas Cook
10 a. "The Terrible"

Long Live the Queen

1901

PAGE 163

Monumental Task

1 Israel
2 The Arc de Triomphe
3 Admiral Nelson
4 Egypt
5 Washington, D.C.
6 Mount Rushmore in the Black Hills of South Dakota
7 Ireland
8 Canberra
9 World War I
10 The Great Fire of London, 1666

Russian Roulette

1 Vikings
2 Catherine the Great
3 Mikhail Gorbachev
4 Ivan the Terrible
5 Romanov
6 15
7 The Crimean War
8 Boris Godunov
9 St. Petersburg
10 Nikita Krushchev

PAGE 164

Vive la France

1 Joan of Arc
2 The Sorbonne, the common name for the University of Paris
3 The Moulin Rouge
4 The Palace of Versailles
5 Bonnie Tyler
6 Laurent Blanc
7 Marseilles
8 The Tricolour
9 Vichy France
10 The Pyrenees

When in Rome

1 Chariots
2 Plebeians (plebs)
3 Pompeii
4 Christianity—he was the first Christian emperor
5 A legion
6 The town hall
7 Jupiter, also known as Jove
8 A large catapult for throwing boulders
9 Central heating, using a fire to send warm air under floors and between walls
10 A dome, the largest in the Ancient World

PAGE 165

French 202

1 A railway station
2 The French Revolution
3 "The Marseillaise"
4 Cardinal
5 The fleur-de-lis
6 Strasbourg
7 Calais
8 A defense system that was designed, but failed, to keep out the Germans in 1940
9 The Channel Tunnel
10 As France's first female prime minister

It's Not Easy Being Green

1 Saint Patrick
2 Bloody Sunday
3 James Connolly
4 Mary Robinson
5 Leprechauns
6 Oliver Cromwell
7 The Battle of the Boyne
8 Bobby Sands
9 Trinity College
10 Eamon de Valera (the term came into use with the Constitution of 1937)

Let's Have a Party!

Toga

PAGE 166

It's All Greek to Me!

1 a. Spartans
2 b. Leonidas
3 a. Plato
4 a. Columns
5 a. A foot soldier—it was a very long spear
6 c. Athens
7 a. Herodotus
8 c. Thucydides
9 a. Delphi
10 a. Socrates

PAGE 167

The World's Largest Continent

1 Vietnam
2 Japan
3 Pol Pot
4 Sri Lanka
5 China
6 Thailand
7 Pakistan
8 The Taliban
9 Iran

The Land of the Rising Sun

1 Shogun (meaning "general")
2 The legendary first emperor of Japan (about 660 BC)
3 Holland's
4 Aum Shinrikyo (Supreme Truth) cult
5 The U.S. Navy, led by Commodore Matthew Perry
6 Meiji
7 The Russian fleet
8 Manchuria
9 An earthquake
10 Akihito

War in the Pacific

1 a. Battle of Midway
2 b. February
3 c. Battle of the Coral Sea
4 a. Bomb-carrying balloons
5 a. General Douglas MacArthur
6 c. Leyte Gulf
7 a. Cowra, New South Wales
8 b. Okinawa
9 a. USS *Indianapolis*
10 b. August

A Strangely Delicious Fact

Spaghetti

Out of Africa

1 Karen Blixen (her real name was Isak Dinesen), played in the film by Meryl Streep
2 Sudan
3 Mali
4 C. S. Forester
5 Toto
6 Abyssinia, which is now called Ethiopia
7 Zanzibar
8 Cairo, the capital of Egypt
9 Nigeria
10 Botswana

Even *More* About Africa

1 Malawi
2 Khartoum
3 Lesotho
4 Idi Amin
5 Atlantic Ocean
6 Equatorial Guinea
7 South Africa
8 Five
9 Togo

African Matchup

1 Malawi
2 Ghana
3 Kush
4 Benin
5 South Africa
6 Zambia
7 Germany
8 Liberia
9 Algeria
10 Zanzibar

Australian Prime Ministers

1 b. Edmund Barton
2 a. William Morris Hughes
3 c. James Henry Scullin
4 a. John Curtin
5 a. United Australia Party
6 b. Portsea
7 a. John Grey Gorton
8 c. Gough Whitlam
9 a. James Lee
10 b. Paul Keating

Aboriginal Australia

1 Bennelong, who served as a go-between for the British and indigenous cultures
2 1830s; 12 ex-convict settlers rounded up and killed 28 Aborigines
3 Hermannsburg (in 1902); Namatjira was known for his watercolor desert landscapes
4 Charles Perkins led the Freedom Rides, protesting discrimination in New South Wales
5 Sir Doug Nicholls
6 Neville Bonner
7 Canberra; activists promoted the rights of Aborigines on the lawn of the Old Parliament House
8 1970s
9 Eddie Mabo, a Torres Strait Islander, campaigned for the landmark decision that clarified native property rights

Australian Affairs

1 Richard Seddon, who fell ill and died suddenly aboard the ship *Oswestry Grange*, en route to New Zealand
2 The Australia, New Zealand, United States Security Treaty (or ANZUS Treaty)
3 1975
4 1947
5 New South Wales
6 Arthur Phillip
7 1985; a photographer drowned, and two agents pleaded guilty to manslaughter
8 Henry Sewell
9 Edward Gibbon Wakefield
10 1965

NZ PMs

1 Richard Seddon
2 William Massey
3 Michael Savage
4 Sir Keith Holyoake
5 Norman Kirk
6 Sir Robert Muldoon
7 David Lange
8 Michael Moore
9 Jennifer Shipley

Australia Emerges

1 c. Sir Henry Parkes
2 a. New Zealand
3 c. Western Australia
4 b. Centennial Park
5 a. Lord Hopetoun
6 a. Seven
7 b. Melbourne
8 c. 1927
9 c. 1953

Answers

Maori History

1 Kumara, or sweet potato
2 Rūaumoko
3 Maui, a demigod with magical powers
4 Alcohol
5 England
6 Potatau Te Wherowhero
7 The British Crown
8 1908
9 1960s
10 Seven

Fly Me

Koala

Around South America

1 Chile
2 Venezuela
3 Suriname
4 Montevideo
5 Argentina
6 Rio de Janeiro
7 Paraguay
8 Lake Titicaca
9 Sucre
10 Colombia

Getting to Know the Ancient Mexicans

1 Aztecs
2 Their language—Nahuatl
3 Mexico City
4 Conquistadors
5 Diseases that the Spanish brought with them, particularly smallpox
6 Converting natives to Catholicism
7 Horses and dogs
8 Montezuma, or Moctezuma

Test Yourself with These Great Mexican Mind Benders

1 True
2 False; Mexico shares borders with Belize and Guatemala to the southeast
3 True
4 False; crowned in 1822, Augstin de Iturbide was the one and only emperor of Mexico—and his reign lasted only eight months
5 True
6 True
7 False; 90 percent is Roman Catholic
8 False; 70 percent of Mexico's population lives in the country's cities

Scattered Points South

1 Simon Bolivar (Bolivia)
2 The Incas
3 Haiti
4 United States, after Spain's defeat in the war of 1898
5 Peru
6 Jamaica
7 Spain and Portugal
8 Chile
9 Brazil
10 Nicaragua

Heads of State

1 a. Nepal
2 c. Bulgaria
3 b. Oman
4 c. Spain
5 a. Queen Elizabeth II
6 b. Cambodia
7 a. Afghanistan's
8 a. Simón Bolivar
9 b. Burkina Faso
10 a. Thailand

Governing Bodies

1 a. Athens
2 c. Russia
3 a. England in the 1600s, under Charles I and Cromwell
4 a. Iceland—its Althing
5 c. Fidel Castro of Cuba
6 a. England and Portugal
7 a. Tonga
8 b. United States
9 b. The European Commission

Do You Have the Right?

Switzerland

Taking a Royal Challenge

1 Colonel Gaddafi
2 Moffitt
3 Jamaica
4 Clark Gable
5 Rudyard Kipling
6 *King Lear*
7 B. B. King
8 *The King and I*
9 King Kong
10 George III, who reigned for 59 years

Titles and Entitlement

1 Purple
2 Sultana
3 John Wayne
4 Princess Leia
5 Thailand
6 Viscount; barons are the lowest rank
7 Cleopatra
8 Lord Lucan
9 Humphrey Bogart
10 The British armed forces

Risings and Revolutions

1 The collapse of the Berlin Wall
2 Fulgencio Batista's
3 Spartacus
4 Stars and Stripes flag of the United States of America
5 Paris
6 Dublin
7 Mao Zedong
8 Napoleon
9 Ayatollah Khomeini
10 Lenin

States and Provinces

1 Al-Fashir
2 KwaZulu Natal
3 Prince Edward Island
4 Baja California
5 Poland
6 Alsace
7 Guatemala
8 Victoria
9 Serbia and Montenegro
10 Baden-Württemburg

PAGE 180

Getting the Vote

1 a. Florida
2 c. East Timor, which elected Xanana Guamao
3 c. Benazir Bhutto, in Pakistan
4 c. Rhodesia
5 a. Jean-Bertrand Aristide
6 a. Franklin D. Roosevelt
7 b. Richard M. Nixon
8 a. Pierre Trudeau
9 a. India
10 b. The Philippines

PAGE 181

Water, Water, Everywhere

1 Panama Canal
2 Moriarty, enemy of Sherlock Holmes
3 A tidal wave
4 The Bund
5 Thailand
6 Enya
7 The Baltic Sea
8 "Bridge Over Troubled Water," by Simon and Garfunkel
9 Yangtze River
10 The Amazon River, with a flow 60 times greater than that of the Nile and a depth of more than 406 feet, at its deepest point

Peak Achievements

1 Rip Van Winkle, in the story by Washington Irving
2 Mount McKinley
3 The Eiger
4 "Over the Hills and Far Away"

5 *Cliffhanger*
6 Mount Sinai
7 Vinson Massif, 16,066 feet
8 Salzburg
9 Turkey
10 In the Blue Ridge Mountains of Virginia

PAGE 182

Pick the Biggest

1 b. Asia
2 a. Sardinia
3 c. Pacific Ocean
4 c. Ukraine
5 a. Nigeria
6 d. Tokyo
7 d. Lake Victoria
8 d. Poland
9 a. Cumbria

Snowcapped and Steep

The Himalayas

Islands on the Screen

1 Robert Newton
2 The Swiss Family Robinson
3 *Lord of the Flies*
4 Colchis
5 *Fantasy Island*
6 Pianosa
7 Tasmania
8 H. G. Wells
9 Crete
10 Yul Brynner

PAGE 183

Bodies of Water

1 The sword Excalibur
2 *Loch Ness*
3 Lake Victoria
4 Veronica Lake
5 The Caspian Sea (A lake is any body of water surrounded by land, and very large lakes are sometimes called seas.)
6 The Sea of Galilee
7 The Cowsills
8 Lake Ontario
9 The Winter Olympics
10 Crocodile

I'm from Longuyland

A peninsula

Compass Points

1 Mali
2 Colombia
3 Somalia
4 Puerto Rico
5 South
6 Cameroon
7 Antarctica
8 Iran
9 The Tropic of Cancer
10 Yemen

PAGE 184

Going with the Flow

1 True
2 True
3 False; the Lena is in Russia
4 *Oui,* quite true
5 True
6 False; the Missouri is longer
7 True
8 True
9 True
10 False; the Amazon is the second-longest

Informative Island Issues

1 Dodecanese (its name means "12 islands")
2 *Papillon*
3 Richard Branson owns Neckar Island, in the Virgin Islands.
4 Martinique
5 Tony Bennett
6 Barbados
7 R. M. Ballantyne
8 Grenada
9 Chris Blackwell
10 "I Am a Rock," by Simon and Garfunkel
11 Norfolk Island
12 Jersey or Guernsey
13 Maldives
14 Kodiak
15 Marquesas
16 Iceland
17 Easter Island
18 Madagascar
19 Cyprus

Answers

Lost Worlds

1 b. Peru
2 a. Java
3 b. Turkey
4 a. Mexico
5 a. Tunis
6 b. Cambodia
7 a. Athens
8 b. Turkey
9 a. Guatemala
10 c. Ireland

A Tribal Gathering

1 d. Brazil
2 c. New Zealand
3 a. Africa
4 b. Survival
5 c. Niger Delta
6 a. Kenya
7 c. Sahara Desert
8 b. Central Africa
9 a. Angola
10 b. Ethiopia

Tongues and Places

1 Hebrew
2 Portuguese
3 Hungarian
4 Flemish/Dutch
5 Serbo-Croatian
6 Arabic
7 Bengali
8 Kurdish
9 Latvian
10 Nepali

Secret Societies

1 True
2 True
3 True
4 False; the Cosa Nostra is thought to have originated in Sicily
5 True
6 False; Carbonari was a secret society that fought for Italian independence in the 1800s

7 True
8 True
9 False; that describes the Mozart opera *The Magic Flute*
10 True

Color My World...

1 Blue, as in Johann Strauss's famous waltz, "The Blue Danube"
2 Red Crescent
3 China
4 Black
5 Vietnam
6 The Purple Heart
7 White
8 Purple
9 Ginza
10 *Just William*

What's in a Nickname?

1 Damascus
2 Albert DeSalvo
3 John Sousa
4 Jack Dempsey
5 Andrew Jackson
6 Bryan Adams
7 Doris Day
8 Babe Ruth
9 James I

Journeys and Destinations

1 *Journey to the Center of the Earth*
2 Gérard Depardieu
3 Keanu Reeves
4 *Seaview*
5 Dame Peggy Ashcroft
6 *The Road to Hong Kong*, 1962
7 *The French Connection*
8 Newfoundland
9 Bolivia

Discoveries

1 China
2 The Egyptians
3 The Vikings
4 Sir Walter Raleigh
5 Captain James T. Kirk and the *Starship Enterprise*

6 Abel Tasman
7 Cape of Good Hope
8 Lake Victoria
9 America
10 Ferdinand Magellan

Captain Cook

1 True
2 False; he took three voyages to the South Pacific
3 True
4 False; that's why Cook went to Tahiti
5 True
6 False; he was off modern-day Victoria
7 True
8 True
9 False; Banks was a botanist
10 True

Ages of Discovery

1 He sailed around the world
2 Prince Henry, son of Portugal's King Jão I
3 Marco Polo
4 Vasco da Gama
5 Sir Francis Drake
6 Bartolomeo Diaz
7 Charles Darwin
8 Sebastian and John Cabot
9 Sir Walter Raleigh
10 Ferdinand Magellan

Who Sailed *The Dove*?

Robin Lee Graham circumnavigated the globe

All Iced Up

1 Ice Age
2 Iceland
3 Ice shelf
4 Iceberg
5 Icefall
6 Iceblink
7 Icebreaker
8 Ice sheet
9 Ice jam
10 Ice needles

Arctic Living

1 Eskimos
2 Reindeer
3 Established as the Inuit home-land in 1999; has a population of 29,000
4 4,000 years
5 The coldest permanently inhab-ited place on Earth; record low temperatures of -96° Fahrenheit
6 Greenland (Siorapaluk)
7 The U.S. nuclear submarine *Nautilus*
8 The first woman to reach the North Pole on foot

PAGE 192

The Truth About Antarctica

1 True
2 True
3 False; 98 percent is ice-covered
4 False; it was once in the tropics
5 False; Mount Erebus is the world's most southerly active volcano
6 True
7 True
8 True

The Cold Facts About Antarctica

1 a. Scientists and support staff
2 b. The Madrid Protocol
3 c. Bans mining, protects plant and animal life, and regulates waste disposal
4 a. About 40 nations have signed—became law in 1998
5 a. Vostok Research Station, East Antarctica, where in 1983 Rus-sian scientists recorded -128.6° Fahrenheit
6 c. James Cook
7 b. Ice crushed his ship
8 b. Discovered the South Magnetic Pole

6 Religion and Mythology

Of the approximately 1,200 official religions of the world, 12 are classified as major religions by the Parliament of World Religions. Of these 12, the "Big Five" are Buddhism, Christianity, Hinduism, Islam, and Judaism. In this chapter, questions range over the religions of the world.

Early Civilizations: Ancient Beliefs and Rituals

Long before there was Christianity, mankind had gods and deities that it worshipped and revered—and evil spirits that it actively feared and sought to foil. See how much you know about the religions and beliefs of ancient cultures.

Myths of the Americas

Many civilizations flourished in North and South America, and long before the arrival of the Europeans, there were highly developed religious and mythological beliefs. What do you know about these cultures?

1 Which Native American chief of the 18th century, whose name is recalled in a famous American car, united the Indians of the Great Lakes against the European invaders?

2 Which civilization came first: the Toltecs or Aztecs?

3 On which continent did the native people believe in a great spirit called Manitou?

4 Which Mexican people worshiped a god in the form of a plumed serpent, a god previously worshiped by the Toltecs?

5 What "s" word is the more proper term for a medicine man?

6 What is the ritualistic item *peyote*: a heraldic emblem, a hallucinogenic drug, or a magic wand?

7 Which South American civilization built Machu Picchu?

8 Which northern people once revered a goddess named Sedna?

9 Which Central American people worshiped a god called Itzamna?

10 What was the term for the pipe smoked by the North American Plains Indians in honor of the Great Spirit?

11 In Aztec myth, who is the brother of the principal deity Quetzalcoatl: Xolotl or Zolotl?

12 Which celestial feature was called the World Tree or the White-Boned Serpent by the Maya of Central America?

13 Inti Raymi was a feast dedicated to a god in which civilization?

14 Which animal was most commonly sacrificed by the Incas?

Gods of Egypt

Despite countless images, most of us know little about the myths surrounding these gods. Can you answer these true or false questions?

1 Ra was the sun god and creator of the world, who traveled across the sky in his boat during the daylight hours.   TRUE ○   FALSE ○

2 One of the earliest deities, Hathor was the goddess of joy, love, and motherhood, who looked after woman. She was usually depicted as a horned deer with the sun between her horns.   TRUE ○   FALSE ○

3 The jackal-headed Anubis attended to funeral rites and guided the newly dead to the hall of judgment, where he weighed their hearts in the scales against the Feather of Truth.   TRUE ○   FALSE ○

4 The divine scribe who recorded the weighing of the hearts of the dead, Thoth was the god of the moon, as well as the god of learning and the inventor of hieroglyphs.   TRUE ○   FALSE ○

5 Isis, the supreme mother goddess, is often depicted with wings spread as a protective gesture over Egypt, holding her son, Seth.   TRUE ○   FALSE ○

6 Osiris was the founding deity of the Egyptian pantheon, whose reign was wholly benevolent; he taught mankind to make bread, build cities, and practice religion.   TRUE ○   FALSE ○

7 Sekhmet, god of war, was depicted with the head of a lion.   TRUE ○   FALSE ○

8 Bes was an ugly giant god who protected women and children.   TRUE ○   FALSE ○

9 The god of storms who came to personify evil and who struggled for power with his benevolent brother, Osiris, was called Amon.   TRUE ○   FALSE ○

10 Taweret, the goddess of childbirth and maternity, was usually depicted as a hippopotamus.   TRUE ○   FALSE ○

Pre-Columbian Gods

The inhabitants of pre-Columbian America had a large range of gods, some very bloodthirsty. Try to pair the god with its characteristic.

Quetzalcoatl_____

Tezcatlipoca_____

Huitzilopochtli_____

Xilonen_____

The Staff God
(a deity holding
a staff)_____

A The most powerful Aztec god, also known as "Smoking Mirror"

B The Aztec maize goddess

C An important Andean god, images of whom have been dated back to 2250 BC, one of the earliest known images of a deity

D Aztec god of Sun and War

E A feathered serpent and the Toltec god of agriculture, arts, and wisdom

Either...Or

Choose the right answer from the two offered.

1 Shinto is: a Chinese board game or a Japanese ancestral religion?

2 An imam is: a Muslim teacher or an African king?

3 The Buddhist religion originated in: India or Japan?

4 The Muslim commander and sultan of Egypt who fought against the armies of the Third Crusade was called: Alladin or Saladin?

5 The Islamic Abbasid Dynasty had its capital at: Mecca or Baghdad?

The Origins of Belief in Truth (or Fib)

Uncover the truth about the background behind many religions and ideas.

1 The word shaman originated among the ethnic people of Siberia.   TRUE ○   FALSE ○

2 Modern-day lacrosse is closely based on a sacred game of the Iroquois Indians.   TRUE ○   FALSE ○

3 The people of many ancient cultures created and wore talismans to ward off enemies.   TRUE ○   FALSE ○

4 In indigenous cultures, the shaman often held dual roles as doctor and chief.   TRUE ○   FALSE ○

5 As part of a healing process, many shamans will put their subjects into a trance.   TRUE ○   FALSE ○

6 Vodun, formerly known as Voodoo, is the official religion of both Haiti and Benin.   TRUE ○   FALSE ○

7 In the British Isles, a folk tradition from the ancient past is still practiced whereby participants decorate wells and springs with flowers and charms to incur the goodwill of water spirits.   TRUE ○   FALSE ○

8 In Europe and the United States, an ox skull is hung over doorways as a talisman bringing good luck to a home.   TRUE ○   FALSE ○

9 Every year on November 5, the small British town of Ottery St. Mary holds a festival where burning tar barrels are rolled or carried through the streets, a tradition that originated as a pagan fire ritual to ward off evil spirits.   TRUE ○   FALSE ○

10 People in parts of Greece, Turkey, and Egypt wear blue beads to protect themselves from evil spirits.   TRUE ○   FALSE ○

Persecution Through the Ages

Religious minorities have been vulnerable to persecution throughout history. Do you know how?

1 In 1597, 26 Christians were crucified in what Asian city?

2 From AD 284 to 305, what Roman emperor actively sought to destroy Christians?

3 In the 13th century, what was the name of the ascetic sect in Southern France that was avidly persecuted and killed?

4 In 1210, members of a heretical sect, the Amalricians, were burned at the stake just outside what major European city?

5 The medieval Christian church ordered the isolation in special houses of what type of people?

6 Witch hunting went on from the 1450s until well into the 18th century (and beyond in some places). In one common test, supposed witches were flung into water. If they floated, were they guilty or innocent?

7 The idea of a literal scapegoat—a live goat expelled from the city carrying the burden of the inhabitants—goes back to what ancient Jewish ritual?

8 In what country did King Langdarma kill thousands of Buddhists in the ninth century?

Off with Their Heads!

Can you name at least one famous cathedral in France that is surrounded by religious iconic statues that had their heads "removed" during the French Revolution?

Household Gods

Many cultures have long had gods or spirits specifically associated with the home. Open your hearth to these questions.

1 The *Lares Familiares* represented family ancestors who watched over the homes of what ancient culture?

2 The *Penates*, who represented plenty and prosperity, were the domestic deities of what part of the house?

3 In Russian and Eastern Europe, the *Domovoi* were benevolent spirits who protected inside the house, but what were *Dvorovoi*?

4 Since the first millennium BC, the Chinese have attributed a mystic significance to the shapes and forms of the earth (geomancy). What Chinese system of interior design stems from this belief?

5 A household shrine, visited by the family members each day to perform an act of *puja*, or worship, to the household deities is common in what religion?

6 In what country did families traditionally sacrifice sweets to the hearth god, Tsao Wang, and smear sugar across his paper image to encourage his continued goodwill over the coming year?

7 What peoples have the saying regarding visitors, "Ahlan wa sahlan," meaning, "You will be welcome as if in your own family and fed as though in the fertile plains"?

8 In parts of what country was a guest seen as a visitor sent from God, with the host having a duty to entertain the guest?

Myths and Mythology

The ancient Greeks and Romans had a highly evolved pantheon of gods and goddesses, many with extremely human failings and foibles. But so, too, did the Nordic people of ancient times and many other cultures. How much do you know about the myths and mythology of other lands—many of which continue to permeate our own culture today?

Creation Stories

Match the explanation for how the earth came to be with the religion or culture from which it sprang.

The earth was once a vast sleeping plain; then the eternal ancestors arose and the paths they trod became sacred songlines. Finding humans half-made from animals and plants, the ancestors finished them._____   **A** Japanese

The present universe was once a primeval ocean, into which the Divine Will set a golden egg, from which came the creator god Brahma, who took the form of a boar and lifted earth from the water on his tusks._____   **B** Egyptian

The goddess Izanami gave birth to the "eight-island country" after she and her husband descended from the Floating Bridge of Heaven._____   **C** Chinese

The sun god Atum rose from the endless sea called Nun and brought forth Shu, god of air, and Tefnut, goddess of water, who had two offspring: earth god Geb and sky goddess Nut._____   **D** Aboriginal

From the void Chaos came the earth goddess Gaia who gave birth to the sky, Uranus, which sent back rain to Gaia, filling her hollows to make lakes and seas._____   **E** Greek

God created the earth in one week, saying on the first day, "Let there be light" and so on, resting on the seventh day._____   **F** Maori

The earth goddess Papa and the sky god Rangi were so in love that they could not separate and so no light could enter the world, until one of their offspring pushed them apart, allowing light to enter and plants to grow. Rangi's bitter tears created the rivers and seas._____   **G** Hindu

All the universe was contained in an egg, which also held the giant Pangu. After 18,000 years, Pangu broke out, and the lighter part of the egg rose to be the sky and the heavier part sank to become the earth. For 18,000 years, Pangu held the two apart, but then he died, and his eyes became the sun and moon, and the fleas on his body became the first men._____   **H** Christian

Myth and Fable

Let's start off easy with a review of some classic legends.

1 If the Elysian Fields were heaven to ancient Greeks, where was heaven to Norsemen?
   a. Iceland
   b. Niflhel
   c. Valhalla

2 Which king unwittingly married his mother?
   a. Oedipus
   b. Hamlet
   c. King Lear

3 Which legendary warrior pulled a sword from a stone to demonstrate his kingly aptitude?
   a. Beowulf
   b. King Arthur
   c. Genghis Khan

4 In which country's mythology are dragons usually friendly and bearers of good fortune?
   a. Thailand
   b. England
   c. China

5 From which continent do the stories of Hiawatha and Paul Bunyan originate?
   a. Asia
   b. North America
   c. Europe

6 Which Greek hero's weak spot was his heel—the only part not protected when his mother dipped him in the River Styx?
   a. Achilles
   b. Paris
   c. Narcissus

7 In the fable, how did the wolf trick the shepherd to get a meal?
   a. It wore Grandma's nightgown as a disguise
   b. It repeatedly howled "wolf!" and laughed when help came
   c. It wore a sheepskin

8 According to legend, who were the twins, suckled by a wolf, who founded Rome?
   a. Castor and Pollux
   b. Romulus and Remus
   c. Mars and Venus

9 According to the mythology of Aborginal peoples of northern Australia, which colorful reptile fashioned the earth during the Dreaming?
   a. The rainbow serpent
   b. The chameleon
   c. The crocodile

Greece Is the Word

Here's a round of questions on the theme of Ancient Greece.

1 Which Greek hero was the son of the nymph Thetis?

2 To which god was the Delphic Oracle dedicated?

3 By what name are Clotho, Lachesis, and Atropos collectively known?

4 What was the 12th Labor of Hercules?

5 Who is the Greek goddess of the hearth?

6 Which Cyclops was blinded in his cave by Odysseus?

7 Who is the Greek goddess of the dawn?

8 By what title was the priestess of the Oracle at Delphi known?

9 By what name are the three companions of Aphrodite—Aglaia, Thalia, and Euphrosyne—collectively known?

10 Which king of Thessaly was condemned by Zeus to roll a boulder uphill forever?

Ye Gods

Can you find the answers to these supremely tough questions?

1 Which Norse god gave his name to Wednesday?

2 Whose brother was Pluto, king of the underworld?

3 Which Greek goddess was deadly with her bow?

4 Who was the son of the Egyptian couple Osiris and Isis?

5 Who in Norse mythology was always playing tricks on the gods?

6 Which people of the Americas worshipped a god named Tezcatlipoca?

7 Where in Asia did an ancient people pray to a sun god called Tankun?

8 In which religion was Agni, god of fire, portrayed with three legs and a thousand eyes?

9 Who was the Roman goddess of love?

10 Which Roman god, whose name is remembered in the first month of the year, was literally two-faced?

It's a Classic

Try out these puzzlers that come via the ancient world.

1 Who is the Roman god of business?

2 What word, now used to mean total disorder, is the Greek term for the void that existed before the creation of the world?

3 In Greek myth, what fate befell people who looked directly at the gorgon Medusa?

4 Which prophetess foresaw the fall of Troy?

5 After the Greek giant Argus was killed, the goddess Hera bestowed his many eyes on which bird?

6 In Greek mythology, what is Moros?

7 Which Greek god is said to shoot arrows that cause people to fall in love?

8 By what name was the Greek hero Heracles known to the Romans?

9 Who was abducted by Hades, god of the underworld?

10 What is the Roman name for the Greek god Hermes?

Myths of Africa and Oceania

Most African concepts are different from European beliefs, but many of the themes are the same, such as mankind's role in the universe. Are you savvy enough to answer these questions?

1 Who wrote *The Songlines*, a book that explores the myths of Australian Aborigines?

2 Oldoinyo Oibor, Masai for "white mountain," is also known by what name?

3 Which warlike African people acknowledge a creator god called Unkulunkulu?

4 Which English term is used to translate the Aboriginal word *alchera*, referring to the remote era when the ancestral spirits walked the earth, leaving songlines in their wakes?

5 In ancient Tahiti, what creatures were euphemistically called "long-legged fish"?

6 Which way do the statues on Easter Island mostly face—inland or out to sea?

7 According to legend, what weapon was invented by the ancestral snake Bobbi-Bobbi, who formed the first one out of one of his own ribs?

Beliefs from Other Lands

Select the right answer from the four options.

1 In Russian myth, what was Bannik the spirit of?
a. The bakery
b. The brewery
c. The bathhouse
d. The belfry

2 In Norse mythology, what form does the bridge called Bifrost take?
a. A rainbow
b. A giant snake
c. A golden sword
d. A cloud

3 What is a *havhest*?
a. A magic Viking helmet
b. A sea monster
c. A Swedish pixie
d. A Danish festival

4 Where, according to the ancient Greeks, does a dryad reside?
a. In an animal
b. In a lake
c. In a rock
d. In a tree

5 Which Polynesian god is said to have fished up the islands with a fishhook and given fire to mankind?
a. Maui
b. Rangi
c. Papa
d. Tane

6 The trickster god known as Anansi Spider in the West Indies originated on what continent?
a. South America
b. Australia
c. North America
d. Africa

7 Thoth, the Egyptian god of learning, was often depicted as what animal?
a. A wolf
b. A baboon
c. An owl
d. A monkey

8 What mythical Chinese animal was said to have the horns of a deer, the head of a camel, the claws of an eagle, and the feet of a tiger?
a. The phoenix
b. The sphinx
c. The dragon
d. The griffin

9 What, in Irish myth, is the Fianna?
a. A screaming witch
b. A royal bodyguard
c. An enchanted sword
d. A festival

10 Which Egyptian god presides over funeral rites and has the head of a jackal?
a. Anubis
b. Seth
c. Isis
d. Toth

Man, Is It Hot Down There

Can you name both the Roman and Greek gods of the underworld?

Celtic Myths

The Celts once occupied a territory that encompassed Britain, most of France and Spain, and even some of Greece and Turkey. Now mainly their heroic myths live on.

1 Which Irish saint is said to have gone on a sea journey in search of the Land of Promise?

2 According to Irish myth, how many eyes did the giant Balor have?

3 Finn MacCool gained wisdom by tasting a fabled fish—was it the Trout of Truth, the Walleye of Wisdom, or the Salmon of Knowledge?

4 The ferocious warrior hero Cuchullain defended Ulster against what fabled queen of Connaught?

5 *The Mabinogion*, a 19th-century translation of the 14th-century *Red Book of Hergest*, collects the epic myths of what country?

6 What son of Finn MacCool was considered the greatest poet in all Ireland?

7 Which Irish fairy foretells a death?

8 Kissing which Irish stone is said to impart eloquence to the tongue?

9 Who is the Irish goddess of death in battle, who often assumed the shape of a crow or raven?

10 What is the name of the reddish stone at the center of Stonehenge?

11 Which island in the North Sea is sometimes known as Holy Island?

12 What Celtic sorceress was a half-sister of King Arthur and queen of Avalon, the island where Arthur was interred?

Christianity Through the Centuries

From its simple beginnings with Jesus and his apostles, Christianity spread rapidly across places, peoples, and the centuries. What can you remember about Christianity's beginnings and about developments among the community of believers since then?

Jesus' Teachings and Miracles

Can you answer these questions about this miraculous man?

1 What was the public discourse in which Jesus gave his disciples the Lord's Prayer (or the Our Father Prayer)?

2 The figures of what two Bible characters appeared with Jesus in a vision at the Transfiguration?

3 What did the "wicked and slothful servant" of Jesus' Parable of the Talents do with his master's money?

4 What miracle did Jesus perform at a wedding celebration?

5 According to Jesus, what would be easier than a rich person's entering the Kingdom of God?

6 Jesus told his disciples to "beware of the leaven of the Pharisees and of" whom?

7 In one of Jesus' parables, a traveler shows himself to be a good neighbor by helping a Jew who has been beaten up by robbers. What was the nationality of that helpful neighbor?

8 The night before his death, what personal service did Jesus perform for his disciples?

Characters in the Gospel Accounts

Do you know the Gospel truth? Let's find out.

1 Mary, the mother of Jesus, and one of her relatives were pregnant at the same time. What was the name of this relative, and who was her son?

2 What was the trade of Mary's husband, Joseph?

3 What did the apostles argue about after the Last Supper on the night before Jesus' death?

4 What was the name of the criminal that Pilate released in place of Jesus during Jesus' trial?

5 What was the name of the friend that Jesus resurrected, who had been dead for four days?

6 What kind act did Jesus perform for his mother just before his death?

7 How many Bible books are traditionally attributed to Jesus' beloved apostle, John?

8 How many wise men, also known as *magi*, are traditionally thought to have visited Jesus as a young child?

Good Book Learning

Test your knowledge of the Bible and its stories by answering true or false.

1 In the book of Genesis, Eve was fashioned from Adam's right hand. TRUE ○ FALSE ○

2 In Exodus, Moses demonstrates God's power to the Israelites by turning his staff into a lion and back. TRUE ○ FALSE ○

3 A swarm of frogs, a swarm of gnats, and a swarm of bats were among the 10 plagues visited on the Egyptians. TRUE ○ FALSE ○

4 King David's first battle as a young soldier in the king's army was with the Philistine giant, Goliath. TRUE ○ FALSE ○

5 When Uzzah touched the Ark of the Covenant with unconsecrated hands, he was struck dead. TRUE ○ FALSE ○

6 Branches from the cedar trees of Lebanon were laid on the road before Jesus when he rode a donkey into Jerusalem. TRUE ○ FALSE ○

7 Jesus rebuked the sisters Mary and Martha for not listening to his teachings when he visited their home. TRUE ○ FALSE ○

8 Jesus spoke of a rich man in hell who longed for a drop of water. TRUE ○ FALSE ○

Do You Know the Apostles?

Match the following descriptions to the name of one of Jesus' apostles. Choose answers from the list below.

Which apostle was the brother of James?_____   A Thomas

Which apostle was also called Simon?_____   B Philip

Which apostle was the brother of Peter?_____   C James

Which apostle was called Zelotes, meaning "the zealot" or "the zealous one"?_____   D Matthew

Which apostle was the brother of John?_____   E Peter

Which apostle was the son of Alphaeus?_____   F Simon

Which apostle was seen by Jesus under a tree?_____   G Judas

Which apostle later doubted?_____   H Andrew

Which apostle was a tax collector?_____   I Nathanael (Bartholomew)

Which apostle was Nathanael's friend?_____   J John

Which apostle was also called Thaddeus?_____

Which apostle betrayed Jesus?_____

Do You Know These Church Figures?

Match each of the following descriptions with the correct name from the list below.

A spiritual originator of Unitarianism, denounced by John Calvin and executed for heresy in Switzerland in 1553 for denying the Trinity and infant baptism_____

A Martin Luther

A Christian teacher, known as one of the Apostolic Fathers, who knew the apostle John personally and died as a martyr near the middle of the second century for refusing to burn incense to the Roman emperor_____

B Polycarp of Smyrna

A 16th-century French theologian who became an influential religious figure through his development of reformed theology and his work in Geneva and Strasbourg_____

C Michael Servetus

The fourth- to fifth-century scholar responsible for the Latin Vulgate translation of the Bible_____

D John Wesley

The 18th-century Anglican minister known for founding Methodism_____

E Jerome

The 16th-century church reformer famous for nailing 95 theses to the church door at Wittenberg_____

F John Calvin

A New England Puritan minister who was influential during the witchcraft trials in Salem, Massachusetts, in the 1600s_____

G Isaac Newton

The 17th- to 18th-century physicist and mathematician who wrote more about theology than science and was possibly an anti-Trinitarian heretic in secret_____

H Cotton Mather

Even More Church History

As the centuries went on, Christianity formed many branches. How much history do you know?

1 Who was the English monarch who broke away from the Catholic hierarchy to form the Church of England?

2 Who was the Frankish king crowned emperor by Pope Leo III on Christmas Day in AD 800, an event that is often viewed as the beginning of the Holy Roman Empire?

3 What was the name of the followers of 14th-century English theologian John Wycliffe, who believed the authority of the Bible was higher than the authority of the clergy?

4 What fourth-century Roman emperor declared himself a Christian and arranged for the church's clergy to receive financial support from the government?

5 The English name of what modern-day spring-time religious festival is likely based on the name of the Anglo-Saxon goddess of spring?

6 Who was the 11th-century pope who authorized the First Crusade?

7 Who was the 10th-century king known as a convert to Christianity, as a uniter of hostile tribes, and, today, as the name of a popular cell-phone technology?

8 What is the collective name for the 12th-century religious movement, still in existence, that was founded by a merchant from Lyons and was known for voluntary poverty, its itinerant lay preachers, its use of the Bible in the vernacular, and its persecution as a heretical sect?

Christianity's Beginnings

In the first century following Christ's crucifixion and resurrection, the budding religion spread quickly. Can you answer these questions correctly?

1 According to the resurrected Christ, what should be more important to Peter than his secular work as a fisherman?

2 What was the name of the apostle chosen to replace Judas Iscariot?

3 In what city was the term *Christians* first used?

4 What was the meaning of the Greek word on which the English word *martyr* is based?

5 Who was the young Christian recruited as a missionary companion by the apostle Paul in the city of Lystra in Asia Minor?

6 Just before ascending to heaven, Christ prophesied that his followers would do what under the power of the Holy Spirit?

7 In whose household did the conversion of the first Gentiles to Christianity take place?

8 How did the apostle Paul support himself during his missionary work?

Events of Jesus' Life

Certain events from Jesus' youth and adulthood are specifically documented in the Bible. Do you know the details?

1 As a youth of 12, Jesus became separated from his parents, who later found him in the temple conversing with the Jewish teachers. At which festival did this occur?

2 What two kinds of food did Jesus give to the crowd that he fed miraculously near the city of Bethsaida?

3 The night before his death, Jesus prophesied that Peter would deny him before a rooster had crowed how many times?

4 At what kind of celebration for Herod was John the Baptist executed?

5 At Jesus' baptism, the Holy Spirit appeared in the form of what animal?

6 How much money was Judas paid to betray Jesus?

7 How did Jesus demonstrate that he had power over natural forces during a boat ride on the Sea of Galilee?

Saints Preserve Us!

It's all Christian saints, all the time, in this highly devout quiz.

1 Which saint founded a famous order in Assisi?

2 Which English saint's shrine made Canterbury a place of pilgrimage?

3 Which female saint did the English execute in 1431?

4 Members of the Church of Jesus Christ of the Latter-day Saints are also called what?

5 Which U.S. city, named after a saint, hosted the World's Fair in 1904?

6 On which saint's day were hundreds of Parisian Protestants massacred in 1572?

7 Which saint said that it was a "dishonor" for a woman to pray with her head uncovered?

8 Which medieval saint wrote the *Summa Theologica*?

9 The parish of St. Giles, notorious for its slums, was in what English city?

10 What area of Scotland, the site of modern-day golf pilgrimages, was the goal of many a medieval religious pilgrimage?

A Good Look at "The Good Book"

The Bible is a unique collection of historical accounts, poetry, teachings, and praise to God. A study of the Bible can be a lifetime undertaking, but you may be able to answer many of the following questions without that.

People of the Bible

Is your memory good enough to answer these questions?

1 What was the name of the woman who betrayed her lover Samson?

2 Name the writers of the four Gospels and Acts.

3 Where did Cain go to dwell when he left the garden of Eden?

4 Ruth, Abigail, Deborah: which was a wife of King David?

5 Who was the Israelite judge who, with only 300 men, saved the nation from a large army of enemies?

6 On the road from Jerusalem to Gaza, Philip the evangelizer preached to a Jewish proselyte and baptized him. What was the nationality of that proselyte?

7 Who was Abraham's firstborn son?

8 Who was the son of Jacob who was sold as a slave by his own brothers?

9 What was the name of the giant Philistine warrior killed by David before he became king?

10 Which one of Noah's sons was an ancestor of Jesus?

11 Out of the 12 Israelites who spied on the Promised Land before Israel's first attempt at an invasion, who were the only two spies who gave an accurate report of conditions in the land?

12 Who was the last king of Judah before the Jews were taken to exile in Babylon?

13 What was the name of the beautiful Jewish woman who became queen of Persia?

14 Who was the foreign conqueror prophesied by Isaiah to liberate God's people from Babylon?

Under the Olive Tree

What were the names of at least four women who appeared in the Old Testament?

Do You Know the Bible Writers?

Match each of the following descriptions to the Bible writer it describes.

Which Bible writer told King Saul that Jehovah was going to depose him?_____   **A** Solomon

Which writer started out as a farm worker, not a prophet?_____   **B** Moses

Which writer had been a violent opposer of God's worshippers?_____   **C** Luke

Which Bible writer started out as a good and wise ruler, but eventually turned to the worship of false gods?_____   **D** Jeremiah

Who survived a sleepover with some big cats?_____   **E** Amos

Which Bible writer was the cupbearer of Artaxerxes, the king of Persia?_____   **F** Paul

Who didn't think he could speak for God because he was only a boy?_____   **G** David

Which writer was a physician?_____   **H** Nehemiah

Which Bible writer grew up in the household of the world ruler of the time?_____   **I** Samuel

Who was forgiven for adultery and murder?_____   **J** Daniel

Religions at Large

Let's take a random stroll through the religions of the world.

1 What name is given to the period of 40 days that precedes Easter?

2 What profession was followed by Peter, Jesus' disciple?

3 In Judaism, what day of the week is the Sabbath?

4 In Judaism, on what day of the week does the Sabbath actually begin, and when?

5 In which river was Jesus baptized?

6 What are the two main religions in Japan?

7 How many pillars of Islam are there?

8 What is the third book of the New Testament?

9 What six-letter word is the official title of an ambassador from the Pope?

Chapter and Verse

How well do you know the specifics?

1 Which peak was the final resting place for Noah's Ark?

2 Which was the only miracle performed by Jesus to be mentioned in all four Gospels?

3 Who was the first person to see Jesus after his resurrection?

4 Who replaced Judas as one of the 12 apostles?

5 What collective name is given to the first five books of the Bible?

6 Which two words make up the shortest verse in the Bible?

7 What is the Decalogue otherwise known as?

8 Which book of the Bible tells us that the number of the beast is 666?

9 In which garden was Jesus betrayed by Judas?

Biblical Times

Here are some historical questions coming straight from the Bible.

1 Who was the Roman governor who ordered the crucifixion of Jesus Christ?
a. Pliny the Younger
b. Pontius Pilate
c. Herod Agrippa

2 Which book of the Bible tells the story of the creation of the world?
a. Exodus
b. Leviticus
c. Genesis

3 Who was the oldest son of Adam and Eve?
a. Cain
b. Abel
c. Daniel

4 Goliath, slain by David, belonged to which tribe of people?
a. Canaanites
b. Philistines
c. Assyrians

5 What was the first task God gave to Adam?
a. To name the animals
b. To find a big leaf
c. To find food for Eve

6 Name the archangel who announced to Mary that she was to be the mother of Jesus.
a. Gabriel
b. Raphael
c. Michael

Is It War or Feast?

The Battle of Agincourt, commemorated most dramatically by Shakespeare in *Henry V*, was notable for being one of the first times the crossbow was used to decidedly turn the outcome of a battle. It was fought in 1415, on October 25, which is also the feast day of two early Christian martyrs. Name them.

7 How many people ate at the Last Supper?
a. 10
b. 12
c. 13

8 Which day in the calendar year is celebrated by Christians as the anniversary of Christ's crucifixion?
a. Good Friday
b. Easter
c. Christmas

9 In the Bible, who is named as "the father of the Jewish race"?
a. Moses
b. Abraham
c. Solomon

A Scripture Quiz

Test your knowledge!

1 Which one of the Ten Commandments includes a promise?

2 Finish this quote: "If any would not work, neither should he..." do what?

3 Who were the sizable community of Canaanites who took the side of the Israelites during the time of Joshua, and thus were allowed to continue living in the Promised Land?

4 What did Moses's law require for anyone who took another's life?

5 How did the violent Assyrian inhabitants of Nineveh react when the prophet Jonah delivered God's condemnatory message to them?

6 What reason does the Bible give for Job having to undergo so many troubles?

7 According to the apostle Paul, at least how many people saw the resurrected Jesus?

8 The Jews spent how many years in exile in Babylon before being allowed to return to their homeland?

Judaism

The world's oldest monotheistic religion, Judaism arose among the wandering Hebrew tribes of Israel. Test your knowledge of this culture that spread from the plains of the Middle East throughout the world.

Major Jewish Holidays

The Jewish calendar is based on the Hebrew calendar, which is calculated differently from the Gregorian calendar. Do you know the names of these holidays, no matter what their dates?

1 What is the name of the New Year and the start of the Hebrew calendar year, generally falling in late September or early October?

2 Ten days after the New Year comes this holiday, when people fast for 25 hours, attend special services, and reflect on their deeds of the previous year. What is this Day of Atonement called?

3 Which holiday, falling five days after the Day of Atonement, includes the erecting of a small tent or outdoor shelter as part of the commemoration of the 40 years that ancient Jews spent wandering in the desert?

4 What is the name of the holiday on which the annual cycle of reading the Torah is over and the cycle begins again for the year?

5 This Festival of Lights commemorates the miracle at the temple in Jerusalem, when only enough oil for one night lasted for eight nights. What is the name of this holiday when people light candles on a menorah and eat special foods?

6 Which festive holiday, celebrated with parties, special food, and children's costumes, commemorates the story told in Esther of the deliverance of the Jews from the massacre plotted by Haman?

7 What is the eight-day holiday when people gather together for a special meal called a seder, which commemorates the ancient Jews' exodus from Egypt?

8 Many Jewish communities take a day that usually falls in late April or early May to commemorate a tragic event in Jewish history. What is this holiday called?

9 Which holiday commemorates the gift of the Torah on Mount Sinai?

10 What is the name of the holiday that observant families celebrate every Friday night and Saturday throughout the year?

Jewish Mix

Can you answer this series of wide-ranging questions on Judaism throughout history?

1 What is the approximate number of adherents of Judaism around the world: 8 million, 18 million, or 80 million?

2 The sole surviving part of the Temple of Herod, what is the name of this sacred place for Jews?

3 The *Mishneh Torah*, also known as the *Yad Ha-Hazaqah*, meaning "the mighty arm," was written by Maimonides around 1180 and is a summary of Jewish what?

4 The groom in a Jewish wedding does what with a glass from which he and his bride have both drunk?

5 Jewish dietary code forbids the eating of pork, shellfish, mixing dairy with meat, and other food considered in the Book of Leviticus to be not *kosher*, a word meaning what?

6 What is the spiritual leader of a Jewish congregation called?

7 Eight days after birth, baby boys are circumcised in a ritual traditionally performed by a man called a what?

8 At the age of 13, a boy is considered an adult in the Jewish community, an event celebrated at what two-word ceremony literally meaning "son of the commandment"?

9 After a death, a Jewish family has extensive prescribed mourning rituals, meant to comfort those left behind and honor the dead. The ritual a newly bereaved family follows for the first seven days is called "sitting..." what?

10 What is the central text of mainstream Judaism?

Who Are the Prophets of Old?

Name these major prophets of Judaism.

1 Considered the greatest of prophets, it was said that this man foresaw all the other prophets, as well as the whole of the Torah.

2 The first Jew, he was one of the three patriarchs and the physical and spiritual ancestor of Judaism.

3 One of the patriarchs of Judaism, his father was about to sacrifice him when an angel stopped the event.

4 This man exchanged a bowl of lentil stew for his brother Esau's birthright.

5 The wife of Abraham and one of the matriarchs of Judaism, this woman was one of seven noted female prophets, and the Talmud reports her prophetic abilities were superior to her husband's.

Root and Branch

Judaism today has four major divisions, from adherents who believe that all laws of the Torah are binding to those who observe Judaic rituals as part of their daily lives. Name these four divisions of Judaism.

Anti-Semitism in History

The Holocaust is obviously the most horrific example in modern history of the persecution that Jews have suffered, but there are other grievous examples dating back centuries. If to know history is to avoid repeating it, match the events with the dates below.

The Jews are expelled from France._____   **A** 1190

A wave of "pogroms"—attacks on Jews—begins in Russia._____   **B** 1290

Besieged by a mob in the English town of York, 150 Jews commit suicide._____   **C** 1394

More than 150,000 Jews are forced to uproot from Spain._____   **D** 1492

The Empress Elizabeth expels Russian Jews from the area around Moscow._____   **E** 1742

The Jews are expelled from England._____   **F** 1881

The World's Major Religions

In addition to the "Big Five" religions, ranked by number of adherents around the world, there are many other religions with large groups of followers. How much do you know about beliefs around the world?

The Rise of Islam

Islam began in AD 610 in Mecca, when the Prophet Muhammad began hearing the word of God spoken by the Angel Gabriel, becoming the basis of a new monotheism alongside Judaism and Christianity.

1 What do Muslims call God?

2 What do Muslims call the pilgrimage to Mecca?

3 What is an imam?

4 The majority of Muslims are which of the two sects of Islam: Shiite or Sunni?

5 The Islamic Abbasid dynasty had its capital where?

6 How many pillars, or main principles, of Islam are there?

7 What were North African converts to Islam known as?

8 What is the name of Islam's holy book?

9 What name is given to the Islamic holy month set aside for fasting?

10 How many times each day are appointed for prayer under Islam?

11 What name is given to the emigration of Muhammad and his followers from Mecca in 622?

12 Who took over as leader of Islam after Muhammad's death in 632?

13 Before he experienced his first holy visions, what work did Muhammad do?

14 Where did Muhammad and his followers go when forced to leave Mecca?

15 Arab artists focused on abstract ornamentation, calligraphy, and architecture because Muhammad prohibited representation of what in art?

The Hindu Deities

Try to untangle the branches of the vast family tree of Hindu gods and goddesses. True or false?

1 Brahma, the creator god and senior member of the Hindu trinity (along with Vishnu and Shiva), is usually depicted with four heads, which he grew to always see his beautiful wife Saraswati. — TRUE ○ FALSE ○

2 Vishnu, the preserver, who seeks to allow good to triumph over evil, has five alternate forms, or avatars. — TRUE ○ FALSE ○

3 Shiva is the personification of destruction and often is shown wearing a necklace of skulls, but he also has a creative principle and is a divine yogi whose meditation keeps the world in existence. — TRUE ○ FALSE ○

4 The monkey god Hanuman was the root of wisdom and learning, but was also the general of a monkey army which aided the hero Rama in his fight with the demon Ravana. — TRUE ○ FALSE ○

5 Ganesha, the elephant-headed god, is the son of Shiva and Parvati and came by his unusual head when he enraged his father who decapitated him, only to find Parvati so grieved that Shiva replace his son's head with the nearest he could find: an elephant's. — TRUE ○ FALSE ○

6 Kali, the personification of the life force who has four arms, holds a sword in one hand, a severed head in another, and raises the other two in blessing. — TRUE ○ FALSE ○

7 The cobra god Shesha has 1,000 heads, and earthquakes occur when he yawns. He is also known as Ananta, meaning "limited." — TRUE ○ FALSE ○

8 Krishna is the eighth avatar of Vishnu and does not have the status of a god in his own right. — TRUE ○ FALSE ○

In Good Faith

Test your basic knowledge of world religions.

1 Which of these Indian religions has been most recently formed: Buddhism, Jainism, Sikhism, Hinduism?

2 Would a Jew from Spain describe himself as either Ashkenazic or Sephardic?

3 Under the Ottoman Empire, what title was borne by the religious official with the ability to issue fatwas?

4 In Buddhism, what is the name given to the state of absolute blessedness reached through the extinction of all worldly desires and concerns?

5 Which English king rejected the authority of Rome in 1527, founding the Anglican church?

6 Which sect of Islam sees divine authority as being vested in its imams?

7 Who was the founder of Sikhism?

8 India's Mughal emperors belonged to which faith: Buddhism, Hinduism, or Islam?

9 Who was the first Catholic president of the United States?

10 In which year were women ordained as priests in the Church of England for the first time: 1994 or 1998?

Religion and Mythology

Test of Faiths

Select the correct option from four possible answers.

1 Which is the world's oldest organized religion still practiced today?
   a. Confucianism   b. Hinduism
   c. Judaism   d. Zoroastrianism

2 Shinto is the native religion of what country?
   a. Korea   b. China
   c. Japan   d. Burma

3 For which religious group is Jerusalem *not* a holy city?
   a. Muslims   b. Christians
   c. Sikhs   d. Jews

4 What is the sacred text of the Sikh religion?
   a. The Vedas   b. The Koran
   c. The Torah   d. The Adi Granth

5 Which is the fastest growing of the "Big Five" classic religions?
   a. Islam   b. Christianity
   c. Buddhism   d. Hinduism

6 Which is the largest Christian church?
   a. Eastern Orthodox   b. Protestant
   c. Anglican   d. Roman Catholic

7 Which religion does not teach the doctrine of the rebirth of souls?
   a. Hinduism   b. Jainism
   c. Buddhism   d. Bahaism

8 In which religion is Jesus Christ not a key figure?
   a. Christianity   b. Daoism
   c. Islam   d. Bahaism

9 When is Buddha thought to have lived?
   a. Circa 2000 BC   b. Circa 550 BC
   c. AD 500   d. AD 622

10 Which religion has the largest number of adherents?
   a. Christianity   b. Islam
   c. Confucianism   d. Hinduism

The Enlightened One: Buddhism

Founded around 560 BC by a prince named Siddhartha, Buddhism grew to the status of a world religion. How much do you know about it?

1 What in Buddhism is dharma?

2 What is the literal meaning of "Buddha"?

3 What is a bodhisattva?

4 Who was the Buddha's mother?

5 What is a mantra, a sacred word, used for?

6 What is the Buddhist term for the cycle of birth, death, and rebirth?

7 The idea that a person's deeds are rewarded or punished in their next cycle of reincarnation is called what?

8 After sitting under the fig, or Bodhi, tree at Bodh Gaya for five weeks, what did the one-time prince Siddhartha understand that transformed him into the Buddha?

9 In Buddhist legend, when a child wanted to make an offering to the Buddha, what innocent gift did he bring in his cupped hands?

10 Influenced by Hinduism, a form of Buddhism called Lamaism developed in what country?

Ranked by Mass

Name the top three religions of the world, largest on down, in terms of overall adherents.

Beliefs of China and Japan

Challenge your knowledge of belief systems in the Far East.

1 Which Chinese philosopher, born in the sixth century BC, was declared a god in 1907?

2 What does the word *tao* in Taoism mean?

3 Japan's monarch is traditionally said to govern from what floral throne?

4 What fish symbolizes strength and endurance in China and the samurai virtue of fortitude in Japan?

5 What is the meaning of *Shinto*?

6 In what country is the supreme god known as the August Personage of Jade?

7 The title Lao Tzu was given to the founder of Taoism. Does it mean Old Master or Wise One?

8 The *I Ching*, or "Book of Changes," is a Chinese method of divining what?

9 Lao Tzu's poetical work, the *Tao Te Ching*, advocates a joyful attitude to life, submissiveness, and what?

10 As the national religion of Japan, Shinto recognizes thousands of kami—gods or spirits who inhabit objects, places, and natural phenomena. Until recently, who was regarded as a living kami?

Answers

Myths of the Americas

1 Pontiac
2 Toltecs
3 North America
4 The Aztecs
5 Shaman
6 A hallucinogenic drug
7 The Incas
8 The Inuit
9 The Maya
10 The pipe of peace
11 Xolotl
12 The Milky Way
13 The Inca
14 The llama; white ones were sacrificed to ask for blessings; black ones to bring rain

Gods of Egypt

1 True
2 False; she was depicted as a cow with the sun between her horns
3 True
4 True
5 False; her son is Horus
6 True
7 False; she was the goddess of war, with the head of a lioness
8 False; Bes was a dwarf
9 False; the evil god was Seth
10 True

Pre-Columbian Gods

1 A feathered serpent and the Toltec god of agriculture, arts, and wisdom
2 The most powerful Aztec god, also known as "Smoking Mirror"
3 Aztec god of Sun and War
4 The Aztec maize goddess
5 An important Andean god, images of whom have been dated back to 2250 BC, one of the earliest known images of a deity

Either...Or

1 A Japanese ancestral religion
2 A Muslim teacher
3 India

4 Saladin
5 Baghdad

The Origins of Belief in Truth (or Fib)

1 True
2 True
3 False; talismans were originally worn to ward off evil spirits
4 False; most shamans were more of priests/doctors and rarely the sole leader of a tribe or group
5 True
6 True
7 True
8 False; many people still hang a horseshoe
9 True
10 True

Persecution Through the Ages

1 Nagasaki, Japan
2 Diocletian
3 The Cathars, or Albigensians
4 Paris
5 Lepers
6 Guilty; the water was "rejecting" them as impure
7 Yom Kippur, the Day of Atonement
8 Tibet

Household Gods

1 The Romans
2 The storeroom or pantry
3 Maligned spirits who haunted the yards and gardens
4 Feng shui
5 Hindu
6 China
7 The Arabs
8 India

Creation Stories

1 Aboriginal
2 Hindu
3 Japanese

4 Egyptian
5 Greek
6 Christian
7 Maori
8 Chinese

Myth and Fable

1 c. Valhalla
2 a. Oedipus
3 b. King Arthur
4 c. China
5 b. North America
6 a. Achilles
7 c. It wore a sheepskin ("a wolf in sheep's clothing")
8 b. Romulus and Remus
9 a. The rainbow serpent

Greece Is the Word

1 Achilles
2 Apollo
3 The Fates
4 To bring Cerberus up from the Underworld
5 Hestia
6 Polyphemus
7 Eos
8 The Pythoness
9 The Graces
10 Sisyphus

Ye Gods

1 Woden (Odin)
2 Zeus's
3 Diana
4 Horus
5 Loki
6 The Aztecs
7 Korea
8 Ancient Hinduism
9 Venus
10 Janus

It's a Classic

1 Mercury
2 Chaos
3 They turned to stone
4 Cassandra

5 The peacock
6 God of Fate or Destiny
7 Cupid
8 Hercules
9 Persephone
10 Mercury

Myths of Africa and Oceania

1 Bruce Chatwin
2 Mount Kilimanjaro
3 The Zulus
4 Dreamtime
5 Human beings
6 Inland
7 The boomerang

PAGE 208

Beliefs from Other Lands

1 c. The bathhouse
2 a. A rainbow
3 b. A sea monster
4 d. In a tree
5 a. Maui
6 d. Africa
7 b. A baboon
8 c. The dragon
9 b. A royal bodyguard
10 a. Anubis

Man, Is It Hot Down There

Roman: Pluto
Greek: Hades

PAGE 209

Celtic Myths

1 Saint Brendan
2 One
3 The Salmon of Knowledge
4 Queen Medb (or Maeve)
5 Wales
6 Oisin
7 A banshee
8 The Blarney Stone
9 Morrigan
10 The Slaughter Stone
11 Lindisfarne
12 Morgan Le Fay

PAGE 210

Jesus' Teachings and Miracles

1 The Sermon on the Mount
2 Moses and Elijah (The *King James Version* uses the name Elias instead of Elijah)
3 Buried it in the ground
4 Turned water into wine
5 A camel going through the eye of a needle
6 The Sadducees
7 A Samaritan
8 Washed their feet

Characters in the Gospel Accounts

1 Elizabeth, the mother of John the Baptist
2 A carpenter (Jesus also was a carpenter, a trade he must have learned from Joseph.)
3 They argued about which of them was the greatest
4 Barabbas
5 Lazarus
6 He turned her over to the care of the apostle John
7 Five: The gospels of John, 1 John, 2 John, 3 John, and Revelation
8 Three—although in fact the Bible does not give the number of magi who visited Jesus

PAGE 211

Good Book Learning

1 False; from his rib
2 False; he turned it into a snake
3 False; there was no swarm of bats
4 False; David was not a soldier but only a shepherd boy
5 True
6 False; palms were laid on the road
7 False; Martha complained that Mary was not helping her with her work but Jesus said in listening to him, Mary was choosing the better way
8 True

Do You Know the Apostles?

1 John
2 Peter
3 Andrew
4 Simon
5 James
6 James
7 Nathanael (Bartholomew)
8 Thomas
9 Matthew
10 Philip
11 Judas
12 Judas

PAGE 212

Do You Know These Church Figures?

1 Michael Servetus
2 Polycarp of Smyrna
3 John Calvin
4 Jerome
5 John Wesley
6 Martin Luther
7 Cotton Mather
8 Isaac Newton

Even More Church History

1 Henry VIII
2 Charlemagne
3 Lollards or Wycliffites
4 Constantine I
5 Easter
6 Urban II
7 Harald Bluetooth
8 Waldensians or Waldenses, named after the group's founder, Peter Waldo

PAGE 213

Christianity's Beginnings

1 Caring for Jesus' sheep
2 Matthias
3 Antioch in Syria
4 A witness
5 Timothy
6 They would be witnesses for him throughout the earth
7 Cornelius's
8 As a tentmaker

Events of Jesus' Life

1 At Passover
2 Bread and fish
3 Three times
4 A birthday party
5 A dove
6 Thirty pieces of silver
7 He calmed a great storm

Saints Preserve Us!

1 Saint Francis
2 Thomas Becket
3 Joan of Arc
4 Mormons
5 St. Louis
6 Saint Bartholomew's Day
7 Saint Paul
8 Saint Thomas Aquinas
9 London (the area is now modern-day Bloomsbury)
10 St. Andrews

PAGE 214

People of the Bible

1 Delilah
2 Matthew, Mark, Luke, and John (Luke is understood to be the writer of Acts as well.)
3 The Land of Nod
4 Abigail
5 Gideon
6 Ethiopian
7 Ishmael
8 Joseph
9 Goliath
10 Shem
11 Joshua and Caleb
12 Zedekiah
13 Esther
14 Cyrus

PAGE 215

Do You Know the Bible Writers?

1 Samuel (Samuel is traditionally known as the writer of Judges, Ruth, and 1 Samuel.)
2 Amos
3 Paul, formerly Saul of Tarsus (Paul is known as the writer of many of the New Testament epistles.)
4 Solomon (Solomon is credited with the books of Ecclesiastes and Song of Solomon, as well as parts of Proverbs.)
5 Daniel
6 Nehemiah
7 Jeremiah (Jeremiah is credited with the book bearing his name, as well as 1 Kings, 2 Kings, and Lamentations.)
8 Luke (Luke is known as writer of the gospel that bears his name, as well as Acts.)
9 Moses (Moses is credited with the Torah—that is, the first five books of the Bible, as well as Job. He is also credited with Psalm 90 and possibly 91.)
10 David

Religions at Large

1 Lent
2 Fisherman
3 Saturday
4 Friday night, at sundown
5 Jordan
6 Shinto and Buddhism
7 Five
8 Luke
9 Nuncio

Chapter and Verse

1 Mount Ararat
2 The feeding of the 5,000
3 Mary Magdalene
4 Matthias
5 Pentateuch
6 "Jesus wept"
7 The Ten Commandments
8 Book of Revelation
9 The Garden of Gethsemane

PAGE 216

Biblical Times

1 b. Pontius Pilate
2 c. Genesis
3 a. Cain
4 b. Philistines
5 a. To name the animals
6 a. Gabriel
7 c. 13
8 a. Good Friday
9 b. Abraham

A Scripture Quiz

1 The Fifth Commandment (sometimes considered the fourth), which says "Honor thy father and thy mother," with the promise "that thy days may be long in the land which Jehovah thy God giveth thee."
2 Eat
3 The Gibeonites
4 Capital punishment
5 They expressed repentance and turned around from their bad ways
6 Satan sought to prove that a righteous man could be forced to curse God
7 At least 500
8 70 years

PAGE 217

Major Jewish Holidays

1 Rosh Hashanah
2 Yom Kippur
3 Sukkot
4 Simchat Torah
5 Hannukah
6 Purim
7 Pesach, or Passover
8 Yom Hashoah, or Holocaust Remembrance Day
9 Shavu'ot
10 Shabbat

PAGE 218

Jewish Mix
1 18 million
2 The Wailing Wall, or Western Wall
3 Jewish law
4 Crushes it under his foot
5 "Proper"
6 A rabbi, or rebbe
7 A mohel
8 Bar mitzvah
9 Shiva
10 The Talmud

Who Are the Prophets of Old?
1 Moses
2 Abraham
3 Isaac
4 Jacob
5 Sarah

Root and Branch
Orthodox, Conservative, Reform, Reconstructionist

PAGE 219

Anti-Semitism in History
1 1394
2 1881
3 1190
4 1492
5 1742
6 1290

PAGE 220

The Rise of Islam
1 Allah
2 The Hajj
3 A Muslim teacher
4 Sunni
5 Baghdad
6 Five
7 Moors
8 The Koran (or Qur'an)
9 Ramadan
10 Five
11 The Hijra
12 His father-in-law, Abu Bakr
13 A merchant
14 Yathrib (or Medina, its modern name)
15 People and animals (it usurped Allah's role as sole creator)

PAGE 221

The Hindu Deities
1 True
2 False; he has 10 avatars
3 True
4 True
5 True
6 False; Kali is the personification of death
7 False; Ananta means infinite
8 False; Krishna is Vishnu's eighth avatar but also a separate god

In Good Faith
1 Sikhism
2 Sephardic
3 Mufti
4 Nirvana
5 Henry VIII
6 Shiah
7 Shri Guru Nanak Dev Ji
8 Islam
9 John F. Kennedy
10 1994

PAGE 222

Test of Faiths
1 b. Hinduism
2 c. Japan
3 c. Sikhs
4 d. The Adi Granth
5 a. Islam
6 d. Roman Catholic
7 d. Bahaism
8 b. Daoism
9 b. circa 550 BC
10 a. Christianity

The Enlightened One: Buddhism
1 Spiritual truth
2 "Enlightened One"
3 One who is on the path to becoming a Buddha but may postpone enlightenment to guide others
4 Queen Maya
5 It is chanted to aid meditation
6 Samsara
7 Karma
8 That desire is the root of all suffering
9 Dust
10 Tibet

Ranked by Mass
Christianity, Islam, Hinduism

PAGE 223

Beliefs of China and Japan
1 Confucius
2 The way (or path)
3 The Chrysanthemum Throne
4 Carp
5 "The way of the gods"
6 China
7 Old Master
8 The future
9 Frugality
10 The emperor

Science

We are able to explain how the world works because of the scientists who've invested countless hours observing it and testing their theories. See how much you know about the world around you with these scientific stumpers.

Amazing Animals

The animal kingdom is a fascinating place to begin your knowledge quest, and this section is written for those who would describe themselves as wild at heart. It covers everything from the big cats in Africa to the curious platypus of Australia. Good luck!

Noah's Ark

Loading them up two-by-two was probably the easy part. Consider all the other intricacies involved in the animal kingdom and see how you would fare in Noah's shoes.

1 What is the largest species of penguin?

2 What is the name of the shelter a hedgehog builds to live in through the winter?

3 What is the name of the fungal delicacy sought out by pigs?

4 According to folklore, what does it mean when swallows are flying high?

5 Is a thorny devil a reptile or an insect?

6 What is the name of the repellant acid produced by ants?

7 What is the main food of salmon, which gives them their pink-tinted flesh?

8 What is the common name for the egg cases of skates and rays, which are often found washed up on beaches?

9 Which ancient people actually ate the edible dormouse and considered it a delicacy?

10 What color is the skin of a polar bear?

11 What is the name of the world's heaviest insect?

12 After the two species of elephant, what is the next largest land mammal?

Gone but Not Forgotten

Unfortunately, numerous plants and animals live on only in our collective memory. Do you know where many of our favorite extinct and endangered species came from? See if you can you match the following to their correct continent.

Tasmanian wolf_____	**A** Africa
Passenger pigeon_____	**B** Asia
Golden bamboo lemur_____	**C** Australia
Lar gibbon_____	**D** North America
Andean tapir_____	**E** South America
Barbary lion_____	
Short-tailed chinchilla_____	
Javan rhino_____	
Kemp's Ridley sea turtle_____	
Amur leopard_____	

Cool Cats

Cats may be our most popular pet with over 600 million estimated to be in homes all over the world. How well do you know your favorite felines?

1 What feature does a Manx cat lack?
a. Vocal cords
b. A tail
c. Fur
d. Whiskers

2 Which member of the big cat family is the world's fastest animal on land?
a. Cheetah
b. Leopard
c. Panther
d. Lion

3 Which is the largest of the big cats?
a. Tiger
b. Lion
c. Jaguar
d. Wildcat

4 Which of the big cats can be found in both cold and warm climates?
a. Cougar
b. Tiger
c. Leopard
d. Snow leopard

5 What is distinctive about the Sphynx cat?
a. Its hairlessness
b. Its almond-shaped eyes
c. Its especially long incisors
d. Its ability to understand Egyptian

6 Which big cat is unique in not being able to retract its claw?
a. Cheetah
b. Lion
c. Tiger
d. Cougar

7 Which spotted cat, found in the lowland areas from Texas to northern Argentina, has short, smooth fur patterned with black-edged spots?
a. Manx
b. Mountain lion
c. Ocelot
d. Cheetah

8 What breed of domestic cat can be fully colored blue, brown, chocolate, lilac, red, or tortoiseshell?
a. Persian
b. Burmese
c. Abyssinian
d. Siamese

9 Which modern breed of domestic cat is considered to be closest to the cats of ancient Egypt?
a. Abyssinian
b. Siamese
c. Burmese
d. Rex

10 Which of the following is not a wild species of cat in Europe?
a. Lynx
b. Wildcat
c. Manx
d. Tabby

The Terriers Have It!

The Airedale is the largest dog in the terrier family. Can you name five others?

It's a Dog's World

It seems as if dogs know no borders since our four-legged friends are loved the world over. Match the correct breeds with the place they were named after.

A hound from a war-torn Asian country_____   **A** Afghan hound

A terrier from a valley in Yorkshire, England_____   **B** Airedale terrier

A spotty dog from the Yugoslav coast_____   **C** Chihuahua

A terrier from a northeastern county of England_____ **D** Dalmatian

A tiny dog from a Mexican province_____   **E** German pointer

A very large Scandinavian dog_____   **F** Great Dane

A pointer from a large European country_____   **G** Labrador

A terrier from Cumbria, England_____   **H** Lakeland terrier

A terrier from the Midlands, England_____   **I** Staffordshire pit bull terrier

A retriever from the Canadian east coast_____   **J** Yorkshire terrier

---

Hickory Dickory Dock

These questions are all about clock-loving mice and their mischievous cousins. Try to spot as many as you can running around the following riddles.

1 Which rodent can store food in its cheeks?

2 Which rodents are reputed (wrongly) to throw themselves off cliffs in huge herds?

3 Which rodents live in a drey?

4 Which large aquatic rodent can fell trees?

5 Which hibernating rodent is proverbially sleepy?

6 What was the rodent-like nickname of the British Eighth Army, which fought in North Africa in World War II?

7 Which North American rodent digs tunnels in river banks and is noted for its strong, musky smell?

8 Bank and field are types of which rodent?

9 Which common rodent is known scientifically as *rattus rattus*?

10 Which rodent, now a popular pet, is sometimes called the sand rat?

Going Ape!

This nighttime show host was renowned for having animals on his show. Can you name the host and five of the animals he shared the stage with?

Identity Parade

Can you pick the right animal from the imposters? Choose from the following to know for sure.

1 What is a tup?
a. A ram
b. A tit
c. A hen
d. A mouse

2 What is a gemsbok?
a. An antelope
b. An Asian shrew
c. A yellow bird found in Corsica
d. A four-footed lizard from Sardinia

3 What is ambergris?
a. A butterfly found in Papua, New Guinea
b. A substance produced in the sperm whale's gut
c. A squirrel found in Northern Europe
d. A substance produced from the sap of a tree that usually contains insects

4 What are gentoos?
a. Whales
b. Sharks
c. Penguins
d. Wooly mammoths

5 What is a potto?
a. An Asian wild pig
b. A Scottish rodent
c. A West African lemur
d. The trough used to feed a herd of sacred cows in India

6 What is a smelt?
a. A fish
b. A cat related to the jaguar and leopard
c. A young eel
d. A wild piglet

7 What is a belemnite?
a. A type of mite particular to elephants
b. Extinct squid-like animals
c. Bacteria that lives in limestone
d. An infant zebra

8 A nestling is the offspring of which of the following:
a. A polecat
b. A snake
c. A rabbit
d. A fox

9 What is a caecilian?
a. A type of earthworm
b. A type of snake
c. A legless, amphibious creature with a backbone
d. A hairless bunny

10 Where do basilisk lizards live?
a. In trees
b. Underground
c. In water
d. In basil plants

Vets Out of Practice

The doctor is in! How much do you know about the world of veterinary medicine? Use the following questions to see for yourself.

1 What pen name did the vet James Alfred Wight adopt?

2 Why do farms fear the FMD virus?

3 If a vet was asked to examine a horse's fetlock, where would he look?

4 Rinderpest is a disease of which farm animals?

5 Which viral disease of the dog shares its name with a type of paint?

6 From which disease was a vaccine for human smallpox developed in 1796?

7 Psittacosis is a disease of which type of animal?

8 What is the more common name for bovine spongiform encephalopathy?

9 What type of parasite causes mange?

10 What animals suffer from scrapie?

Biology Showdown

Here's a random sampling of basic questions that will determine whether you're science savvy or need to spend a little more time hitting the books.

1 On what do all newborn mammals feed?

2 What kind of animal is a caribou?

3 Which wild cat has the loudest roar?

4 What connects Charles Darwin to the cartoon character Snoopy?

5 Koi is a variety of which freshwater fish, much prized in Japan?

6 In prehistoric times, how did pterosaurs get around?

7 What body part is lacking in agnathan fish?

8 What bird flies the farthest when it migrates?

9 Where does a female bitterling, a fish, lay her eggs?

10 Alpacas are domesticated breeds of which wild South American animal?

Birds of a Feather

Do you have a favorite fine-feathered friend? This mix of questions is designed to see if you can fly high with your knowledge of the bird world.

1 What bird has the largest wingspan?

2 What is a baby pigeon called?

3 Who created the character Woody Woodpecker?

4 What color are parakeets in the wild?

5 What is the alternative name for the butcherbird?

6 What is the name of the world's smallest bird?

7 What is the fastest-moving bird?

8 How many eyelids do birds have?

9 What enables swiftlets to fly in the dark?

10 How many songs can a wood thrush sing at one time?

A Matched Set

Unlike the human tradition of sharing names with a mate, often the male and female member of many species are known by different names. See if you can name the female for each animal in the following list.

Boar_____	**A** Cow
Ass_____	**B** Doe
Giraffe_____	**C** Ewe
Hare_____	**D** Goose
Zebra_____	**E** Hen
Sheep_____	**F** Jenny
Rooster_____	**G** Mare
Fox_____	**H** Queen
Gander_____	**I** Sow
Tomcat_____	**J** Vixen

As the Birds Fly...

Who directed the 1963 classic film *The Birds*?

Bird Words

Our language is rich with references to our feathered friends in symbols and figures of speech. Listen to the following clues and see if you can tell which birds fit the following descriptions.

1 Someone who hoards objects

2 A coward

3 In cricket, scoring no runs

4 In golf, two under par

5 In golf, three under par

6 Someone who ignores danger, hoping it will go away

7 Suddenly giving up alcohol or drugs is called what?

8 Someone who stays up all night is a night___?

9 A greedy person who gulps his food might be accused of being which large white seabird?

10 Someone who is especially vain and dresses in overly elaborate clothes may be known as what?

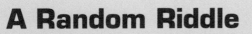

A Random Riddle

Which Eagles hit begins with the line: "On a dark desert highway, cool wind in my hair"?

Cool Things About Chemistry

Be careful—a few of these questions might be considered explosive!

Symbolic Science

Every element on the periodic table is abbreviated to make scientific notations easier to follow. Can you name the correct element based on its symbol?

1 Ar
 a. Argon
 b. Arsenic
 c. Americium

2 Br
 a. Bohrium
 b. Boron
 c. Bromine

3 Ca
 a. Carbon
 b. Californium
 c. Calcium

4 Co
 a. Copper
 b. Cobalt
 c. Chlorine

5 S
 a. Sulphur
 b. Sodium
 c. Selenium

6 Ag
 a. Gold
 b. Silver
 c. Argon

7 Pt
 a. Platinum
 b. Plutonium
 c. Potassium

8 Ni
 a. Nitrogen
 b. Niobium
 c. Nickel

9 Rh
 a. Rhodium
 b. Rhenium
 c. Ruthenium

10 Pb
 a. Polonium
 b. Lead
 c. Phosphorus

Melting Metals

Every element has a different melting point. Can you rearrange this list so they're in the correct order, from lowest to highest?

1 Aluminum

2 Cadmium

3 Copper

4 Manganese

5 Nickel

6 Platinum

7 Plutonium

8 Silver

9 Tin

10 Zinc

Lighter than Air!

What gas is responsible for making birthday balloons a delightful part of any party?

Why, It's Elementary!

How well do you remember high school chemistry? See if you're still the ace in the class with the following questions.

1 Which is the only radioactive element that is a gas at normal room temperature and pressure?

2 What name was given to the fruitless search for a process by which base metals could be converted to gold?

3 According to Chinese philosophy, how many elements are there?

4 Which common element evolved from a rare commodity into metal due to the Bayer process?

5 Name the smallest particle of an element that can be identified as that element.

6 Which is the most reactive gas—so reactive that even water will burn in it?

7 Which element has close to 10 million known compounds?

8 Name the semiautobiographical work written by Primo Levi.

9 What is the only metal that is liquid at room temperature?

10 Which is the most common element in the earth's crust?

Domestic Science

If you stop and think about it, the modern home is a showcase of scientific achievement. Can you answer the following?

1 Where might you find a tungsten filament?

2 Magnetrons are devices used in radar transmitters. Where would you find one in the kitchen?

3 What do the initials VCR stand for?

4 What role does sodium hydrogen carbonate have in the making of cakes?

5 Which 1967 invention made use of bacteria to brighten clothes?

6 In what form might you have live bacteria lactobacilli in your refrigerator?

7 In some countries, what form of abbreviation tells you which additives have been added to prepared foods?

8 Alva Fisher's 1906 invention changed Mondays in the home forever. What was the invention?

9 What product first used by ancient Egyptians is still used by some women today to enhance their eyes, though is not sold in the United States because of safety concerns?

10 What name is given to the process by which yeast converts sugar to alcohol?

Chemical Compounds

Most common everyday items have a scientific name. How many matches can you make in the following list?

Dihydrogen oxide_____	A Aspirin
Calcium sulphate_____	B Bleach
Sodium hydroxide_____	C Caustic soda
Acetic acid_____	D Epsom salt
Magnesium sulphate_____	E Methylated spirits
Sodium hypochlorite_____	F Milk of Magnesia
Magnesium hydroxide_____	G Plaster of paris
Acetylsalicylic acid_____	H Vinegar
Ascorbic acid_____	I Vitamin C
Methyl alcohol_____	J Water

Nature's Chemistry Set

Many chemicals and medicines are extracted from plants, as the following statements reveal. Can you tell what's true in the following list?

1 Quinine is used to treat cholera.　　　　　　　　　　　　　　　　　TRUE ○　FALSE ○

2 The leaf of the dock plant can be used to soothe nettle stings.　　　TRUE ○　FALSE ○

3 Digitalis, a drug found in foxgloves, is used to treat arthritis.　　　TRUE ○　FALSE ○

4 The plant pigment carotene is green.　　　　　　　　　　　　　　　TRUE ○　FALSE ○

5 Poppy is a flower that produces the painkilling drug morphine.　　　TRUE ○　FALSE ○

6 The main traditional commercial use for tannin, which is extracted from bark and other　TRUE ○　FALSE ○
plant material, is papermaking.

7 Dandelion is a diuretic.　　　　　　　　　　　　　　　　　　　　TRUE ○　FALSE ○

8 Taxol is extracted from American yew trees and is the source of a valuable drug for　TRUE ○　FALSE ○
treating liver disease.

9 Aspirin is derived from willow bark.　　　　　　　　　　　　　　　TRUE ○　FALSE ○

10 Belladonna is a poisonous plant.　　　　　　　　　　　　　　　　TRUE ○　FALSE ○

Making the Most of M

It's time to roll up your sleeves and test your vocabulary skills. Just remember that all of the answers begin with the letter M.

1 The temperature at which a solid substance becomes liquid

2 The quantity of matter as determined by weight or motion

3 The process of determining dimension, weight, or quantity of something

4 Gold, silver, and copper are all types of this

5 The only metallic element that is liquid at room temperature

6 The smallest physical unit of an element or compound

7 Equivalent to 0.03937 inch

8 An error in calculation

9 A combination of two or more substances that can be physically separated

General Science

Get ready to rev up your intellectual engine. The mixed bag of questions in this section is designed to challenge you on all facets of science, from anthropology and astronomy to physics and biology, as well as everything in between.

Odds and Ends

You have to be lightning fast to know all the answers to this general round of tricky questions.

1 With which part of their body do snakes and lizards smell?

2 What do pangolins eat?

3 The loofah is used to wash your back in the bath, but what is it?

4 As well as stunning their prey, for what do electric eels use their unique attribute?

5 Can you name a type of animal that has a spinneret?

6 During the mating season, what color are male stickleback breasts?

7 What is a ring ouzel?

8 Where do you find phloem and xylem?

9 What, zoologically, is a monitor?

10 What is odd about the swimming posture of the shrimpfish, also known as razorfish?

M Is for Moo

Don't spend too much time chewing your cud over these answers—they all begin with the letter *M*.

1 Tiny relatives of spiders

2 The commonest wild duck

3 A member of the cabbage family, its seeds are used to make a hot condiment

4 An insect resembling someone at prayer

5 Field, sugar, and Norway are varieties of this tree

6 A dangerous type of eel, brightly colored and found in tropical waters

7 An evolutionary strategy whereby an animal protects itself by having the same markings as a more dangerous species

8 A relative of the starling that can copy human voices

9 A mythical Cretan creature, half bull, half human

10 Sand, house, and crag are all varieties of this bird

Dinosaur Dilemmas

The study of fossils has yielded many important insights into the prehistoric period when dinosaurs ruled the earth. See if you can sort out the truth from fiction in the following statements.

1 In 1824 *Megalosaurus* was the first dinosaur to be named, aside from birds. TRUE ○ FALSE ○

2 *Compsognathus*, a carnivorous dinosaur from the Jurassic period, is notable because it lived underwater. TRUE ○ FALSE ○

3 Charles Darwin coined the term *dinosaur*, meaning "terrible lizard" in 1841. TRUE ○ FALSE ○

4 *Ankylosaurus* had a large club tail. TRUE ○ FALSE ○

5 Dinosaurs became extinct 10 million years ago. TRUE ○ FALSE ○

6 The *Utahraptor* was the largest of the raptors. TRUE ○ FALSE ○

7 *Tyrannosaurus rex* had the largest brain. TRUE ○ FALSE ○

8 Unlike most dinosaurs, the *Iguanodon* did not have thumbs. TRUE ○ FALSE ○

9 *Diplodocus* is another name for the *Brontosaurus*. TRUE ○ FALSE ○

The Appliance of Science

A rose by any other name may smell as sweet, but scientists have to know the right terms to convey their findings accurately. Could you keep up with their conversation?

1 In medicine, what do the initials CAT stand for?

2 What device allows a car's driving wheels to turn at different speeds from each other?

3 Which celestial object, once seen as a harbinger of doom, will be seen again in 2062?

4 What is it called when a rocket can overcome the force of Earth's gravity?

5 What name is given to the simple paint mark that stops ships from being overloaded?

6 What name is given to muscles that cannot be consciously controlled, such as the heart?

7 What aid to motoring safety was invented in 1934 by Percy Shaw?

8 What is the connection between soot, pencil leads, and diamonds?

9 What was the first commonly used plastic?

10 What are drugs known as ACE inhibitors used to control?

A Totally Terrific Tally of Beasts

From tapirs to thrushes, there are tons of animals whose names begin with the letter *T*. Can you name 20 of them?

Wild Word Power

This round is dedicated to some of the odder words in the plant and animal kingdoms. If you get fewer than four out of 10, you are probably guessing.

1 What is a hamadryad?
a. A poisonous Indian snake
b. A bird of prey
c. A sub-Saharan flowering bush

2 What is brooklime?
a. The name of a slug's trail
b. A water plant related to the speedwells
c. The seedpod of a spotted rock rose

3 What is a cardoon?
a. A plant related to the artichoke
b. The ancestor of the horse
c. A species of pygmy antelope

4 What type of animal is an onager?
a. A Russian bird
b. An American shrew
c. An Asian wild ass

5 Where on a duck would you find its speculum?
a. Its beak
b. Its underbelly
c. Its wing

6 From what is jojoba derived?
a. Sperm whale
b. A desert shrub
c. Avocado pear

7 What is a crested caracara?
a. A colobus monkey
b. A European newt
c. An American bird of prey

8 What are genets and civets?
a. Mammals related to the mongoose
b. Songbirds
c. Squirrels

9 What is a wart-biter?
a. A leech
b. A bush cricket
c. An African wading bird

10 What is an amethyst deceiver?
a. A migratory butterfly
b. A lizard
c. Type of fungus

Four of a Kind

Being well-rounded in science also requires knowing about the square. In honor of four-sided shapes, all of the answers in this round are four-letter words.

1 What name is given to the smallest creature in a litter?

2 Common, gray, monk, harp, and hooded are all types of what?

3 What color is the easy-to-grow perennial known as speedwell?

4 What type of animal is said to rut?

5 What do you call the state of dangerous frenzy in male elephants?

6 What is a baby whale called?

7 Royal, male, lady, and buckler are all types of what?

8 In biology what is composed of cytoplasm and a nucleus? (Hint: It begins with the letter C.)

9 Hercules carried the skin of which fearsome animal?

10 What common herb has a name that also means a wise man?

Dig It, Dino!

What distinction was shared in the 1820s by William Buckland, a clergyman, and Gideon Mantell, a physician?

The Human Body

Few creatures are as complex and fascinating as the human animal. Crack these quizzes and you'll have proven a better understanding of your own body, as well as mind.

Body Bits

This random round is about all the many parts and pieces of our anatomy.

1 What are you suffering from if you have spasms of your diaphragm, technically called singultus?

2 Where and when does air from your body reach hurricane speed?

3 Where on the male body does human hair grow the fastest?

4 Where would you find your umbilicus?

5 Borborygmus is the scientific name for which embarrassing bodily function?

6 Which bony rings surround and protect your spinal cord?

7 What is the common name for you trachea?

8 How heavy is the average human brain?

9 Approximately how fast in miles per hour does a signal travel through the nervous system?

10 If you can see your epidermis, what are you looking at?

Food as Medicine

How well do you know your digestive system and what you put into it?

1 What process, beginning in your mouth, is finally completed in your colon?

2 What do cows have four of and humans have one?

3 Apart from bones, what other part of the body uses most of the calcium in your diet?

4 What causes the uncomfortable condition of a "stitch" during exercise?

5 What mineral is the main constituent of red blood cells?

6 Which brown-green secretion helps you to digest fat?

7 In England, the government hid the development of radar technology during World War II by using which vegetable to explain their pilots' successes?

8 Rickets is caused by a lack of which vitamin?

9 A high level of what naturally occurring substance in the bloodstream is an important cause of the hardening of the arteries?

10 What vitamin did Linus Pauling advocate in high doses?

Them Bones

Sure the leg bone is connected to the ankle bone, but do you know what your doctor calls those bones? Match the following body part with the appropriate scientific name.

Carpal_____   A Arm

Humerus_____   B Breast

Tibia_____   C Collar

Scapula_____   D Ear

Phalanges_____   E Fingers

Clavicle_____   F Hand

Ilium and ischium_____   G Hip

Malleus and incus_____   H Lower leg

Sternum_____   I Shoulder

Femur_____   J Thigh

Doctor, Doctor

Do you have the right answers to these slippery questions tucked away in your medicine bag?

1 What painkiller is related to the cricket bat?

2 Who might use a nebulizer?

3 What is the ancient Chinese practice of sticking fine needles into a person called?

4 What poisonous garden plant is used to produce a powerful heart medicine?

5 What invention of Wilhelm Roentgen revolutionized modern medicine by allowing doctors to see inside the human body?

6 Alexander Fleming is credited with discovering which antibiotic after studying the growth of mold?

7 In alternative medicine, what name is given to the practice of exposing the body to ultra-dilute solutions?

8 Warfarin, once used as a rat poison, is used to treat what medical condition?

9 For what surgical procedures is Dr. Magdi Yacoub famous?

10 By what name is nitrous oxide more commonly known?

11 How many bones does a normal adult have?

12 What is the name of the last part of the small intestine?

13 What condition causes the skin to turn yellow?

The Heart of the Matter

See if you can get to the bottom of these true and false puzzlers.

1 Platelets are the blood component responsible for getting oxygen to your muscles. TRUE ○ FALSE ○

2 Like insulin, lipids are a component of the blood that usher glucose in the cells of the body. TRUE ○ FALSE ○

3 The human heart has two chambers, the ventricle and the atrium. TRUE ○ FALSE ○

4 The cornea is the only living part of the body without a blood supply. TRUE ○ FALSE ○

5 If you have AB blood, the only type of blood you can safely receive in a transfusion is AB blood. TRUE ○ FALSE ○

6 The heart is the only muscle in the body that never tires. TRUE ○ FALSE ○

7 Leeches, a blood-sucking parasite once widely used to treat various medical conditions, have fallen out of favor completely in the medical world. TRUE ○ FALSE ○

8 The femoral artery is the largest blood vessel in your body. TRUE ○ FALSE ○

9 If a patient is having a myocardial infarction, they are having a heart attack. TRUE ○ FALSE ○

10 Over a typical life span of 76 years, the heart will beat nearly 2.8 billion times. TRUE ○ FALSE ○

Thicker Than Water

Though a little less technical than the other quizzes in this section, you'll still want to tread carefully through these questions. Everything in this round is all about the red stuff that's coursing through your veins.

1 Who played Dracula in the 1992 film *Bram Stoker's Dracula*?

2 What are the smallest blood vessels in the body called?

3 What is the term for an obstruction in a blood vessel due to clot or an air bubble?

4 What color is Mr. Spock's blood?

5 Which military leader acquired the nickname of "Old Blood and Guts"?

6 Who was the child from Kokomo, Indiana, who was not allowed to attend school in 1984 because he had contracted AIDS?

7 What name was given to January 30, 1972, to describe what happened that day in Derry, Northern Ireland?

8 What is another name for black pudding?

9 According to U.S. regulations, how often can a person donate whole blood?

10 About how much blood does an average adult have circulating in the body?

Take Him to Heart!

Which pioneering South African surgeon conducted the world's first heart transplant in 1967?

Disease!

Will you score a healthy knowledge of medicine with this round? Simply choose the correct answer from the following questions to know for sure.

1 Which disease killed more people in 1918 than died in World War I?
a. Influenza
b. German measles
c. Smallpox
d. Cowpox

2 What common insect helped to spread the "Black Death" throughout the Middle Ages?
a. Mosquito
b. Flea
c. Fly
d. Worm

3 What is commonly called "the kissing disease"?
a. Mononucleosis
b. Strep throat
c. Mumps
d. Chicken pox

4 What sort of virus causes cold sores?
a. Herpes
b. Chicken pox
c. Polio
d. AIDS

5 What is the only disease that affects humans to have been completely eradicated from the population?
a. Smallpox
b. Polio
c. Leprosy
d. Dropsy

6 What disease, introduced during World War II, made the Scottish island of Gruinard uninhabitable?
a. Leprosy
b. Influenza
c. Anthrax
d. Chicken pox

7 Which viral disease is characterized by a violent fear of water?
a. Malaria
b. Rabies
c. Cholera
d. Mononucleosis

8 What is the term for a disease prevalent among animals?
a. Pandemic
b. Epizootic
c. Epidemic
d. Plague

9 What is the oldest known infection?
a. Leprosy
b. Staph
c. Bubonic Plague
d. Mumps

10 Which branch of medicine deals with the diseases and care of old people?
a. Geriatrics
b. Obstetrics
c. Oncology
d. Pediatrics

Name That Tune!

What is the hip bone connected to in the famous ditty "Dry Bones"?

Purely Plants

Scientists estimate that over 300,000 plant species call this planet home. Fortunately for you, most of questions in this section concentrate on those that could be growing in your own backyard. If you've spent enough time in the garden, you should have no trouble at all keeping things under control.

G Is for Garden

Are you gifted with a green thumb? If so, you'll likely have an easy time plowing your way through these clues for words that begin with *G*.

1 This is a term for plants placed in areas where grass is difficult to grow.

2 Having a few of these in your garden is said to bring good luck.

3 Every fence needs one of these.

4 Orchids and other delicate plants grow best in these.

5 This is what a seed does when it begins to sprout.

6 This is a term for plants when they're used to fertilize the soil.

7 This is another name for locusts.

8 These are considered among the most reliable flowering plants in any home garden.

9 A piece of this rhizome is called a "hand."

10 Chlorophyll is the reason many plants have this color.

Flower Power

Have a favorite flower? Take your pick of the patch from this colorful bunch of questions.

1 In what habitat does edelweiss grow?

2 How many flowering seasons does a biennial plant have?

3 What plant is often nicknamed granny's bonnet?

4 In which family is the group of plants known as chamomile, many of which have medicinal and herbal uses?

5 Why are daylilies so called?

6 'Peace' is a yellowish-gold variety of what common garden plant?

7 How did the corpse flower get its name?

8 By what romantic name is the amaranth or tassel flower known, so called for its long tassels of crimson-purple flowers?

9 What is the national flower of the Netherlands?

10 According to tradition, what message is baby's breath meant to convey in a bouquet?

Planted Evidence

Here's a mixed bag of questions to challenge your mastery of the plant world.

1 Which plant flavors gin?
a. Anise
b. Juniper
c. Lingonberry

2 What is a perennial plant?
a. One that lives for more than one season
b. One that blossoms year-round
c. One that lives for about one month after flowering

3 Sitka and Norway are types of which coniferous tree?
a. Maple
b. Spruce
c. Oak

4 Who saw: "...a crowd, a host, of golden daffodils"?
a. William Wordsworth
b. William Blake
c. William Holden

5 What color are gorse flowers?
a. Pink
b. White
c. Yellow

6 What does a deciduous tree do with its leaves in winter?
a. It keeps them
b. It sheds them
c. Neither—this type of tree doesn't have leaves

7 From what plant is opium extracted?
a. Poppy
b. Crocus
c. Willow bark

8 Busy Lizzie, jewelweed, and touch-me-not are all common names for what type of flower?
a. Impatiens
b. Geranium
c. Begonia

9 What color are fresh coconuts?
a. Yellow
b. Green
c. Brown

10 What plant is the national flower of Northern Ireland?
a. Wild Irish rose
b. Marsh marigold
c. Shamrock

Hello, Weed

Technically any plant that grows where it's not wanted can be classified as a weed. See if you can pull the right answer out of this particular patch.

1 What eastern-sounding creeper grows so fast it can smother other plants and even buildings?

2 What is the common name of convolvulus?

3 What common weed is a source of food for butterflies and can be made into soup?

4 What common weed is extremely poisonous to horses and cattle but not sheep?

5 What is glyphosate?

6 What common lawn weed, with white and yellow flowers, shares its name with the largest plant family?

7 The weed Herb Robert is a relative of which common garden plant?

8 What do you call the layer of compost, peat, manure, or other organic matter applied to smother weeds?

9 What weed is a traditional remedy for nettle stings?

10 What color are the flowers of willowherb?

Fruit Mix

Here's a delicious round of questions that are packed with flavor. Match the right fruit to the right clue.

What fruit is so stinky that it is banned from upscale hotels in Singapore?_____   **A** Apricot

What fruit is the most popular item to put on a pizza?_____   **B** Coconut

What fruit is best eaten unripe in Asian salads?_____   **C** Breadfruit

What fruit, when sliced, has a pit that's in the shape of a cross?_____   **D** Plantain

This fruit's inner bark is transformed into canoes, in the South Seas._____   **E** Green papaya

What fruit has a bumpy skin that can be either green or black?_____   **F** Tomato

This fruit is known as "the golden seed of the sun."_____   **G** Durian

What fruit grows all over the deserts of Mexico and the American southwest?_____   **H** Avocado

What fruit can only be eaten when cooked?_____   **I** Passion fruit

This popular fruit's name translates to the word "grimace."_____   **J** Prickly cactus

Flower Arranging

Many plants are given especially descriptive names. Can you spot the right flowers from these cryptic clues?

1 Part of an eye

2 Woman's footwear

3 An easy way to get a fortune

4 A flower between the hills

5 What the shepherds watched while seated on the ground

6 Buddy gets followed by this

7 The results from Cupid's arrow

8 A lover's request

9 What's the story...

10 Neat ranks

Bite the Fruit, Snow White!

Can you name the fruit that the Wicked Queen wanted Snow White to take a bite of, to make her sleep?

Pots and Pansies

Here's a random round to see how well you keep up when the questions fly in all directions. Good luck!

1 Who wrote the novel *Keep the Aspidistra Flying?*

2 What is the name of the Japanese art of growing miniature trees?

3 What is the name for the Japanese art of flower arranging?

4 What color are the flowers of the bottlebrush?

5 *Echinocereus, Opuntia*, and *Mammillaria* are all genus of what prickly plant?

6 What is the general name for plants with fleshy leaves that grow in dry places?

7 What is the more common name for *Philodendron pertusum*, noted for its glossy, perforated leaves slashed to the margins?

8 What color are the upper leaves of poinsettia?

9 According to his poem, what common flower did William Wordsworth encounter when he "wandered lonely as a cloud"?

10 What is the name for a small posy of flowers, as pinned to a woman's dress on a special occasion?

Boys' Brigade

All the answers in this round contain boys' names. How many do you know?

1 What wildflower, also known as goldenrod, is named after the brother of Moses?

2 Jacob's youngest son gives his name to which tree that yields the resin known as benzoin?

3 What popular spiky house plant is named after Eve's husband?

4 Which common garden weed shares a name with the founder of the London police force?

5 By what other name is the goat's beard known?

6 What family of yellow-flowered plants takes its name from the man who baptized Christ?

7 Which son of Isaac and father of the Jewish nation gave his name to a small white or blue flower found in the stony Arctic or alpine soils?

8 Which lily, also known as the paradise lily, shares its name with a make of tobacco?

9 The owner of Winnie-the-Pooh shares a name with which perennial white-flowered garden plant?

10 Which biblical figure, a perfect example of poverty and patience, gives his name to loosely tufted annual grass?

Space Odyssey

Launched October 1, 1958, the U.S. space program has enabled scientists to push the boundaries of human exploration, but clearly we weren't the first to become enraptured with unraveling the mysteries of the cosmos. Can you figure out your place in the universe with the following questions?

Earmarked for Exploration

As Captain Kirk always described it, space is the final frontier. So to see if you are ready for a trip through deep space, try your hand at figuring out all the related words from the following clues. And here's a hint: They all begin with the letter *E*!

1 The planet that spins about 92.9 million miles away from the sun

2 A closed, symmetric curve shaped like an oval

3 The imaginary circle around the Earth's surface that is equidistant from the North and South poles

4 March 21 and September 22 mark these two spots on Earth's calendar

5 A means for measuring mountains

6 What *E* represents in the equation $E=mc^2$

7 A mistake

8 A large satellite of the planet Jupiter that is exceptionally smooth

9 A way to express extremely large numbers in an equation

10 Recipient of the Nobel Prize in physics in 1921

Stars in Their Eyes

Look up! Is it a bird or a plane? Don't give up—you can probably figure out the right answer from the following clues.

1 By what name is the Polaris Star better known?

2 What super-telescope orbiting in space went embarrassingly wrong in 1990?

3 What is a light year?

4 What name is given to a star that has collapsed so far in on itself that nothing, not even light, can escape its gravitational pull?

5 Which British theoretical physicist wrote the bestselling science book *A Brief History of Time*?

6 What do the initials NASA stand for?

7 What name is given to stars that are grouped together and form an imaginary outline?

8 What are the 12 astrological signs collectively known as?

9 Approximately how old is the solar system?

10 What name is given to the dark patches that are seen on the surface of the sun?

11 Which song opens with the line: "Starry, starry night / Paint your palette blue and grey"?

A Fact-Finding Mission

Your goal, should you choose to accept it, is to figure out which of the following statements are true and which are false. May the facts be with you.

1 Though Mars is much smaller than Earth, its surface area is about the same as the land surface area of Earth. TRUE ○ FALSE ○

2 Neptune's orbit is the most nearly circular of any planet's, with an eccentricity of less than 1 percent. TRUE ○ FALSE ○

3 The pressure of Venus's atmosphere at the surface is about the same as the pressure at the top of Mount Everest. TRUE ○ FALSE ○

4 Venus is quite dry, although it likely once had large amounts of water similar to Earth. TRUE ○ FALSE ○

5 Jupiter sends out more energy than it receives from the sun. TRUE ○ FALSE ○

6 Mercury, known since the third millennium BC, was sometimes given different names for its appearance as a morning star and as an evening star. TRUE ○ FALSE ○

7 Saturn has a barely detectable magnetic field. TRUE ○ FALSE ○

8 Of all the planets, Saturn is the least dense. TRUE ○ FALSE ○

9 Mercury has been photographed by two U.S. spacecraft, Mariner 10 and MESSENGER. TRUE ○ FALSE ○

10 Jupiter is about 10 percent hydrogen and 90 percent helium. TRUE ○ FALSE ○

Astronomical Animals

As the ancient Romans viewed the night sky, they saw many shapes emerge, and so they named them accordingly. Match the correct animal with its constellation.

What animal is associated with the constellation Taurus?_____ **A** Bear

What animal is associated with the constellation Delphinus?_____ **B** Bull

What animal is associated with the constellation Ursa Major and Ursa Minor?_____ **C** Dolphin

What animal is associated with the constellation Lacerta?_____ **D** Eagle

What animal is associated with the constellation Capricorn?_____ **E** Fox

What animal is associated with the constellation Vulpecula?_____ **F** Goat

What animal is associated with the constellation Sirius?_____ **G** Horse

What type of animal was Pegasus, after which a constellation was named?_____ **H** Lizard

What animal is associated with Aquila?_____ **I** Swan

What animal is associated with the constellation Cygnus?_____ **J** Dog (the Dog Star)

Sun, Moon, and Stars

Look to the sky for the answers to this astrological round.

1 What is the name of the Egyptian god of the sun?
a. Ra
b. Osiris
c. Tut

2 Which rock musical featured the song "Good Morning Starshine"?
a. *Jesus Christ Superstar*
b. *Tommy*
c. *Hair*

3 In *Star Wars Episode VI: Return of the Jedi*, which monstrous villain was choked to death by Princess Leia?
a. Boba Fet
b. Jabba the Hutt
c. Admiral Ackbar

4 How many astronauts have walked on the moon?
a. 39
b. 7
c. 12

5 Which country has a symbol called the Sun of May at the center of its flag?
a. Argentina
b. Greece
c. Japan

6 In Greek mythology, whose wings melted when he flew too close to the sun?
a. Hermes
b. Icarus
c. Prometheus

7 Who wrote the novel *The Moon and Sixpence*?
a. Somerset Maugham
b. Theodore Dreiser
c. Aldous Huxley

8 Kenney Jones replaced Keith Moon in which pop group?
a. The Oak Ridge Boys
b. Pink Floyd
c. The Who

9 Sun Myung Moon is the leader of what?
a. South Korea
b. The Unification Church
c. Hyundai

10 Who starred in the 1954 version of *A Star Is Born*?
a. Judy Garland and James Mason
b. Marlene Dietrich and Mickey Rooney
c. Doris Day and Rock Hudson

Space, the Final Frontier

Set a course for adventure and test your knowledge of deep space with this quick round of questions.

1 What was the American astronaut Alan B. Shepard Jr.'s unique achievement?

2 Christa McAuliffe died when the *Challenger* exploded. What kind of spaceship was it?

3 Around 1900, astronomer Percival Lowell thought he saw what on the surface of Mars?

4 What rocket was used to launch the *Apollo* moon missions in the 1960s and 1970s?

5 Which country launched the first satellite?

6 What was the first living creature sent into space?

7 What name is given to the course of an object circling a planet or the sun?

8 Soviet cosmonaut Valentina Tereshkova achieved what first for her country on June 16, 1963?

9 What was the name of the first space shuttle?

10 Which *Apollo* mission went disastrously wrong, resulting in the famous radio transmission: "Houston, we've had a problem"?

11 What was the name of the U.S. space probe launched toward Jupiter in 1989?

12 What is the name of Doctor Who's home planet?

The Planet Suite

Here's a straightforward round that won't take you light years to complete.

1 The orbit of which recently de-classified planet takes it farthest from the sun?

2 Which planet is named after the Roman god of the sea?

3 In which year did man land on the moon?

4 What name is given to the group of planets that orbit the sun?

5 Which planet has prominent rings around it?

6 Which planet is known as the Red Planet?

7 Which planet is the brightest object in the sky after the sun and the moon?

8 Which is the third planet from the sun?

9 Rocks that fall from space and collide with Earth are known as what?

10 Which is the hottest planet in our solar system?

11 In the *Superman* series, in which city is *The Daily Planet* located?

12 Which planet's moons are named mainly after characters from Shakespeare plays?

13 Who composed *The Planets* suite?

14 Who directed the 2001 remake of *Planet of the Apes*?

15 Which is the second largest planet in our solar system?

16 From what are Saturn's rings made?

17 Titan is a satellite of which planet?

18 Who was the first man to walk on the moon?

Water World

Where to begin with the water section? The biodiversity our oceans hold, as well as how much remains to be discovered from them, means there's no shortage of trivia questions here. Whether you're a confirmed landlubber or passionate about being near the ocean, you'll find plenty of room to test your sea legs with this round.

Something Fishy

Having a hard time picking out your favorite seafood? You'll need to know the low-down on all kinds of species to make it through this round.

1 From which fish does caviar come?

2 Which unusual fish can climb trees?

3 What is krill?

4 What is the largest species of ray fish?

5 What does a male sea horse have that makes it unique among male sea creatures and helps it to rear its young?

6 How does an archer fish catch its insect prey?

7 For what do whales use baleen?

8 What does a fish use to extract oxygen from water?

9 Under what name is dogfish usually sold for human consumption?

10 What snake-like fish migrate from Europe to the Sargasso Sea?

11 What is the name of a female salmon?

Another Name for Agua

We're talking water, here...and all you really need to know to make it through this round is that all the answers begin with the letter A.

1 Another name for fish tank

2 An underground layer of water

3 An album released by Jethro Tull in 1971

4 A two-word term that describes precipitation with elevated pH levels

5 A type of microscopic, rootless plant life that grows in the water

6 Lobsters have these, just like many insects

7 This covers approximately one-fifth of Earth's surface

8 A collective name for the greater part of the West Indies in the Caribbean Sea

9 What a sponge will do with water

10 A sedentary sea animal seen around coral

Pond Life

Henry David Thoreau spent years gazing on the placid reflection of Walden Pond, but just how well do you think he would have fared with the following clever questions?

1 How does a sergeant fish get its name?

2 What type of fish is a wobbegong?

3 Does a coconut sink or float in salt water?

4 To which class of mammal does the duck-billed platypus belong?

5 Which appropriately named fish is entirely transparent?

6 Which flightless bird of the Southern Hemisphere lives in rookeries?

7 Who wrote *Moby Dick*?

8 Which sea animal moves through the water by a form of jet propulsion?

9 Who wrote *The Little Mermaid*?

10 Which fish has species known as three-spined and ten-spined?

I Can See the Sea

Tread carefully to see if you're quick enough to keep up with these marine creatures.

1 What sea-going animal, with a small trunk-like nose, shows the greatest difference in size between the male and female?

2 What is a Portuguese man-o-war?

3 In winter, what color is the plumage of the ptarmigan, an Arctic bird?

4 Name an arthropod that moves sideways?

5 What is the largest type of seaweed?

6 What shark has a bizarre head with eyes at the end of wing-like flaps?

7 Are sea cucumbers animals or plants?

8 Blue and humpback are types of what animal?

9 What fish is called a kipper when it is filleted and dried?

10 What name is given to the thick layer of fat that insulates a whale's body?

Giants of the Sea

If you were to measure the males from tip to tail, could you put the following whales in the right order from longest to shortest?

1 Fin whale

2 Humpback whale

3 Minke whale

4 Blue whale

5 Orca (or killer) whale

6 Right whale

7 Sei whale

8 Sperm whale

A Whale of a Role

Whales through the ages have shown up everywhere in literature and on the silver screen. Can you name 10 movies or books that have featured a whale as a main character?

Legends of the Deep

Can you match the following descriptions with the right sharks? Go easy—their teeth are all razor sharp!

This shark has yellowish skin so it can blend in with the sandy bottoms of shallow water regions_____

This coral-loving shark hunts at night and can sit motionless on the ocean floor for hours_____

Swimming at speeds up to 22 mph, they have been called "the peregrine falcons of the shark world"_____

These gentle giants can weigh up to 8,000 pounds_____

An incredibly large tail, sometimes accounting for one-third of its body weight, helps this shark create mini-whirlpools to trap its prey_____

Their drive to feast seems insatiable, but so does their urge to travel (one tagged shark was tracked from New York to Brazil)_____

Though no one has ever been able to get this shark on a scale, estimates suggest it weighs over 13 tons_____

These deep-water sharks have dorsal fins lined with spines that contain a mild poison_____

Thought to be the most abundant shark in the world, these are among the most frequently studied sharks_____

This unusual looking shark is especially fond of stingrays for its prey_____

A Basking shark

B Black dogfish shark

C Blue shark

D Great hammerhead shark

E Lemon shark

F Shortfin mako shark

G Spiny dogfish shark

H Thresher shark

I Whale shark

J Whitetip reef shark

The Ways of Water

Water is such a powerful force of nature, some might even describe it as being wild. But it's clear you know how to get to the bottom of it all if you can make it through this last round.

1 What natural force produces an invisible skin on the surface of water?

2 Water forms approximately what percentage of the mass of the adult human body?

3 Name the science of flowing liquids.

4 Why does a frozen water pipe split?

5 What is the oldest known method of harnessing power from water?

6 What is the energy that is created by water flowing through turbines in a dam called?

7 On average, how many centimeters of snow make one centimeter of water?

8 What name is given to a whirlwind that occurs over water and results in a spiraling column of spray and mist?

9 What entry in the *Guinness Book of World Records* makes the North Fork Roe River in Montana unique?

10 What percentage of the world's water is not salt water?

Answers

Noah's Ark

1 Emperor
2 Hibernaculum
3 Truffles
4 Good weather is on the way
5 A reptile; an Australian lizard
6 Formic acid
7 Shrimp
8 Mermaids' purses (or devil's purses)
9 The Romans
10 Black
11 The Goliath beetle or elephant beetle
12 The hippopotamus

Gone but Not Forgotten

1 Australia
2 North America
3 Africa
4 Asia
5 South America
6 Africa
7 South America
8 Asia
9 North America
10 Asia

Cool Cats

1 b. A tail
2 a. Cheetah
3 a. Tiger
4 c. Leopard
5 a. Its hairlessness
6 a. Cheetah
7 c. Ocelot
8 b. Burmese
9 a. Abyssinian
10 c. Manx

It's a Dog's World

1 Afghan hound
2 Airedale terrier
3 Dalmatian
4 Yorkshire terrier
5 Chihuahua
6 Great Dane
7 German pointer
8 Lakeland terrier
9 Staffordshire pit bull terrier
10 Labrador

Hickory Dickory Dock

1 Hamster
2 Lemmings
3 Squirrel
4 Beaver
5 Dormouse
6 The Desert Rats
7 Muskrat
8 Vole
9 Black rat (also known as house rat, roof rat, and ship rat, among other names)
10 Gerbil

Identity Parade

1 a. A ram
2 a. An antelope (or oryx)
3 b. A substance produced in the sperm whale's gut
4 c. Penguins
5 c. A West African lemur
6 a. A fish
7 b. Extinct squid-like animals
8 c. A rabbit
9 c. A legless, amphibious creature with a backbone
10 a. In trees

Vets Out of Practice

1 James Herriot
2 FMD stands for foot-and-mouth disease
3 Just above the hoof
4 Cattle
5 Distemper
6 Cow pox
7 Birds (especially parrots)
8 Mad cow disease (or BSE)
9 A mite
10 Sheep and goats

Biology Showdown

1 Milk
2 A large deer
3 Lion
4 Beagle: Snoopy is a beagle; Darwin sailed in HMS *Beagle*
5 Carp
6 They flew
7 Jaws
8 Arctic tern
9 Into the cavity of freshwater mussels
10 Llamas

Birds of a Feather

1 Albatross
2 Squab
3 Walter Lantz
4 Green
5 Shrike
6 Bee hummingbird
7 Peregrine falcon
8 Three
9 Echolocation
10 Two

A Matched Set

1 Sow
2 Jenny
3 Cow
4 Doe
5 Mare
6 Ewe
7 Hen
8 Vixen
9 Goose
10 Queen

As the Birds Fly...

Alfred Hitchcock

PAGE 234

Bird Words

1 Magpie
2 Chicken
3 Duck
4 Eagle
5 Albatross
6 Ostrich
7 Cold turkey
8 Owl
9 Gannet
10 Peacock

A Random Riddle

"Hotel California"

PAGE 235

Symbolic Science

1 a. Argon
2 c. Bromine
3 c. Calcium
4 b. Cobalt
5 a. Sulphur
6 b. Silver
7 a. Platinum
8 c. Nickel
9 a. Rhodium
10 b. Lead

Melting Metals

1 Tin
2 Cadmium
3 Zinc
4 Plutonium
5 Aluminum
6 Silver
7 Copper
8 Manganese
9 Nickel
10 Platinum

Lighter than Air!

Helium

PAGE 236

Why, It's Elementary!

1 Radon
2 Alchemy
3 Five: wood, fire, metal, earth, and water
4 Aluminum
5 An atom
6 Fluorine
7 Carbon
8 *The Periodic Table*
9 Mercury
10 Oxygen; most of it is bound in compounds with other elements, not free in the air

Domestic Science

1 In a lightbulb
2 In a microwave oven
3 Video cassette recorder
4 It is the chemical name for baking soda, a leavening agent
5 Biological washing powder
6 Yogurt
7 E numbers
8 The washing machine
9 Kohl, an eyeliner made of salts of heavy metals, such as antimony and lead
10 Fermentation

Chemical Compounds

1 Water
2 Plaster of paris
3 Caustic soda (or lye)
4 Vinegar
5 Epsom salt
6 Bleach
7 Milk of Magnesia
8 Aspirin
9 Vitamin C
10 Methylated spirits

PAGE 237

Nature's Chemistry Set

1 False
2 True
3 False
4 False
5 True
6 False
7 True
8 False
9 True
10 True

Making the Most of M

1 Melting point
2 Mass
3 Measure
4 Metal
5 Mercury
6 Molecule
7 Millimeter
8 Mistake
9 Mixture

PAGE 238

Odds and Ends

1 Their tongues
2 Ants and termites
3 The fibrous fruit of the tropical loofah plant, a type of gourd
4 For navigation in much the same way a bat uses sound
5 Spiders, caterpillars, or silkworms
6 Red
7 A bird in the thrush family, typically found in moorland and rocky hills of western and central Europe
8 In plant stems and trunks; they are the vessels that carry water and food
9 A type of large lizard
10 It swims head-down

Answers

M Is for Moo

1 Mites
2 Mallard
3 Mustard
4 Mantis
5 Maple
6 Moray
7 Mimicry
8 Mynah
9 Minotaur
10 Martin

Dinosaur Dilemmas

1 True
2 False; it is notable for being the smallest dinosaur yet found—about the size of a chicken
3 False; it was Sir Richard Owen
4 True
5 False; it was 65 million years ago
6 True
7 True
8 False; it had a pointed spike-like thumb
9 False; *Apatosaurus* is another name for the *Brontosaurus*

The Appliance of Science

1 Computerized axial tomography
2 Differential
3 Halley's Comet
4 Escape velocity
5 Plimsoll line (or mark)
6 Involuntary muscle
7 Road reflectors known as cat's-eyes
8 They are all forms of carbon
9 Bakelite
10 Blood pressure

Wild Word Power

1 a. A poisonous Indian snake
2 b. A water plant related to the speedwells
3 a. A plant related to the artichoke
4 c. An Asian wild ass
5 c. Its wing
6 b. A desert shrub
7 c. An American bird of prey
8 a. Mammals related to the mongoose
9 b. A bush cricket
10 c. Type of fungus

Four of a Kind

1 Runt
2 Seal
3 Blue (also in shades of purple and pink)
4 Deer
5 Must
6 Calf
7 Fern
8 Cell
9 Lion
10 Sage

Dig It, Dino!

They discovered fossil dinosaur bones

Body Bits

1 Hiccups
2 In your nose, when you sneeze
3 The beard
4 On your belly—it is your belly button
5 Tummy rumbling
6 Vertebrae
7 Windpipe
8 About three pounds
9 Approximately 225 mph
10 Skin

Food as Medicine

1 Digestion
2 Stomachs
3 Teeth
4 A stitch is a cramp of the diaphragm muscle
5 Iron
6 Bile
7 Carrots; the British said their pilots were eating carrots to improve their night vision
8 Vitamin D
9 Cholesterol
10 Vitamin C

Them Bones

1 Hand
2 Arm
3 Lower leg
4 Shoulder
5 Fingers
6 Collar
7 Hip
8 Ear
9 Breast
10 Thigh

Doctor, Doctor

1 Aspirin, which is derived from substances found in willow bark (cricket bats are traditionally made of willow)
2 Someone with asthma
3 Acupuncture
4 Foxglove (digitalis)
5 X-rays
6 Penicillin
7 Homeopathy
8 Stroke and thrombosis; it's an anticoagulant
9 Heart and lung transplants
10 Laughing gas—a painkiller
11 206
12 Ileum
13 Jaundice

PAGE 243

The Heart of the Matter

1 False; it's hemoglobin
2 False
3 False; it has four chambers
4 True
5 False; AB is known as the universal receiver
6 True
7 False; they are still used
8 False; the aorta is largest
9 True
10 True

Thicker Than Water

1 Gary Oldman
2 Capillaries
3 Embolism
4 Green
5 General George S. Patton
6 Ryan White
7 Bloody Sunday
8 Blood sausage or blood pudding
9 Once every 56 days
10 5 liters

Take Him to Heart!

Dr. Christiaan Barnard

PAGE 244

Disease!

1 a. Influenza
2 b. Flea
3 a. Mononucleosis
4 a. Herpes
5 a. Smallpox
6 c. Anthrax
7 b. Rabies
8 b. Epizootic
9 a. Leprosy
10 a. Geriatrics

PAGE 245

G Is for Garden

1 Ground cover
2 Gnomes
3 Gate
4 Greenhouse
5 Germinate
6 Green manure
7 Grasshoppers
8 Geraniums
9 Ginger
10 Green

Flower Power

1 On alpine slopes
2 Two
3 Columbine or *Aquilegia*
4 The daisy family
5 Their flowers last one day
6 Rose
7 It smells like rotting flesh
8 Love-lies-bleeding
9 Tulip
10 Happiness

PAGE 246

Planted Evidence

1 b. Juniper
2 a. One that lives for more than one season
3 b. Spruce
4 a. William Wordsworth
5 c. Yellow
6 b. It sheds them
7 a. Poppy
8 a. Impatiens
9 b. Green
10 c. Shamrock

Hello, Weed

1 Russian vine
2 Bindweed or morning glory
3 Nettles
4 Common ragwort
5 A weed killer
6 Daisy
7 Geranium
8 Mulch
9 Dock
10 Pink to purplish

PAGE 247

Fruit Mix

1 Durian
2 Tomato
3 Green papaya
4 Passion fruit
5 Breadfruit
6 Avocado
7 Apricot
8 Prickly cactus
9 Plantain
10 Coconut

Flower Arranging

1 Iris
2 Lady's slipper
3 Marigold
4 Lily of the valley
5 Phlox
6 Holly
7 Bleeding heart
8 Forget-me-not
9 Morning Glory
10 Primrose

Bite the Fruit, Snow White!

Apple

PAGE 248

Pots and Pansies

1 George Orwell
2 Bonsai
3 Ikebana
4 Most commonly orange-red (also may be white, greenish, pink, or yellow)
5 Cacti
6 Succulents
7 Swiss cheese plants
8 Red (also may be pink, white, yellow, or marbled)
9 Daffodil
10 Corsage

Answers

Boys' Brigade

1 Aaron's rod
2 Benjamin bush or tree
3 Adam's needle
4 Herb Robert
5 Jack-go-to-bed-at-noon
6 St. John's wort
7 Jacob (Jacob's ladder)
8 St. Bruno's lily
9 Herb Christopher
10 Job (Job's tear)

Earmarked for Exploration

1 Earth
2 Ellipses
3 Equator
4 Equinox
5 Elevation
6 Energy
7 Error
8 Europa
9 Exponential
10 Einstein

Stars in Their Eyes

1 The Pole Star (also Northern Star or North Star)
2 The Hubble telescope
3 The distance light travels in a year (5,880 billion miles)
4 A black hole
5 Stephen Hawking
6 National Aeronautics and Space Administration
7 Constellation
8 The zodiac
9 4.6 billion years old
10 Sun spots
11 "Vincent" by Don McLean

A Fact-Finding Mission

1 True
2 False
3 False
4 True
5 True
6 True
7 False
8 True
9 True
10 False; it's about 90 percent hydrogen and 10 percent helium

Astronomical Animals

1 Bull
2 Dolphin
3 Bear
4 Lizard
5 Goat
6 Fox
7 Dog (the Dog Star)
8 Horse
9 Eagle
10 Swan

Sun, Moon, and Stars

1 a. Ra
2 c. *Hair*
3 b. Jabba the Hutt
4 c. 12
5 a. Argentina
6 b. Icarus
7 a. Somerset Maugham
8 c. The Who
9 b. The Unification Church
10 a. Judy Garland and James Mason

Space, the Final Frontier

1 He was the first American in space
2 Space shuttle
3 Canals
4 Saturn V
5 The USSR launched Sputnik in 1957
6 The dog Laika in 1957
7 Orbit
8 She was the first woman in space
9 *Enterprise*
10 *Apollo 13*
11 *Galileo*
12 Gallifrey

The Planet Suite

1 Pluto
2 Neptune
3 1969
4 The solar system
5 Saturn
6 Mars
7 Venus
8 Earth
9 Meteorites
10 Mercury
11 Metropolis
12 Uranus
13 Gustav Holst
14 Tim Burton
15 Saturn
16 Primarily ice
17 Saturn
18 Neil Armstrong

Something Fishy

1 Sturgeon
2 Mudskipper
3 A small shrimp-like animal that is plentiful in the ocean and is fed on by whales and other animals
4 Manta ray
5 A pouch in his abdomen, where the young are hatched
6 It knocks them off overhanging leaves by squirting a jet of water
7 To filter water for small animals on which they feed
8 Gills
9 Rock salmon
10 Eels
11 Hen

Another Name for Agua

1 Aquarium
2 Aquifer
3 *Aqualung*
4 Acid rain
5 Algae
6 Antennae
7 Atlantic Ocean
8 Antilles
9 Absorb
10 Anemone

PAGE 254

Pond Life

1 From the five stripes that resemble a sergeant major's insignia
2 A shark
3 Float, as a form of seed dispersal
4 Monotremes
5 Glassfish
6 Penguins
7 Herman Melville
8 Octopus
9 Hans Christian Andersen
10 Stickleback

I Can See the Sea

1 Elephant seals; females are a third the size of males
2 Jellyfish
3 White, to camouflage itself in the snow
4 Crab
5 Giant kelp
6 Hammerhead shark
7 Animals
8 Whale
9 Herring
10 Blubber

Giants of the Sea

1 Blue whale
2 Fin whale
3 Sperm whale
4 Humpback whale
5 Sei whale
6 Right whale
7 Minke whale
8 Orca (or killer) whale

PAGE 255

Legends of the Deep

1 Lemon shark
2 Whitetip reef shark
3 Shortfin mako shark
4 Basking shark
5 Thresher shark
6 Blue shark
7 Whale shark
8 Black dogfish shark
9 Spiny dogfish shark
10 Great hammerhead shark

The Ways of Water

1 Surface tension
2 About 55 to 60 percent
3 Hydraulics
4 Because water expands as it freezes
5 Water wheel
6 Hydroelectric power
7 About 10 centimeters
8 Waterspout
9 At 200 feet long, it is the world's shortest river
10 About 3 percent

8 The Wonderful World of Business

Would you rather take your chances playing *Who Wants to Be a Millionaire* or sweating it out to see who's fired next in Donald Trump's boardroom? The questions you'll find here prove hands down that there are many ways to become wealthy.

Legends of Industry

Covering everything from inspired inventions to Wall Street tycoons, this section gets off with a round of inspired inventions to get the creative juices flowing.

MBA Magic

Are you considered a master of business affairs? Then test your mettle and put on your thinking cap—all of the answers to the following clues begin with the letter *M*.

1 A person of great influence, importance, or standing in a particular enterprise or field of business.

2 No business leader gets out of bed without this in the morning—it's what propels them to succeed.

3 A five-letter word that describes the quality of mind that allows one to face danger or hardship resolutely.

4 A message or announcement to employees can take this written form.

5 A type of stock or bond fund that pools money from many investors.

6 A person to whom employees report in a business.

7 A type of bonus for an employee whose work is superior and whose services are valued.

8 Any place where buyers and sellers meet to sell things.

9 Making this is the goal of most businesses.

10 These are held in order for people to gather for a specific purpose.

Mega-Mansions

Many of the following landmark homes, built by some of America's leading political and industrial families, are notable for their displays of unparalleled wealth. Do you know who called each of the following estates home?

The Breakers_____   A Cornelius Vanderbilt II

Rosecliff_____   B Elvis Presley

Longwood Gardens_____   C Franklin D. Roosevelt

Montpelier_____   D James Madison

Kykuit_____   E John D. Rockefeller

Springwood_____   F Originally Edsel Ford, now Martha Stewart

Graceland_____   G Pierre Samuel du Pont II

Monticello_____   H Theresa Fair Oelrichs

Skylands_____   I Thomas Jefferson

What Did the Neighbors Think?

What film was shot on location of newspaper magnate William Randolph Hearst's palatial mansion in San Simeon, California?

Generous Giants and Landmark Deals

Many of the world's wealthiest are long-remembered not just for their millions, but also for their decisions to share their fortunes with the rest of the world, as this round of questions will reveal.

1 Already the world's wealthiest charitable foundation with assets of more than $30 billion, what philanthropic institution more than doubled its size in 2006 when investor Warren Buffet donated an additional $31 billion to it?

2 Who organized a Christmas initiative in South Africa to provide food, clothing, shoes, school supplies, books, and toys to 50,000 children?

3 In 1997, media mogul Ted Turner announced to the world that he would give $1 billion to what international institution for its programs?

4 Who made possible the founding of the University of Chicago through gifts totaling more than $80 million?

5 Although Donald Trump has sealed numerous multimillion dollar deals, he is afraid of germs and famous in the business world for his objection to what common gesture?

6 In 1892, a merger of Edison General Electric Company and Thomson-Houston Electric Company created what company?

7 In 1901 who astounded Wall Street by creating a billion-dollar merger resulting in the U.S. Steel Corporation?

8 Which government agency was created in 1914 to prevent unfair methods of competition among businesses?

9 What nickname did Andrew Carnegie, John D. Rockefeller, and J. P. Morgan share?

10 What was the title of Ayn Rand's magnum opus published in 1957?

11 How much money were the core cast members paid per episode for the 9th and 10th seasons of the television comedy *Friends*?

12 Who was the philanthropist who climbed his way to the top of the world and later established the Himalayan Trust in 1962?

13 Who is the Hungarian-born philanthropist who openly said in 2003 that removing President George W. Bush from office was one of his main priorities?

14 Which landmark museum, designed by Frank Lloyd Wright, opened its doors on October 21, 1959, thanks to the generosity of the industrialist family that bears its name?

15 Who is the notable philanthropist who spent years tending to his extensive gardens and donating millions to Delaware's public schools after his retirement as chairman of General Motors in 1929?

Still Making Green

According to *Forbes Magazine*, the top 10 dead celebrities with the highest incomes total over $226 million dollars based on pretax earnings from licensing agreements and book and record sales. How many can you name?

A Walk on Wall Street

Take a stroll through the center of the financial universe with this collection of questions only an insider trader would know.

1 What term is used to describe a trader or investor who is pessimistic about a market, stock, or position, and believes that prices will drop?

2 Name the only company listed in the Dow Jones Industrial Index today that was also included in the original index in 1896?

3 What term is used to describe a trader or investor who is optimistic about a market, stock, or position, and believes that prices will rise?

4 What is the name of Dow Jones's flagship publication, founded in 1889?

5 At her death in 1916, Henrietta Howland Robinson Green left a fortune that today would be worth about $3.5 billion, which she largely amassed through investing. What was her nickname in the finance world?

6 October 29, 1929, is known as the worst day in stock market history. What day of the week was it?

7 Who served orange juice and brioche to traders the morning of October 19, 1999, to celebrate shares of her company being sold to the public?

8 If you were to go to 11 Wall Street, where would you be?

9 Which president was inaugurated on the steps of a building on Wall Street?

10 In which city was the first stock exchange in America founded in 1790?

Sold to the Highest Bidder!

What price would you pay for something you really wanted? The following auction items prove the sky is the limit for some!

1 What was the title of the painting that was sold at Sotheby's New York for nearly $54 million on November 11, 1987?

2 The famed Christie's auction house in New York facilitated the sale of this rare instrument known as "The Lady Tennant" for a record $2.03 million in 2005. What was it?

3 What popular PBS television show enables people to have long-lost items from their attics appraised by top auctioneers and experts?

4 When was the antique Persian rug that the Newport Restoration Foundation paid close to $4.5 million for in 2008 estimated to have been made?

5 Pop star George Michael purchased John Lennon's upright walnut Steinway piano for $2.08 million. What mark from Lennon does the piano still bear?

6 Whose prized Stratocaster became the most expensive guitar ever to sell at auction when it went on the block at Christie's in June 2004?

7 On November 9, 1999, a nude painting by which Spanish master was sold at auction by Christie's for $45.1 million dollars?

8 Which Hollywood director purchased the sled used in Orson Welles's 1941 masterpiece, *Citizen Kane*, for $55,000?

9 What was someone trying to auction on the Internet auction site Ebay on September 2, 1999, when the company decided to close it down? Bidding had reached a hefty price tag of $5,750,100.

The Wonderful World of Business

Eureka!

You may feel just as jubilant as the bright minds mentioned in this quiz...if you know all the right answers, that is!

1 What kind of tool was invented by Charles Moncke?

2 What connects the man who discovered penicillin with the creator of James Bond?

3 What did Belgian-born Jean Joseph Étienne Lenoir create in 1860 that paved the way for the first automobile to eventually develop?

4 What did American industrialist George Mortimer Pullman develop around 1859?

5 Which model of car did Henry Ford name after his son?

6 In the 1870s, inventor Elisha Gray and another man both rushed their respective designs for this communication device to the patent office within hours of each other and eventually entered into a famous legal battle to see who owned the rights. Gray lost. Who was the other man?

7 What swept through the U.S. Patent Office on December 15, 1836, destroying all of the patent drawings to that date?

8 In 1897, Felix Hoffman invented an improved method of synthesizing acetylsalicylic acid that the Bayer Company eventually realized they could market as what?

9 What did Art Fry invent in the early 1970s when he wanted a bookmark that wouldn't fall out of his church hymnal?

10 What name did the B. F. Goodrich Company give to its version of an innovation originally patented as "Automatic, Continuous Clothing Closure"?

Modern Moguls

Do you have a head for business? Test your knowledge of these legendary entrepreneurs to find out.

1 What New York tycoon is credited as saying, "As long as you're going to be thinking anyway, think big"?

2 Although he dated leading ladies Ava Gardner and Katharine Hepburn, which legendary billionaire dropped from public view in later life?

3 At the age of 19, which technology industrialist founded a computer software company with Paul Allen?

4 With the purchase of a large studio production facility in Chicago, Oprah Winfrey became the third woman in American entertainment history to own her own studio. Can you name the two others?

5 Which computer company was founded by a self-made entrepreneur who dropped out of the University of Texas in Austin at the age of 19 to start it?

6 Who borrowed some of the techniques he learned as a trader at Salomon Brothers in the 1970s to use with his team when he was elected to New York's highest office?

7 Who was America's first billionaire?

8 Which former CEO of General Electric is married to a former editor of the *Harvard Business Review*?

9 Which business mogul was born in Scotland and spent his formative years in Allegheny, Pennsylvania, learning about the railroad, oil, and steel business? When he died in 1919, over half of his $500 million fortune was distributed to nonprofit organizations.

10 Who is one of the largest private landowners in the United States with about 1.75 million acres in New Mexico, Montana, South Dakota, and Nebraska? (Hint: In Montana, his ranch operations raise bison.)

The Glass Ceiling

You've come a long way, baby! See if you can match these milestones for U.S. women to the correct year when they occurred.

A graduate of New England Female Medical College, Rebecca Lee Crumpler becomes the first black woman to receive an MD degree_____   **A** 1809

Muriel "Mickey" Siebert becomes the first woman to own a seat on the New York Stock Exchange and the first woman to lead one of its member firms_____   **B** 1864

Novelist Edith Wharton becomes the first woman to win a Pulitzer for fiction, winning for her novel *The Age of Innocence*_____   **C** 1869

Juanita Kreps becomes the first woman director of the New York Stock Exchange and later becomes the first woman named Secretary of Commerce_____   **D** 1896

Lettie Pate Whitehead joins Coca-Cola's board of directors and becomes the first American woman to serve as a director of a major corporation_____   **E** 1921

Mary Kies patents a method of weaving straw with silk, becoming the first woman to receive a patent_____   **F** 1933

Arabella Mansfield gets permission to practice law in Iowa, making her the first woman lawyer_____   **G** 1934

Geraldine Ferraro becomes the first woman to run for vice president on a major party ticket_____   **H** 1967

Alice Guy Blaché shoots the first of her more than 300 films, making her the first American woman film director; it was a short feature called *La Fee aux Choux* (*The Cabbage Fairy*)_____   **I** 1972

Frances Perkins is appointed secretary of labor by President Franklin D. Roosevelt, becoming the first woman member of a presidential cabinet_____   **J** 1984

From Here to There

There are so many ways to get around these days, and each mode of transportation plays an important role in the business world, whether they're making machines, testing their limits, or charging us a fee for their use.

Pedal Power

Hold tight in the turns and see if you can keep up on this quick round—it's the fastest thing on two wheels!

1 Who said: "I think it [bicycling] has done more to emancipate women than anything else in the world."

2 What piece of cycling equipment is rarely worn in China?

3 Which city claims the sixth-highest quality of life in the world and is also home to the world's most successful community bicycle program?

4 Which city in the Pacific Northwest has a bicycle network that's grown from 60 to over 260 miles since the early 1990s?

5 Known as the bicycle capital of Europe, which port city also reports that bicycles account for 40 percent of all traffic movements on its streets?

6 Which city in California enables more than 40,000 of its residents to commute to work regularly by bicycle because it maintains over 63 miles of municipal bicycle lanes and paths?

7 Selling close to a million bikes a year, which Wisconsin-based company claims to be the world's largest manufacturer of bicycles sold by specialty retailers?

8 With two-wheeled delivery fleets now numbering 37,000, what has been delivered to homes across the United Kingdom since 1880?

9 In 1899 Charles Minton Murphy (aka "Mile-a-Minute Murphy") became the first cyclist to ride a mile in under a minute when he rode behind what type of transportation device to benefit from its wind draft?

10 Which European country was the last to maintain a regiment of bicycle troops, disbanding the unit in 2003?

Baby, You Can Drive My Car

What stainless steel car appeared in a series of movies starring Michael J. Fox and Christopher Lloyd, and what were the names of those movies?

On the Road Again!

Americans love their cars—in fact, we can't get enough of them! See how many of the following questions you can correctly answer.

1 In what year did Henry Ford begin to mass produce cars using assembly lines?

2 In 1965, who wrote *Unsafe at Any Speed*, a best-selling indictment of the auto industry and its poor safety standards?

3 Which car company was the first to introduce the modern three-point seatbelt as a standard feature in its cars?

4 In 1985, which car company was the first to introduce a driver side air bag to the U.S. market?

5 What town does the folk-rock group Crash Test Dummies call home?

6 On what model car did Japanese automaker Toyota spend an estimated $1 billion to develop before putting it on sale in December 1997?

7 How did California governor Arnold Schwarzenegger retrofit his trademark Hummer to be more environmentally responsible?

8 In which country did Saab cars originate?

9 Who wrote the bohemian odyssey *On the Road*?

10 What's the name of the National Public Radio show hosted by Tom and Ray Magliozzi?

Time for T

Test your boundaries with a tour of all these transportation-related words. To make your travel a little easier, try to remember that all of them begin with the letter *T*. Name:

1 A path or course made or laid out for some particular purpose

2 The part of a car that allows the motor to shift gears

3 To work from home using a computer

4 When this is heavy, everyone gets jammed

5 Another name for the truckers' union

6 Small and powerful, this is what's used to push and pull ships and barges

7 If you visit San Francisco, you could still have an opportunity to ride one of these

8 Built in 1969, this fast track is the pride of Alabama

9 Roads, runways, and parking lots are all paved with this material

10 Eighteen-wheelers are one of many types

Muscle Madness

Considered by many to be as American as apple pie, muscle cars paved the way for the modern road warrior. Can you match the manufacturer to these classic models?

Charger_____	A Chevrolet
Camaro_____	B Dodge
Wedge_____	C Ford
GTO_____	D Mercury
Road Runner_____	E Plymouth
Torino Cobra_____	F Pontiac
Barracuda_____	
Cougar_____	
Firebird Trans Am_____	
Impala_____	

Flying High

You're sure to make a smooth landing if you can score the right answer on all of these curious airplane questions.

1 Who piloted the *Spirit of St. Louis*, from Roosevelt Field, New York, to Le Bourget Field outside Paris in 1927 to make the world's first solo nonstop transatlantic flight?

2 Where did Captain Chesley Sullenberger make an emergency landing of US Airways flight 1549 on January 15, 2009?

3 Who was Bessie Coleman?

4 In 2006, what did the U.S. Travel and Security Administration mandate for all carry-on baggage as a security measure?

5 What model of jumbo jet has flown more than 3.5 billion passengers around the world since launching in the early 1970s?

6 Who was born on July 24, 1897, and was believed to have died in 1937 on a flight between New Guinea and Howland Island?

7 Conceived in 1962, the supersonic Concorde jet was an unlikely collaboration between which two governments?

8 How many passengers could the early corporate-style jets such as the Lear 23 carry as a full load?

9 Which city is served by Santa Cruz airport?

10 What is the name of the biggest plane built in Britain?

11 At more than $2 billion each, what is the world's most expensive aircraft?

12 What name is given to the design of aircraft with the tail wing in front of the main wing?

13 At the 1973 Paris Air Show, the Soviet version of the Concorde crashed. By what nickname was the plane better known?

14 Britain was the first country to introduce a jet passenger line. What was its name?

15 Name the fastest aircraft capable of vertical takeoff.

16 Apart from being the fastest aircraft when built, what is the other unique claim to fame of the rocket-powered X-15?

17 What 1960s vintage aircraft still holds the record for the fastest operational manned flight?

18 During World War II, how did one join the "caterpillar club"?

Which Is Farthest?

Can you guess which destination is farthest from the first city mentioned? You could earn your wings if you do.

1 Berlin to Cape Town or Caracas?

2 Honolulu to Buenos Aires or Calcutta?

3 Hong Kong to London or Los Angeles?

4 Paris to Istanbul or Lisbon?

5 San Francisco to Hong Kong or Manila?

6 Warsaw to Istanbul or London?

7 Mexico City to New York or Rio de Janeiro?

8 Sydney to Stockholm or Warsaw?

9 New York to Shanghai or Tokyo?

10 Cairo to Tokyo or Washington, D.C.

Former High Flyers

In the 1990s, a handful of famous international air carriers went out of business. Can you name five of them?

All Aboard!

It's time for a little train spotting. Try your hand at matching the right name of these well-traveled trains with their respective routes and descriptions.

This train travels the highest routes in the world._____   **A**   Blue Train

Traveling 5,778 miles, this is the longest regular train trip in the world._____   **B**   Bullet Train

This glorious train trip travels from Paris to Istanbul, passing through six countries in between._____   **C**   Chattanooga Choo Choo

Making its debut in 1902, this luxury train traveled between Chicago and New York City._____   **D**   Flying Scotsman

This train ran from Chicago to Los Angeles._____   **E**   Indian Pacific

Traveling from Sydney to Perth, this train from down under lays claim to the world's longest stretch of straight track._____   **F**   Orient Express

On this luxury train, you can get your hair done in the salon while making the trip from London to Edinburgh._____   **G**   Peruvian Central Railway

This South African train makes its run between Cape Town and Pretoria._____   **H**   Super Chief

Built in 1964 with special tracks and minimal curves to enable high speeds, this train is known also as Shinkansen by its creators._____   **I**   TGV

This electric train can make its way from Paris at speeds regularly reaching 186 mph._____   **J**   20th Century Limited

A popular Glenn Miller Orchestra song from the 1940s romanticized a ride on what train?_____   **K**   Trans-Siberian Express

Getting Around Underground

Public transportation systems have enabled cities to grow at an amazing rate. How well do you know what's beneath some of the largest metropolitan cities in the world?

1   In February 1870, where did Alfred Beach open a "Pneumatic Transit," as the system was known, consisting of a 312-foot wind tunnel and a 22-passenger car propelled over the tracks by a 100-horsepower fan?

2   In terms of number of riders, which former Eastern-bloc city has the largest train system in the world?

3   Which American city was the first to officially open its underground system, nicknamed the "T," on September 1, 1897?

4   Which European city is credited with having the most track in its subway system?

5   Which Midwestern town spent $6 million dollars between 1920 and 1925 constructing a subway system that it never finished?

6   Which city opened a 2.5-mile electric subway in 1896, using single cars with trolley poles, making it the first subway on the European continent?

7   If you were riding a SEPTA subway, where would you be riding?

8   What is the underground system in Paris called?

9   What is the underground system in Berlin called?

10   In 2000, which baseball teams competed in what was often described as the subway series?

Great Ships

Get ready to set sail with these seaworthy questions!

1 What name is given to the powered water buses on the canals in Venice?

2 What was the name of the oil tanker that sank off the coast of Brittany in 1978?

3 What is the name of the cruise ship that German forces sank off the coast of Ireland in 1915?

4 Who directed *Amistad*, the 1998 film that told the story of a slave ship revolt that landed its passengers in Long Island instead of Africa?

5 In what river did more than 1,500 former Union POWs die in the explosion of the steamship *Sultana* in 1865?

6 What was the name of the ship that ultimately rescued 705 people from the sinking *Titanic*?

7 What slammed into the starboard side of the *Andrea Doria* just after 11 p.m. on the night of July 25, 1956?

8 Before it became known as one of the world's most luxurious ocean liners, what was the *Queen Mary* used to transport in World War II?

9 With a price tag of $10 million earning it a reputation as one of the most expensive productions in Broadway history, what musical won five Tony Awards in June 1997, including Best Musical?

10 What was the name of the ship Christopher Jones commanded when it set sail from Southampton, England, on September 16, 1620?

11 Built in 1911 and weighing 5,909 tons, this was the biggest sailing vessel ever built.

12 This clipper broke records regularly between 1885 and 1895 on the Australia-England route.

13 Name the largest passenger vessel ever built.

14 This giant liner was supposed to have been called *Queen Victoria*, but had to be renamed due to a misunderstanding.

15 Built in 1957, this Soviet icebreaker was also the first nuclear-powered surface ship.

16 *Titanic's* sister ship, which also sank tragically and mysteriously during World War I, was called by this name.

17 Laid down in 1914, this was the first aircraft carrier.

18 Which was the fastest-ever clipper ship on the China tea route?

Flights of Fancy

In 1991 who flew about 6,700 miles from Japan to Canada with Per Lindstrand on the world's first successful transpacific hot-air balloon flight?

An Entertaining Bit of Business

How do we define fun? Whether it's visiting an amusement park, watching a movie, enjoying a good meal, or visiting the sights of a new town, the entertainment business is built around the common human desire to just have a good time.

Twist and Turn

Roller coasters are the focal point of many amusement parks, and not for the feint of heart. Do you dare to venture a guess on this round of hair-raising true and false questions?

1   LaMarcus A. Thompson introduced his Switchback Gravity Pleasure Railway at Coney Island in 1884. This device was recognized as the first true roller coaster in America.   TRUE ○   FALSE ○

2   It was at Chicago's Columbian Exposition that the famous George Ferris Giant Wheel was introduced in 1893. A true wonder of the then modern world, the Ferris wheel weighed in at over 4 million pounds and was 264 feet high.   TRUE ○   FALSE ○

3   Disneyland, the nation's first theme park, was built at an initial cost of $1.7 million and drew 500,000 visitors to its five themed areas during its first season in 1955.   TRUE ○   FALSE ○

4   Walt Disney World opened in 1971 after Disney made the biggest investment ever for an amusement resort, a whopping $250 million.   TRUE ○   FALSE ○

5   Kings Island theme park near Cincinnati, Ohio, opened in 1972 and is credited with building the first all-steel roller coaster, which they named The Racer.   TRUE ○   FALSE ○

6   The Twister opened at Six Flags Great America in Gurnee, Illinois, in 1992. The first inverted roller coaster, in which the cars travel underneath the structure, was an immediate hit and soon parks around the world were building them.   TRUE ○   FALSE ○

7   In 1997 when the Superman ride opened at Six Flags Magic Mountain, Valencia, California, it broke records for the tallest roller coaster (415 feet tall) and fastest speed (100 miles per hour).   TRUE ○   FALSE ○

8   Leap-The-Dips, built in 1902 for Lakemont Park in Altoona, Pennsylvania, is the world's oldest operating wooden roller coaster and was designated a National Historic Landmark in 1996.   TRUE ○   FALSE ○

9   Perhaps the best-known roller coaster, the Cyclone, was opened at Walt Disney World Island in 1972.   TRUE ○   FALSE ○

10   In the 1987 film, *Roller Coaster*, George C. Scott plays a technical supervisor caught up in a mysterious plot that involves terrorist bombs placed around roller coasters.   TRUE ○   FALSE ○

The Wonderful World of Business

Dining Hot Spots

These days the restaurant business represents a big portion of the entertainment landscape, too. See how well you score in matching these notable restaurants—and don't forget to leave a good tip!

This restaurant, launched by Alice Waters in 1971, was a pioneer in developing the concept of local eating._____

You might want to drop in on this legendary spot after you see a Broadway show._____

This New York restaurant is run by Thomas Keller, the same gifted chef who started California's famed The French Laundry._____

A landmark restaurant since the 1880s, it's been under the supervision of the Brennan family since 1974._____

Originally housed in the Mayfair Hotel, this restaurant's reputation for fine dining has inspired generations._____

If you prefer authentic Mexican food over gourmet, head next door to Frontera Grill, the sister restaurant to this high-end institution, the next time you're in Chicago._____

The next time you're visiting Greenwich Village, you'll want to drop in on this Food TV Network's restaurant for a delicious bite._____

This is the restaurant that Louella Parsons and Hedda Harper claimed as their unofficial headquarters._____

In 1970 Chef Georges Perrier's created this Philadelphia restaurant to be an international destination._____

An NFL legend lent his name to this line of restaurants serving top-shelf steaks._____

A Babbo

B Brown Derby

C Chez Panisse

D Commander's Palace

E Le Bec-Fin

F Le Cirque

G Per Se

H Sardi's

I Shula's

J Topolobampo

It's a Small World, After All

Some people take classes before planning a trip to the Magic Kingdom. Would you need to do the same to answer these tricky questions correctly?

1 Covering 40 square miles, less than 35 percent of the property at Walt Disney World Resort has been developed. How has 25 percent of the land been allocated?

2 In Epcot Center, what attraction weighs 16 million pounds—more than three times that of a space shuttle fully fueled and ready for launch?

3 To the nearest thousands, how many people work at Disney World Resort?

4 What geometric shape are the 11,324 aluminum and plastic-alloy pieces that form the outer "skin" of Spaceship Earth?

5 Walt Disney World maintains the third largest fleet of what in Florida?

6 Disney's Wedding Pavilion was designed to give the bride and groom a view of what landmark scene while standing at the altar?

7 Where are more than 30 tons of fruits and vegetables grown on-site and served in Walt Disney World restaurants?

8 What kind of stone was used to build the Cinderella Castle in the Magic Kingdom?

9 What is the tallest mountain attraction at Walt Disney World?

10 What Disney landmark would wear a hat size of 342 3/4?

Legendary Lodgings

The hotel business has always benefited from interesting stories, especially those that are impossible for people to forget. Do you remember enough to name all of these special spots?

1. Esther Williams starred in the 1949 movie *This Time for Keeps*, which was filmed at this Mackinac Island hotel.

2. Located at Fifth Avenue and Central Park South, this New York City hotel is also known as "The Home of Eloise" by Friends of Libraries, USA.

3. This Paradise Island resort, inspired by a lost city, features 50,000 marine animals swimming on site.

4. This swanky Park Avenue luxury spot was originally located on the site of the Empire State Building.

5. This boutique hotel just west of Los Angeles features Swan Lake in its picturesque front lawn.

6. Where was Robert Francis Kennedy shot?

7. What Memphis hotel features a daily parade of marching ducks?

8. Considered the tallest building in New York until 1899, this red-brick landmark played host to many notable artists, including Eugene O'Neill, William Burroughs, Arthur Miller, Jaspar Johns, Leonard Cohen, Janis Joplin, and Bob Dylan, among others.

9. There have been three hotels at the corner of State and Monroe Streets in Chicago. Name the first, which burned down just 13 days after opening in 1871.

10. Originally called the Windsor Hotel, this Memphis sleeping spot is now home to the National Civil Rights Museum.

11. The Eagles won a Grammy for Record of the Year in 1977 for taking us all to this place with their music.

Roll 'Em!

Can you figure out which *A* words belong in the movie business based on the following clues?

1. What the director yells to signal the start of a scene

2. The person who represents the business interests of industry talent

3. According to the Motion Picture Association of America, these are the only people who should be watching R-rated films

4. Cartoons would be one example

5. Only the most elite and sought-after celebrities can make the cut for this

6. Refers to the perspective from which a scene is shot

7. Movie posters are a form of this

8. Errol Flynn and Tyrone Power were masters of this genre

9. In this ceremony, Oscar legends are born

10. Another name for thespians

Room at the Inn?

Hotels are always appearing in movies as the location for wrong-doings—some murderously wrong. How many hotels can you name that appeared in frightening feature films?

Taking a Grand Tour

Would you be able to survive in the travel and tourism business? See how well you can navigate these European landmarks by matching each place to its rightful location.

Kampa Island—This island is accessible if you cross the Charles Bridge that spans the Vlatva River_____

Englischer Garden—This park, Europe's largest city-owned park, is on the scale of Central Park in New York_____

Boboli Gardens—It's where a famous Renaissance family was able to get away from it all_____

Phoenix Park—This European park has housed a zoo since 1830_____

Luxembourg Gardens—Among other attractions, you'll find a pond where you can rent a motorized remote control boat_____

Gellért Hill and Citadella—The large Citadel on top of this hill allowed the Habsburgs to keep an eye on the city_____

Schloss Mirabell—Take a close look and you'll likely recognize several fountains and vistas from scenes in *The Sound of Music*_____

Schönbrunn Palace—This palace, built from 1697 to 1780, was a summer home for the Empress Maria Theresia and other Hapsburg royalty_____

Palais du Prince—Built as a 13th-century fortress, it became the royal residence in the 15th century_____

La Croisette—Palm trees and flowers line his famous boulevard by the beach_____

A Budapest, Hungary

B Cannes, France

C Dublin, Ireland

D Florence, Italy

E Monte Carlo, Monaco

F Munich, Germany

G Paris, France

H Prague, Czech Republic

I Salzburg, Austria

J Vienna, Austria

Who Said That?

Can you match the right legendary talent with their words of wisdom about the entertainment business?

"Broadway has been very good to me. But then, I've been very good to Broadway."_____

"There's no business like show business."_____

"The number of people who will not go to a show they do not want to see is unlimited."_____

"I'm going to stay in show business until I'm the last one left."_____

"I would rather entertain and hope that people learned something than educate people and hope they were entertained."_____

"I was a veteran, before I was a teenager."_____

"Heartthrobs are a dime a dozen."_____

"Career is too pompous a word. It was a job, and I have always felt privileged to be paid for what I love doing."_____

"For the theatre one needs long arms; it is better to have them too long than too short. An artiste with short arms can never, never make a fine gesture."_____

"Hollywood's a place where they'll pay you a thousand dollars for a kiss, and fifty cents for your soul."_____

A Barbara Stanwyck

B Brad Pitt

C Ethel Merman

D George Burns

E Irving Berlin

F Marilyn Monroe

G Michael Jackson

H Oscar Hammerstein

I Sarah Bernhardt

J Walt Disney

Arcade Allure

Generations of kids have grown up with joysticks in their hands trying to beat their latest score. In fact, the video-game industry now represents a multibillion dollar segment of the economy. Can you beat the highest player with these tricky questions?

1 In 1972, which company introduced *Pong* to the arcades?
a. Magnavox
b. Microsoft
c. Atari

2 The original home version of *Pong* was sold exclusively through what store?
a. Sears
b. Kmart
c. Radio Shack

3 When were Game Boys first released?
a. 1980
b. 1989
c. 1991

4 *Super Mario Brothers* was a game invented by which company?
a. Nintendo
b. Atari
c. Sega Genesis

5 Which company was the first to market a 3-D home video game?
a. Nintendo
b. Sony PlayStation
c. Atari

6 How many colors did its makers claim could be displayed on a Game Boy Advance monitor?
a. More than 5,000
b. More than 18,000
c. More than 32,000

7 What company joined the video-game arena in 1982 with its first version of *Flight Simulator*?
a. Microsoft
b. Nintendo
c. Midway

8 What video game did Russian mathematician Alexy Pajitnov develop in 1985?
a. *Tetris*
b. *Pentominos*
c. *Centipede*

9 Which controversial video game was released in 1992 and was the first to use digitized images of real actors to aid in its visual authenticity?
a. *World of Warcraft*
b. *Mortal Kombat*
c. *Street Fighter II*

10 What organization provides the public with ratings and information about video game content?
a. ESRB
b. FTC
c. HBO

Box Office Blowouts

Can you figure out which films scored all-time box office records based on the following clues?

1 Written and directed by Christopher Nolan, this film won two Oscars, including one awarded posthumously.

2 Written and directed by James Cameron, this film won 11 Oscars.

3 George Lucas received an Oscar nomination for Best Director for this work that year, but it went to Woody Allen for *Annie Hall* instead.

4 This animated sequel starring a lovable green ogre actually topped its original by more than $150 million.

5 This Steven Spielberg film was nominated for Best Picture, but it went to *Gandhi* instead.

6 Despite all the money it made, this 2006 film only received one Oscar out of its four nominations; Jack Sparrow might have said he was robbed.

7 From the pages of Marvel comics, this 2002 thriller was spring-loaded with an all-star cast.

The Life of Luxury

The world of the rich and famous is glimmering with fantastic treasures. And, as the saying goes, if you have to ask the price, you probably can't afford it. The same logic doesn't hold true for trivia though. In this round of fun puzzlers, anyone can probably guess the right answer!

A Girl's Best Friend

Sure, diamonds are a girl's best friend, but it's a safe bet that few would turn down any of the fantastic baubles mentioned in this ritzy quiz.

1 According to Hollywood lore, where did Marlene Dietrich accidentally drop her 37.41-carat cabochon emerald ring?
 a. Into a pitcher of cocktails
 b. Into a wishing well
 c. Into the batter of a cake she was making

2 Which jewelry company was the first to lend its creations to a starlet attending the Academy Awards ceremony in 1944?
 a. Harry Winston
 b. Cartier
 c. Tiffany's

3 What color is pure gold?
 a. Yellow
 b. White
 c. Pink

4 Cultured pearls are formed with human intervention, but what are the odds of a pearl being formed naturally?
 a. 1 in every 500 oysters
 b. 1 in every 10,000 oysters
 c. 1 in a million oysters

5 What is another name for the thick coating on the inner shell of the oyster or mollusk?
 a. Mother of pearl
 b. Cultured pearl
 c. Black pearl

6 What is the term for a necklace measuring 28 to 36 inches in length?
 a. Princess length
 b. Opera length
 c. Matinee length

7 Measuring nearly 10 inches in diameter, the Pearl of Lao Tzu is the largest pearl ever found. How much does it weigh?
 a. 3.6 pounds
 b. 9.5 pounds
 c. 14.1 pounds

8 Why are engagement rings traditionally worn on the third finger of the left hand?
 a. Because it's the least used finger of the hand
 b. Because most women wear a size 7
 c. Because the ancient Egyptians believed that the vein in that finger ran directly to the heart

9 Who introduced the metal platinum to jewelry in 1896?
 a. Alfred Cartier
 b. Charles Lewis Tiffany
 c. Diamond Jim Brady

Fabulously Fashionable

Can you strike a pose with the following round? It's clearly designed to reveal who's in or out when it comes to being fashion conscious.

1 This heiress-turned-fashion-model is just as comfortable maneuvering the party scene as she is on the runway.

2 Katharine Hepburn starred in a 1969 Broadway musical about the life of this French fashion designer who created "the little black dress."

3 Held in New York's Bryant Park, this is the event where top designers from around the world reveal their latest creations.

4 This reality television program revolved around weekly competitions among young fashion designers.

5 Which magazine editor's former assistant wrote the book *The Devil Wears Prada*?

6 The 1957 musical *Funny Face*, starring Fred Astaire as the fashion photographer Dick Avery, was a fictional account of the early career of which high-fashion legend?

7 Which European city stunned the fashion world in 2006 by banning from its runways models with a BMI less than 18?

8 Donna Karan and Marc Jacobs both graduated from this legendary school of design.

9 PETA is trying to change people's minds about wearing these.

10 Simon Doonan is the creative director and mastermind window dresser of which fashionable New York shopping destination?

Fine Furniture

Whether you call it a divan, a sofa, or a davenport, the world of fine furnishings is riddled with interesting facts and details.

1 What type of furniture was originally produced in medieval times to store armor?

2 American furniture crafted in the Chippendale style was made from about 1750 to 1780 and was named after cabinetmaker Thomas Chippendale's work. Where was Chippendale from?

3 American furniture crafted in this style dates from the 1720s to about 1750, although the queen it is named after died in 1714. What is it called?

4 What is an English desk and drawer combination called? (Hint: In America the word came to refer to a chest of drawers generally for the bedroom.)

5 What do you call a very thin layer of particularly fine wood that has been glued on to inferior wood to produce a smooth and attractive surface?

6 Why did all of the silver furniture disappear from the royal palaces of France?

7 What German school of art ushered in a new age of furniture design in 1925?

8 In China, fine furniture was often made of lacquered wood pieces inlaid with what precious substance?

Are You Seeing Red?

How many stones—precious and semiprecious—can you name that are red in color?

Luxury Wheels

If the thought of driving a collectible car leaves you feeling weak in the knees, put your skills to the test by seeing how many clues you can match up with the right roadsters on the following list.

Real fame came for this company with the 1907 introduction of a six-cylinder engine inside a silver-painted four-passenger chassis dubbed the Silver Ghost_____

A Aston Martin

The first car from this company was made in post-war Europe and had a rear-mounted, souped-up 40-horsepower Volkswagen engine and parts from wherever the company could find them_____

B Bentley

The first car from this company had the initials "SS" in its name, which stood for "Standard-Swallow." The SS would eventually be dropped because the initials brought up connotations of Nazi Germany_____

C Bugatti

This company's first super-car, introduced in 1966, was named after a line of renowned fighting bulls_____

D Duesenberg

This car manufacturer's brand recognition was at an all-time high when a replica of its 1961 250 GT was featured in the 1986 movie *Ferris Bueller's Day Off*_____

E Ferrari

This company picked up legendary Formula One driver Juan-Manuel Fangio in the 1950s to drive its 250F to a win in the car's debut at the Argentine Grand Prix_____

F Jaguar

This company produced the vehicle of choice for Sean Connery's James Bond in 1964's *Goldfinger*_____

G Lamborghini (the Miura)

The Continental R, which debuted in 1991, was the first car from this company to have its own dedicated body since 1954 because the company had been owned by Rolls-Royce since 1931_____

H Maserati

This American-built car was considered so fine by the general public that they coined the term "It's a Doozy" in its honor_____

I Porsche

The first car designed and built by this Italian visionary had three wheels and two engines_____

J Rolls-Royce

Lifestyles of the Rich and Famous

Looking for a way to spend a lavish afternoon? Let's see if you can learn the language of the ultra-elite. The trick is that they all rely on the letter *L*.

1 Who hosted the television program that inspired the name of this quiz?

2 Who wouldn't want to sit in the lap of this?

3 What is an Italian coffee served with milk?

4 If you buy one of these, you'll need a chauffeur.

5 When you need to revise your will, this is who you'd call.

6 What is the home of the Metropolitan Opera and the New York City Ballet?

7 If you've shopped on Rodeo Drive, you know your way around this town.

8 If you live in the limelight, people will eventually make these up about you.

9 Some people think it's fashionable to arrive this way.

10 More than half of the porcelain in France is made in this town.

Jet Setters

Even if you don't travel everywhere first class, you can probably figure out the right answer to these high-flying questions.

1 What was the name of Elvis Presley's Convair 880 jet?

2 What high-flying rock group began as a trio that called itself Jet Set?

3 Which Hollywood actor began as a "sweat hog" in Mr. Kotter's classroom and eventually became a licensed pilot?

4 In 1972, which company became the first aircraft manufacturer in the world to build 100,000 aircraft?

5 What mega-millionaire businessman owns Virgin Airways?

6 What is another name for the term for the condition known as "desynchronosis"?

7 Who decided to sink a hefty wad of his computer fortune into the development of a civilian rocket known as *SpaceShipOne*?

8 Which reporter, writing under the pen name Cholly Knickerbocker, is credited with coining the term "jet set"?

9 Which country music duo claimed they weren't the jet set, but instead were "the old Chevrolet set"?

10 What supersonic creation had its debut on January 21, 1976?

Top Travel Destinations

Can you name the top 10 states visited in the United States, according to the U.S. Travel Association?

Luxury Events

It's hard to forget some of the fantastic facts that surround these noteworthy parties. Even if you didn't attend, how many details can you remember?

1 Who hosted the legendary Black and White Ball in the Grand Ballroom of the Plaza Hotel in 1966?

2 With whom do debutantes have their first dance when attending Le Debut des Jeunes Filles de la Nouvelle Orleans?

3 Which hip-hop mogul hosts an annual White Party with a dress code that's strictly enforced?

4 How many inaugural balls were held to celebrate the swearing in of President Barack Obama?

5 *Vanity Fair* magazine hosts an annual celebrity-packed party after which awards event?

6 Who hosted the world's most expensive birthday party for himself on July 13, 1996?

7 Whose post-wedding blessing ceremony on April 10, 2005, was attended by more than 800 notable guests, including Prime Minister Tony Blair?

8 Which Hollywood talent agent was as famous for his star-studded Oscar parties as he was for his deal-making?

9 At which New York City event did Waterford Crystal make its mark in 2000?

10 What little bauble did Richard Burton give Elizabeth Taylor for her 40th birthday?

The Days of Wine and Roses

How good are you at sniffing out a suspicious story? Can you tell what's true in the following statements?

1 The Manhattan cocktail, made from whiskey and sweet vermouth, was created by Winston Churchill's mother. TRUE ○ FALSE ○

2 In the 1600s, thermometers were filled with brandy instead of mercury. TRUE ○ FALSE ○

3 Of the 400 species of oak, virtually all are suitable for making the type of high-grade oak barrels necessary for fermenting wine. TRUE ○ FALSE ○

4 The longest recorded champagne cork flight was 177 feet and 9 inches, four feet from level ground at Woodbury Vineyards in New York. TRUE ○ FALSE ○

5 A bottle of wine from approximately AD 325 was found in 1867 when a Roman stone sarcophagus was unearthed near the town of Speyer, Germany. TRUE ○ FALSE ○

6 The first Prohibition law went on the books in Indiana in 1816, forbidding the sale of any alcohol on Sunday. TRUE ○ FALSE ○

7 In 1880, Utah became the first entirely "dry" state. TRUE ○ FALSE ○

8 The first winery in the United States was in Napa, California. TRUE ○ FALSE ○

9 In 1863, a species of native American grapes were taken to Botanical Gardens in England and set the stage for decimating nearly all the vineyards of Europe due to a type of root louse the plants carried (the American varieties were naturally resistant to their effects). TRUE ○ FALSE ○

10 In 1985, one of the most expensive bottles of wine ever sold fetched a record price of $160,000; the bottle was a Bordeaux that had once belonged to Thomas Jefferson. TRUE ○ FALSE ○

11 Dom Perignon invented Champagne. TRUE ○ FALSE ○

The Things We Make

Building a business requires more than simple bricks and mortar. If product must be made, the manufacturing process is critical. And that's precisely why this section begins with the low-down on some factory facts.

Factory Facts

Time to punch the clock and check your speed with this round of fast facts!

1 What company, located in Everett, Washington, is credited with having created the largest factory building in the world?

2 What was the nickname given to Mary Harris Jones, the woman who led protest marches from Kensington, Pennsylvania, to New York City during the Roosevelt administration?

3 What is the title of the 1936 Chaplin masterpiece that depicted man's difficulty living in an industrialized society?

4 Which Roald Dahl novel was made into a movie in 1971 and remade in 2005 by Tim Burton?

5 What was the name of the Los Angeles restaurant David Overton opened in 1978 to celebrate his mother's over-the-top cream cheese desserts?

6 What is the name of the factory device that involves a continuous loop supported by rollers?

7 Where is the largest chocolate factory in the United States located?

8 What term was coined by a Ford Motor Co. engineer around 1946 to describe systems in which mechanical, electrical, or computerized actions are substituted for human effort and intelligence?

9 What name is given to factories where workers are employed at low wages and under unhealthy or oppressive conditions?

10 Some factories contain hundreds of miles of these so they can transport items from place to place (two words).

11 What name is given to a factory that contains several buildings?

The Union Label

Do you remember the words to the famous union label song? If so, sing it now!

The Wonderful World of Business

The Computer Industry

The PC world is based on bits and bytes, which in some ways are similar to true and false statements. That said, can you tell which events really did happen in the evolution of the computer industry? A true or false is all you need to provide.

1   In 1939 Walt Disney Pictures ordered eight Hewlett-Packard Audio Oscillators to generate sound effects for its 1940 movie *Fantasia*   TRUE ○   FALSE ○

2   On election night in 1952, CBS News borrowed a UNIVAC to make a scientific prediction of the outcome of the presidential race between Dwight D. Eisenhower and Adlai Stevenson.   TRUE ○   FALSE ○

3   In 1960, AT&T designed its Dataphone, the first commercial modem for converting digital computer data to analog signals that could be transmitted across its long-distance network.   TRUE ○   FALSE ○

4   In 1976 Steve Wozniak designed a single-board computer called the Apple I.   TRUE ○   FALSE ○

5   In 1977, Tandy Radio Shack's first desktop computer—the TRS-80—sold 50,000 units within a month of its release.   TRUE ○   FALSE ○

6   In 1981, Adam Osborne produced the first portable computer, the Osborne I, which weighed a whopping 24 pounds and cost $1,795.   TRUE ○   FALSE ○

7   In 1980 *Time* magazine varied its annual tradition of naming a "Man of the Year," and instead named the computer its "Machine of the Year."   TRUE ○   FALSE ○

8   In 1984 Apple Computer introduced the Macintosh with a $1.5 million commercial during the 1984 Super Bowl.   TRUE ○   FALSE ○

9   In 1988 Pixar's *Tin Toy* became the first computer-animated film to win an Oscar, winning the award for best animated short film.   TRUE ○   FALSE ○

10 In 1994 Yahoo is founded by Harvard graduate students Jerry Yang and David Filo.   TRUE ○   FALSE ○

United We Stand

Organized labor has been a powerful factor in the growth of the American workforce. How much do you know about these groups?

1   Who was the agrarian labor leader born near Yuma, Arizona, who helped migrant workers by becoming involved in California's self-help Community Service Organization (CSO)?

2   Whose leadership of the coal miners' strike in 1902 secured higher wages and better working conditions in the industry?

3   What 1979 film about the textile industry earned Sally Field her first Oscar award?

4   Who was the longstanding leader of the AFL–CIO who refused to support either candidate in the 1972 presidential elections?

5   What is the largest labor union in the United States not affiliated with the AFL–CIO?

6   Which U.S. holiday was created to honor working people?

7   Who served as president of the International Brotherhood of Teamsters from 1957 to 1971?

8   How much of a pay hike did members of the United Auto Workers receive after their momentous 67-day strike against General Motors in 1970?

9   What group of workers did President Reagan dismiss in August 1981 for holding what he deemed to be an unauthorized strike?

10 What is the term used to describe a worker who crosses a picket line?

Gearing Up!

Simple machines basically have few or no moving parts, but they make work considerably easier. Can you spot what the examples below have in common and match them to the right type?

Clocks, automobiles, and drills use these_____

Staircase, ramp, bottom of a bathtub_____

Flagpole, crane, mini-blinds_____

Ax, zipper, knife_____

Door on hinges, seesaw, hammer, bottle opener_____

Bolt, spiral staircase_____

Doorknob, wagon, toy car_____

A Inclined plane

B Lever

C Pulley

D Gears

E Screw

F Wedge

G Wheel and axle

The Mothers of Invention

Can you figure out what the following women are credited with creating?

1 The corset's reign began to topple when Mary Phelps Jacob invented this instead.

2 As an industrial engineer and mother of 12, Lillian Moller Gilbreth never threw away a good idea, which was a step in the right direction in creating this device.

3 Marie Curie's conscious decision not to patent methods of processing radium or its medical applications led to the development of this radiology miracle.

4 Bette Nesmith Graham, a Dallas secretary and a single mother, originally called her invention "mistake out."

5 In 1959 Ruth Handler invented this iconic toy, named after her own daughter, Barbara.

6 Early in the 19th century, Madame C. J. Walker made her fortune selling these unique products door-to-door to other women.

7 Stephanie Kwolek's research for DuPont led to the development of this synthetic material, which is five times stronger than steel.

8 Marion Donovan's leakproof, disposable, and absorbent invention revolutionized child care and the paper industry.

9 Mary Anderson's invention became standard equipment on all American cars by 1916 and made driving in wet weather considerably safer.

10 Ann Moore's observations of mothers in Africa carrying their babies securely on their backs led her to design this baby toting device in 1969.

Here We Come

Bette Nesmith Graham's son was the stocking-capped lead guitarist in a 1960s television rock band with a simian name. Can you remember the guitarist and the band?

Made in America

Brace yourself. This round of questions is designed to reveal whether you know the nuts and bolts of the manufacturing process. Appropriately enough, all the answers begin with the letter *B*, for business. Name the *B* word for...

1 When a shipment is delayed

2 What an optical scanner reads

3 Any type of physically demanding work could qualify as this

4 Any type of goods transported or sold in large volume versus individual packages

5 An incidental or secondary item created during the manufacturing process

6 A group of things worked on at once

7 A type of container

8 The person who supervises a team

9 When something doesn't work anymore

10 In a textile mill, it's what fabric is wrapped onto

Rosie the Riveter

By 1944, there were 12 million Americans in uniform, and the shape of this country would be forever changed as an unprecedented number of women went to work. How much do you know about the changes that were underfoot?

1 In 1944, war production represented what percent of the gross national product?

2 The Rosie the Riveter painting originally graced the cover of what magazine?

3 What's angelic about the portrait of Rosie that ran on the magazine cover?

4 At the height of World War II, about what percentage of the 100,000-person Richmond Kaiser shipyard workforce were women?

5 Where is the Rosie the Riveter National Historical Park located?

6 What was the name of the nation's first HMO, originally founded to keep California shipyard workers healthy?

7 What was Atchison Village?

8 Whose painting of Rosie the Riveter was auctioned by Sotheby's on May 22, 2002, for $4,959,500?

From Main Street to Wall Street

Wherever business may take you, there are sure to be many rungs to the corporate ladder, each riddled with new challenges and politics. Depending on how well you know how to play the game, you may find yourself climbing to the top before you know it.

A Day at the Office

If Saturday and Sunday are your favorite days of the week, these business riddles are guaranteed to chase away the Monday through Friday blues.

1 Who created *Dilbert*, the cartoon series that features a likeable and extremely nerdy engineer-office worker?

2 Who designed the corporate office space for the Johnson Wax company in Racine, Wisconsin?

3 What character does Rainn Wilson play on *The Office*?

4 Where would you work if your office was located at 233 South Wacker Drive in Chicago?

5 What did West Michigan's Herman Miller Company introduce in 1968 that changed the idea of office forever?

6 How many states are visible from the top of New York's most famous office building?

7 What type of popular office chair replaced a traditional fabric on foam design with "breathable" mesh?

8 In what 1999 movie did Jennifer Aniston play a waitress who befriends a computer software engineer bent on seeking revenge from his company?

9 What had everyone watching the clock when it went into effect October 24, 1940, as part of the Fair Labor Standards Act of 1938?

10 Considered the world's largest office building, what opened January 15, 1943?

Copy Cat!

What was the name of the inky paper used in typewriters to make duplicate copies of a document?

The Wonderful World of Business

Office Antiques

Always seeking bigger and better efficiencies, the following quiz reveals how many excellent office technologies have been scrapped in the name of progress. How many might you remember?

1. In 1874, the original Sholes & Glidden typewriter used the QWERTY keyboard, but typed in what?
   a. Capital letters only
   b. Blue ink
   c. Double-spaced lines

2. Which gun-making company had a hand in producing the world's first typewriter?
   a. Smith & Wesson
   b. E. Remington & Sons
   c. Winchester Guns

3. Early typewriters featured a foot treadle. What was its function?
   a. To advance the paper after every keystroke
   b. To help power the keys
   c. To provide for the carriage return

4. What did Ralph Wedgwood patent in 1806 that allowed office workers to make more than one copy of a document?
   a. An office printing press
   b. Carbon paper
   c. Lithographs

5. In 1965, Xerox introduced a machine to the business world capable of producing how many copies an hour?
   a. 2,400
   b. 600
   c. 60

6. What did inventor Samuel B. Fay patent in 1867 that could literally hold an office together?
   a. The stapler
   b. Rubber bands
   c. The first bent-wire paper clip

7. What were the machines called that were invented beginning in the early 17th century to help people keep their numbers straight?
   a. Calculators
   b. Arithmometers
   c. Addometers

8. Introduced in 1981, what did Texas Instrument's TI-1766 calculator eliminate the need for?
   a. Batteries
   b. Microchips
   c. Adding tape

Principles of Business

Pay attention and you're sure to succeed with this round! All of the following clues point to words that begin with the letter *P*.

1. A list of employees to be paid, with the amount due to each

2. A demonstration, lecture, or welcoming speech

3. The department responsible for recruitment and welfare of staff or employees

4. The monetary gains of a company, less operating expenses

5. A number that expresses the proportion per hundred

6. Salary or wages

7. Everything owned by the company

8. A prize, bonus, or award given to motivate customers to buy something

9. The minimum interest rate charged by a commercial bank on short-term loans

10. An advancement in rank or position

Imaginary Wealth

Sure, we all sit around and wonder what it might be like to win the lottery, but can you figure out who the true fictional tycoons might be from the following clues?

1 This poor little rich boy made his debut as a backup feature in *Little Dot* in 1953.

2 Michael Douglas brought this character to life as a ruthless Wall Street tycoon.

3 This patriotic icon is believed to have been inspired by the initials on the boxes of food that fed the U.S. Army.

4 His kinfolk told him to "move away from there."

5 This brave crime fighter was a pivotal member of the Justice League, as well as the orphaned child of billionaires.

6 Dickens could not have imagined a more miserly character for his most popular Christmas story.

7 Raul Julia almost stole scenes from his wife, played by Anjelica Huston, in this 1991 dark comedy.

8 In 1980 over 90 million American viewers tuned in to see how the cliffhanger involving this larger-than-life Texan would resolve.

9 This reclusive candy maker was originally played on film by Gene Wilder.

10 Which wealthy man spent time as a castaway after *The Minnow* was lost?

Taking Shorthand

Sweet-talking the secretary is often the best way to score an appointment to meet with the big boss. Would you have enough of the inside scoop on the following notable secretaries to charm your way into the inner sanctum?

1 Who was Miss Jane Hathaway?

2 Comedienne Marcia Wallace won an Emmy for her voice work as Bart Simpson's teacher Mrs. Krabappel, but Wallace got her first big break playing a secretary on what popular 1972 sitcom?

3 What television character worked at Winfred-Louder Department Store for the store manager, Mr. Bell?

4 Who was Secretary of State under President Nixon?

5 Which actress plays the character Pam Beesly on *The Office*?

6 What 1988 television comedy about a fictional news series called *FYI* (*For Your Information*) had a running gag about the lead character never being able to keep a secretary?

7 Who played White House Press Secretary C. J. Cregg on *The West Wing*?

8 What was the full name of Colonel Potter's devoted assistant on *M*A*S*H*?

9 Who was nominated for a Grammy in 1982 for her performance of the theme song "Nine to Five"?

10 Who played Tess McGill in the 1990 situation comedy *Working Girl*, based on the film by the same name?

Business School Basics

If you've shopped around business schools before, you probably don't need to hit the books any further to match up the following schools with their respective universities.

Ross School of Business_____	**A** Brigham Young University
The Wharton School_____	**B** Carnegie Mellon University
Booth School of Business_____	**C** Cornell University
Kellogg Graduate School of Management_____	**D** Dartmouth College
Fuqua School of Business_____	**E** Duke University
Sloan School of Management_____	**F** Emory University
Haas School of Business_____	**G** Indiana University, Bloomington
Johnson Graduate School of Management_____	**H** MIT
Tuck School of Business_____	**I** New York University
Stern School of Business_____	**J** Northwestern University
Anderson School of Management_____	**K** Southern Methodist University
Kelley School of Business_____	**L** UCLA
Darden School of Business_____	**M** University of California, Berkeley
Kenan–Flagler Business School_____	**N** University of Chicago
Cox School of Business_____	**O** University of Michigan
Tepper School of Business_____	**P** University of North Carolina at Chapel Hill
Mendoza College of Business_____	**Q** University of Notre Dame
McCombs School of Business_____	**R** University of Pennsylvania
Marriott School of Management_____	**S** University of Texas at Austin
Goizueta Business School_____	**T** University of Virginia

C Is for Cash

All of the following clues point to words that have two things in common: They revolve around money and begin with the letter *C*.

1 In the European Union, the euro is a form of what?

2 When a lender has confidence in a purchaser's ability and intention to pay, what do they issue?

3 Before ATMs, people used to use these more often.

4 This is what you make when you "break" a dollar.

5 A mail-order means to selling merchandise.

6 What is used in a poker game in lieu of money?

7 What were originally issued in gold and silver?

8 What did people receive as part of the Homestead Act?

9 What is a type of check drawn by a bank on its own funds?

10 What is a means of determining how much money you have?

At the Top

Can you match these corporate figures with the companies that they made notable?

Ty Warner_____   A Amazon

Lee Iacocca_____   B Beanie Babies

Jeff Bezos_____   C Berkshire Hathaway

Mark Zuckerberg_____ D Chrysler

Warren Buffet_____   E Condé Nast

Philip Knight_____   F Enron

Sam Walton_____   G Facebook

Ken Lay_____   H Nike

S. I. Newhouse Jr._____ I Oracle

Larry Ellison_____   J Walmart

Media

All corporations depend on the news to help them keep up with the competition, communicate with their markets, and stay abreast of changes that might affect profitability. But as the following quizzes show, the media industry is also a business unto itself with many facts and facets to its own intriguing story.

Read All About It!

They're black and white and read all over, or so that old riddle goes. But how much do you know about those who make the news?

1 What catchphrase did newspaper publisher William Randolph Hearst popularize after the sinking of a U.S. battleship off the coast of Havana?

2 How much did an issue of the *New York Times* cost when it debuted in 1851?

3 Who directed *Citizen Kane*?

4 Which founding father was also brother to the man who first published the *New England Courant*, the first "newspaper" in Boston?

5 What tabloid did Carol Burnett sue in 1981 for printing a story accusing her of public drunkenness?

6 What major newspaper printed its final edition on February 27, 2009, just 55 days shy of its 150th anniversary of publication?

7 Who played Alicia Clark, the hard-driving editor who is out to manage costs in the 1994 film, *The Paper*?

8 Which owner and publisher of a major U.S. newspaper earned a Pulitzer Prize for Biography in 1998?

9 What one-operator machine was introduced to the printing world about 1886 and was used by newspapers for generations?

10 What scandal did Carl Bernstein and Bob Woodward unravel after details were first reported on June 18, 1972?

11 What newspaper is nicknamed "The Old Gray Lady"?

12 Which newspaper first rolled off the presses on September 15, 1982, and was selling more than 1.3 million copies a day nationwide by the end of the following year?

Paying for Page Turners

What was founded in 1926 to sell books at reduced prices by mail on a subscription basis?

The Well-Read Reader

Don't bookmark this page! Just jump right in and see how well you've been staying abreast of the literary landscape.

1 Who was born July 31, 1965, and grew up to write one of the most popular series of children's books of all time?
a. Cornelia Funke
b. Christopher Paolini
c. J. K. Rowling

2 Whose collection forms the cornerstone of the book collection housed at the Bibliothèque Nationale de France?
a. Jean Paul Sartre
b. Victor Hugo
c. Charles V

3 Johannes Gutenberg invented a press that used movable metal type around 1450, but what country to the east had been producing books using carved woodblocks as early as the seventh century?
a. Japan
b. China
c. Korea

4 Which book has sold more than 18 million copies since 1930?
a. *Better Homes and Gardens Cook Book*
b. *Better Homes and Gardens Complete Guide to Quilting*
c. *Better Homes and Gardens Plants for All Seasons*

5 In 1906, what industry did Upton Sinclair expose as a public-health threat in his landmark work, *The Jungle*?
a. Meatpacking
b. Textiles
c. Sugar

6 Who wrote the controversial novel *Satanic Verses* in 1989 and received death threats from Islamic militants?
a. Ayaan Hirsi Ali
b. Michael Ondaatje
c. Salman Rushdie

7 What do J. D. Salinger's *The Catcher in the Rye*, Harper Lee's *To Kill a Mockingbird*, John Steinbeck's *Of Mice and Men*, and Mark Twain's *The Adventures of Huckleberry Finn* have in common?
a. They all won the Pulitzer Prize
b. They've all been used to challenge the First Amendment
c. They've all been nominated for a National Book Award

8 Who wrote *Nickel and Dimed: On (Not) Getting By* in America?
a. Barbara Ehrenreich
b. Barbara Kingsolver
c. Michael Pollen

9 Who wrote *Mr. Peabody's Apples*?
a. Katie Couric
b. Jerry Seinfeld
c. Madonna

10 What was Stephen King's first novel?
a. *Salem's Lot*
b. *Carrie*
c. *The Dark Tower*

Commercial Success

Can you match the right product with its tried-and-true advertising slogan?

Good to the last drop_____   A American Express

Built for the human race_____   B Apple

It's the real thing_____   C AT&T Yellow Pages

Just slightly ahead of our time_____   D Coca-Cola

Breakfast of champions_____   E Gatorade

Takes a licking and keeps on ticking_____   F Life Alert

Let your fingers do the walking_____   G Maxwell House

Don't leave home without it_____   H Nissan

I've fallen and I can't get up_____   I Panasonic

Once you pop, you can't stop_____   J Pringles

Be like Mike_____   K Timex

Think different_____   L Wheaties

Mostly Magazines

You have to be pretty sharp to make it in the magazine business. See if you have what it takes to stay in the game with this glossy round of riddles.

1 What weekly magazine debuted in 1923 and became legendary for its annual Man of the Year cover?

2 What popular men's magazine did Marilyn Monroe grace the cover of when it hit newsstands in 1953?

3 Who was on the cover of the very first *People* magazine in 1974?

4 In what country was the editor of *Vanity Fair*, Graydon Carter, born?

5 Who was 25 when she became editor-in-chief of England's oldest glossy, *The Tatler*?

6 In 1991 which photographer took the cover shot for *Vanity Fair* of a pregnant Demi Moore posing nude?

7 Who publishes *Rolling Stone* magazine?

8 At what women's magazine did Helen Gurley Brown serve at the helm for 32 years?

9 Which Canadian editor served as the editor-in-chief of *Us Weekly*, *Glamour*, *Cosmopolitan*, *Marie Claire*, and *YM*?

10 What was the name of the political magazine launched by the son of a U.S. president in 1995?

Internet Intrigue

Computers work in binary code, meaning everything can be broken down into simple yes-no questions. The same can be said for the following list of brain puzzlers, it's just that these require a true or false to complete.

1 Queen Elizabeth was the first state leader to send an e-mail. TRUE ○ FALSE ○

2 Isaac Asimov coined the term coin "cyberspace" in 1984. TRUE ○ FALSE ○

3 In 1998 an Internet virus temporarily shut down about 10 percent of the world's Internet servers. TRUE ○ FALSE ○

4 A popular interface system that provided point-and-click navigation was created at the University of Minnesota in 1991 and named after the school's mascot. TRUE ○ FALSE ○

5 In 1994 Microsoft creates Netscape and introduces the Navigator browser. TRUE ○ FALSE ○

6 In 1985 Quantum Computer Services debuts its services, featuring e-mail, electronic bulletin boards, news, and other information; later, the company changes its name to America Online. TRUE ○ FALSE ○

7 On July 8, 1997, Internet traffic records are broken as people tune in to watch the first online broadcast of the 68th All-Star Baseball Game. TRUE ○ FALSE ○

8 When America Online bought Time Warner in 2000 for $16 billion, it represented the biggest merger of all time. TRUE ○ FALSE ○

9 In 2003 Apple Computer introduced its Apple iTunes Music Store, where people could download songs for free. TRUE ○ FALSE ○

10 By 2006, the Internet had grown to include more than 600 million Web sites. TRUE ○ FALSE ○

11 In a move to challenge Google's Internet dominance of search and advertising, software giant Microsoft offered to buy Yahoo for $44.6 billion in 2008. TRUE ○ FALSE ○

12 In 2007, World Series tickets prove so popular that the Colorado Rockies' computer system crashes when it receives 8.5 million hits within the first 90 minutes of sales. TRUE ○ FALSE ○

Energy

While there are many types of fuel that can make things run, controlling those resources often translates into real power as the numerous energy crises through the years have shown. How well-versed are you in the different means to power?

Striking It Rich

Vast fortunes have been made and lost in the oil business, making it an endlessly fascinating subject for most.

1 Who made the decision in 1911 to break up John D. Rockefeller's company, Standard Oil?

2 The 2008 film *There Will Be Blood*, about a turn-of-the-century oil prospector and the destructive nature of power, was based on a novel by whom?

3 The Trans Alaska Pipeline System moves oil from the North Slope of Alaska to where?

4 How many gallons are in a barrel of crude oil?

5 What happened on March 24, 1989, in Alaska on Prince William Sound?

6 How much of the world's total oil endowment is thought to be in the Middle East?

7 What year was the largest reservoir of American petroleum north of Mexico discovered in Alaska?

8 What is "Texas Tea"?

9 What is the main type of machinery used in drilling oil?

Blowing in the Wind

We might not find all the answers in this energy source, but figuring out whether the following statements are true or false might shed some light on the matter.

1 Unlike power plants, many wind plants are not owned by public utility companies. TRUE ○ FALSE ○

2 Over 25,000 years ago, the ancient Egyptians used wind to sail ships. TRUE ○ FALSE ○

3 American colonists used windmills to pump water. TRUE ○ FALSE ○

4 Wind is caused by the uneven heating of the earth's surface by the sun. TRUE ○ FALSE ○

5 In Tehachapi, California, the wind blows less from April through October than it does in the winter. TRUE ○ FALSE ○

6 One of the world's largest wind farms, the Horse Hollow Wind Energy Center in Texas, generates enough electricity to power 220,000 homes per year. TRUE ○ FALSE ○

7 To make wind energy feasible, large turbines require wind speeds of at least 20 mph. TRUE ○ FALSE ○

8 The kinetic energy in wind decreases exponentially in proportion to its speed. TRUE ○ FALSE ○

9 In 2007, Texas oil tycoon T. Boone Pickens led a coalition of landowners in planning for the world's largest wind farm. TRUE ○ FALSE ○

Answers

PAGE 263

MBA Magic

1 Magnate
2 Motivation
3 Moxie
4 Memo
5 Mutual funds
6 Manager
7 Merit pay
8 Market
9 Money
10 Meetings

Mega-Mansions

1 Cornelius Vanderbilt II
2 Theresa Fair Oelrichs
3 Pierre Samuel du Pont II
4 James Madison
5 John D. Rockefeller
6 Franklin D Roosevelt
7 Elvis Presley
8 Thomas Jefferson
9 Originally Edsel Ford, now Martha Stewart

What Did the Neighbors Think?

The Godfather

PAGE 264

Generous Giants and Landmark Deals

1 Bill and Melinda Gates Foundation
2 Oprah Winfrey
3 The United Nations
4 John D. Rockefeller
5 Handshakes
6 General Electric
7 J. P. Morgan
8 The Federal Trade Commission
9 Robber Baron
10 *Atlas Shrugged*
11 One million dollars each
12 Sir Edmund Hillary
13 George Soros
14 The Guggenheim Museum
15 Pierre S. du Pont

Still Making Green

1 Kurt Cobain
2 Elvis Presley
3 Charles M. Schulz
4 John Lennon
5 Albert Einstein
6 Andy Warhol
7 Theodore Geisel (Dr. Seuss)
8 Ray Charles
9 Marilyn Monroe
10 Johnny Cash

PAGE 265

A Walk on Wall Street

1 Bear
2 General Electric
3 Bull
4 *The Wall Street Journal*
5 The Witch of Wall Street
6 Tuesday, a day that has come to be known as "Black Tuesday"
7 Martha Stewart
8 The New York Stock Exchange
9 George Washington
10 Philadelphia

Sold to the Highest Bidder!

1 *Irises* by Vincent Van Gough
2 A Stradivarius violin
3 *Antiques Roadshow*
4 1600
5 Cigarette burns
6 Eric Clapton's
7 Picasso
8 Steven Spielberg
9 A human kidney

PAGE 266

Eureka!

1 A monkey wrench
2 They both had the surname Fleming
3 The first practical internal-combustion engine
4 Railroad sleeping car
5 The Ford Edsel
6 Alexander Graham Bell
7 Fire
8 Aspirin

9 Post-it notes
10 Zipper

Modern Moguls

1 Donald Trump
2 Howard Hughes
3 Bill Gates
4 Lucille Ball and Mary Pickford
5 Dell
6 Michael Bloomberg
7 John D. Rockefeller
8 Jack Welch
9 Andrew Carnegie
10 Ted Turner

PAGE 267

The Glass Ceiling

1 1864
2 1967
3 1921
4 1972
5 1934
6 1809
7 1869
8 1984
9 1896
10 1933

PAGE 268

Pedal Power

1 Susan B. Anthony
2 Helmets
3 Copenhagen, Denmark
4 Portland, Oregon
5 Amsterdam, Netherlands
6 San Francisco, California
7 Trek
8 Mail
9 Train
10 Switzerland

Baby, You Can Drive My Car

A DeLorean in *Back to the Future*

PAGE 269

On the Road Again!

1 1914
2 Ralph Nader

3 Volvo
4 Mercedes-Benz
5 Winnipeg, Manitoba
6 Prius
7 He made it run on vegetable oil
8 Sweden
9 Jack Kerouac
10 *Car Talk*

Time for T

1 Track
2 Transmission
3 Telecommute
4 Traffic
5 Teamsters
6 Tugboat
7 Trolley
8 Talladega Superspeedway
9 Tarmac
10 Trucks

Muscle Madness

1 Dodge
2 Chevrolet
3 Plymouth
4 Pontiac
5 Plymouth
6 Ford
7 Plymouth
8 Mercury
9 Pontiac
10 Chevrolet

PAGE 270

Flying High

1 Charles Lindbergh
2 The Hudson River
3 The first black female pilot in the United States. She trained in Paris and received her license in 1921.
4 No liquids or gels would be permitted
5 Boeing 747
6 Amelia Earhart
7 The British and French
8 Five
9 Mumbai
10 Bristol Brabazon built in 1948 to carry about 100 passengers
11 BS Spirit stealth bomber
12 Canard

13 Concordski
14 The Comet
15 The Harrier Jump Jet
16 It was the first aircraft ever to fly into space, in 1967
17 The SR-71 Blackbird spy plane
18 By escaping from an airplane by parachute. The club was named after the silkworm (caterpillar) that provided the parachute silk.

Which Is Farthest?

1 Cape Town
2 Buenos Aires
3 Los Angeles
4 Istanbul
5 Manila
6 London
7 Rio de Janeiro
8 They're the same distance: 9,696 miles
9 Shanghai
10 Tokyo

PAGE 271

All Aboard!

1 Peruvian Central Railway
2 Trans-Siberian Express
3 Orient Express
4 20th Century Limited
5 Super Chief
6 Indian Pacific
7 Flying Scotsman
8 Blue Train
9 Bullet Train
10 TGV
11 Chattanooga Choo Choo

Getting Around Underground

1 New York City
2 Moscow
3 Boston
4 London
5 Cincinnati
6 Budapest
7 Philadelphia
8 Metro
9 U-Bahn
10 New York Yankees and New York Mets

PAGE 272

Great Ships

1 Vaporetti
2 *Amoco Cadiz*
3 *Lusitania*
4 Steven Spielberg
5 The Mississippi
6 *The Carpathian*
7 The bow of another ship, the *Stockholm*
8 British troops
9 *Titanic*
10 *Mayflower*
11 *France II*
12 *Cutty Sark*
13 *Freedom of the Seas, Liberty of the Seas, Independence of the Seas* (all are Royal Caribbean International cruise liners)
14 *Queen Mary*
15 *Lenin*
16 *Britannic*
17 *Argus*
18 *Flying Cloud*

Flights of Fancy

Sir Richard Branson

PAGE 273

Twist and Turn

1 True
2 True
3 False; it cost $17 million and drew 3.8 million visitors
4 True
5 False; The Racer was notable for reviving interest in wooden roller coasters
6 False; the ride was called Batman
7 True
8 True
9 False; the Cyclone was a ride at Coney Island in 1927
10 False

Answers

Dining Hot Spots

1 Chez Panisse
2 Sardi's
3 Per Se
4 Commander's Palace
5 Le Cirque
6 Topolobampo
7 Babbo
8 Brown Derby
9 Le Bec-Fin
10 Shula's

It's a Small World, After All

1 As a wilderness preserve
2 Spaceship Earth
3 62,000; Walt Disney World Resort is the largest single-site employer in the United States
4 Triangles
5 Buses
6 Magic Kingdom's Cinderella Castle
7 The Land Pavilion in Epcot
8 None; the whole shell of the building is fiberglass
9 Expedition Everest at Disney's Animal Kingdom
10 The Earful Tower at Disney's Hollywood Studios

Legendary Lodgings

1 Grand Hotel
2 The Plaza
3 Atlantis
4 Waldorf Astoria
5 Hotel Bel Air
6 Ambassador Hotel
7 The Peabody
8 The Chelsea Hotel
9 The Palmer
10 Lorraine Motel
11 Hotel California

Roll 'Em!

1 Action
2 Agent
3 Adults
4 Animation

5 A-list
6 Angle
7 Advertisement
8 Adventure
9 Academy Awards
10 Actors

Taking a Grand Tour

1 Prague, Czech Republic
2 Munich, Germany
3 Florence, Italy
4 Dublin, Ireland
5 Paris, France
6 Budapest, Hungary
7 Salzburg, Austria
8 Vienna, Austria
9 Monte Carlo, Monaco
10 Cannes, France

Who Said That?

1 Ethel Merman
2 Irving Berlin
3 Oscar Hammerstein
4 George Burns
5 Walt Disney
6 Michael Jackson
7 Brad Pitt
8 Barbara Stanwyck
9 Sarah Bernhardt
10 Marilyn Monroe

Arcade Allure

1 c. Atari
2 a. Sears
3 b. 1989
4 a. Nintendo
5 b. Sony PlayStation
6 c. More than 32,000
7 a. Microsoft
8 a. *Tetris*
9 b. *Mortal Kombat*
10 a. ESRB

Box Office Blowouts

1 *The Dark Knight*
2 *Titanic*
3 *Star Wars*
4 *Shrek 2*

5 *E.T.: The Extra-Terrestrial*
6 *Pirates of the Caribbean: Dead Man's Chest*
7 *Spider-Man*

A Girl's Best Friend

1 c. Into the batter of a cake she was making
2 a. Harry Winston
3 a. Yellow
4 b. 1 in every 10,000 oysters
5 a. Mother of pearl
6 b. Opera length
7 c. 14.1 pounds
8 c. Because the ancient Egyptians believed that the vein in that finger ran directly to the heart
9 a. Alfred Cartier

Fabulously Fashionable

1 Paris Hilton
2 Coco Chanel
3 Fashion Week (recently named Mercedes Benz Fashion Week and moving to Lincoln Center in 2010)
4 *Project Runway*
5 Anna Wintour
6 Richard Avedon
7 Madrid
8 Parsons
9 Furs
10 Barney's

Fine Furniture

1 Armoire
2 London
3 Queen Anne
4 Bureau
5 Veneer
6 In times of war, the silver mountings were melted down and turned into silver coins
7 Bauhaus
8 Mother of pearl

PAGE 280

Luxury Wheels

1 Rolls-Royce
2 Porsche
3 Jaguar
4 Lamborghini (the Miura)
5 Ferrari
6 Maserati
7 Aston Martin
8 Bentley
9 Duesenberg
10 Bugatti

Lifestyles of the Rich and Famous

1 Robin Leach
2 Luxury
3 Latte
4 Limousine
5 Lawyer
6 Lincoln Center
7 Los Angeles
8 Lies
9 Late
10 Limoges

PAGE 281

Jet Setters

1 *The Lisa Marie*
2 The Byrds
3 John Travolta
4 Cessna
5 Richard Branson
6 Jet lag
7 Paul Allen
8 Igor Cassini
9 George Jones and Tammy Wynette
10 The Concorde

Top Travel Destinations

California, Florida, Texas, Pennsylvania, New York, Nevada, Georgia, North Carolina, Virginia, New Jersey

Luxury Events

1 Truman Capote
2 Their fathers
3 Sean Combs
4 10
5 Academy Awards

6 Sultan of Brunei
7 Prince Charles and Camilla Parker Bowles
8 Paul "Swifty" Lazar
9 The New Year's Eve Countdown on Times Square
10 A pendant featuring a 69-carat diamond

PAGE 282

The Days of Wine and Roses

1 True
2 True
3 False
4 True
5 True
6 True
7 False
8 False; the first commercial winery was established in Missouri in 1823
9 True
10 True
11 False; he devised the mushroom cork and metal closure that allowed vintners to keep bubbles in the bottle

PAGE 283

Factory Facts

1 The Boeing Company
2 Mother Jones (also Mother of All Agitators and the Miners' Angel)
3 *Modern Times*
4 *Charlie and the Chocolate Factory*
5 The Cheesecake Factory
6 Conveyor belt
7 Hershey, Pennsylvania
8 Automation
9 Sweatshop
10 Conveyor belts
11 Plant

PAGE 284

The Computer Industry

1 True
2 True
3 True
4 True

5 False; it sold 10,000 in the first month
6 True
7 False; the year was 1982
8 True
9 True
10 False; they were Stanford graduate students

United We Stand

1 Cesar Chavez
2 John Mitchell
3 *Norma Rae*
4 George Meany
5 National Education Association
6 Labor Day
7 James "Jimmy" Hoffa
8 13 percent
9 Air-traffic controllers
10 Scab

PAGE 285

Gearing Up!

1 Gears
2 Inclined plane
3 Pulley
4 Wedge
5 Lever
6 Screw
7 Wheel and axle

The Mothers of Invention

1 The modern bra
2 Trash cans with foot-pedal lids
3 X-ray machines
4 Liquid paper (also called white out and correction fluid)
5 The Barbie doll
6 Beauty products for African American women
7 Kevlar
8 Disposable diapers
9 Windshield wipers
10 Snugli baby carriers

Here We Come

Michael Nesmith of The Monkees

Answers

Made in America

1 Back order
2 Bar code
3 Backbreaking
4 Bulk
5 By-product
6 Batch
7 Box
8 Boss
9 Broken
10 Bolt

Rosie the Riveter

1 44 percent
2 *The Saturday Evening Post*
3 She has a halo floating just above her visor
4 27 percent
5 Richmond, California
6 Kaiser Permanente
7 A housing complex built for the shipyard workers
8 Norman Rockwell's

A Day at the Office

1 Scott Adams
2 Frank Lloyd Wright
3 Dwight Schrute
4 Willis Tower (formerly Sears Tower)
5 The cubicle
6 Five; distances up to 80 miles are visible from the top of the Empire State Building, so you can see New Jersey, Pennsylvania, Connecticut, and Massachusetts, as well as New York
7 Aeron
8 *Office Space*
9 40-hour work week
10 The Pentagon

Office Antiques

1 a. Capital letters only
2 b. E. Remington & Sons
3 c. To provide for the carriage return
4 b. Carbon paper

5 a. 2,400
6 c. The first bent-wire paper clip
7 b. Arithmometers
8 a. Batteries

Principles of Business

1 Payroll
2 Presentation
3 Personnel
4 Profit
5 Percentage
6 Paycheck
7 Property
8 Premium
9 Prime rate
10 Promotion

Imaginary Wealth

1 Richie Rich
2 Gordon Gecko
3 Uncle Sam
4 Jed Clampett
5 Bruce Wayne
6 Ebeneezer Scrooge
7 *The Addams Family*
8 J. R. Ewing
9 Willy Wonka
10 Thurston Howell III

Taking Shorthand

1 Mr. Drysdale's secretary on *The Beverly Hillbillies*
2 *The Bob Newhart Show*
3 Mimi Bobeck from *The Drew Carey Show*
4 Henry Kissinger
5 Jenna Fischer
6 *Murphy Brown*
7 Allison Janney
8 Corporal Walter Eugene "Radar" O'Reilly
9 Dolly Parton
10 Sandra Bullock

Business School Basics

1 University of Michigan
2 University of Pennsylvania
3 University of Chicago

4 Northwestern University
5 Duke University
6 MIT
7 University of California, Berkeley
8 Cornell University
9 Dartmouth College
10 New York University
11 UCLA
12 Indiana University, Bloomington
13 University of Virginia
14 University of North Carolina at Chapel Hill
15 Southern Methodist University
16 Carnegie Mellon University
17 University of Notre Dame
18 University of Texas at Austin
19 Brigham Young University
20 Emory University

C Is for Cash

1 Currency
2 Credit
3 Checkbooks
4 Change
5 Catalog
6 Chips
7 Coins
8 Claims
9 Cashier's check
10 Counting

At the Top

1 Beanie Babies
2 Chrysler
3 Amazon
4 Facebook
5 Berkshire Hathaway
6 Nike
7 Walmart
8 Enron
9 Condé Nast
10 Oracle

Read All About It!

1 Remember the Maine
2 One penny
3 Orson Wells
4 Benjamin Franklin

5 *National Enquirer*
6 *Rocky Mountain News*
7 Glenn Close
8 Katharine Graham
9 Linotype
10 Watergate
11 *The New York Times*
12 *USA Today*

Paying for Page Turners

The Book-of-the-Month Club

PAGE 293

The Well-Read Reader

1 c. J. K. Rowling
2 c. Charles V
3 b. China
4 a. *Better Homes and Gardens Cook Book*
5 a. Meatpacking
6 c. Salman Rushdie
7 b. They've all been used to challenge the First Amendment
8 a. Barbara Ehrenreich
9 c. Madonna
10 b. *Carrie*

PAGE 294

Commercial Success

1 Maxwell House
2 Nissan
3 Coca-Cola
4 Panasonic
5 Wheaties
6 Timex
7 AT&T Yellow Pages
8 American Express
9 Life Alert
10 Pringles
11 Gatorade
12 Apple

Mostly Magazines

1 *Time*
2 *Playboy*
3 Mia Farrow
4 Canada
5 Tina Brown
6 Annie Liebovitz
7 Jann Wenner
8 *Cosmopolitan*
9 Bonnie Fuller
10 *George*

PAGE 295

Internet Intrigue

1 True
2 False; writer William Gibson coined the term
3 False; it was 1988
4 True
5 False; they were introduced by Marc Andreessen and Jim Clark
6 True
7 False; records were broken on that date when the NASA Web site broadcast images taken by *Pathfinder* on Mars
8 True
9 False; tunes cost 99 cents apiece
10 False; there were 92 million Web sites
11 True
12 True

PAGE 296

Striking It Rich

1 The U.S. Supreme Court
2 Upton Sinclair
3 Valdez, Alaska
4 42 gallons
5 The *Exxon Valdez* spilled 11 million gallons of oil
6 41 percent
7 1968
8 A nickname for oil
9 Derrick

PAGE 297

Blowing in the Wind

1 True
2 False
3 True
4 True
5 False; wind speeds are highest in the hot summer months
6 True
7 False; large turbines require wind speeds of at least 13 mph
8 False
9 True

The Arts

You probably know that Vincent Van Gogh cut off his ear, but do you know the two primary kinds of flowers he painted? And do you know how many sonnets Shakespeare wrote? This chapter is bursting with mind-stretching questions about literature, music, dance, architecture, the movies, and more.

Literature

From Charles Dickens to Mark Twain and from Miss Marple to Winnie the Pooh, books are filled with memorable characters, spectacular settings, complex plot lines—and unlimited trivia questions. Try your hand at these!

What the Dickens?

Test your knowledge of the beloved author Charles.

1 Which Dickens novel was set in London and Paris?

2 What was Dickens's three-letter pen name?

3 Which Dickens character has been played on film by Alec Guinness and Ron Moody?

4 In which prison was Amy Dorrit born in *Little Dorrit*?

5 Philip Pirrip is the central character of which novel?

6 Which novel featured the Jarndyce court case?

7 "God bless us everyone" is the last line of which seasonal novel?

8 Who married Madeline Bray?

9 Which Dickens novel is set against the Gordon Riots?

10 Which novel was left unfinished when Charles Dickens died?

Novel Occupations

The following titles all have occupations in the title. Who labored to write each book?

1 *The Mayor of Casterbridge*

2 *The Vicar of Wakefield*

3 *Doctor Jekyll and Mr. Hyde*

4 *The Little Drummer Girl*

5 *The Sailor Who Fell from Grace with the Sea*

6 *Doctor Faustus*

7 *The Virgin Soldiers*

8 *The Postman Always Rings Twice*

9 *The Ambassadors*

10 *A Portrait of the Artist as a Young Man*

From Page to Screen

Novels by Charles Dickens are so colorful that they seem to be written for the big screen. Can you name three Dickens novels that have been made into movies?

Taking a Leaf from Literature

Authors often draw on the natural world in their creations. Can you tell what happens when nature and these written works collide?

1 What plant of the primrose family was the code name of Baroness Orczy's spy character?
a. The Fushia Fandango
b. The Clarkia Rubicunda
c. The Scarlet Pimpernel

2 What is the only insectivorous mammal to appear in the title of a Shakespeare play?
a. The bat
b. The badger
c. The shrew

3 The title of what John Steinbeck novel includes the name of a rodent and a primate?
a. *King Rat*
b. *The Organ Grinder's Monkey*
c. *Of Mice and Men*

4 What group of insects appears in the title of William Golding's reworking of *The Coral Island*?
a. Flies, in *Lord of the Flies*
b. Locusts, in *Day of the Locusts*
c. Ants, in *King of the Ant Hill*

5 Who wrote *The Scarlet Letter*?
a. Nathaniel Hawthorne
b. Henry David Thoreau
c. Washington Irving

6 In the *Ingoldsby Legends*, what thieving bird was cursed by the Cardinal Lord Archbishop?
a. The Jackdaw of Rheims
b. The Altar Boy's Macaw
c. The Bishop's Canary

7 In a movie about Henry II and his wife Eleanor of Aquitaine (based on a Broadway play), Henry was referred to as what large carnivore at what time of year?
a. The bear in springtime
b. The lion in winter
c. The vulture in November

8 What type of whale was the subject of the novel *Moby Dick*?
a. A killer whale
b. A humpback whale
c. A sperm whale

9 Which tree appears in the title of a wintry novel by David Gutterson?
a. Aspen *(The Aspens of Vail)*
b. Cedar *(Snow Falling on Cedars)*
c. Maple *(Maple Syrup, New Hampshire Hotcakes)*
d. Apple *(Apple House Rules)*

10 Which bird appears in a poem by Edgar Allen Poe, where it says repeatedly, "Nevermore"?
a. Mockingbird
b. Raven
c. Parrot

That's a Great Start

Choose from the list below to identify the classic novels from their opening lines.

"It is a truth universally acknowledged, that a single man in possession of a good fortune, must be in want of a wife."_____

"All happy families resemble one another, but each unhappy family is unhappy in its own way."_____

"The past is a foreign country: they do things differently there."_____

"I was born in the city of Bombay...once upon a time."_____

"All children, except one, grow up."_____

"If you really want to hear about it, the first thing you'll probably want to know is where I was born, and what my lousy childhood was like."_____

"As Gregor Samsa awoke one morning from uneasy dreams he found himself transformed in his bed into a gigantic insect."_____

"Mother died today. Or maybe yesterday, I don't know."_____

"I had a farm in Africa at the foot of the Ngong hills."_____

"For a long time, I used to go to bed early."_____

A *The Catcher in the Rye* by J. D. Salinger

B *Out of Africa* by Isak Dinesen

C *The Go-Between* by L. P. Hartley

D *Anna Karenina* by Leo Tolstoy

E *The Metamorphosis* by Franz Kafka

F *Peter Pan* by J. M. Barrie

G *Pride and Prejudice* by Jane Austen

H *The Stranger/The Out-sider* by Albert Camus

I *Midnight's Children* by Salman Rushdie

J *Remembrance of Things Past* by Marcel Proust

Colorful Writing

Most authors avoid purple prose, but they don't banish colors from their works altogether. Can you name the colors in the questions below?

1 What was clockwork in the title of the 1962 novel by Anthony Burgess?

2 What color were the gables in the house where Anne lived?

3 What color is featured in the title of William Least Heat-Moon's 1982 best seller that was subtitled "A Journey into America"?

4 What color is the badge of courage in Stephen Crane's novel about the American Civil War?

5 Which color connects the author of *The Sword and the Stone* and the girl in the fairy tale who meets seven dwarfs?

6 Name Alice Walker's 1982 best seller.

7 What color was the horse in Anna Sewell's children's classic?

8 Which Ian Fleming novel featured a plot to rob Fort Knox?

9 Which savior of the French aristocracy was created by Baroness Orczy?

10 Whose school days did Thomas Hughes write about?

What's in a Name?

A rose is a rose is a rose is a rose: but what if it's called something else? See if you can identify the authors hiding behind other names.

1 Which sisters hid their literary identities under the names Currer, Ellis, and Acton Bell?

2 By what name was the wife of archaeologist Max Mallowan known to her reading public?

3 By what name was Eric Blair celebrated as the writer who warned us of Big Brother?

4 The name George Eliot was used to hide an author's female identity. What was her name?

5 Mark Twain was the pen name of whom?

6 *The Spy Who Came In from the Cold* introduced novelist John Le Carré, whose real name is...?

7 *Primary Colors*, published as Anonymous, was actually written by which U.S. journalist?

8 Which Irish-sounding name connects an American novelist who wrote about the "jazz age" with a 19th-century writer who translated *The Rubáiyát of Omar Khayyám*?

9 Speaking of Irish-sounding names, under what pseudonym did Englishman Richard Patrick Russ write his famous sea stories?

10 By what other name is the crime writer Barbara Vine known?

11 Henry wrote *Tropic of Capricorn*; Arthur wrote *Death of a Salesman*. What last name do they share?

12 Who occasionally writes under the pseudonym Richard Bachman?

Novel Locations

Exotic settings always make a book magical. Match the novel with the country in which it is set, choosing from the list below.

Under the Volcano by Malcolm Lowry_____   A Canada

The Quiet American by Graham Greene_____   B Chile

The Great Fortune by Olivia Manning_____   C Denmark

Smilla's Sense of Snow by Peter Hoeg_____   D Egypt

A House for Mr. Biswas by V. S. Naipaul_____ E Kenya

The Constant Gardener by John le Carré_____ F Mexico

The House of the Spirits by Isabel Allende_____ G Romania

The Blind Assassin by Margaret Atwood_____   H South Africa

Palace Walk by Naguib Mahfouz_____   I Trinidad and Tobago

Cry, the Beloved Country by Alan Paton_____ J Vietnam

Detective Work

Put on your deerstalker, grab your magnifying glass, and track down the answers!

1 The central figure in a great many Dorothy L. Sayers crime novels is Detective...?

2 Which fictional detective potters about the English village St. Mary Mead?

3 Which literary detective, created by P. D. James, was a policeman as well as an amateur poet?

4 Who are detectives Andy and Peter, created by Reginald Hill in *A Clubbable Woman*?

5 Which American crime writer created the character of Dr. Kay Scarpetta?

6 Which priest-detective did G. K. Chesterton create?

7 Which American writer wrote about Philip Marlowe in mysteries such as *The Big Sleep*?

8 Which lawyer in the crime stories by Erle Stanley Gardner is assisted by Della Street?

9 Name France's best-known fictional detective, created by Belgian author Georges Simenon.

10 Which whodunit by Dashiell Hammett features the sleuth Sam Spade?

11 What Cajun sleuth began his long, troubled run when he debuted in 1992's *Neon Rain*?

Novel Sisters

Name one novel written by Charlotte Brontë, one by Emily Brontë, and one by Anne Brontë.

Between the Covers and Around the World

Test your knowledge about literature in other languages and from different cultures in this quick tour around the world.

1 What does the title of Hitler's book *Mein Kampf* mean in English?

2 What is the name of the 16th-century astrologer whose four-line prophecies were published in a volume titled *The Centuries*?

3 Which French novelist wrote *J'accuse*, in defense of the wrongly imprisoned officer Alfred Dreyfus?

4 Who wrote the feminist classic *The Female Eunuch*?

5 Which author wrote *Tales of the Jazz Age* and became a sort of literary laureate for the American 1920s?

6 Which famous novel was written by Miguel de Cervantes?

7 Which Roman historian wrote *Lives of the Caesars*?

8 Which American novelist wrote *For Whom the Bell Tolls*?

9 Which 18th-century radical wrote *The Rights of Man*?

10 Name the philanthropist who endowed hundreds of libraries across America and Britain, many of which are named after him.

From Old to New

Can you tell if these statements about literature—from ancient to modern day—are true or false?

1 There are 32 books in the New Testament.   TRUE ○   FALSE ○

2 Erasmus's most famous work is *The Praise of Folly*.   TRUE ○   FALSE ○

3 The fictional Tom Brown attended the real-life school of Eton.   TRUE ○   FALSE ○

4 Tristram Shandy's real title is *The Life and Opinions of Tristram Shandy, Gentleman*.   TRUE ○   FALSE ○

5 *Revolutionary Road*, the novel, was originally published two years before the movie appeared.   TRUE ○   FALSE ○

Storied Creatures

How much do you know about these much-loved animal characters from children's literature?

1 What sort of animal is Hairy Maclary?
a. Dog
b. Llama
c. Gorilla
d. Tarantula

2 What were Flopsy, Mopsy, and Peter?
a. Animated table settings in *Beauty and the Beast*
b. Butterflies
c. Earthworms
d. Rabbits

3 Which type of creature was Beatrix Potter's Mrs. Tiggy-Winkle?
a. Hedgehog
b. Giraffe
c. Bat
d. Robin

4 In *Alice in Wonderland*, who was having tea with the Mad Hatter and the dormouse when Alice arrived?
a. Spring chicken
b. June bug
c. March hare
d. White rat

5 What sort of animal is Winnie the Pooh's friend Eeyore?
a. Ostrich
b. Warthog
c. Ogre
d. Donkey

6 According to the nursery rhyme, what did Mary have?
a. A little lamb
b. A little pony
c. A little turkey
d. A little cat

7 What is the name of Doctor Dolittle's parrot?
a. Cracker
b. Rainbow
c. Polynesia
d. Polly

8 Which character was surprisingly cowardly in *The Wizard of Oz*?
a. The scarecrow
b. The lion
c. The flying monkey
d. The tin man

9 What was the name of the Darling family's dog in *Peter Pan*?
a. Nana
b. Sparky
c. Scottie
d. Manfred

10 In *The Jungle Book*, what sort of animal was Baghera?
a. A cow
b. A vulture
c. A panther
d. A bear

Poetry

Shakespeare wrote comedies, dramas, sonnets—you know all that, but do you know much about his wife? Poetry and poets offer us comfort, peace, recognition—and lots of trivia! How much do you know?

All About the Bard

Dig deep into your Shakespearean fund of knowledge to answer the questions below.

1 In which English town was Shakespeare born?

2 What relation was Mary Arden to Shakespeare?

3 Which Anne did Shakespeare marry?

4 Which Shakespeare play begins with a Danish prince meeting his father's ghost?

5 In which Shakespeare play does a character begin a funeral speech with the words, "Friends, Romans, countrymen, lend me your ears"?

6 In which play does the Moor of Venice kill his wife in a fit of jealousy?

7 Which London theater, where many of Shakespeare's plays were staged, burned down in 1613 but has been rebuilt?

8 What do the initials RSC stand for in the theater world?

9 The name of which Shakespeare play is never supposed to be said aloud inside a theater for fear of bringing bad luck?

10 In which Shakespeare comedy does a fairy queen fall for a weaver named Bottom?

Ancient Places

Poets are often inspired by the sky, mountains, fields—all sorts of settings. Ponder the places poets use below.

1 Which novel set in Dublin was inspired by Homer's *Odyssey*?

2 Which modern Irish poet wrote poems inspired by Iron Age bog burials in northern Europe?

3 Which English author from Nottingham wrote *Etruscan Places*?

4 Name an epic tale of ancient Mesopotamia.

5 In which Babylonia tale does Utnapishtim escape a great flood?

6 Virgil's *Aeneid* is an account of the founding of which ancient state by Aeneas after the fall of Troy?

The People's Poet

Poets generally don't play a public role, but poet laureates accept a more public position than most. Name two U.S poet laureates.

Poetry as Truth

Poetry may offer us universal truths, but the statements about poetry below aren't necessarily true. Which are true and which are false?

1 Plato's works had been part of the oral tradition before being written down around 800 BC.   TRUE ○   FALSE ○

2 William Shakespeare was born in 1564.   TRUE ○   FALSE ○

3 Many of Shakespeare's sonnets were written for a young man.   TRUE ○   FALSE ○

4 Robert Frost wrote *Do Not Go Gentle Into That Good Night*.   TRUE ○   FALSE ○

5 John Keats wrote *Ode on a Grecian Urn*.   TRUE ○   FALSE ○

Verse of the Ages

Ancient poetry can tell us much about ourselves today. How much do you know about this poetry?

1 Name the epic poems credited to Homer.

2 What work of classical Indian literature is the world's longest epic poem?

3 What is Ovid's most famous work, containing a collection of myths based on the theme of transformation?

4 What is the name of the spirit who serves Prospero in Shakespeare's *The Tempest*?

5 Which epic poem begins with the words, "Of man's first disobedience..."?

6 The mythical poet Orpheus descended into Hades to seek his dead wife Eurydice. How did she die?

Legendary People

Memorable characters emerge from poetry, as do memorable poets. See how much you know about the people below.

1 Which 15th-century poet wrote a romantic account of the life of William Wallace?

2 In which Shakespeare play does what appears to be a statue of the long-dead Queen Hermione come to life?

3 Who is the son of Finn MacCool, said to be the greatest poet in Ireland?

4 Who wrote the poem *Endymion*, about a Greek shepherd's love for Cynthia, the moon?

5 Who wrote *The Songlines* about the culture of Australia's aboriginal peoples?

6 Which English Romantic poet wrote the sonnet *Ozymandias*, the Greek name for Pharaoh Ramses II?

7 Name Virgil's epic poem about a Trojan prince who founded Rome.

Music

Classical, jazz, country and western, hip-hop: what's your favorite style? And who are your favorite artists? See how well-rounded you are in your musical education by tackling the questions below.

Classical Capers

If you know classical music, you'll waltz through these!

1 Who composed the opera *Don Giovanni*?
a. Beethoven
b. J. S. Bach
c. Leonard Bernstein
d. Mozart

2 How is Dvorak's Symphony No. 9 better known?
a. *From the New World*
b. *The Wedding March*
c. *The Lone Ranger* theme song

3 Who composed the classical music on which the pop song "A Whiter Shade of Pale" was based?
a. Puccini
b. J. S. Bach
c. Tchaikovsky

4 The Duke of Mantua is a character in which opera?
a. *The Pirates of Penzance*
b. *Die Fledermaus*
c. *Rigoletto*

5 Which opera is set aboard the HMS *Indomitable?*
a. *Billy Budd*
b. *Mutiny on the Bounty*
c. *The Pirates of Penzance*

6 Who composed the *Peer Gynt Suites*?
a. Edvard Grieg
b. Jacob de Haan
c. Cornelius Dopper

7 What is the title of Beethoven's only opera?
a. *Cosi fan Tutte*
b. *The Marriage of Figaro*
c. *Fidelio*

8 Who composed "The Blue Danube Waltz"?
a. Johann Strauss
b. J. S. Bach
c. Frederic Chopin

9 What is the alternative name for Bach's Air from Suite No. 3?
a. Air on a G String
b. "Afternoon Etude"
c. "Amsterdam Air"

10 What does the musical direction rallentando signify?
a. Play slurs between the notes indicated
b. Suddenly play very fast
c. Slow the music

Time to Play

These statements about instruments are true. Or are they false? You decide.

1 A spinet is a woodwind instrument.	TRUE ○	FALSE ○
2 The only stringed instrument of a symphony orchestra not played with a bow is a harp.	TRUE ○	FALSE ○
3 A guitar can be Spanish, acoustic, or electric.	TRUE ○	FALSE ○
4 Itzhak Perlman and Joshua Bell are both famous for playing the cello.	TRUE ○	FALSE ○
5 A piece of paper is useful if you want to play music on a comb.	TRUE ○	FALSE ○
6 The zither originated in Canada.	TRUE ○	FALSE ○

What a Classic!

Do you know the score in the musical world?

1 What does the conductor of a symphony orchestra hold in his hand?

2 How many reeds does an oboe have?

3 In which capital city is the Bolshoi Theater?

4 Does the musical term allegro signify a slow tempo or a quick tempo?

5 In which century did Tchaikovsky live?

6 From where do Gilbert and Sullivan's pirates hail, according to the title of an 1879 operetta?

7 What musical instrument connects Isaac Stern, Vanessa Mae, and Yehudi Menuhin?

8 What instrument was named after its inventor, John Sousa?

9 On which river does the Manaus Opera House in Brazil stand?

10 By what name is Beethoven's Ninth Symphony more commonly known?

Movie Music

You may be able to sing along with these songs, but can you name the movie-song connections?

1 Which movie starring Madonna featured the song "Into the Groove"?

2 Which film featured the song "Anything You Can Do, I Can Do Better"?

3 The national flower of Austria inspired which song in *The Sound of Music*?

4 "Food, Glorious Food" is the opening song in which musical?

5 The musical *Camelot* was based on the life of which legendary king?

6 Which 1982 movie featured "Eye of the Tiger" by Survivor?

Bang the Drum Slowly

Name five percussion instruments in an orchestra.

Bach to the Classics

Dig deep into your fund of musical knowledge to find the answers to the questions below.

1 Which of the following was composed by Aram Khachaturian?
a. "Foil Dance"
b. "Sabre Dance"
c. "Epee Dance"

2 Who was known as "The Waltz King"?
a. Johann Strauss
b. Laurence Welk
c. John Phillip Sousa

3 What year provides the title for the overture by Tchaikovsky to commemorate the defeat of Napoleon?
a. 1814
b. 1812
c. 1776

4 What does the musical term forte mean?
a. Loud
b. Soft
c. Do your best

5 Which symphony by Beethoven was used in the Second World War because its opening four notes are similar to the Morse code for V?
a. Symphony No. 3
b. Symphony No. 9
c. Symphony No. 5

6 Mozart was born in:
a. Vienna
b. Salzburg
c. Strasburg

7 Stradivarius is a famous maker of which musical instrument?
a. Clarinet
b. Violin
c. Cello

8 What is the highest singing female voice?
a. Soprano
b. Tenor
b. Alto

9 Which orchestra is sometimes referred to by the initials NYPO?
a. Neil Young's Polytechnic Orchestra
b. New York Philharmonic Orchestra
c. New York Pops Orchestra

10 What name is given to the principal female singer in an opera?
a. Carlotta
b. Diva
c. Prima donna

Tuned to the Classics

Classical music is one thing; the details surrounding the music quite another. How broad is your classical knowledge?

1 Who founded the Proms concerts, first held in London in 1895?

2 Who are "prommers" at the Proms concerts in London?

3 Which female cellist was married to the pianist Daniel Barenboim and died tragically young of multiple sclerosis?

4 What nationality was composer Dimitri Shostakovich?

5 Who composed *Enigma Variations*?

6 Beethoven's Symphony No. 3 is better known as what?

7 How many crotchets are there in a minim?

8 What instrument accompanies a piano, a violin, and a viola in a piano quartet?

9 Which opera singer appeared in an Italian court in 2001, charged with tax evasion?

10 What is the name of the opera house in Milan that was built in 1778 on the site of a church?

11 Which American composer wrote "Fanfare for the Common Man"?

Instrumental Instruments

You may not be a proficient trumpet or piano player, but chances are you know something about these instruments. Do you know something about the instruments here?

1 Who wrote the song "Mr. Tambourine Man"?

2 For playing which musical instrument was Liberace famous?

3 What instrument does Jack Lemmon play in the 1959 comedy *Some Like It Hot*?

4 What instrument shares its name with a kitchen device used for slicing vegetables?

5 What instrument was played by the "boogie woogie...boy of Company B"?

6 What is the smallest woodwind instrument in a symphony orchestra?

Opening Lines

Check out these opening lines, and then name that tune!

1 Which song from a famous movie starts with the line: "I got chills; they're multiplying"?

2 Which Michael Jackson hit starts with: "It's close to midnight"?

3 Which Abba hit begins: "I work all night, I work all day"?

4 Which song by The Beatles opens with the line: "Oh yeah, I'll tell you something I think you'll understand"?

5 Which duet starts with Cher singing: "They say we're young and we don't know"?

6 Which song begins with: "And now, the end is near, and so I face the final curtain"?

Strike Up the Band

Start your toes tapping with these questions about movie musicals.

1 Which was the first movie musical to win 10 Oscars?

2 Which Oscar-winning 1972 musical movie was set in pre-war Berlin at the Kit Kat Club?

3 In which musical did we first meet the character of Fanny Brice?

4 Which 1969 musical had Clint Eastwood singing "They call the wind Mariah"?

5 What were Rodgers's and Hammerstein's first names?

6 Where, according to the title of the 1944 musical starring Judy Garland, were you to meet?

7 Judy Garland and James Mason both won Oscar nominations for their roles in which 1954 musical directed by George Cukor?

8 With which cartoon character did Gene Kelly dance in the movie *Anchors Aweigh*?

9 Where was Gene Kelly, an American, according to the title of the 1951 movie directed by Vincente Minnelli?

Country Roads

Swing your partner (and then ask your partner to help with these country and western questions)!

1 Which country singer starred in the movies *9 to 5* and *Steel Magnolias*?

2 Which country star had hits with "Welcome to My World" and "I Love You Because"?

3 Who played country singer Loretta Lynn in the film *Coal Miner's Daughter*?

4 Whose autobiography is titled *Stand by Your Man*?

5 Who sang about a boy named Sue?

6 "Coward of the Country" was a transatlantic hit for which country legend?

7 Who recorded the best-selling album *Come on Over* in 1997?

8 Who wrote the song "Crazy," a hit for Patsy Cline?

9 Which country and western star appeared alongside John Wayne in the film *True Grit*?

10 Who wrote the song "Take Me Home, Country Roads"?

TV Music Box

How well do you remember these musical moments from TV?

1 Which U.S. sitcom used the song "Love and Marriage" sung by Frank Sinatra as its theme?

2 Who sang the theme to *The Love Boat*?

3 The Rembrandts recorded the song "I'll Be There for You" as its theme for which hit TV series?

4 Al Jarreau had a hit with the theme for which 1980s TV series?

5 Which real-life rocker appeared in *Happy Days* as the character Leather Tuscadero?

6 Which singer played Sonny Crockett's wife in *Miami Vice*?

7 What is the name of the saxophonist in *The Muppet Show* band?

8 Which singer provided the theme and some of the incidental music for *Ally McBeal*?

The Movies

What's better than a night at the movies? The stars, the glitz, the glamour...the popcorn! See how much you know about this most magical form of entertainment.

Movie Menagerie

Lions and tigers and bears! Oh my! How good are you at answering movie questions that have something to do with animals?

1 In the 1989 film *Turner and Hooch*, what type of animal was Tom Hanks's slobbery partner?

2 Which 1963 film told the true story of two dogs and a cat that traveled hundreds of miles to be reunited with their owners?

3 Who played the Bond girl Pussy Galore?

4 A Thomas Harris novel became a 1991 box-office smash for Jodie Foster and Anthony Hopkins. What was the movie?

5 "Just when you thought it was safe to go back in the water" was the catchphrase for which film sequel?

6 Clyde the orangutan shares the screen with which lead actor in *Every Which Way but Loose*?

7 Ben, from the 1972 movie of the same name, was what type of creature?

8 What is the panther's name in *The Jungle Book*?

9 Which 1966 movie recounted the true story of a lioness called Elsa?

10 Simba, Mufasa, Timon, and Pumbaa were all stars of which 1994 Disney animation?

Cat-egory

Here's a new movie category: Name three movies with the word "cat" in the title.

The Christmas Movie

Christmas comes only once a year, but the questions about Christmas movies can be asked year-round!

1 Who played Scrooge in the 1988 film *Scrooged*?
a. John Belushi
b. Will Farrell
c. Bill Murray

2 Who played Santa in the 1994 film *Miracle on 34th Street*?
a. Richard Dreyfus
b. Richard Attenborough
c. Billy Crystal

3 In which 1946 film did James Stewart attempt to commit suicide at Christmas?
a. *It's a Wonderful Life*
b. *The Philadelphia Story*
c. *Harvey*

4 Which Bond film features Dr. Christmas Jones?
a. *Dr. No*
b. *Moonraker*
c. *The World Is Not Enough*

5 Which film sees Arnold Schwarzenegger attempting to buy a Turbo Man doll for his son's Christmas present?
a. *The Santa Claus*
b. *Bad Santa*
c. *Jingle All the Way*

6 Who played Scrooge in *The Muppet Christmas Carol*?
a. Michael Caine
b. Steve Martin
c. Tim Curry

7 In which 1998 film does Michael Keaton play a deceased father who comes back to life as a snowman?
a. *Desperate Measures*
b. *Jack Frost*
c. *The Paper*

8 The 1982 animated film *The Snowman* featured which boy soprano singing "Walking in the Air"?
a. Yves Abel
b. Peter Auty
c. Aled Jones

9 Which wrestler played the title role in the 1996 film *Santa with Muscles*?
a. Hulk Hogan
b. Mickey Rourke
c. Rocky Johnson

10 Who played Mr. Lawrence in the 1983 film *Merry Christmas Mr. Lawrence*?
a. Tom Hanks
b. Tom Cruise
c. Tom Conti

Roll the Credits

Which films close with the following memorable lines?

1 "Sir, if any of my circuits or gears will help, I'll gladly donate them." "He'll be all right."

2 "For a moment there I thought we were in trouble."

3 "I do wish we could chat longer, but...I'm having an old friend for dinner."

4 "Attaboy, Clarence."

5 "Well, nobody's perfect."

6 "Louis, I think this is the beginning of a beautiful friendship."

7 "All right, Mr. DeMille, I'm ready for my close-up."

8 "He finally got to the top of the world...and it blew right up in his face."

9 "Throw that junk in."

10 "This is Ripley, last survivor of The Nostromo, signing off."

Great Children's Films

The movies are for children, but the questions are not childishly simple.

1. Who played the title role in the 1971 film adaptation of Roald Dahl's *Willy Wonka & the Chocolate Factory*?

2. In the movie *The Wizard of Oz*, what color are Dorothy's slippers?

3. R. Lee Ermey, who starred in *Full Metal Jacket*, plays what part in Disney's 1995 *Toy Story*?

4. Which author, more famous for writing spy novels, wrote *Chitty Chitty Bang Bang*?

5. Which eight-times married actress starred in the 1944 film *National Velvet*?

6. Which little elephant with big ears learned to fly in a Disney film?

7. Which child star was "home alone" in 1990?

8. Angela Lansbury played a trainee witch who helped repel a German invasion of Britain in which 1971 children's film?

9. Who provides the voice for Mushu, the Demoted One in Disney's 1998 *Mulan*?

10. Which 1999 children's movie was advertised with the slogan: "The Little family just got bigger"?

Magnificent Seven

The number seven is lucky for some, unlucky for others. How lucky is it for you in this quiz?

1. In how many James Bond films did Sean Connery play 007?

2. Who played the leader of *The Magnificent Seven* in the original film?

3. In which 1995 thriller were Morgan Freeman and Brad Pitt chasing Kevin Spacey?

4. Which famous literary sleuth was lured to Vienna to cure his cocaine addiction in the movie *The Seven-Per-Cent Solution*?

5. Which 1954 movie musical featured the song "Bless Yore Beautiful Hide"?

6. Name the film in which Marilyn Monroe's skirt was blown upward by air from a grating.

7. In the 1964 movie *Robin and the 7 Hoods*, who sang "My Kind of Town"?

8. In which year was the first full-length animated film *Snow White and the Seven Dwarfs* released?

9. Where did Brad Pitt spend seven years, according to the title of a 1997 movie?

10. Who directed the movie *The Seven Samurai*, on which *The Magnificent Seven* was based?

Double Trouble

Name two movies featuring a pair of twins.

Just Plane Crazy

It's true that all these statements are linked to aircraft. But is it true that they're true? Answer true or false.

1 Cary Grant starred in Hitchcock's 1959 movie *North by Northwest*. TRUE ○ FALSE ○

2 George Peppard and James Mason starred in *Grey Skies*, a 1966 movie about German pilots. TRUE ○ FALSE ○

3 Nicolas Cage shared a plane with criminals led by John Malkovich in the 1997 movie *Con Air*. TRUE ○ FALSE ○

4 Katharine Hepburn and Spencer Tracy appeared in *Flying Down to Rio*. TRUE ○ FALSE ○

5 The 1956 movie *Reach for the Sky* told the story of Douglas Bader, a British Second World War ace. TRUE ○ FALSE ○

6 *Planes, Trains and Automobiles*, starring Steve Martin, ended with Paul Young's hit "Every Time You Go Away." TRUE ○ FALSE ○

7 Arthur Hailey's novel *Airport* was made into a 1970 blockbuster featuring Burt Lancaster, Jacqueline Bisset, and George Kennedy. TRUE ○ FALSE ○

8 Charles Lindbergh's life story was chronicled in the film *The Spirit of St. Louis*. TRUE ○ FALSE ○

9 Cary Grant was nicknamed "The Baron of Beefcake" and made his debut in the 1948 film *Fighter Squadron*. TRUE ○ FALSE ○

10 The last line of *Beauty and the Beast* was: "It wasn't the airplanes. It was beauty killed the beast." TRUE ○ FALSE ○

B Movies

They're not second-rate movies, but they all start with the letter "B".

In which 1956 movie did Marilyn Monroe play a café singer?_____ **A** *Barbarella*

In which 1955 classic did Sidney Poitier play a schoolteacher in an inner-city school?_____ **B** *Basic Instinct*

What was the title of the 1975 movie in which John Wayne played a Chicago policeman sent to London to arrest a gangster?_____ **C** *Beauty and the Beast*

Which 1987 movie, directed by Blake Edwards, costarred Bruce Willis and Kim Basinger?_____ **D** *Blackboard Jungle*

The song "Be Our Guest" was sung by a candlestick in which Disney film?_____ **E** *Blind Date*

Which Oscar-winning film of 1995 told the story of William Wallace?_____ **F** *Brannigan*

Which 1968 movie starring Jane Fonda and set in the 41st century featured a blind angel?_____ **G** *Braveheart*

Which 1976 movie, set among New York gangsters in 1929, starred a teenage Jodie Foster?_____ **H** *Bugsy Malone*

In which 1992 film costarring Sharon Stone did Michael Douglas investigate a murder?_____ **I** *Bus Stop*

Maybe Baby

Go back in time and answer some very child-ish questions.

1 In which 1968 movie did Mia Farrow give birth to the son of Satan?

2 Which *Star Trek* actor directed the movie *Three Men and a Baby*?

3 What sort of animal was Baby in the movie *Bringing Up Baby*, starring Cary Grant?

4 Name the 1987 movie in which Diane Keaton played an executive who acquires a baby.

5 Which actor-director named his son Satchel?

6 The life of which sporting legend was chronicled in the 1992 film *The Babe*?

7 What was the title of the 1998 sequel to the 1995 movie *Babe*?

8 Who starred alongside Holly Hunter in the 1987 movie *Raising Arizona*?

9 Which comedy duo assisted Santa Claus in the 1934 movie *Babes in Toyland*?

10 In which movie sequel did Rick Moranis inadvertently expose his two-year-old son to a ray that made him grow excessively?

Birds of a Feather

What do you know about bird-related movies?

1 Which brothers starred in the movie *Duck Soup*?

2 What sort of bird accompanied a cat in the title of a 1939 Bob Hope movie?

3 What was the name of the parrot that taught Doctor Dolittle to talk to the animals?

4 In which 1978 movie did Richard Burton lead a troop of mercenaries?

5 Which 1969 movie, starring Clint Eastwood, was based on a novel by Alistair Maclean?

6 What was the name of the character played by John Wayne in the movie *True Grit*?

7 Which 1970 Robert Altman film, named after its main character, had that character searching for the secret of flight?

8 On whose poem was the 1963 horror film *The Raven* based?

9 In which film did Kris Kristofferson play Rubber Duck?

10 What was Anthony Edwards's call sign in the 1986 movie *Top Gun*?

Technicolor Trivia

Red and yellow and pink and blue: Which color of the rainbow is part of the question or answer below?

1 During which war was the 1968 movie *The Green Berets* set?

2 Which Quentin Tarantino film features the characters Mr. Orange, Mr. Pink, and Mr. White?

3 In which 1990 movie did Sean Connery play a defecting Soviet submarine commander?

4 Oprah Winfrey made her big-screen debut in which award-winning dramatic film?

5 Which movie introduced Peter Sellers as the bumbling Inspector Clouseau?

6 In which 1968 animated feature film were the villains called the Blue Meanies?

7 Which 1986 movie features Eddie Murphy as the bodyguard to a child with supernatural powers?

8 The movie *Black Beauty* was based on a novel by which author?

Novel Ideas

Which did you like better: the book or the movie? Here you get to think about books turned into movies.

1 Which 1991 movie has the same title as a 1986 novel by Anthony Powell?
a. *The Fisher King*
b. *From a View to a Death*
c. *Afternoon Men*

2 Who did Sir Anthony Hopkins play in *Shadowlands*?
a. J. R. R. Tolkien
b. W. B. Yeats
c. C. S. Lewis

3 On whose book was *The Name of the Rose* based?
a. Stephen King
b. John Updike
c. Umberto Eco

4 Who wrote the novel *The Godfather*, on which the Mafia movies were based?
a. Mario Puzo
b. Francis Ford Coppola
c. Gay Talese

5 The book *Enemy Coast Ahead* was adapted into which war film?
a. *The Dam Busters*
b. *Full Speed Ahead*
c. *Damn the Torpedoes!*

6 Gregory Peck starred in *To Kill a Mockingbird*. Who wrote the best-selling book it was based on?
a. Truman Capote
b. Harper Lee
c. Ralph Ellison

7 Dustin Hoffman starred as *The Graduate*. Who wrote the novel?
a. Charles Webb
b. Buck Henry
c. Calder Willingham

8 Which novel by Kazuo Ishiguro became a 1993 movie starring Emma Thompson and Sir Anthony Hopkins?
a. *The English Patient*
b. *A Room with a View*
c. *The Remains of the Day*

9 Which Thomas Hardy character was played by Nastassja Kinski in a 1979 movie?
a. Lucy Honeychurch
b. Tess of the D'Urbervilles
c. Dorothea Brooke

A Winning Performance

Can you give an Oscar-winning performance when you answer these questions?

1 Which movie shares, with *Titanic*, the most number of Oscar nominations in the 20th century?

2 Which 1980 movie earned Robert Redford an Oscar for Best Director?

3 For which movie did George C. Scott refuse his Oscar?

4 How old was Jessica Tandy, the oldest actress to win an Oscar, in *Driving Miss Daisy*?

5 On what does an Oscar statuette stand?

6 Which Oscar-winning movie of 1956 was based on a novel by Jules Verne?

7 How was Pu Yi known in the title of a movie that won nine Oscars?

8 Who was the first-ever actor to win Best Actor Oscars in two consecutive years?

9 Director Baz Luhrmann's wife won a Best Art Direction Oscar in 2002 for *Moulin Rouge*. What is her name?

10 Which was the first non-Hollywood movie to win an Oscar for Best Motion Picture?

What a Disaster!

Trouble on the seas, in the air, and at a nuclear power plant: can it get worse? Choose from the list of movies below to test your disaster-movie knowledge.

Which 1974 movie featuring a host of stars had Steve McQueen playing Fire Chief Michael O'Hallorhan?_____   **A** *Armageddon*

Name the 1972 movie in which Shelley Winters and Gene Hackman perished at sea._____   **B** *The China Syndrome*

Morgan Freeman played the president of the United States in this 1998 disaster film._____   **C** *Dante's Peak*

Kate Winslet was cast into the spotlight after taking the lead in which 1997 movie?_____   **D** *Deep Impact*

In which 1998 space film did Bruce Willis play oil driller Harry Stamper, who saves the world?_____   **E** *The Hindenburg*

Which 1975 film told the true story of a 1937 disaster involving an airship?_____   **F** *Independence Day*

Which 2000 movie saw George Clooney battling against the elements of the sea?_____   **G** *The Perfect Storm*

Pierce Brosnan played the volcano expert in this 1997 movie._____   **H** *The Poseidon Adventure*

In which 1979 movie did Jack Lemmon and Jane Fonda avert a nuclear power plant disaster?_____   **I** *Titanic*

Jeff Goldblum played a computer genius in this 1996 movie._____   **J** *The Towering Inferno*

Days Like These

It's just one of those days. In fact, each answer includes the word "day."

1 Which film saw Arnold Schwarzenegger battling against Satan in the shape of Gabriel Byrne?

2 In which film did the Marx Brothers assist a young girl who owned a sanatorium and a racehorse?

3 In which 1990 movie did Tom Cruise play a stock car driver?

4 Which 1962 film is based on John Wyndham's book about giant plants taking over the world?

5 Which 1973 movie shared its title with a 1957 hit for Buddy Holly and the Crickets?

6 In which 1969 film did Richard Burton play Henry VIII in pursuit of his second wife?

7 What was the 1998 movie in which Harrison Ford crash-landed a plane on a deserted island?

8 George Clooney fell in love with Michelle Pfeiffer in which 1996 move?

9 In which movie did Sir Anthony Hopkins play a butler named Stevens?

10 In which 1996 movie does Will Smith play a U.S. Air Force pilot battling against alien invaders?

Visual Arts

Whether you love paintings, sculpture, or theater, you'll probably love many of the questions about visual arts in this section. The question is: will you love the answers?

All the World's a Stage

Watching live theater is a thrilling experience. Showing off your knowledge about theater can be fun, too. How much do you know about it?

1 Kathleen Turner, Jerry Hall, Anne Archer, Amanda Donohoe, and Linda Gray have all appeared naked on London's West End stage, playing which character?

2 Which brothers composed *Porgy and Bess*?

3 The stage musical and film *The King and I* concerned the king of which country?

4 Which musical features the song "Getting to Know You"?

5 Which play is referred to as "The Scottish play"?

6 On whose poetry is the stage musical *Cats* based?

7 In which country is the play *Miss Saigon* set?

8 Which street is the home of New York theater?

9 Which musical is based on the legend of King Arthur?

10 Name the two rival gangs in *West Side Story*.

A Monumental Task

Monuments and sculpture have a lot in common; sometimes they're one and the same. See how much you know about these contemporary monuments.

1 In which country is Yad Vashem a memorial to the six million Jews killed during the Holocaust?

2 Which arch in Paris bears the names of 386 of Napoleon's generals?

3 Who is commemorated by the statue at the top of the column in London's Trafalgar Square?

4 In which American city is the Lincoln Memorial?

5 Which mountain in the United States is carved with the likenesses of presidents Washington, Jefferson, Lincoln, and Roosevelt?

6 In which country was a monument to Lord Nelson destroyed by a bomb in 1966?

7 In which Australian city is the Tomb of the Unknown Soldier located?

8 The Menin Gate, where Belgian firefighters sound the "Last Post" every night, is a monument to the fallen of which war?

9 What incendiary event does the Monument, in London, commemorate?

A Brush with Beauty

Test your knowledge about paintings and painters from around the world with these detailed questions.

1 The French artist Monet is famous for depicting which kind of pond plant?

2 In addition to irises, which flowers are associated with the artist Vincent van Gogh?

3 What name describes paintings of fruit, flowers, food, dead birds, and other inanimate things?

4 Which surrealist often featured strange and twisted clocks in his painting?

5 Which Dutch master painted a picture of the pleasures of the land of Cockaigne?

6 Which medieval Dutch painter is known for nightmarish depictions of the torments of hell?

7 Which painting by Sandro Botticelli depicts a mythical version of the coming of spring?

8 Which great Venetian painter was described as "the sun amidst small stars"?

9 Which American artist was the impetus behind the 1960s Pop Art movement?

10 Which 20th-century Spanish artist was strongly influenced by African art?

Where Did You See It?

Museums here and there hold some of the greatest treasures of art. Name three world-famous art museums.

Sing and Dance

In which stage musicals have you heard the following songs? Choose from the list below.

"On the Street Where You Live"_____	A *Annie*
"All I Ask of You"_____	B *Godspell*
"The Movie in My Mind"_____	C *Hair*
"I Don't Know How to Love Him"_____	D *Jesus Christ Superstar*
"I Am What I Am"_____	E *The King and I*
"It Ain't Necessarily So"_____	F *La Cage Aux Folles*
"Getting to Know You"_____	G *Miss Saigon*
"Aquarius"_____	H *My Fair Lady*
"Day by Day"_____	I *Phantom of the Opera*
"It's the Hard-Knock Life"_____	J *Porgy and Bess*

Made to Last

Is your knowledge about sculpture as long-lasting as the sculptures themselves?

1 Which East African people are known for their sculptures?

2 Which Zimbabwean people are famed for their wood sculptures?

3 Which native hardwood is commonly used by African peoples for carvings?

4 Which famous 20th-century British sculptor was influenced by the art of Melanesia?

5 Which sculptor created the statue known as *The Three Graces*?

Very Visual

Which of these statements about the varied visual arts are true? Which are false?

1	The French artist Paul Gauguin painted in Tahiti in the 1890s.	TRUE ○	FALSE ○
2	A penguin (as a logo) first appeared on a paperback book in 1935.	TRUE ○	FALSE ○
3	Saint Christopher is the patron saint of artists.	TRUE ○	FALSE ○
4	The Louvre opened in 1893.	TRUE ○	FALSE ○
5	The Russian-born artist Marc Chagall designed a memorial peace window for the headquarters of the United Nations.	TRUE ○	FALSE ○
6	Michaelangelo's statue of *David* is located in Rome.	TRUE ○	FALSE ○
7	Marcel Duchamp painted *Nude Descending a Staircase*.	TRUE ○	FALSE ○
8	Italy produced the painters Giotto, Raphael, and Canaletto.	TRUE ○	FALSE ○
9	Molière wrote his plays in Italy.	TRUE ○	FALSE ○
10	Gainsborough painted *The Blue Boy*.	TRUE ○	FALSE ○

Dance

What is Marie Antoinette's connection to dance? What dance did Chubby Checker make very popular? And how much do you know about this subject? Test yourself below to find out!

Smooth Moves

Can you answer these questions about bodies in motion?

1 Which energetic dance was popularized by Chubby Checker in the 1950s?

2 Which British dancer, often partnered with Nureyev, became president of the Royal Academy of Dancing in 1954 and died in 1991?

3 Which popular 1960s teen dance was named after an African tribe?

4 How many dancers perform a pas de deux?

5 Which dance craze was a hit record for Little Eva and Kylie Minogue?

6 Which dance represents the letter "F" in the phonetic alphabet?

7 Which dance troupe entertained television viewers with their kaleidoscopic patterns on *The Jackie Gleason Show*?

8 What dance-inspired water sport has been a Summer Olympic Games event since 1984?

9 John Barry wrote the score for which Oscar-winning Western starring Kevin Costner?

10 Which Cuban dance style strongly influenced salsa?

Dance-o

Dances often have exotic and fun-to-pronounce names. Can you name two dances that end in "o"?

Take Your Partner

Dance around the dance floor—and around the world. Check out these globe-trotting questions about dance.

1 Which famous Scottish dance was originally performed by a warrior over his shield?
   a. The Highland Fling
   b. Reel of Tulloch
   c. The Cake Walk

2 Salsa evolved from Puerto Rican dance music and which other musical style?
   a. Western line dancing
   b. The Aboriginal didgeridoo
   c. Jazz

3 For which Pacific Islanders is Laka the goddess of dance?
   a. Hawaiians
   b. Samoans
   c. Fijians

4 Which athletic street dance was popular in the 1980s among urban teenagers in U.S. and U.K. cities?
   a. Electric bugaloo
   b. Break dancing
   c. Hip-hop dancing

5 Rangda the witch is the Queen of Evil in the dance-drama of which Indonesian island?
   a. Bali
   b. Java
   c. Borneo

6 In which African traditional religion are spirits called Orishas worshipped in dancing and drumming ceremonies?
   a. Yoruba
   b. Azande
   c. Santeria

7 Arabic dancing is accompanied by music played on which stringed instrument, the forerunner of the lute and mandolin?
   a. The lyre
   b. The oud
   c. The sitar

8 What showman visited with entertainer Sammy Davis Jr. on his deathbed and then described Davis pretending to toss him a basketball?
   a. Jay Leno
   b. Bill Cosby
   c. Gregory Hines

Let's Dance

This bunch will keep you on your toes!

1 Which dancer died when her scarf caught in the wheel of a car in which she was traveling?

2 What was the full name of the character played by John Travolta in the film *Saturday Night Fever*?

3 Which Irishman took upon himself the title of "Lord of the Dance" in the 1990s?

4 Which film told the story of Lieutenant John Dunbar?

5 Which dancer's last words were, "Get my swan costume ready"?

6 What is the name of the national dance of Poland?

7 By what name is Virginia McMath better known?

8 In which decade of the 20th century were the Charleston and Black Bottom dances most popular?

9 Which biblical character performed the dance of the seven veils?

10 What is the name of the court dance made popular by Marie Antoinette?

On Your Feet!

Feel like cutting a rug? Spot the fibs and label each statement true or false.

1 The 1987 chart-topper for Australian singer Kylie Minogue, "The Locomotion," was written by pop megastar Madonna. TRUE ○ FALSE ○

2 "Do You Wanna Dance?" has been a hit for Bobby Freeman, the Beach Boys, Cliff Richard, Del Shannon, The Mamas and the Papas, and Bette Midler. TRUE ○ FALSE ○

3 Katharine Hepburn was known for singing, "I Could Have Danced All Night" in the film *My Fair Lady*. TRUE ○ FALSE ○

4 According to the lyrics, Abba's dancing queen was age 17. TRUE ○ FALSE ○

5 "Twist and Shout" has been a hit for Johnny O'Keefe, The Beatles, and the Jamaican duo Chaka Demus & Pliers. TRUE ○ FALSE ○

6 Leo Sayer sang "You Make Me Feel Like Dancing" in 1976. TRUE ○ FALSE ○

7 American disco kings the Bee Gees were in a "Boogie Wonderland" in 1979. TRUE ○ FALSE ○

8 In 1997 Michael Jackson released the album *Moonwalk*. TRUE ○ FALSE ○

9 The Van Goghs backed Martha Reeves on her recording of 1964's "Dancing in the Street." TRUE ○ FALSE ○

Architecture

Architecture is all around us, though you may never really have noticed particular buildings. But maybe you did—and can answer the questions below.

Standing Tall

They may be tall, they may be short—but these questions are all about buildings.

1 Which Kuala Lumpur skyscrapers are symbolic of Malaysia's economic growth?

2 Architects in which U.S. city built the first skyscrapers?

3 Which New York skyscraper was briefly the world's tallest building in 1930?

4 Who is the architect of the building that will replace New York's World Trade Center?

5 Which famous New York art museum was designed by Frank Lloyd Wright?

6 The architecture of Florence is one of the city's principal attractions for visitors. What period is it from?

7 Ebenezer Howard founded which English garden city to provide a healthy environment?

8 Which Barcelona suburb did Ildefonso Cerdà design for healthy living?

9 Who designed the major public buildings of Brasilia?

Famous Buildings

You know these buildings, but who designed them? Choose from the list below.

Bank of China Tower, Hong Kong, China_____ **A** Gustave Eiffel

Chrysler Building, New York_____ **B** James Hoban

White House, Washington, D.C._____ **C** Renzo Piano

Guggenheim Museum, Bilbao, Spain_____ **D** César Pelli

Tjibaou Cultural Centre, New Caledonia_____ **E** Le Corbusier

Chek Lap Kok Airport, Hong Kong, China_____ **F** Norman Foster

Eiffel Tower, Paris, France_____ **G** I. M. Pei

Petronas Towers, Kuala Lumpur, Malaysia_____ **H** Frank Gehry

Greenwich Hospital, Greenwich, England_____ **I** Sir Christopher Wren

United Nations Headquarters, New York_____ **J** William Van Alen

Architects with Style

Test yourself with these facts about great builders and their great buildings.

1 Which English architect, noted for his London churches, features in a Peter Ackroyd novel?

2 Which architect designed Paris's Pompidou Centre and London's Millennium Dome?

3 Where did Italian architect Filippo Brunelleschi see his great new dome rise over a city cathedral in the early 1400s?

4 Which Chinese architect designed the East Wing of Washington's National Gallery?

5 The album, *Bridge Over Troubled Water,* was about which architect?

6 Which architect founded the Bauhaus School of Modern Design in Germany in 1919?

7 Which U.S. president was also an architect, whose buildings include the University of Virginia?

8 Which famous architect planned and designed buildings in the Sydney, Australia, suburb of Castlecrag?

9 Which Spanish architect designed the church of the Sagrada Familia in Barcelona?

10 Which Indian city was largely designed and built by Sir Edwin Lutyens?

Big Apple Bridges

There are 2,027 bridges in New York City. Can you name five?

Monumental Matters

Can you answer these big questions about ancient temples and other special buildings?

1 Which of the Seven Wonders of the Ancient World was destroyed by earthquakes in the 14th century?

2 Which king of Judea built the last temple of Jerusalem, of which the Western (or "Wailing") Wall is all that remains?

3 Which Roman emperor started the construction of the Colosseum?

4 What is the name of the highest surviving Roman aqueduct, which brought water to Nimes?

5 Which of the Seven Wonders of the Ancient World, located in what is now Turkey, did Herostratus destroy in his quest for fame in 356 B.C.?

6 Which Mesoamerican city had two temple platforms now known as the Pyramids of the Sun and Moon?

7 Which Greek sculptor supervised the design and building of the Parthenon?

8 Which Roman emperor built a palace near Split in modern Croatia?

9 Which city in northeastern Italy, famed for its churches decorated with mosaics, was the last capital of the Western Roman Empire?

10 In which country do the Colossi of Memnon stand as reminders of the pharaohs?

Across the Board

Can you tell which statements about a wide variety of architectural subjects are true and which are false?

1 "Buildering" is the term for demolishing tall buildings.   TRUE ○   FALSE ○

2 The Temple of Zeus, one of the Seven Wonders of the Ancient World, was located in Delphi.   TRUE ○   FALSE ○

3 Europe's oldest surviving university is in Paris.   TRUE ○   FALSE ○

4 The snake-shaped earthwork in Ohio, built by early people of the Eastern Woodlands, is called the Serpent Mound.   TRUE ○   FALSE ○

5 Italian renaissance architect Andrea Palladio triggered a long-lasting fashion for classical buildings.   TRUE ○   FALSE ○

6 The dome of Rome's Pantheon was made of stone.   TRUE ○   FALSE ○

Building Bridges

This whimsical round will test your knowledge of all kinds of bridges.

1 Which duo sang "Bridge Over Troubled Water" in 1970?

2 The Bosphorus Bridge connects Europe with which other continent?

3 In which American city is the Golden Gate Bridge?

4 Name the acting father of Jeff and Beau Bridges.

5 In which Italian city is the Bridge of Sighs?

6 Who directed the film *The Bridge on the River Kwai*?

Where Are They?

They're hard to miss when you see them, but you need to know where they are in order to see them. Name the cities in which the following buildings and monuments are found.

1 The Eiffel Tower

2 St. Paul's Cathedral

3 The Statue of Liberty

4 The White House

5 The Kremlin

6 Disney World

7 The Vatican

8 The Acropolis

9 Petronas Towers

10 The Little Mermaid Statue

Home Sweet Home

They may not be McMansions, but they're home to plenty of people. Can you answer the questions about these types of houses?

1 What are the snow houses called that Arctic peoples build as temporary hunting shelters?

2 What is the name for round huts made from animal skins used by Asian peoples?

3 What type of dwelling do Bedouins traditionally live in?

4 What do the Aymara of Lake Titicaca, South America, use to build their houses?

5 What is unusual about the hotel in Coober Pedy, South Australia?

6 Which town in southern Spain is famous for its underground houses?

7 What is the unusual feature of many houses built in marshy areas and on river deltas?

Historic Houses

Sometimes a building becomes more famous than its occupants. Can you answer these questions about well-known historic houses?

1 Which U.S. President designed his own house, called Monticello, in Virginia?

2 In which city is Holyroodhouse?

3 Which German ruler built the fairy-tale castle of Neuschwanstein?

4 Which famous architect wanted to rebuild Hampton Court Palace in the 1600s, but never got to finish the job?

5 Who lived in a chalet at Obersalzberg above Berchtesgaden?

6 Potala Palace, the traditional seat of the Dalai Lama, is situated in which Tibetan city?

7 The Moorish palace known as the Alhambra is situated in which Spanish city?

8 What is the name of the imperial palace complex in the heart of Beijing?

9 What is the name of the U.S. presidents' retreat in the Appalachian Mountains?

10 In which French palace was the treaty that officially ended the First World War signed?

Decorative Arts

From delicate willow patterns in china to ornate wood inlay in furniture, the decorative arts are a welcome part of everyday living, from Bauhaus to your house. See how much you know about decorative arts by answering the questions below.

Early Decorative Arts

Can you spot the correct answer about ancient art?

1 What did the Phoenecians use to make purple dye?
a. Tree bark
b. Flowers
c. Shellfish
d. Spices

2 Which craft technology is not associated with ancient China?
a. Iron casting
b. Jade carving
c. Silk weaving
d. Glassblowing

3 What is our main source of knowledge about Etruscan arts?
a. Pottery
b. Tombs
c. Temples
d. Scrolls

4 What distinguishing feature was given to Assyrians on Assyrian relief sculpture?
a. Beards
b. Trousers
c. Shaved heads
d. Spectacles

5 Which of these was not characteristic of Celtic design?
a. Spirals
b. Interlacing curves
c. Cameos
d. Enamel

6 What is the term for the small blocks of stone used to make Roman mosaics?
a. Tessitura
b. Tesserae
c. Terzetti
d. Tetrastichs

7 Which of the following identifies the Lapita culture of the South Pacific islands?
a. Wood carving
b. Shell money
c. Pottery
d. Outrigger canoes

High Style

From lowly bricks to the heights of Queen Victoria's empire, here are several statements about the decorative arts. Are they true or false?

1 Bricks made from mud and dried in the sun are called "terra-cotta."	TRUE ○	FALSE ○
2 The willow pattern for china was designed in England.	TRUE ○	FALSE ○
3 The technique of lacquering is first thought to have been used under the Zhou dynasty.	TRUE ○	FALSE ○
4 Queen Victoria's empire gave rise to the Empire Style in interior design.	TRUE ○	FALSE ○
5 William Morris was known for stained glass as well as for textiles.	TRUE ○	FALSE ○
6 The Minoan civilization is particularly famous for wall paintings, or frescoes.	TRUE ○	FALSE ○
7 The discovery of King Tut's tomb influenced Art Deco design.	TRUE ○	FALSE ○
8 Indian sculpture was directly influenced by Greek sculpture.	TRUE ○	FALSE ○
9 In weaving, the warp goes crossways and the weft goes lengthways.	TRUE ○	FALSE ○
10 Egyptian mummy masks were made of plaster and linen or papyrus.	TRUE ○	FALSE ○

Arts and Crafts

Not just for children, Arts and Crafts is serious business. How well will you do in this round about design and the decorative arts?

1 Which New York store became famous for its Art Nouveau lamps, jewelry, and glassware?

2 What is the term for the use of Chinese styles and motifs in Western furniture and fabrics?

3 What type of decorative flooring were the Romans famous for?

4 What U.S. religious group created furniture still admired for its simplicity, robustness, and craftsmanship?

5 Which 19th-century English artistic and social movement influenced the 20th-century Bauhaus style?

6 Which decorative technique involves inlaying small pieces of wood, bone, or ivory on furniture to create ornate patterns?

7 Which interior design style of the Victorian era harked back to the architecture of medieval times?

8 Which civilization on the Mekong River was noted for its craftsmanship?

9 Which London museum specializing in decorative arts opened in 1852 as the Museum of Manufacturers?

On the Make

Check out these questions about long-ago crafts, including some on how they're made.

1 Which toolmaking technique was developed around 250,000 years ago?

2 What was the name of both the city house and the country manor where English architect, designer, and writer William Morris lived?

3 Who set up his workshop in St. Martin's Lane, London, in 1753?

4 What was once made by heating animal fat with wood ash or another alkali?

5 Which Peruvian culture, based on the Pacific coast south of modern Lima, was famous for its exquisite textiles?

6 Morris & Company began to sell what in Boston in 1873?

7 What term is used for a Greek or Roman brooch made of two-colored stone?

8 The term black-figure and red-figure refer to what form of Greek art?

9 The Moche people of Peru produced sculpted pots or "jars" with a spout named after which piece of horse-riding equipment?

10 Which ancient European civilization is noted for its terra-cotta sarcophagi portraying couples on a couch?

Answers

PAGE 305

What the Dickens?
1 *A Tale of Two Cities*
2 Boz
3 Fagin
4 Marshalsea Prison
5 *Great Expectations*
6 *Bleak House*
7 *A Christmas Carol*
8 Nicholas Nickleby
9 *Barnaby Rudge*
10 *The Mystery of Edwin Drood*

Novel Occupations
1 Thomas Hardy
2 Oliver Goldsmith
3 Robert Louis Stevenson
4 John Le Carré
5 Yukio Mishima
6 Thomas Mann
7 Leslie Thomas
8 James M. Cain
9 Henry James
10 James Joyce

PAGE 306

Taking a Leaf from Literature
1 c. The Scarlet Pimpernel
2 c. The shrew
3 c. *Of Mice and Men*
4 a. Flies, in *Lord of the Flies*
5 a. Nathaniel Hawthorne
6 a. The Jackdaw of Rheims
7 b. The lion in winter
8 c. A sperm whale
9 b. Cedar (*Snow Falling on Cedars*)
10 b. Raven

PAGE 307

That's a Great Start
1 *Pride and Prejudice* by Jane Austen
2 *Anna Karenina* by Leo Tolstoy
3 *The Go-Between* by L. P. Hartley
4 *Midnight's Children* by Salman Rushdie
5 *Peter Pan* by J. M. Barrie
6 *The Catcher in the Rye* by J. D. Salinger
7 *The Metamorphosis* by Franz Kafka
8 *The Stranger/The Outsider* by Albert Camus
9 *Out of Africa* by Isak Dinesen
10 *Remembrance of Things Past* by Marcel Proust

Colorful Writing
1 Orange—*Clockwork Orange*
2 Green—*Anne of Green Gables* by L. M. Montgomery
3 Blue—*Blue Highways*
4 Red—*The Red Badge of Courage*
5 White—T. H. White and Snow White
6 *The Color Purple*
7 Black—*Black Beauty*
8 *Goldfinger*
9 The Scarlet Pimpernel
10 Tom Brown

PAGE 308

What's in a Name?
1 Charlotte Brontë, Emily Brontë, and Anne Brontë
2 Agatha Christie
3 George Orwell
4 Mary Anne Evans
5 Samuel Clemens
6 David Cornwall
7 Joe Klein
8 Fitzgerald—the novelist F. Scott and the English translator Edward
9 Patrick O'Brian
10 Ruth Rendell
11 Miller
12 Stephen King

Novel Locations
1 Mexico
2 Vietnam
3 Romania
4 Denmark
5 Trinidad and Tobago
6 Kenya
7 Chile
8 Canada
9 Egypt
10 South Africa

PAGE 309

Detective Work
1 Lord Peter Wimsey
2 Miss Marple
3 Adam Dalgliesh
4 Dalziel and Pasco
5 Patricia D. Cornwell
6 Father Brown
7 Raymond Chandler
8 Perry Mason
9 Jules Maigret
10 *The Maltese Falcon*
11 Dave Robicheaux, created by James Lee Burke

Between the Covers and Around the World
1 My Struggle
2 Nostradamus
3 Émile Zola
4 Germaine Greer
5 F. Scott Fitzgerald
6 *Don Quixote*
7 Suetonius
8 Ernest Hemingway
9 Thomas Paine
10 Andrew Carnegie

PAGE 310

From Old to New
1 False; there are 27
2 True
3 False; he attended Rugby
4 True
5 False; the book was originally published in 1961, and the movie appeared in 2008

Storied Creatures
1 a. Dog
2 d. Rabbits
3 a. Hedgehog
4 c. March hare
5 d. Donkey
6 a. A little lamb
7 c. Polynesia
8 b. The lion
9 a. Nana
10 d. A bear

PAGE 311

All About the Bard

1 Stratford-upon-Avon, Warwick-shire, England
2 His mother
3 Anne Hathaway
4 *Hamlet*
5 *Julius Caesar*—the speech is by Mark Antony
6 *Othello*
7 The Globe
8 Royal Shakespeare Company
9 *Macbeth*
10 *A Midsummer Night's Dream*

Ancient Places

1 *Ulysses*
2 Seamus Heaney
3 D. H. Lawrence
4 *The Epic of Gilgamesh*
5 *The Epic of Gilgamesh*
6 The Roman state

PAGE 312

Poetry as Truth

1 False; Homer's works is correct
2 True
3 True
4 False; Dylan Thomas wrote it
5 True

Verse of the Ages

1 *The Iliad* and *The Odyssey*
2 *Mahābhārata*
3 *Metamorphoses*
4 Ariel
5 Milton's *Paradise Lost*
6 From a snake bite

Legendary People

1 Blind Harry
2 *The Winter's Tale*
3 Oisin
4 John Keats
5 Bruce Chatwin
6 Percy Bysshe Shelley
7 *The Aeneid*

PAGE 313

Classical Capers

1 d. Mozart
2 a. *From the New World*
3 b. J. S. Bach
4 c. *Rigoletto*
5 a. *Billy Budd*
6 a. Edvard Grieg
7 c. *Fidelio*
8 a. Johann Strauss
9 a. Air on a G String
10 c. Slow the music

PAGE 314

Time to Play

1 False; it is a keyboard instrument
2 True
3 True
4 False; they are famous for playing the violin
5 True
6 False; it originated in China

What a Classic!

1 A baton
2 One double reed
3 Moscow
4 Quick tempo
5 19th century
6 Penzance (*The Pirates of Penzance*)
7 Violin
8 Sousaphone
9 Amazon
10 *The Choral Symphony*

Movie Music

1 *Desperately Seeking Susan*
2 *Annie Get Your Gun*
3 "Edelweiss"
4 *Oliver*
5 King Arthur
6 *Rocky III*

PAGE 315

Bach to the Classics

1 b. "Sabre Dance"
2 a. Johann Strauss
3 b. 1812
4 a. Loud

5 c. Symphony No. 5
6 b. Salzburg
7 b. Violin
8 a. Soprano
9 b. New York Philharmonic Orchestra
10 c. Prima donna

Tuned to the Classics

1 Sir Henry Wood, the conductor credited with expanding the summer tradition
2 Standing-room ticket holders who are allowed to stroll, or "promenade," about the Royal Albert Hall
3 Jacqueline du Pré
4 Russian
5 Edward Elgar
6 *Eroica*
7 Two
8 Cello
9 Luciano Pavarotti
10 La Scala
11 Aaron Copland

PAGE 316

Instrumental Instruments

1 Bob Dylan
2 Piano
3 Double bass
4 Mandolin
5 Bugle
6 Piccolo

Opening Lines

1 "You're the One That I Want"
2 "Thriller"
3 "Money, Money, Money"
4 "I Want to Hold Your Hand"
5 "I Got You Babe"
6 "My Way"

Strike Up the Band

1 *West Side Story*
2 *Cabaret*
3 *Funny Girl*
4 *Paint Your Wagon*
5 Richard and Oscar
6 St. Louis (*Meet Me in St. Louis*)
7 *A Star Is Born*
8 Jerry from *Tom and Jerry*
9 Paris (*An American in Paris*)

Answers

Country Roads

1 Dolly Parton
2 Jim Reeves
3 Sissy Spacek
4 Tammy Wynette
5 Johnny Cash
6 Kenny Rogers
7 Shania Twain
9 Glen Campbell
10 John Denver

TV Music Box

1 *Married with Children*
2 Jack Jones
3 *Friends*
4 *Moonlighting*
5 Suzi Quatro
6 Sheena Easton
7 Zoot
8 Vonda Shepard

Movie Menagerie

1 A dog
2 *The Incredible Journey*
3 Honor Blackman
4 *Silence of the Lambs*
5 *Jaws 2*
6 Clint Eastwood
7 A rat
8 Bagheera
9 *Born Free*
10 *The Lion King*

The Christmas Movie

1 c. Bill Murray
2 b. Richard Attenborough
3 a. *It's a Wonderful Life*
4 c. *The World Is Not Enough*
5 c. *Jingle All the Way*
6 a. Michael Caine
7 b. *Jack Frost*
8 b. Peter Auty
9 a. Hulk Hogan
10 c. Tom Conti

Roll the Credits

1 *Star Wars*
2 *Butch Cassidy and the Sundance Kid*
3 *Silence of the Lambs*
4 *It's a Wonderful Life*
5 *Some Like It Hot*
6 *Casablanca*
7 *Sunset Boulevard*
8 *White Heat*
9 *Citizen Kane*
10 *Alien*

Great Children's Films

1 Gene Wilder
2 Ruby
3 Sergeant, a plastic soldier
4 Ian Fleming
5 Elizabeth Taylor
6 Dumbo
7 Macaulay Culkin
8 *Bedknobs and Broomsticks*
9 Eddie Murphy
10 *Stuart Little*

Magnificent Seven

1 Seven
2 Yul Brynner
3 *Seven*
4 Sherlock Holmes
5 *Seven Brides for Seven Brothers*
6 *The Seven Year Itch*
7 Frank Sinatra
8 1937
9 Tibet *(Seven Years in Tibet)*
10 Akira Kurosawa

Just Plane Crazy

1 True
2 False; it was called *The Blue Max*
3 True
4 False; it starred Fred Astaire and Ginger Rogers
5 True
6 True
7 True
8 True
9 False; the actor was Rock Hudson
10 False; the movie was *King Kong*

B Movies

1 *Bus Stop*
2 *Blackboard Jungle*
3 *Brannigan*
4 *Blind Date*
5 *Beauty and the Beast*
6 *Braveheart*
7 *Barbarella*
8 *Bugsy Malone*
9 *Basic Instinct*

Maybe Baby

1 *Rosemary's Baby*
2 Leonard Nimoy
3 A leopard
4 *Baby Boom*
5 Woody Allen
6 Babe Ruth
7 *Babe: Pig in the City*
8 Nicolas Cage
9 Laurel and Hardy
10 *Honey, I Blew Up the Kid*

Birds of a Feather

1 The Marx Brothers
2 Canary
3 Polynesia
4 *The Wild Geese*
5 *Where Eagles Dare*
6 Rooster Cogburn
7 *Brewster McCloud*
8 Edgar Allan Poe
9 *Convoy*
10 Goose

Technicolor Trivia

1 The Vietnam War
2 *Reservoir Dogs*
3 *The Hunt for Red October*
4 *The Color Purple*
5 *The Pink Panther*
6 *Yellow Submarine*
7 *The Golden Child*
8 Anna Sewell

Novel Ideas

1 a. *The Fisher King*
2 c. C. S. Lewis
3 c. Umberto Eco
4 a. Mario Puzo
5 a. *The Dam Busters*
6 b. Harper Lee
7 a. Charles Webb
8 c. *The Remains of the Day*
9 b. Tess of the D'Urbervilles

A Winning Performance

1 *All About Eve*
2 *Ordinary People*
3 *Patton*
4 80 years old
5 A reel of film
6 *Around the World in 80 Days*
7 *The Last Emperor*
8 Spencer Tracy
9 Catherine Martin
10 Laurence Olivier's 1948 version of *Hamlet*

What a Disaster!

1 *The Towering Inferno*
2 *The Poseidon Adventure*
3 *Deep Impact*
4 *Titanic*
5 *Armageddon*
6 *The Hindenburg*
7 *The Perfect Storm*
8 *Dante's Peak*
9 *The China Syndrome*
10 *Independence Day*

Days Like These

1 *End of Days*
2 *A Day at the Races*
3 *Days of Thunder*
4 *The Day of the Triffids*
5 *That'll Be the Day*
6 *Anne of the Thousand Days*
7 *Six Days Seven Nights*
8 *One Fine Day*
9 *The Remains of the Day*
10 *Independence Day*

All the World's a Stage

1 Mrs. Robinson in *The Graduate*
2 George and Ira Gershwin
3 Siam (now Thailand)
4 *The King and I*
5 *MacBeth*
6 T. S. Eliot's
7 Vietnam
8 Broadway
9 *Camelot* (honorable mention if you answered *Spamalot*, the Monty Python farce)
10 The Jets and the Sharks

A Monumental Task

1 Israel
2 The Arc de Triomphe
3 Admiral Nelson
4 Washington, D.C.
5 Mount Rushmore in the Black Hills of South Dakota
6 Ireland
7 Canberra
8 First World War
9 The Great Fire of London, 1666

A Brush with Beauty

1 Water lilies
2 Sunflowers
3 Still life
4 Salvadore Dali
5 Bruegel the Elder
6 Hieronymus Bosch
7 *Primavera*
8 Titian
9 Andy Warhol
10 Pablo Picasso

Sing and Dance

1 *My Fair Lady*
2 *Phantom of the Opera*
3 *Miss Saigon*
4 *Jesus Christ Superstar*
5 *La Cage Aux Folles*
6 *Porgy and Bess*
7 *The King and I*
8 *Hair*
9 *Godspell*
10 *Annie*

Made to Last

1 The Makonde
2 The Shona
3 Ebony
4 Henry Moore
5 Canova

Very Visual

1 True
2 True
3 False; it's Saint Luke
4 False; it opened in 1793
5 True
6 False; it's in Florence
7 True
8 True
9 False; he wrote them in France
10 True

Smooth Moves

1 The Twist
2 Dame Margot Fonteyn
3 The Watusi
4 Two
5 Locomotion
6 Foxtrot
7 The June Taylor Dancers
8 Synchronized swimming
9 *Dances with Wolves*
10 Mambo

Take Your Partner

1 a. The Highland Fling
2 c. Jazz
3 a. Hawaiians
4 b. Break dancing
5 a. Bali
6 a. Yoruba
7 b. The oud
8 c. Gregory Hines

Answers

Let's Dance

1 Isadora Duncan
2 Tony Manero
3 Michael Flatley
4 *Dances with Wolves*
5 Anna Pavlova
6 Mazurka
7 Ginger Rogers
8 1920s
9 Salome
10 Gavotte

On Your Feet!

1 False; Carole King wrote "The Locomotion"
2 True
3 False; Audrey Hepburn sang it
4 True
5 True
6 True
7 False; "Boogie Wonderland" was recorded by Earth Wind & Fire
8 False; the album's title was *Blood on the Dance Floor*
9 False; the Vandellas did the backup

Standing Tall

1 The Petronas Towers
2 Chicago
3 The Chrysler Building
4 Daniel Libeskind
5 The Guggenheim
6 The Renaissance
7 Letchworth Garden City
8 Eixample
9 Oscar Niemeyer

Famous Buildings

1 I. M. Pei
2 William Van Alen
3 James Hoban
4 Frank Gehry
5 Renzo Piano
6 Norman Foster
7 Gustave Eiffel
8 César Pelli

9 Sir Christopher Wren
10 Le Corbusier

Architects with Style

1 Nicholas Hawksmoor (1661–1736)—the novel *Hawksmoor* appeared in 1985
2 Richard Rogers
3 Florence
4 I. M. Pei
5 Frank Lloyd Wright—in the song "So Long, Frank Lloyd Wright"
6 Walter Gropius
7 Thomas Jefferson
8 Burley Griffin
9 Antoni Gaudi
10 New Delhi

Monumental Matters

1 The Lighthouse of Alexandria
2 Herod the Great
3 Vespasian
4 The Pont du Gard
5 The Temple of Artemis at Ephesus
6 Teotihuacán
7 Phidias
8 Diocletian
9 Ravenna
10 Egypt

Across the Board

1 False; it's the term for climbing tall buildings
2 False; it was in Olympia
3 False; the correct answer is Bologna
4 True
5 True
6 False; it was made of concrete

Building Bridges

1 Simon and Garfunkel
2 Asia
3 San Francisco
4 Lloyd Bridges
5 Venice
6 David Lean

Where Are They?

1 Paris
2 London
3 New York
4 Washington
5 Moscow
6 Orlando
7 Rome
8 Athens
9 Kuala Lumpur
10 Copenhagen

Home Sweet Home

1 Igloos
2 Yurts or gers
3 A tent
4 Reeds
5 It is underground
6 Guadix
7 They are on stilts

Historic Houses

1 Thomas Jefferson
2 Edinburgh
3 King Ludwig II of Bavaria
4 Christopher Wren
5 Adolf Hitler
6 Lhasa
7 Granada
8 The Forbidden City
9 Camp David
10 Palace of Versailles

Early Decorative Arts

1 c. Shellfish
2 d. Glassblowing
3 b. Tombs
4 a. Beards
5 c. Cameos
6 b. Tesserae
7 c. Pottery

High Style

1 False; they are called "adobe"
2 True
3 True
4 False; the style rose during Napoleon I's empire
5 True
6 True
7 True
8 True
9 False; it's the other way around
10 True

Arts and Crafts

1 Tiffany & Co.
2 Chinoiserie
3 Mosaic
4 The Shakers
5 The Arts and Crafts Movement
6 Marquetry
7 Gothic Revival
8 The Funan
9 The Victoria and Albert Museum

On the Make

1 The Levallois technique
2 Kelmscott
3 Thomas Chippendale
4 Soap
5 The Paracas
6 Wallpaper
7 Cameo
8 Pottery
9 Stirrups
10 The Etruscans

10 Word Play

You may think of words simply as devices that help you read, but they are surprisingly thoughtful, meaningful, helpful...and even funny! These questions will stretch your mind and test your knowledge.

Word Origins

Scratch the surface of a common word and you'll find gods and goddesses, temples, colors of the rainbow, and so much more bubbling beneath. Test your knowledge of these long-ago sources with these questions brimming with history.

Ancient Origins

How much do you know about how these words and expressions started?

1 What is the original Greek meaning of the term *hieroglyph*?
a. Sacred carving
b. Secret writing
c. Hidden meaning

2 What word means a Roman spirit that guides someone from life to death and has come to mean someone who has exceptional talents?
a. Scholar
b. Prodigy
c. Genius

3 What did the word *philosophy* originally mean in Greek?
a. Learning
b. Love of wisdom
c. Thinker

4 The origin of the word *Phoenician* may come from the Greek *phoinikes*—referring to a color. Which color?
a. Blue
b. Purple
c. Pink

5 Whose mathematical law says: "The square of the hypotenuse of a right-angled triangle is equal to the sum of the squares of the other two sides"?
a. Pythagoras
b. Blaise Pascal
c. Albert Einstein

6 What is a Maecenas?
a. Musician
b. Greek scholar
c. Patron of the arts

7 What is the Breton word for an ancient monument that means "long stone"?
a. Menhir
b. Stonehenge
c. Bravig

8 Which ancient civilization is recalled in the word *augury*?
a. Greek
b. Mesopotamian
c. Roman

9 The name of Carthage's citadel is the Byrsa. What does the word *byrsa* mean?
a. Lamb's wool
b. Ox hide
c. Sheepskin

Word Play

In the Beginning...

Here are the origins of words—and their original meanings: true or false?

1 *Mesopotamia* means "land between rivers."	TRUE ○	FALSE ○
2 The name *Etruscan* is recalled in a modern region of Italy: Venice.	TRUE ○	FALSE ○
3 The term *Buddha* means "The Simple One."	TRUE ○	FALSE ○
4 Tannin, a naturally occurring chemical used in leather-making, shares its derivation with the word *tanning*.	TRUE ○	FALSE ○
5 The word *sphinx* comes from Greek.	TRUE ○	FALSE ○
6 The original meaning of *cubitum*, the Latin word from which the ancient unit of measurement known as the cubit is derived, is knee.	TRUE ○	FALSE ○
7 Jewelry worn on the chest is called pectoral, derived from the Latin for *breast* or *stomach*.	TRUE ○	FALSE ○

The People Name Game

The answers may be common terms, but they're not as simple as you might think.

1 After whom was the Julian calendar named?

2 What is the meaning of the Latin expression from which the word *Aborigine* is derived?

3 Which ancient people gave constellations their names?

4 To whom was the Pantheon in Rome dedicated?

5 The people who took over from the Hopewell in North America, after about AD 600, are named after the biggest river flowing through their territory. What is it?

6 How did people of the Bronze Age Urnfield Culture dispose of their dead?

7 The San people are descendants of southern Africa's original hunter-gatherers. By what other name are they commonly known?

8 The Greek "father of medicine" gave his name to an oath traditionally sworn by doctors. What is that oath called?

9 Which Mediterranean people first used the laurel wreath as a victor's crown?

10 Which month of the year is named after the first Roman emperor?

11 Which people, now associated with Scotland, Wales, and Ireland, celebrated festivals called Beltane and Samhain?

12 By what name are the Mochica people of northern Peru also known?

Be Afraid, Be Very Afraid

If you're not too scared, name three phobias (from the Greek *phobos*, meaning fear) that begin with *A*.

I Didn't See That Coming!

These words and customs hark back to long ago. Can you name them now?

1 What distinguished homo habilis from previous hominids: the ability to stand upright or to use tools?

2 Which English word for the way in which a year is divided comes from the Roman name for the first day of each month?

3 Which bloody form of Roman entertainment may be the origin of the thumbs-down gesture?

4 What word comes from an imitation of the way in which—according to the Greeks—uncouth non-Greeks spoke?

5 The Vedic period of Indian history is named after the Vedas, the oldest sacred writings of Hinduism. What does *veda* mean?

6 What does Punic mean, as in the Punic Wars?

So Close!

Sometimes modern-day words come from similar-sounding roots. Can you name them?

1 Which Roman goddess is referred to in the word *cereal*?

2 What word did Mausolus of Caria give to the English language?

3 Which wealthy Greek colony in southern Italy gave rise to the word *sybaritic,* meaning luxurious and sensuous?

4 Parsis are followers of the Zoroastrian religion. What does *Parsi* mean?

5 Saturday is named after which Roman god?

Two of Twelve

Name the two months on the calendar derived from the names of Roman gods.

Back to the Future

Wordsmiths reach back to the past to answer questions about words today. Can you look far enough back to answer these questions on the origins of names, words, and phrases?

1 Which culture gave us the word *draconian*?

2 The press is often said to "pillory" personalities: where does this phrase come from?

3 Why were lanterns originally called *lanthorns*?

4 Which Roman name for a popular eatery has endured into modern times as a word for a pub or bar?

5 From which religion does the idea of the "sacred cow" originate?

6 A person who eats well is sometimes called a "hearty trencherman": what, at the medieval table, was a *trencher*?

7 Which penal institution is so called because it was originally designed to produce penitence?

8 Which famous design style was named after an exhibition held in 1925?

What's in a Place Name?

How did yesterday's words turn into today's cities, mountains, and waterways? See if you know!

1 Which Spanish city was founded by the Phoenicians as Gades?

2 The alliance of city-states led by Athens and founded in 478 BC was named after which Greek island?

3 With which mountain range is the Chavin culture associated?

4 To which dynasty does China owe its name?

5 After which ancient people is the Tyrrhenian Sea named?

6 What is the name of the region straddling the India-Pakistan border where the Aryans first settled, and whose name in Sanskrit means "five rivers"?

7 By what name do we know the area of southern France that corresponds to the Roman's Provincia Romana?

8 Which ancient Mesopotamian city had a name that meant "Gate of God," referring to its god Marduk?

9 What Latin word was the origin of the "chester" or "cester" in English place names?

10 Which temple in Athens was dedicated to the goddess Athena?

11 In which country is the port of Mocha, famous for the export of coffee?

12 Which Spanish seaport gave its name to an alcoholic drink?

Famous Quotes

From the dire warnings about war to the wickedly funny jabs at lawyers, the quotes below are sure to make you think and make you laugh. But can you answer questions about who said what?

Say What?

Did these people really say that? Which is true and which is false?

1 Dorothy Parker said, "Men seldom make passes at girls who wear glasses." TRUE ○ FALSE ○

2 Jerry Lewis said, "I never forget a face, but in your case I'll be glad to make an exception." TRUE ○ FALSE ○

3 Benjamin Franklin said, "A foolish consistency is the hobgoblin of little minds." TRUE ○ FALSE ○

4 Albert Einstein said, "Only two things are infinite, the universe and human stupidity, and I'm not sure about the former." TRUE ○ FALSE ○

5 Karl Marx said, "Man was born free, and he is everywhere in chains." TRUE ○ FALSE ○

Funny Bones

Match each humorous quote with its speaker, choosing from the list below.

"I don't care to belong to any club that will have me as a member."_____ **A** Mark Twain

"If Hitler invaded hell, I would make at least a favorable reference to the devil...."_____ **B** Dorothy Parker

"If there were no bad people, there would be no good lawyers."_____ **C** Robert Bloch

"A classic—something that everybody wants to have read and nobody wants to read."_____ **D** Margaret Thatcher

"Being powerful is like being a lady. If you have to tell people you are, you aren't."_____ **E** Charles Dickens

"That woman speaks 18 languages and can't say 'no' in any of them."_____ **F** Winston Churchill

"I have the heart of a child. I keep it in a jar on my shelf."_____ **G** Erma Bombeck

"It goes without saying that you should never have more children than you have car windows."_____ **H** Groucho Marx

Name the Speaker

Which person famously uttered the following? Choose from the list below.

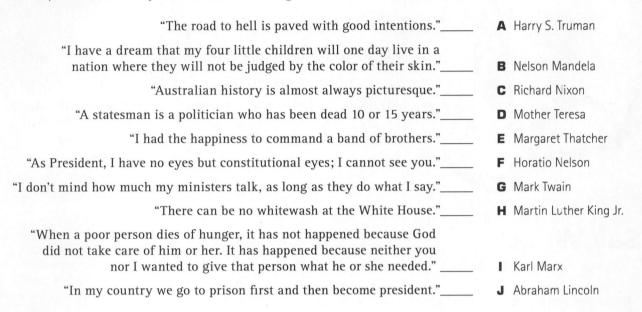

"The road to hell is paved with good intentions."_____

"I have a dream that my four little children will one day live in a nation where they will not be judged by the color of their skin."_____

"Australian history is almost always picturesque."_____

"A statesman is a politician who has been dead 10 or 15 years."_____

"I had the happiness to command a band of brothers."_____

"As President, I have no eyes but constitutional eyes; I cannot see you."_____

"I don't mind how much my ministers talk, as long as they do what I say."_____

"There can be no whitewash at the White House."_____

"When a poor person dies of hunger, it has not happened because God did not take care of him or her. It has happened because neither you nor I wanted to give that person what he or she needed." _____

"In my country we go to prison first and then become president."_____

A Harry S. Truman

B Nelson Mandela

C Richard Nixon

D Mother Teresa

E Margaret Thatcher

F Horatio Nelson

G Mark Twain

H Martin Luther King Jr.

I Karl Marx

J Abraham Lincoln

...And Phrases for All!

What does it mean? Who said it? Where was it said? Do you know the answers?

1 What does René Descarte's dictum *cogito ergo sum* mean?

2 Complete this quotation: "Workers of the world unite. You have nothing to lose but your _____."

3 What fiscally minded slogan was the main rallying cry of the American Revolution?

4 The rallying cry "Liberty, Equality, Fraternity" was first coined during which revolution?

5 On which monument will you find the words: "Give me your tired, your poor, your huddled masses yearning to breathe free...."?

6 "From ____ in the Baltic to Trieste in the Adriatic"–in which Baltic city did Churchill's "iron curtain" start?

7 Complete this saying of Mao Zedong: "All reactionaries are paper ____."

8 Louis XIV declared: *L état, c'est moi.* What does this mean?

9 Complete this quote from a poem by Rupert Brooke: "That there's some corner of a foreign field/ That is ____ ____."

10 In the 1960s young people were exhorted to "Turn on, tune in, and ____ ____."

Notable and Quotable

How well do you know the background of these famous wordsmiths?

1 Dorothy Parker, known for her cynicism, depression, and suicide attempts, died at age 73:
   a. Of a heart attack
   b. From falling off the curb of a New York City street
   c. From an overdose of sleeping pills

2 How did Benjamin Franklin enter the publishing business?
   a. Roaming the Pennsylvania countryside for articles to put in *Poor Richard's Almanak*
   b. He printed political leaflets to distribute in Philadelphia
   c. As an apprentice to his brother; he was a full-fledged printer by age 17

3 How does Douglas Adams's *Hitchhiker's Guide to the Galaxy* begin?
   a. Dirk Gently finds an alien communication device
   b. The main character wins a tour of the galaxy on a spaceship
   c. Aliens destroy Earth to make way for an intergalactic highway

4 The popularity of humorist Erma Bombeck's column, At Wit's End, soared when she wrote about what in the 1950s?
   a. Travel destinations within a two-day drive of Columbus, Ohio
   b. Her frustration with the housewife role and housekeeping
   c. California's beach culture

5 What was the original inspiration for Garrison Keillor's radio show, *A Prairie Home Companion*?
   a. *The Three Stooges*
   b. *The Grand Ole Opry* country music show
   c. *The Roy Rogers Show*

6 Best known as the host of the comedy quiz show *You Bet Your Life*, Groucho Marx avoided the use of:
   a. Insults
   b. Sexual innuendo
   c. Profanity

7 Multitalented Oliver Wendell Holmes was famous as the author of the poem "Old Ironsides," for his humor and opinions published in *Atlantic Monthly,* and for his books (three novels and two biographies). However, he was also:
   a. A Harvard-trained physician
   b. A renowned astronomer
   c. A letter-carrier for the Postal Service

8 Woody Allen, the famed comedian, writer, and film director, was the subject of a documentary, *Wild Man Blues*, that focused on a singular aspect of his career. What did that film feature?
   a. A literature discussion group that's the source of many of Allen's comedic ideas
   b. His performances as a jazz clarinetist
   c. Behind-the-scenes practical jokes during the making of a movie

O Brother, Who Art Thou?

The Marx Brothers (at least those who speak) are known for their witty sayings. Name the five Marx Brothers.

Who Said That?

The sayings are famous. The people are famous. But is each saying attributed to the right person? Choose true or false.

1 Benjamin Spock said, "You know more than you think you do." TRUE ○ FALSE ○

2 Tom Wolfe proclaimed, "We are now—in the Me Decade...." TRUE ○ FALSE ○

3 Thomas Edison noted, "Science without religion is lame, religion without science is blind." TRUE ○ FALSE ○

4 Linda Evangelista said, "We don't wake up for less than $10,000 a day." TRUE ○ FALSE ○

5 John F. Kennedy proclaimed, "Ask not what your country can do for you—ask what you can do for your country." TRUE ○ FALSE ○

6 Robert Frost said, "Silence the pianos and with muffled drum/Bring out the coffin, let the mourners come." TRUE ○ FALSE ○

7 Bill Gates remarked, "Fancy being remembered around the world for the invention of a mouse!" TRUE ○ FALSE ○

8 Nelson Mandela observed, "True reconciliation does not consist in merely forgetting the past." TRUE ○ FALSE ○

My Country, 'Tis of Thee

My country, your country? Which country completes each quote? Choose from the list below.

"Poor _____, so far from God and so close to the United States." (Attributed to Porfirio Diaz) **A** Africa

"_____ always brings us something new." (Pliny the Elder) **B** Australian

"From _____'s icy mountains...." (Reginald Heber) **C** Brazilian

"Nothing in _____ is identifiable, the mere asking of a question causes it to disappear or to merge in something else." (E. M. Forster) **D** England

"In all directions stretched the Great _____ Emptiness, in which the mind is the least of possessions." (Patrick White) **E** German

"Scratch a _____ and you find a Tartar." (proverb) **F** Greenland

"If I were a _____ without land or money or the means to feed my children I would be burning the rain forest too." (Sting) **G** India

"America is a land whose center is nowhere; _____ one whose center is everywhere." (John Updike) **H** Mexico

"I speak Spanish to God, Italian to women, French to men, and _____ to my horse." (Emperor Charles V) **I** Russian

"To win in _____ we will have to exterminate a nation." (Benjamin Spock) **J** Vietnam

War and Peace

War may be hell, but it's also great fodder for quotes. Who made the following statements? Choose from the list below.

"Mankind must put an end to war or war will put an end to mankind." _____

"To jaw-jaw is always better than to war-war." _____

"Political power grows out of the barrel of a gun." _____

"The only thing necessary for the triumph of evil is for good men to do nothing." _____

"A man cannot be too careful in the choice of his enemies." _____

"There never was a good war, or a bad peace." _____

"Never forget that everything Hitler did in Germany was legal." _____

"We cannot afford another victory like that." _____

A Benjamin Franklin

B Oscar Wilde

C Edmund Burke

D Martin Luther King Jr.

E John F. Kennedy

F Winston Churchill

G Pyrrhus

H Mao Zedong (Tse-tung)

Gone Missing

The quotes below are useless without your help. Supply the missing words to complete the quotes.

1 "That is no country for _____."

2 "Happiness _____ many things."

3 "One man may ____ a horse, while another may not look over a hedge."

4 "Our body is a ____ for living."

5 "____ is the girl's prison and the woman's workhouse."

6 "The place is very well and quiet and the _____ only scream in a low voice."

7 "Phone for the ____-____, Norman As Cook is a little unnerved."

8 "Soap and ____ are not as sudden as a massacre, but they are more deadly in the long run."

9 "Dark house, by which once more I stand/Here in the long unlovely ____."

10 "Vice came in always at the door of ____, not at the door of inclination."

One Last Time!

Writers, economists, philanthropists: they all have something important to say. Can you figure out who said what?

1 According to the playwright George Bernard Shaw, the "great advantage of a hotel is that it's a refuge from ____ ____."

2 Who, in the 1920s, said that houses were "machines for living"?

3 Which Victorian writer called for a revival of the spirit that had built the cathedrals of medieval Europe?

4 Which economist claimed that no famine had ever occurred in a democracy?

5 Who said, "Heaven helps those who help themselves"?

6 Which philanthropist said he believed in giving "wholesale and not retail"?

7 What do Hindu parents whisper into their newborn infant's ear just after birth?

8 "All they that love not tobacco and boys be fools" are lines attributed to which playwright?

Quote, UnQuote

Puzzle out the people who made these dramatic statements.

1 Which archaeologist declared: "Everywhere the glint of gold"?

2 Which king was Byron referring to in his poem that begins, "The Assyrian came down like the wolf on the fold"?

3 Who gave the greeting: "We who are about to die salute you!"?

4 Which statement of Christian beliefs begins, "We believe in one God, the Father, the Almighty, maker of heaven and earth...."?

5 Of whom did Jesus say: "Upon this rock I will build my church"?

6 Who was Wilfred Owen quoting when he wrote: "The old lie: Dulce et decorum est pro patria mori" ("It is sweet and fitting to die for one's country")?

7 Who said, "I found Rome a city of brick and left it a city of marble"?

8 "O my son Absolom, my son, my son Absolom! Would God I had died for thee." Which grieving father said this?

9 Who is supposed to have said, "O Lord make me chaste, but not yet"?

10 Which Latin author and orator was the source of the exclamation, "O tempora! O mores!" (What times! What customs!)

In a Manner of Speaking

Words are fun to play with, and expressions even more so. Can you answer the following questions about familiar expressions?

1 Who, according to the playwright Christopher Marlowe, had "the face that launched a thousand ships"?

2 What epic poem begins with the words that can be translated, "Sing, O goddess, the anger of Achilles son of Peleus...."?

3 Which country was known as the "granary of the ancient world"?

4 The Roman poet Horace is credited with the expression "Carpe Diem." What does it mean?

5 "Raised to the purple" was an expression used for the appointment of Roman emperors. Which people traded in the purple dye used for emperors' robes?

6 "Beware the Ides of March," says a Shakespearean soothsayer. Who was killed on this day?

7 At whose feast did the words "Mene, Mene, Tekel, Upharsin" appear on the wall?

8 "Mandate of Heaven" is applied to the rulers of which country?

9 "To cut the Gordian knot" means to resolve a difficulty by taking strong action. Who cut the Gordian knot?

Witty and Wise

Are you as wise as the people who made the following statements? Choose the speaker from the list below.

"If you want to know what God thinks of money,
just look at the people he gave it to."_____   **A**   Douglas Adams

"I know not with what weapons World War III will be fought,
but World War IV will be fought with sticks and stones."_____   **B**   Groucho Marx

"I love deadlines. I like the whooshing sound they make as they fly by."_____   **C**   Oliver Wendell Holmes

"The funniest line in English is 'Get it?' When you say that, everyone chortles."_____   **D**   Albert Einstein

"Outside of a dog, a book is man's best friend.
Inside of a dog it's too dark to read."_____   **E**   Garrison Keillor

"Some people are so heavenly minded that they are no earthly good."_____   **F**   Ronald Regan

"Government is like a baby: An alimentary canal with a big appetite
at one end and no sense of responsibility at the other."_____   **G**   Dorothy Parker

Foreign Words

Words travel, just as people do, and many have made long trips around the world. So pack your bags and grab a ticket to exciting destinations, courtesy of the English language!

Foreign Food

Culture hitches a ride with words when they travel, and food is the best surprise in that hitchhiker's suitcase. Can you answer the questions below without getting hungry?

1 What Swedish word meaning "sandwich table" is sometimes used to mean an all-you-can-eat buffet?

2 What is the English name for the sweet cubes, flavored with rosewater, known as *lokum*?

3 Which Italian bread derives its name from its slipper-like shape?

4 What Italian pudding has a name that means "pick-me-up"?

5 By what scientific name is the natural sugar in milk known?

6 With which word do the French toast a person's health?

7 What word is used for food considered unfit to eat under Islamic dietary law?

In Translation

Some answers are in English, some are in foreign languages. How versatile are you?

1 Which German school of design had a name that translates as "house of building"?

2 By what name is the cha-no-yu ceremony known in English?

3 For what disease is the bacterium *Yersinia pestis* responsible?

4 By what name were China's *Yi he quan* known in English?

5 Whose translation of the Bible was first published in 1534?

6 In 17th-century North America, what was an "indenture": a contract to work for someone for a fixed term or a grant of land?

7 Which Jewish festival means "head of the year"?

8 What does the title "Mahatma" mean?

Lost in Translation

Word meanings often get lost or forgotten when words travel. Can you help recover their lost baggage?

1 What is the literal meaning of the name Nova Scotia?
a. New Scotland
b. New Scooter
c. Scottish Hatchback
d. Scottish Star

2 What does the name Sierra Leone mean in Spanish?
a. Desert Lions
b. Stormy Desert
c. Lion Mountains
d. Long Coast

3 Which island's name means "rich port" when translated?
a. Madagascar
b. Puerto Rico
c. Barbados
d. Singapore

4 Which Central American country's name incorporates the Spanish word for *water*?
a. Honduras
b. El Salvador
c. Panama
d. Nicaragua

5 Which one of the following countries' names derives from the Phoenician word for *refuge*?
a. Malta
b. Italy
c. Belgium
d. New Zealand

6 Which European country's name means "eastern kingdom"?
a. Bulgaria
b. Austria
c. Albania
d. Germany

7 Which Caribbean island was named after a day of the week?
a. Jamaica
b. Grenada
c. Cuba
d. Dominica

8 Which country's name means "resplendent land" in Sanskrit?
a. India
b. Sri Lanka
c. Myanmar
d. Iran

9 Which island's name means "terraced bay" in Mandarin?
a. Taiwan
b. Hainan
c. Honshu
d. Hokkaido

10 Zimbabwe is a Shona word meaning what?
a. Land of kings
b. River people
c. Settled country
d. House of stone

Language Class

Do you perk up when you hear a foreign word or do you tune it out? You'll find out when you try to answer the questions below.

1 In India, what is the occupation of a *dhobi-wallah*?

2 By what English word is the Jewish rite of "brit" or "bris" usually known?

3 What is the English equivalent of an *autobahn*?

4 What German word meaning "children's garden" is another term for nursery school?

5 True or false? In France, a *cru* is a haircut.

6 True or false? Desert nomads wear headgear called a *tagelmoust*.

A World of Words

You'll recognize the words from Russia, Japan, Germany, France—but what do they mean?

1 What does the name Argentina mean?

2 What name is given to very brief, descriptive Japanese poems in which some scene or moment is captured in just a couple of lines?

3 What Russian word, usually translated as "openness," described Gorbachev's policy of limited free speech and media reform?

4 What is the meaning in English of the phrase *Deutschland über alles,* the title of the German national anthem in the 1930s?

5 The Croix de Feu was a fascist organization in France before World War II. What does *Croix de Feu* mean in English?

6 What does the title Ataturk mean?

7 What is the literal meaning of the word *apartheid*?

8 What does the word *intifada* mean?

9 From which Roman name is the Russian title *tsar* derived?

10 *Lebensraum* is the Nazi idea that Germany was cramped and needed more territory. What does the term mean literally?

War of Words

How much do you know about the words of war politics below?

1 In 1834, 17 German states joined the *Zollverein*. What does this word mean?

2 In the *Reconquista*, Christian armies reconquered which country?

3 What word meaning "resurgence" or "revival" is the name given to the Italian nationalist movement of the 19th century?

4 The mass attack on German Jews in 1938 is often called "the night of the broken glass" in English. What is its German name?

5 By what name are the Falkland Islands known in Argentina?

6 In which Middle Eastern country is the parliament called the *knesset*?

7 What German term is used to describe the German bombing of British cities from 1940 onward?

8 What Russian word meaning "fortress" is often used to denote the seat of government in Moscow?

9 What Russian word, usually translated as "restructuring," describes Gorbachev's program of reform?

Hello! Hi! Hey!

You can probably say hello several ways in your native tongue. Can you name four ways to say hello in languages other than English?

Latin Test

Latin words and phrases pop up in courts, in art studios, and especially in schools. Will you get a good grade on the test below?

1 Which Latin legal term translates as "you must have the body"?

2 What did a large letter "F" branded into the forehead of some Roman slaves stand for?

3 What does the Latin phrase *Memento mori,* much used in the Middle Ages, mean?

4 A famous 15th-century study of witchcraft bore the title *Malleus Maleficarum.* What did this name mean?

5 Which English philosopher considered the child a *tabula rasa* ("blank tablet") to be written on?

6 The Latin phrase *rus in urbe* might be applied to a town garden. What does it mean?

7 What special substance, used to decorate wood, is obtained from the tree *Rhus vernicifera?*

8 What Latin name is given to the underfloor heating system used by the Romans?

9 If you take a person's words *cum grano salis,* what are you taking them with?

10 What does the Latin phrase "*Mens sana in corpore sano*" mean?

Single Letters and Words

You've mastered expressions and sayings, phrases and words: How well will you do with initials, acronyms, and missing letters? Test your knowledge of the essential building blocks of words—individual letters—with the questions below.

Take a Letter

What's your initial response to these questions?

1 Which letter is associated with the actor Desmond Llewelyn in the James Bond films?
a. X
b. Q
c. Z

2 Which letter of the alphabet represents 100 in Roman numerals?
a. C
b. D
c. L

3 Who directed the 1954 thriller *Dial M for Murder*?
a. Steven Spielberg
b. Alfred Hitchcock
c. Billy Wilder

4 What does the letter *G* stand for in the classification of movies?
a. General showing
b. General audiences
c. General exhibition

5 Which TV series features the characters Mulder and Scully?
a. *X Men*
b. *X Women*
c. *The X-Files*

6 What does the *H* stand for in H. G. Wells?
a. Harold
b. Humphrey
c. Herbert

7 What does the *P* stand for in ESP?
a. Potential
b. Perception
c. Possibility

8 What does the *C* stand for in Washington, D.C.?
a. Columbia
b. Center
c. Charter

9 The letter *D* is the international car registration plate for which country?
a. Germany
b. France
c. Italy

10 What does the *I* stand for in IQ test?
a. Information
b. Instant
c. Intelligence

Bloody Good Answer

Try not to be squeamish, and name all four blood types.

Initial Queries

What do the following sets of initials stand for?

1 HBO		**11** GDP	
2 CBS		**12** GATT	
3 ICBM		**13** TGV	
4 OBE		**14** Soweto	
5 CNN		**15** LDC	
6 AIDS		**16** ETI	
7 UNHCR		**17** WHO	
8 SARS		**18** UNICEF	
9 OPEC		**19** UAE	
10 NAFTA		**20** UFO	

As Easy as ABC

It's always easiest to start at the beginning—in this case, with your ABCs.

1 What *A* is the study of celestial bodies and the universe?

2 What *A* is a flowering plant known for its licorice-like flavor?

3 What *B* is the name of a horse's head harness?

4 What *B* is the name given to whale fat?

5 What *C* is a breed of dog that can be bearded and border?

6 What *C* changes gas into vapor in a car engine?

Short for...

LOL (lots of luck) with these three-letter acronyms!

1 In the world of computers and the Internet, what does FTP stand for?

2 The Soviet secret police was the Komitet Gosudarstvennoi Bezopasnosti (KGB). What does that mean in English?

3 In the British police force, what does CID stand for?

4 In the world of stamp-collecting, what is an FDC?

5 The underground network of which city includes a service called the RER?

6 What does RMS stand for when referring to a ship—as in the RMS *Queen Mary 2?*

7 In the world of accident and emergency, what does SAR stand for?

8 In the jargon of the advertising world, what does USP stand for?

9 In an airport, what important function is known by the acronym ATC?

10 In home technology, what does the acronym VCR stand for?

11 In text messages and e-mails, what do the initials BTW mean?

12 The military forces of which country are known as the PLA?

13 What does FBI stand for?

14 What does the first *D* in DVD stand for?

15 Which airport has the code LHR?

16 What do the initials of the elite force SAS stand for?

Wedding Bells

The initial letters are given—can you complete the names?

1 Before she was carried off to Troy by Paris, Helen was married to King M___ of Sparta.

2 In the Greek pantheon, Zeus was married to Hera. Her name in the Roman religion was J___.

3 King S___ of Israel is reputed to have had 1,000 wives and concubines.

4 The Emperor Augustus's wife of 51 years was called L___.

5 Julia, the daughter of Julius Caesar, was married to P___.

6 The Egyptian goddess I___ was the wife of Osiris.

7 Alexander the Great had a wife called R___.

8 King Prasutagus's more famous widow, a queen of the native Britons, was called B___.

9 In Greek mythology, Haephaestus was the long-suffering husband of the goddess A___.

10 Messalina was the notoriously scandalous third wife of the emperor C___.

Short on Politics and Diplomacy

How well do you know your political and diplomatic abbreviations?

1 Which three European countries came together in a customs union known as Benelux in 1948?

2 In which African country did KANU hold power for nearly 40 years from 1963 to 2002?

3 What do the letters *VJ* in VJ Day stand for?

4 What does the acronym MAD stand for in the context of the nuclear arms race of the 20th century?

5 What four-letter abbreviation is usually used for the National Socialist German Workers' Party?

6 What do the letters CND stand for in the name of this anti-war protest group?

7 What does the acronym PLO stand for?

8 What does NATO stand for?

9 What do the letters *EEC* stand for?

First and Last

Each answer begins and ends with the same letter. Name:

1 South America's second-longest river.

2 A poor, war-torn country in southwest Africa.

3 The world's largest continent.

4 An arid state in the southwest United States.

5 The capital city of Norway.

6 The United States' northernmost state.

7 The term that describes someone who practices the religion of Islam.

8 A peninsula, to the east of the Red Sea, where most of the oil states lie.

9 The most sparsely populated continent on Earth.

10 Asia's largest freshwater lake and the world's deepest.

A Is for...

You may be able to list 10 countries whose names all begin with *A*, but can you match the questions with the right *A* country?

The world's largest island, discovered by the Europeans in the 1600s._____   **A** Addis Ababa

This Asian country has been war-ravaged since the Soviets invaded in 1979._____   **B** Afghanistan

A North African desert republic, formerly a French colony._____   **C** Albania

The capital city of Ethiopia._____   **D** Algeria

This country fought the United Kingdom in 1982 in a war over possession of offshore islands._____   **E** Andorra

____ and Barbuda: Elizabeth II remained queen of this Caribbean state in the Lesser Antilles after its independence in 1981._____   **F** Antigua

A European state on the Adriatic, sandwiched between Greece and Yugoslavia._____   **G** Argentina

This former Soviet republic, wedged between Muslim states in the Caucasus region, claims to have been the first officially Christian country._____   **H** Armenia

A bishop and the President of France are co-princes of this Pyrenean principality._____   **I** Australia

This Alpine republic was the core of a vast European empire until 1918._____   **J** Austria

More Than a K-9

True or false? "K-12" is a shorthand term in computer programming.

Many-Lettered Words

It's time to think beyond single letters and concentrate on three-letter words, four of a kind, and so on. It's something like poker! How well will you play your cards?

Four-Letter Words

No, no, none of the answers is objectionable—but they do have four letters. Count 'em!

1 What name is given to the smallest creature in a litter?

2 Common, gray, monk, harp, and hooded are types of what?

3 In which organ of the body would you find bronchioles?

4 What mammal is also a chemical measure, a spy, and a breakwater?

5 What is the name given to the state of dangerous frenzy in male elephants?

6 What is a baby whale called?

7 What part of a gymnosperm is naked?

8 What *C*, in biology, is composed of cytoplasm and a nucleus?

9 What common herb has a name that also means a wise man?

To Cap It All

All six answers begin with the letters *cap*.

1 What word can be a small cloak or a headland?

2 What word means to overturn, especially when applied to a boat?

3 Which star sign does a goat represent?

4 What name is given to the detachable compartment of a spacecraft?

5 What name is given to a domestic cock that is castrated and fattened for eating?

6 What name is given to a revolving barrel for winding in cable?

To Cap It Off

You've named six: Now name four more words that start with *cap*.

A Call to Arms

All six answers begin with the letters *arm*.

1 Of which European country is Yerevan the capital?

2 What South American burrowing animal has a body encased in bony plates?

3 In the Bible, what battle will take place at the end of the world?

4 What name is given to an agreement to stop fighting and negotiate peace?

5 In the human body, how is the axilla known?

6 What is the name for defensive clothing worn during battle?

Links of Three

Can you find the common factor in each of these lists?

1 Ki-Nubi, Norfuk, Papiamento

2 Barhee, Khadrawy, Halawy

3 Munich, Sydney, Barcelona

4 Inupiat, Chukchi, Aleuts

5 Vietnam, Laos, North Korea

6 Criollo, bagual, cimarron

7 Alice Springs, Australia; Medina, Saudi Arabia; Palm Springs, California

8 Jiao, jeon, kobo

9 Ilocano, Fulfulde, Oromo

Three-Letter Words

The questions are long, but the answers are short—only three letters. What are they?

1 In some card games, which card can be either high or low?

2 Which drink is flavored with juniper berries?

3 Which cooking vessel is also the name of the pipe-playing Greek god of shepherds?

4 What name is given to grass cuttings that are dried to make animal fodder?

5 What is the principal monetary unit of Japan?

6 What island and island group is the most westerly in the Federated States of Micronesia?

"More" Four-Letter Words

Here are more four-letter words: an "echo" of the quiz above. What are the words?

1 Which pop group was founded by George Michael and Andrew Ridgeley?

2 What flower is England's national symbol?

3 Which Andrew Lloyd Webber musical features the song "Memory"?

4 In Scotland, what name is given to a lake?

5 Pb is the chemical symbol for what?

6 In imperial measurements, 1,760 yards is equivalent to one what?

Double-Duty Words

It's fun to play with words, and here you'll find words that are playful on their own. Check out these quizzes about puns, homophones, and words with double meanings.

Take a Second Look

Think twice before you answer these questions about words that can be taken two ways!

1 Which drink is also the name for one side of a ship?

2 Which writing instrument can also be an animal enclosure?

3 What short word can apply to a water barrier and a foal's mother?

4 Which *G* word means a narrow opening between hills and to eat greedily?

5 What does a wrestler use on opponents that is also the name for a storage area on a ship?

6 What word for a rain garment also means "more slippery"?

7 What verb that pertains to fatigue is also a car part?

8 What word for a group of people assembled for an official purpose also is the name for a sheet of rigid material?

9 What tough natural material shares its name with side-to-side motion?

Talking to the Trees

Sometimes you can't see the forest for the trees, and sometimes the trees have nothing to do with a forest. Can you figure out what other meanings these tree names have?

1 This tree's name also means to long for something.

2 This tree sounds like a coating of hairs.

3 This tree's name also means burned wood.

4 This tree sounds like an old respected person.

5 This tree's name is also a very poisonous plant.

6 This tree sounds like a Mediterranean island.

7 Take one letter away from this tree and it sounds sacred.

8 This tree's name also means smart or dapper.

9 This tree sounds like the second person (singular or plural).

10 This tree's name is also an ingredient of margaritas.

It's Not Funny!

Some people may think this round is "punny"; others may just groan. Here are puns, ranging from poor to truly awful.

1 Which Pacific "boy" from off of South America plays periodic havoc with the world's weather?

2 Why were William Shakespeare's London performances *not* "out of this world"?

3 What did the Victorian pugilist Tom Sayers and the Chinese *yi he quan* movement have in common?

4 How did scarification leave its mark on people?

5 Which dramatic form got a big "yes" from Japanese audiences, despite its negative-sounding name?

6 Why were all economics once home economics?

7 Why might it be said that kitchen innovator Denis Papin responded well to pressure?

8 Why was Franz Liszt reputedly such a smashing pianist?

9 Which manufacturer first got "saucy" in 1876?

10 At an Aztec wedding ceremony, "tying the knot" meant the couple literally tied what together?

Missing Links

One word, many meanings: Find the word that can fill all three blanks.

1 Fair ____, ____ barrier, ____ war.

2 ____ garden, ____ town, farmers' ____.

3 Mega____, ____ state, ____ center.

4 Micro____, ____sman, city ____.

5 Shanty ____, ____ship, ____ hall.

6 High-speed ____, camel ____, tractor ____.

7 Farm____, stilt ____, ____holder.

8 ____burden, national ____, ____repayment.

9 Hague ____, Geneva ____, biological weapons ____.

10 Renewable ____, ____ expenditure, ____ efficiency.

Vowels

Vowels may be fewer in number than consonants, but they hold more power. How powerful are you when it comes to answering questions about vowels?

A Is for...

The *answers* in this quiz begin with the letter *A*. Can you name them *all?*

1 What is the 11th sign of the zodiac?

2 By what other name is a German shepherd dog commonly known?

3 Which seven-letter word means to withhold a vote from an election?

4 For what crime was Anne Boleyn executed in 1536?

5 What is the name of the largest dam on the River Nile?

6 Of which region in southern Spain is Seville the central city?

7 What is the middle name of inventor Thomas Edison?

8 What flavor is ouzo, the national drink of Greece?

9 What name is given to the fear of heights?

10 Which film featured a spacecraft called the *Nostromo?*

11 In the Bible, who was married to Sarah and Keturah?

12 What is the collective name for a group of frogs?

13 Which team won soccer's World Cup in 1978?

14 In which country is the Pushtu language spoken?

15 Globe and Jerusalem are both varieties of what?

16 In Anglican church hierarchy, what rank is immediately below a bishop?

17 What is the name of the wax-like substance obtained from sperm whales and used in perfumes?

18 What is the birthstone for March?

19 In mythology, who was the beautiful youth loved by Venus?

20 What is the name of the princess in *Sleeping Beauty?*

E Is for...

All answers begin with the letter *E*. Can you name *each* and *every* one?

1 From what are black piano keys traditionally made?

2 What is the national flower of Austria?

3 In which part of the human body would you find the smallest bones?

4 Which Christian festival is celebrated on January 6?

5 What is the second book of the Old Testament?

6 Quito is the capital of which country?

7 Who phoned home in a 1982 film?

8 What is the name of the European single currency?

9 Which river ran through the ancient city of Babylon?

10 Which is the smallest of the three Baltic states?

11 Julius Caesar, Vincent Van Gogh, and Edward Lear all suffered from which disease?

12 In which Jane Austen novel did Henry Knightley marry Miss Woodhouse?

13 What was Che Guevara's real first name?

14 What name is given to a person who carries out the instructions of a will?

15 What is the name of the disease that causes massive and grotesque swelling of the limbs?

16 Which objects in the British Museum, originally taken from the Parthenon in Athens, does Greece want back?

17 Who was Orpheus attempting to rescue when he traveled down to Hades?

18 What name is given to a group of larks?

19 What is the alternative name for Beethoven's Third Symphony?

20 Sea urchins and starfish both belong to which marine animal group?

Time for a Consonant

Let's not leave out consonants altogether! Name two colors of purple that start with *L*.

I Is for...

Only very *intelligent* people will be able to answer all these questions. All answers begin with the letter *I*.

1 What name is given to the front teeth between the canines?

2 What color falls between blue and violet in the spectrum?

3 In which sport is the Stanley Cup a trophy?

4 What is the medical term for sleeplessness?

5 Which country won eight Olympic gold medals in the 20th century for men's field hockey?

6 Diabetes is caused by a lack of what?

7 Springfield is the capital of which state?

8 What is the Russian equivalent for the name John?

9 What is dyspepsia more commonly known as?

10 What is Spain's national airline called?

11 Which rock group started life as The Farriss Brothers?

12 What name is given to a large heated box for hatching eggs?

13 What is the capital city of Pakistan?

14 What is the name given to a scientist who studies fish?

15 Which 1987 film starring Dustin Hoffman and Warren Beatty was a major box-office flop?

16 Who was the only survivor of the shipwrecked *Pequod*, in the novel *Moby Dick*?

17 What was the title of the painting that was sold at Sotheby's New York for $49 million on November 11, 1987?

18 On which river does the city of Mandalay stand?

19 What is the name of the last part of the small intestine?

20 What name is given to the Japanese art of flower arranging?

O Is for...

Are the answers *obvious?* They all begin with the letter *O*.

1 What nickname is given to the gold-plated figurines awarded annually by the Academy of Motion Picture Arts and Sciences?

2 Which is the only bird from which leather can be obtained?

3 What sort of branch symbolizes peace?

4 What name is given to the elliptical course of a planet?

5 What kind of angle is between 90 degrees and 180 degrees?

6 Which four-letter word is the name of a semi-precious stone characterized by striped layers?

7 What name is given to a brief biography of a person who has died?

8 Which three-letter word is the name of the unit for electrical resistance?

9 What do coin collectors call the head side of a coin?

10 Which mountain was the home of the Greek gods?

11 Which six-letter word means the opposite of transparent?

12 What name is given to the study of birds?

13 Which animal is the only marsupial native to the Americas?

14 What is the last letter of the Greek alphabet?

15 What word with musical associations is the singular of the Latin word *opera*?

16 What name is given to an infection of the ear?

17 What name is given to the study of eggs?

18 Which historical empire shares its name with a cushioned, backless seat?

19 What are beasts with eight feet called?

20 What name is given to a scientist who studies diseases of the eye?

U Is for...

All answers begin with the letter *U*. Do you *understand?*

1 What does the *U* stand for in the abbreviation UFO?

2 Which African nation was ruthlessly led by Idi Amin?

3 Which mythical beast was a horse with a horn on its head?

4 Which actress, whose first name begins with *U*, costarred in *Pulp Fiction*?

5 What is the milk-secreting organ of a cow called?

6 Which group of crime fighters was led by Eliot Ness?

7 Which veteran heavy metal band was named after a character in a Charles Dickens novel?

8 What is the medical name for the womb?

9 What name was given to German submarines during the Second World War?

10 Which mythological hero was played in a 1954 film by Kirk Douglas?

11 What is cosmology the study of?

12 Salt Lake City is the capital of which state?

13 Which gray, radioactive metallic element is used to fuel reactors and nuclear bombs?

14 In mythology, Rhea is the daughter of whom?

15 What name was given to Schubert's Symphony No. 8 in B Minor?

16 If cat equals feline, what word equals bear?

17 What name is given to the underground railway system in Berlin?

18 What name is given to the two dots placed over a letter in the German language to indicate the pronunciation of a word?

19 What is the name given to animals with hooves?

20 What five-letter word is the name given to the shadow of the Earth on the moon?

...And Sometimes Y

Yes, it's true: All answers start with the letter *Y*.

1 Which song contains the line "Suddenly, I'm not half the man I used to be"?

2 What it Fred Flintstone's catchphrase?

3 Which mammal lives at the highest altitude?

4 Which stringed toy was originally used as a weapon by native tribes of the Philippines?

5 What is the main unit of currency in Japan?

6 Which cartoon character claims that he is "smarter than the average bear"?

7 What kind of singing, originating in Switzerland, was popularized by the singer Frank Ifield?

8 What name is given to the veil worn by Muslim women that covers the face so that only the eyes remain exposed?

9 By what name is the "Abominable Snowman of the Himalayas" known?

10 What is the name of the industrial port located next to Tokyo?

Missing Vowels

Find the missing vowels and find your answer!

1 S*RF A term for a medieval peasant.

2 SCR*B*S The clerks and record-keepers of the ancient world.

3 P*RK* A hooded fur jacket traditionally worn by the Inuit.

4 G**CH*S Cowboys from Argentina.

5 *PPR*NT*C* One who learned his trade by assisting a master craftsman.

6 P*DDL*R The name given to a person who went from place to place selling small items.

7 R*CK*F*LL*R Surname of John, who made his fortune from oil.

8 TR**B*D**R A traveling poet or storyteller in medieval Europe.

9 G**LDS Medieval associations of merchants or craftsmen.

10 B*RR*LS What a cooper makes.

Where Did the Vowels Go?

Vowels become even more important when they're missing. Use the clues to help you fill in the gaps.

1 CH*RTR**S* A green or yellow liqueur.

2 T*N*M*NT A type of housing often found in slum areas.

3 W*RKH**S* Where the poor were accommodated in Victorian England.

4 P*PR*K* A spicy ingredient of Hungarian goulash.

5 S*C*LY This island was an important source of grain for the ancient Mediterranean world.

6 S*M*V*R This device was used in Russia for making tea.

7 B*RD***X A French wine-making region.

8 *C*P*NCT*R* This is a traditional Chinese form of medicine.

9 T*RR*G*N This herb was traditionally chewed to give relief from a toothache.

10 G**RG* *RW*LL The author of a satirical novel on communism.

A Quiz About P**PL*

Find the vowels and find the groups of people.

1 BR*HM*NS The highest rank in India's ancient caste system.

2 Q**K*RS A religious group that pioneered prison reform in Britain and America.

3 L*P*RS People who suffer from a disease that rots the flesh and skin.

4 *RM*N**NS A minority people who came under attack in Turkey in 1894.

5 L*V*LL*RS A political movement in 17th-century England accused of wanting to "level men's estates."

6 FR*NC*SC*NS A religious order founded in 1209.

7 B**RS Farming people who waged guerrilla wars against the British in South Africa in the late 19th century.

8 S*M*R** The warrior elite in Japanese society from the 12th to the 19th century.

9 C*TH*RS A religious cult that took its name from the Greek word for "pure."

10 P*R*T*NS Strict English Protestants of the 16th and 17th centuries.

More Y

Y always gets short shrift, so here's another Y question. Name two animals that start with Y.

Grammar

I or me? Him or he? Us or we? Whether you know which is correct because of grammatical rules or simply because it sounds right, you want to write and speak properly. How well do you know your collective nouns? Your adjectives? Your pronouns? Take the test below to find out!

Got a Red Pen Ready?

Catch the common mistake in each sentence.

1 The kids were anxious to put on their swim-suits and enter the pool.

2 None of the vases look good in that living room.

3 Charlie has been leaving work early alot.

4 Can I borrow the car tonight?

5 Smokey the Bear reminds us, "Only you can prevent forest fires."

6 The judges' panel is comprised of company department heads.

7 Let me know whether or not the porch light is on.

8 It goes without saying that we all had a great time at the party.

You Done Good!

You may have done well on the previous gram-matical test—how well will you score on this one? Spot the common error in each sentence.

1 I need to visit the ATM machine.

2 This brand of paper towels boasts excellent absorbtion.

3 The little girl accidently stepped into a deep mud puddle.

4 We'll stick to the speed limit alright, because that's the law.

5 While crossing the fence, a field hand snagged his pants on barb wire.

6 The weight lifter rolled up her right sleeve to reveal a well-toned bicep.

7 The customer forked a buttery Brussel sprout and popped it into his mouth.

8 Since the park lies along the flyway, Canadian geese stop there frequently.

You and Me (or Is It I?)

The following statements are grammatically correct—true or false?

1 Stan and me are going to the store.   TRUE ○   FALSE ○

2 Stand near Ellen and I for the photo.   TRUE ○   FALSE ○

3 Us girls are planning a party.   TRUE ○   FALSE ○

4 You and he are going to win.   TRUE ○   FALSE ○

5 She and Diana got into a fight.   TRUE ○   FALSE ○

Adjectivally Yours

To what animal do these adjectives refer?

Bovine_____	**A** Ape
Caprine_____	**B** Bear
Aquiline_____	**C** Cow
Simian_____	**D** Eagle
Ursine_____	**E** Goat
Porcine_____	**F** Horse
Ovine_____	**G** Lion
Murine_____	**H** Mouse
Equine_____	**I** Pig
Leonine_____	**J** Sheep

All Together Now

No man is an island, and more than one man is "men." That's easy. But here's something harder: What collective nouns are given to groups of the following things?

1 Crows

2 Widows

3 Flies

4 Monkeys

5 Angels

6 Sheep

7 Bears

8 Dolphins

9 Coyotes

10 Cobras

Alphabetical Order

Everything in its place, and a place for everything—that phrase may date back to the 1800s and refer to cleanliness, but it works equally well for the alphabet and all the words in it. If you like order, you'll love this section!

A(lphabetical) (B)rainteasers...

This quiz is doubly tough! You need to know the right answers, and then list them in alphabetical order. Name:

1 The Seven Dwarfs

2 The planets in our solar system

3 The continents

4 The colors of the rainbow

5 The stars in our solar system

6 The five major oceans

7 The five major Romance languages

The First Six

Here's a clue to help you get started on this round: the first six answers correspond to the first six letters of the alphabet.

1 What *A* is the name given to a large cage or building where birds are kept?

2 Sofia is the capital of which country?

3 Which *C* is one-hundredth of a euro?

4 What is the name of the line that cuts a circle in half?

5 What seven-letter word is the name given to a territory surrounded by a foreign dominion?

6 From which plant is linseed obtained?

The G(oa)L

Now try to reach your goal of giving answers that range from *G* to *L*.

1 What *G* is the name of an armored glove thrown down as a challenge?

2 What does the *H* stand for in the medical treatment HRT?

3 What *I* word can precede curtain, lady, and lung?

4 In what sport does an ippon score 10 points?

5 In which state is Fort Knox?

6 Which EU country has the smallest population of all the EU states?

Middle Range

Why is this quiz called "Middle Range"? Because the answers stretch from *M* to *R*!

1 On which Mediterranean island did the British actor Oliver Reed die?

2 What three-letter word precedes the names of four American states?

3 What name is given to a musical composition for eight singers or players?

4 Andorra lies in which mountain range?

5 What word is given to a porcupine's sharp spines?

6 Which Alex Haley novel features the character Chicken George?

The End

And finally, questions with answers that range from *S* to *Z*.

1 Which London thoroughfare is famous for high-quality men's tailoring?

2 What is the capital city of Albania?

3 Which African country borders the north shore of Lake Victoria?

4 What has a person lost if suffering from aphonia?

5 What name is given to a Native American's tent?

6 How is 19 written in Roman numerals?

7 What mysterious Himalayan animal is also known as the Abominable Snowman?

8 Which actor, born in 1915, intended to be a painter, was blacklisted in the McCarthy era, and won three Tony Awards?

Ancient Origins

1 a. Sacred carving
2 c. Genius
3 b. Love of wisdom
4 b. Purple
5 a. Pythagoras
6 c. Patron of the arts
7 a. Menhir
8 c. Roman
9 b. Ox hide

In the Beginning...

1 True
2 False; Tuscany is correct
3 False; the Enlightened One is right
4 True
5 True
6 False; elbow is right
7 True

The People Name Game

1 Julius Caesar
2 In the beginning
3 The Greeks
4 All the gods
5 The Mississippi
6 They cremated them
7 Bushmen
8 Hippocratic oath
9 The Greeks
10 August
11 The Celts
12 Moche

I Didn't See That Coming!

1 The ability to use tools
2 Calendar
3 Gladiator contests
4 Barbarian
5 Knowledge
6 Carthaginian

So Close!

1 Ceres
2 Mausoleum
3 Sybaris

4 Persian
5 Saturn

Two of Twelve

March (from Mars) and January (from Janus)

Back to the Future

1 Ancient Greece
2 The public punishment at the pillory
3 The "windows" were made from horn
4 Tavern
5 Hinduism
6 A piece of bread
7 Penitentiary
8 Art Deco

What's in a Place Name?

1 Cádiz
2 Delos
3 The Andes
4 Qin, or Ch'in
5 The Etruscans
6 Punjab
7 Provence
8 Babylon
9 *Castra*
10 The Parthenon
11 Yemen
12 Jerez (sherry)

Say What?

1 True
2 False; it was Groucho Marx
3 False; it was Ralph Waldo Emerson
4 True
5 False; the correct person is Jean-Jacques Rousseau

Funny Bones

1 Groucho Marx
2 Winston Churchill
3 Charles Dickens
4 Mark Twain
5 Margaret Thatcher
6 Dorothy Parker
7 Robert Bloch
8 Erma Bombeck

Name the Speaker

1 Karl Marx
2 Martin Luther King Jr.
3 Mark Twain
4 Harry S. Truman
5 Horatio Nelson
6 Abraham Lincoln
7 Margaret Thatcher
8 Richard Nixon
9 Mother Teresa
10 Nelson Mandela

...And Phrases for All!

1 I think, therefore I am
2 Chains
3 No taxation without representation
4 The French
5 The Statue of Liberty
6 Stettin
7 Tigers
8 "I am the state"
9 Forever England
10 Drop out

Notable and Quotable

1 a. Of a heart attack
2 c. As an apprentice to his brother; he was a full-fledged printer by age 17
3 c. Aliens destroy Earth to make way for an intergalactic highway
4 b. Her frustration with the housewife role and housekeeping
5 b. The Grand Ole Opry country music show
6 c. Profanity; Groucho Marx was famous for his insults and sexual innuendo
7 a. A Harvard-trained physician
8 b. His performances as a jazz clarinetist

O Brother, Who Art Thou?

Chico, Harpo, Groucho, Gummo, Zeppo

Who Said That?

1 True
2 True
3 False; Albert Einstein said it
4 True
5 True
6 False; W. H. Auden said it
7 False; Walt Disney said it
8 True

My Country, 'Tis of Thee

1 Mexico
2 Africa
3 Greenland
4 India
5 Australian
6 Russian
7 Brazilian
8 England
9 German
10 Vietnam

War and Peace

1 John F. Kennedy
2 Winston Churchill
3 Mao Zedong (Tse-tung)
4 Edmund Burke
5 Oscar Wilde
6 Benjamin Franklin
7 Martin Luther King Jr.
8 Pyrrhus

Gone Missing

1 Old men
2 Washes away
3 Steal
4 Machine
5 Home
6 Children
7 Fish-knives
8 Education
9 Street
10 Necessity

One Last Time!

1 Home life
2 Le Corbusier
3 John Ruskin

4 Amartya Sen
5 Samuel Smiles
6 John D. Rockefeller Sr.
7 The call to prayer
8 Christopher Marlowe

Quote, UnQuote

1 Howard Carter
2 Sennacherib
3 Gladiators
4 The Nicene Creed
5 Simon Peter
6 Horace
7 Augustus Caesar
8 King David
9 Augustine of Hippo
10 Cicero

In a Manner of Speaking

1 Helen of Troy
2 *The Iliad*
3 Egypt
4 Seize the day
5 The Phoenicians
6 Julius Caesar
7 Belshazzar
8 China
9 Alexander the Great

Witty and Wise

1 Dorothy Parker
2 Albert Einstein
3 Douglas Adams
4 Garrison Keillor
5 Groucho Marx
6 Oliver Wendell Holmes
7 Ronald Regan

Foreign Food

1 Smorgasbord
2 Turkish delight
3 Ciabatta
4 Tiramisu
5 Lactose
6 *Santé*
7 *Haram*

In Translation

1 Bauhaus
2 The (Japanese) tea ceremony
3 Bubonic plague
4 Boxers
5 Martin Luther's
6 A contract to work for someone
7 Rosh Hashanah
8 Great Soul

Lost in Translation

1 a. New Scotland
2 c. Lion Mountains
3 b. Puerto Rico
4 d. Nicaragua
5 a. Malta
6 b. Austria
7 d. Dominica
8 b. Sri Lanka
9 a. Taiwan
10 d. House of stone

Language Class

1 Washing clothes
2 Circumcision
3 Motorway or freeway
4 Kindergarten
5 False; it's a vineyard (literally "growth")
6 True

A World of Words

1 "Land of silver"
2 Haiku
3 Glasnost
4 Germany above all
5 Fiery Cross
6 Father of the Turks
7 Separateness
8 Uprising (literally, "shaking off")
9 Caesar
10 Living space

Answers

War of Words

1 Customs union
2 Spain
3 *Risorgimento*
4 *Kristallnacht*
5 Las Malvinas
6 Israel
7 The Blitz
8 Kremlin
9 *Perestroika*

Latin Test

1 *Habeas corpus*
2 *Fugitivus*
3 Remember that you must die
4 Hammer of Witches
5 John Locke
6 Country in the city
7 Lacquer
8 Hypocaust
9 A grain of salt
10 "A healthy mind in a healthy body" or "A sound mind in a sound body"

Take a Letter

1 b. Q
2 a. C
3 b. Alfred Hitchcock
4 b. General audiences
5 c. *The X-Files*
6 c. Herbert
7 b. Perception
8 a. Columbia
9 a. Germany
10 c. Intelligence

Bloody Good Answer

A, B, AB, O

Initial Queries

1 Home Box Office
2 Columbia Broadcasting System
3 Intercontinental ballistic missile
4 Officer of the Order of the British Empire
5 Cable News Network
6 Acquired Immune Deficiency Syndrome
7 United Nations High Commissioner for Refugees
8 Severe Acute Respiratory Syndrome
9 Organization of the Petroleum Exporting Countries
10 North American Free Trade Agreement
11 Gross domestic product
12 General Agreement on Tariffs and Trade
13 *Train à Grande Vitesse*
14 South West Township
15 Least (or less) developed country
16 Ethical Trading Initiative
17 World Health Organization
18 United Nations Children's Fund
19 United Arab Emirates
20 Unidentified flying object

As Easy as ABC

1 Astronomy
2 Anise
3 Bridle
4 Blubber
5 Collie
6 Carburetor

Short for...

1 File Transfer Protocol
2 Committee of State Security
3 Criminal Investigation Department
4 First-day cover
5 Paris
6 Royal Mail Steamer
7 Search and rescue
8 Unique selling proposition (or point)
9 Air traffic control
10 Videocassette recorder
11 By the way
12 China
13 Federal Bureau of Investigation
14 Digital
15 London Heathrow
16 Special Air Service

Wedding Bells

1 Menelaus
2 Juno
3 Solomon
4 Livia
5 Pompey
6 Isis
7 Roxane
8 Boudicca
9 Aphrodite
10 Claudius

Short on Politics and Diplomacy

1 Belgium, Netherlands, Luxembourg
2 Kenya
3 Victory in Japan
4 Mutually assured destruction
5 Nazi
6 Campaign for Nuclear Disarmament
7 Palestine Liberation Organization
8 North Atlantic Treaty Organization
9 European Economic Community

First and Last

1 Orinoco
2 Angola
3 Asia
4 Arizona
5 Oslo
6 Alaska
7 Muslim
8 Arabia
9 Antarctica
10 Lake Baikal

A Is for...

1 Australia
2 Afghanistan
3 Algeria
4 Addis Ababa
5 Argentina
6 Antigua
7 Albania
8 Armenia
9 Andorra
10 Austria

More Than a K-9

False; it's an educational term

PAGE 364

Four-Letter Words

1 Runt
2 Seal
3 Lung
4 Mole
5 Must
6 Calf
7 Seed
8 Cell
9 Sage

To Cap It All

1 Cape
2 Capsize
3 Capricorn
4 Capsule
5 Capon
6 Capstan

PAGE 365

A Call to Arms

1 Armenia
2 Armadillo
3 Armageddon
4 Armistice
5 Armpit
6 Armor

Links of Three

1 Creole languages
2 Commercial varieties of date
3 All have hosted the Olympic Games
4 Arctic peoples
5 Marxist states
6 South American horse breeds
7 Oasis towns
8 Currencies
9 Languages

Three-Letter Words

1 Ace
2 Gin
3 Pan
4 Hay
5 Yen
6 Yap

"More" Four-Letter Words

1 Wham!
2 Rose
3 *Cats*
4 Loch
5 Lead
6 Mile

PAGE 366

Take a Second Look

1 Port
2 Pen
3 Dam
4 Gorge
5 Hold
6 Slicker
7 Tire
8 Panel
9 Rock

Talking to the Trees

1 Pine
2 Fir
3 Ash
4 Elder
5 Hemlock
6 Cypress
7 Holly
8 Spruce
9 Yew
10 Lime

PAGE 367

It's Not Funny!

1 El Niño
2 Because they were in the Globe
3 Both were "boxers"
4 Literally scarred them
5 Noh
6 Because "economics" is derived from Greek root for "house"
7 He invented the pressure cooker
8 He was said to break the pianos he played
9 Heinz
10 Their garments

Missing Links

1 Trade
2 Market
3 City
4 State
5 Town
6 Train
7 House
8 Debt
9 Convention
10 Energy

PAGE 368

A Is for...

1 Aquarius
2 Alsatian
3 Abstain
4 Adultery
5 Aswan
6 Andalucia
7 Alva
8 Aniseed (Anise)
9 Acrophobia
10 *Alien*
11 Abraham
12 Army
13 Argentina
14 Afghanistan
15 Artichoke
16 Archdeacon
17 Ambergris
18 Aquamarine
19 Adonis
20 Aurora

Answers

PAGE 369

E Is for...

1 Ebony
2 Edelweiss
3 Ear
4 Epiphany
5 Exodus
6 Ecuador
7 E.T.
8 Euro
9 Euphrates
10 Estonia
11 Epilepsy
12 *Emma*
13 Ernesto
14 Executor
15 Elephantiasis
16 Elgin Marbles
17 Eurydice
18 Exaltation
19 *Eroica*
20 Echinoderms

PAGE 370

I Is for...

1 Incisors
2 Indigo
3 Ice hockey
4 Insomnia
5 India
6 Insulin
7 Illinois
8 Ivan
9 Indigestion
10 Iberia
11 INXS
12 Incubator
13 Islamabad
14 Ichthyologist
15 *Ishtar*
16 Ishmael
17 *Irises*, by Vincent Van Gogh
18 Irrawaddy
19 Ileum
20 Ikebana

O Is for...

1 Oscars
2 Ostrich
3 Olive
4 Orbit
5 Obtuse
6 Onyx
7 Obituary
8 Ohm
9 Obverse
10 Olympus
11 Opaque
12 Ornithology
13 Opossum
14 Omega
15 Opus
16 Otitis
17 Oology
18 Ottoman
19 Octopods
20 Ophthalmologist

PAGE 371

U Is for...

1 Unidentified (flying object)
2 Uganda
3 Unicorn
4 Uma Thurman
5 Udder
6 Untouchables
7 Uriah Heep
8 Uterus
9 U-boats
10 Ulysses
11 Universe
12 Utah
13 Uranium
14 Uranus
15 *Unfinished Symphony*
16 Ursine
17 U-Bahn
18 Umlaut
19 Ungulate
20 Umbra

PAGE 372

...And Sometimes *Y*

1 "Yesterday," by the Beatles
2 Yabba-Dabba-Doo
3 Yak
4 Yo-yo
5 Yen
6 Yogi Bear
7 Yodeling
8 Yashmak
9 Yeti
10 Yokohama

Missing Vowels

1 Serf
2 Scribes
3 Parka
4 Gauchos
5 Apprentice
6 Peddler
7 Rockefeller
8 Troubadour
9 Guilds
10 Barrels

PAGE 373

Where Did the Vowels Go?

1 Chartreuse
2 Tenement
3 Workhouse
4 Paprika
5 Sicily
6 Samovar
7 Bordeaux
8 Acupuncture
9 Tarragon
10 George Orwell

A Quiz About P**PL*

1 Brahmans
2 Quakers
3 Lepers
4 Armenians
5 Levellers
6 Franciscans
7 Boers
8 Samurai
9 Cathars
10 Puritans

PAGE 374

Got a Red Pen Ready?

1 Better to say "eager" rather than "anxious," which implies anxiety or fear.
2 Change "look" to "looks." When *none* is used as a singular noun (standing for "not one"), match it with a verb in singular form.

3 Use "a lot" as two words.

4 Use *may* (implying permission) rather than *can* (which implies ability).

5 It's actually "Smokey Bear," without "the" in the middle. Songwriters added "the" to give the name more of a lyrical rhythm in 1952. However, despite the popular song, it's simply "Smokey Bear."

6 Change "is comprised of" to "comprises" (meaning *includes* or *is made up of*).

7 The phrase *or not* is extraneous. "Or not" is already implied by the use of the word *whether*.

8 Shorten the sentence to "We all had a great time at the party." (If it truly "goes without saying," why bother saying it at all?)

You Done Good!

1 The initials ATM stand for "Automatic Teller Machine," making "machine" in the sentence redundant.

2 "Absorb" is the word's root, but it's actually spelled *absorption*.

3 The correct word is *accidentally*.

4 It's *all right*—two words.

5 Those grabby strands of fencing are actually called *barbed* wire.

6 That upper arm muscle, even when you're speaking of just one, is called a biceps.

7 Those bitter little morsels are named after the Belgian city, so it's *Brussels sprout*.

8 The bird species is *Canada* geese.

PAGE 375

You and Me (or Is It I?)

1 False; Stan and I

2 False; Ellen and me

3 False; We girls

4 True

5 True

Adjectivally Yours

1 Cow
2 Goat
3 Eagle
4 Ape
5 Bear
6 Pig
7 Sheep
8 Mouse
9 Horse
10 Lion

All Together Now

1 Murder (or storytelling)
2 Gaggle
3 Swarm
4 Troop (or tribe or cartload)
5 Host
6 Flock (or down, drove, fold, hurtle, trip)
7 Sleuth (or sloth)
8 Pod
9 Band
10 Quiver

PAGE 376

A(lphabetical) (B)rainteasers...

1 Bashful, Doc, Dopey, Grumpy, Happy, Sleepy, Sneezy

2 Earth, Jupiter, Mars, Mercury, Neptune, (Pluto), Saturn, Uranus, Venus

3 Africa, Antarctica, Asia, Australia, Europe, North America, South America

4 Blue, green, indigo, orange, red, violet, yellow

5 The sun (and only the sun!)

6 Arctic, Atlantic, Indian, Pacific, Southern (also known as Antarctic Ocean)

7 French, Italian, Portuguese, Romanian, Spanish

The First Six

1 Aviary
2 Bulgaria
3 Cent
4 Diameter
5 Enclave
6 Flax

PAGE 377

The G(oa)L

1 Gauntlet
2 Hormone
3 Iron
4 Judo
5 Kentucky
6 Luxembourg

Middle Range

1 Malta
2 New
3 Octet
4 Pyrenees
5 Quills
6 *Roots*

The End

1 Savile Row
2 Tirana
3 Uganda
4 Voice
5 Wigwam
6 XIX
7 Yeti
8 Zero Mostel